AF842124

NORFOLK RECORD SOCIETY
founded 1930

Patron:
HER MAJESTY QUEEN ELIZABETH, THE QUEEN MOTHER

President:
TIMOTHY COLMAN, Esq., D.C.L.

Vice-Presidents:
The Most Hon. THE MARQUESS TOWNSHEND OF RAYNHAM
The Right Rev. THE LORD BISHOP OF NORWICH
The Very Rev. THE DEAN OF NORWICH
SIR EDMUND BACON, Bt., K.G., T.D.
The Rt. Hon. LORD BLAKE, F.B.A., J.P.

The Council:
C.B.Jewson, Esq., J.P., F.S.A. (Chairman)
A.P.Baggs, M.A., F.S.A.
Mrs.T.R.C.Blofeld
I.Cresswell, F.S.A.
S.E.Gurney
D.E.H.James, M.A.
Mis J.M.Kennedy, B.A.
D.P.Mortlock, F.L.A.
M.V.B.Riviere, M.A.
F.S.A., T.D.
M.J.Sayer, M.A., B.Litt.
W.R.Serjeant, B.A., F.R.Hist.S.
The Right Rev. Abbot A.Watkin, M.A.,
F.S.A., F.R.S.A., F.R.Hist.S.

Hon. Secretary:
R.C.Frostick, M.A., LL.B., 425, Unthank Road, Norwich,
NR4 7QB

Joint Hon. Editors:
A.Hassell Smith, B.A., Ph.D., F.R.Hist.S.
and
R.Virgoe, B.A., Ph.D., F.R.Hist.S.,
Centre of East Anglian Studies,
University of East Anglia,
Norwich, NR4 7TJ

Hon. Treasurer:
K.S.Dugdale, M.A., F.C.P., 2, The Close,
Norwich, NR1 4DJ

NORFOLK RECORD SOCIETY

PUBLICATIONS

The following volumes have been published and are on sale at prices which will be quoted on applications to the Hon. Secretary. Those marked with an asterisk are currently in stock: others can sometimes be obtained.

Vol. I	Calendar of Frere MSS: Hundred of Holt. Muster Roll, Hundred of North Greenhoe, circa 1523. Norwich subscriptions to the Voluntary Gift of 1662.
Vol. II	St. Benet of Holme, 1020-1210. The eleventh and twelfth century sections of Cott. MS. Galba E ii. The Register of the Abbey of St. Benet of Holme. Part I.
Vol. III	St. Benet of Holme, 1020-1210. Introductory Essay on the eleventh and twelfth century sections &c. Part II.
Vol. IV	The Visitation of Norfolk, 1664. Part I.
Vol. V	The Visitation of Norfolk, 1664. Part II.
Vol. VI	The Musters Returns for divers Hundreds in the County of Norfolk, 1569, 1572, 1574, and 1577. Part I.
Vol. VII	The Musters Returns for divers Hundreds in the County of Norfolk, 1569, 1572, 1574, and 1577. Part II.
Vol. VIII	A Norfolk Sessions Roll, 1394-1397. The Maritime Trade of the Port of Blakeney, Norfolk, 1587-1590. A Norfolk Poll List, 1702.
Vol. IX	Records of the Gild of St. George in Norwich, 1389-1547.
Vol. X	Norwich Consistory Court Depositions, 1499-1512 and 1518-1530.
Vol. XI	The First Register of Norwich Cathedral Priory.
Vol. XII	The Norfolk Portion of the Chartulary of the Priory of St. Pancras of Lewes.
Vol. XIII	East Anglian Pedigrees.
Vol. XIV	The Correspondence of Lady Katherine Paston, 1603-1627.
***Vol. XV**	Minutes of Norwich Court of Mayoralty, 1630-1631.
Vol. XVI	Part I. Index of Wills Proved in the Consistory Court of Norwich, 1370-1550 (A to Hi). Part II. Index of Wills Proved in the Consistory Court of Norwich, 1370-1550 (Hi to Ro). Part III. Index of Wills Proved in the Consistory Court of Norwich, 1370-1550 (Ro to Z).
Vol. XVII	Post-Reformation Royal Arms in Norfolk Churches. Cellarer's Roll, Bromholm Priory, 1415-16. Subsidy Certificates, 1581.
Vol. XVIII	Bishop Redman's Visitation, 1597.
***Vol. XIX**	*Part I. Archdeaconry of Norwich: Inventory of Church Goods temp. Edward III. Part II. Archdeaconry of Norwich: Inventory of Church Goods temp. Edward III.
Vol. XX	The Knyvett Letters, 1620-1644.
Vol. XXI	Index of Wills Proved in the Consistory Court of Norwich, 1550-1603.
Vol XXII	Baptisms in Church Book of Old Meeting House, Norwich, 1657-81. Baptisms and Deaths in Church Book of Gt. Yarmouth Independent Church, 1643-1705. Account Book of 'Baptised' Church in City of Norwich, 1726-45.

PUBLICATIONS

Vol. XXII **cont'd.**	Notes on Blomefield MSS. in Bodleian Library. Progress Notes of Warden Woodward relating to the Norfolk Property of New College, Oxford, 1659-1675.
***Vol.** XXIII	The Freemen of Norwich, 1714-1752.
***Vol.** XXIV	Extracts from the two earliest Minute Books of the Dean & Chapter of Norwich Cathedral, 1566-1649.
Vol. XXV	Registers of Passengers from Gt. Yarmouth to Holland and New England, 1637-1639.
Vol. XXVI	Norfolk Quarter Sessions Order Book, 1650-1657.
***Vol.** XXVII	The Correspondence of Thomas Corie, Town Clerk of Norwich, 1664-1687. The Visitation of Norfolk, 1664: Observations and Comments.
Vol. XXVIII	Index of Wills Proved in the Consistory Court of Norwich, 1604-1686.
Vol. XXIX	An Index of the Indentures of Norwich Apprentices enrolled with the Norwich Assembly, Henry VII-George II.
Vol. XXX	Norfolk Lieutenancy Journal, 1676-1701.
***Vol.** XXXI	The Ames Correspondence, 1837-47.
***Vol.** XXXII	The Registrum Vagum of Anthony Harrison. Part I.
***Vol.** XXXIII	The Registrum Vagum of Anthony Harrison. Part II.
***Vol.** XXXIV	Index of Wills Proved in the Consistory Court of Norwich, 1687-1750.
***Vol.** XXXV	A Cartulary of Creake Abbey.
***Vol.** XXXVI	Minutes of the Norwich Court of Mayoralty, 1632-1635.
Vol. XXXVII	Mary Hardy's Diary.
***Vol.** XXXVIII	Index of Wills Proved in the Consistory Court of Norwich, 1751-1818.
***Vol.** XXXIX	Great Yarmouth Assembly Minutes, 1538-1545. The Norwich Accounts for the Customs on Strangers' Goods and Merchandise, 1582-1610.
***Vol.** XL	The Norwich Census of the Poor, 1570.
***Vol.** XLI	Communer Rolls of Norwich Cathedral Priory.
***Vol.** XLII	Faden's Map of Norfolk.
***Vol.** XLIII	The Letter Book of John Parkhurst, Bishop of Norwich, compiled during the years 1571-5.
***Vol.**XLIV	Crime in East Anglia in the Fourteenth Century: Norfolk Gaol Delivery Rolls, 1307-1316.
***Vol.** XLV	Norfolk Lieutenancy Journal, 1660-1676.
***Vol.** XLVI	The Papers of Nathaniel Bacon of Stiffkey: Vol I. 1556-1577.

NORFOLK RECORD SOCIETY

Report of the Council for 1978

1. During the year we have welcomed as new members of the Society Mrs.D.J.Baker, Mr.D.J.Brentnall, Dr.D.C.Cornish, The Bavarian State Library, Munich, The Brighton Polytechnic and The University of California. Unfortunately, as always, we lost a few of our members by death or resignation, and we ended the year with 251 subscriptions, a net increase of 1.
2. We much regret that during the course of the year Sir Edmund Bacon indicated to us that he felt the time had come for him to give up his office as President. Sir Edmund accepted the Presidency in 1968 following the death of Lord Evershed, and during his term of office took a keen and lively interest in the activities of the Society, bringing to them a wide experience of public and business life coupled with a deep interest in the history of the County, in which many of his own family had played a distinguished part. Sir Edmund's retirement coincides with his retirement as Lord Lieutenant of the County of Norfolk and the Council is pleased to be able to report that his successor as Lord Lieutenant Mr. Timothy Colman has agreed to succeed him as the President of this Society.
3. In our Report for 1977 we said that our 1978 Volume would be the first of the series of Volumes of the Papers of Nathaniel Bacon edited by Dr. Hassell Smith. During the course of the year it became apparent that this first Volume would be much longer than originally expected and that it would therefore be convenient to offer it as a double Volume for 1978 and 1979.
4. The Council has endeavoured to keep the Society's subscriptions to a minimum consistent with maintaining the high standard which members have rightly come to expect. While deciding to hold the present subscription levels for 1979, the Council reluctantly decided that increased costs of printing and postage made an increase in 1980 inevitable. The new subscription rates will be £4.50 for individual members and £5.50 for institutional members in the United Kingdom and Eire, with an overseas membership subscription of £6.00. The Council hope that members will feel that even at these increased levels members are getting extremely good value for their subscriptions.

C.B.Jewson
(Chairman)

THE NORFOLK RECORD SOCIETY

INCOME AND EXPENDITURE ACCOUNT

For the year ended 31st December 1978

1977 £	Expenditure	1978 £	£
	Printing and despatching		
1,996	Volume XLV	2,280.30	
	Less: Provision made in		
1,996	1977	2,180.30	
-			100.30
	Provision for printing and		
2,180	despatch of Volume XLVI		1,000.00
87	Postage and Sundries		53.00
210	Purchases - Books		112.00
	British Record Society		
7	Subscription		7.50
33	Editorial Expenses		-
(46)	Surplus/(Deficit) for year		534.70
£2,471			£1,808.00

1977 £	Income	1978 £
919	Subscriptions	897.43
992	Sale of Publications	427.99
193	Interest	205.92
42	Income Tax Refund	48.46
200	Grants	200.00
20	Royalties	28.20
105	Legacy and Donation	-
£2,471		£1,808.00

THE NORFOLK RECORD SOCIETY

BALANCE SHEET

31st December 1978

1977 £	Fund and Liabilities	1978 £	£	1977 £	Assets	1978 £
	Fund				£934.05 9% Treasury Stock	
778	At 31st December 1977	732.22		649	at cost (Market Value £719.22)	649.10
(46)	Add: Surplus for 1978	534.70			Cash at Bank	
				260	Current Account - Barclays	181.31
732			1,266.92		Trustee Savings Bank of	
79	Subscriptions in Advance		51.52	2,082	Eastern England	1,488.03
	Provision for Printing &					
2,180	Despatch of Volume XLVI		1,000.00			
£2.991			£2,318.44	£2,991		£2,318.44

TO THE MEMBERS OF THE NORFOLK RECORD SOCIETY

We have examined the foregoing Accounts and certify them to be in accordance with the books and vouchers of the Society.

PEAT, MARWICK, MITCHELL & CO.
CHARTERED ACCOUNTANTS
NORWICH
30th April 1979

NORFOLK RECORD SOCIETY

Report of the Council for 1979

During the year we have welcomed as new members of the Society Dr.B.Baxter, Mr.S.Naunton, Mrs.A.Fenner and the University of Essex. We regret having to report a higher than usual number of deaths and resignations, as a result of which the total number decreased for the first time for a number of years to a year end figure of 245. We are pleased to say that following the end of the year a number of new members have joined us, so we hope that the decline is only a temporary one.

During the year the first volume of the Papers of Nathaniel Bacon was published as a double volume of the Society for the years 1978/79. A ceremony was held at the University of East Anglia to mark the publication, which was a joint venture of the University's Centre of East Anglian Studies and this Society. Work on the next volume is already well in hand and it is hoped that this will be published in 1982 or 1983.

The Society is not alone in being extremely concerned at the rapidly increasing cost of printing and it is a cause of great regret that the traditional letterpress printing now appears to be beyond the resources of the Society. The Council is nevertheless anxious to maintain the high standards which have existed in the past and every effort will be made to ensure that the use of alternative modern printing methods do not predjudice the overall standard of the Society's work.

At the same time the Council will endeavour to maintain membership subscription at the lowest possible level. Increases for 1980 were announced last year but the Council must warn members that in view of the continued high rate of inflation a further increase seems inevitable in the near future.

C.B.Jewson
(Chairman)

THE NORFOLK RECORD SOCIETY

INCOME AND EXPENDITURE ACCOUNT

For the year ended 31st December 1979

1978 £	Expenditure	1979 £	£	1978 £	Income	1979 £
	Printing and despatching			897	Subscriptions	977
2,280	Volume XLVI	1,671		428	Sale of Publications	548
	Less: Provision made in			206	Interest	236
2,180	1978	1,000		49	Income Tax Refund	52
100			671	200	Grants	200
	Provision for printing and			28	Royalties	32
1,000	despatch of Volume XLVII		1,000	-	Legacy and Donation	7
53	Postage and Sundries		69			
113	Purchases - Books		200			
	British Record Society					
7	Subscription		15			
	Contribution towards					
-	Reception		25			
535	Surplus for year		72			
£1,808			£2,052	£1,808		£2,052

THE NORFOLK RECORD SOCIETY

BALANCE SHEET

31st December 1979

1978 £	Fund and Liabilities	1979 £	£	1978 £	Assets	1979 £
	Fund				£934.05 9% Treasury Stock 1994	
732	At 31st December 1978	1,267		649	at cost (Market Value £657.38)	649
535	Add: Surplus for 1979	72			Cash at Bank	
				181	Current Account - Barclays	361
1,267			1,339		Trustee Savings Bank of	
51	Subscriptions in Advance		145	1,488	Eastern England	1,474
	Provision for Printing &					
2,180	Despatch of Volume XLVII		1,000			
£2,318			**£2,484**	**£2,318**		**£2,484**

TO THE MEMBERS OF THE NORFOLK RECORD SOCIETY

In accordance with the instructions given to us, we have prepared the attached accounts from the accounting records of The Norfolk Record Society and from information and explanations given to us. We have not carried out an audit and accordingly express no opinion thereon.

PEAT, MARWICK, MITCHELL & CO.
CHARTERED ACCOUNTANTS
NORWICH
6th May 1980

NORFOLK RECORD SOCIETY

Hon. General Editors:

A.Hassell Smith, B.A., Ph.D., F.R.Hist.S.

and

R.Virgoe, B.A., Ph.D., F.R.Hist.S.

VOL. XLVII

INDEX
of
WILLS PROVED
in the
CONSISTORY COURT OF NORWICH
1819-1857
and now preserved in the
NORFOLK RECORD OFFICE

Compiled by

MRS CLAIRE FROSTICK

with a foreword by

MISS JEAN KENNEDY, B.A.

Norfolk Record Society
1980

Published for the Norfolk Record Society
by
Geo Abstracts Ltd
Regency House
34 Duke Street
Norwich

Copyright Norfolk Record Society 1982

ISBN 0 9501370 7 3

CONTENTS

FOREWORD

This volume completes the series of indexes to wills proved in the Norwich Consistory court. Ecclesiastical jurisdiction in testamentary matters was abolished from 12 January 1858 by the Court of Probate Act and wills in England and Wales were thereafter proved in the Principal Probate or 40 local District Probate Registries.

In 1819 the diocese of Norwich comprised the archdeaconries of Norfolk, Norwich, Sudbury and Suffolk. On 30 May 1837 the archdeaconry of Sudbury covering the western part of Suffolk and the rural deanery of Fordham in Cambridgeshire was transferred to the diocese of Ely. Wills of testators from these parishes however continued to be proved in the Norwich Consistory court and after this date we find for example 21 wills from Burwell, 12 from Bury St. Edmund's, 11 from Fordham, 36 from Newmarket and eight from Sudbury; the numbers in every case exceeding those proved in the earlier part of the period covered.

It should be remembered that wills of persons holding property in the area were also proved in the archdeaconry and peculiar courts as well as the Prerogative Court of Canterbury. Details of the records of these courts and their present location are to be found in Wills and their Whereabouts by A. J. Camp or A Simplified Guide to Probate Jurisdictions by J. S. W. Gibson. Regulations concerning the court in which a will should have been proved, depending on the jurisdiction or jurisdictions within which the testator held property, had never been strictly observed. It can however be of interest to discover why the wills of people described as being of places well outside its area were registered or proved in the Consistory court. John Thirkettle of New Orleans and Jonathon Spurling of Bolton-Le-Moors, Lancashire, both held property in the diocese and had their wills registered in the Norwich Consistory court after they had been proved by the British Consul for New Orleans and the Bishop of Chester respectively, by virtue of requisitions sent to them. George Dawson flour merchant of South Shields, Co. Durham also held property in the diocese and his will which was correctly proved in the Norwich Consistory court, unless, as would seem likely, he additionally owned property in South Shields, has a prefixed note saying that the testator lived and died at Weybourne. Elizabeth Thornhill Howell is described as being of Hybla Castleknock, Co. Dublin, widow, and her will, which has no real property specified in it, is also prefixed by a note to the effect that she lived and died at the Bishop's Palace, Norwich. A legacy of £100 to her son the Reverend Doctor Samuel Hinds makes it clear that she was the Bishop's mother and her will had been drawn up in April 1848 before she moved to Norwich and while her son was the Vicar and a prebendary of Castleknock.

The system of the Registry remained unchanged. There is a bundle of original wills and a register for each year. The 1819 register is bound with that for 1818, but otherwise they are large and distinct. They have as previously been named after the first will recorded in them, but the court and year alone will serve as an adequate reference. Where a will has not been registered the number of the original will (O.W.) is given and a few names appear only in the manuscript index.

Similar surnames such as Haward and Hayward; Paine and Payne; Simmons, Simonds and Symonds have not been grouped together or cross-referenced. Therefore when seeking a particular entry all variants should be tried.

For the first time in the will index series, the volume incorporates an index of occupations and these show an increasing variety of nomenclature and more specialized descriptions. Besides alehouse keepers, inn holders or keepers, victuallers and vintners, we now also find beerhouse keepers, beer sellers, publicans and tavern keepers. As well as apothecaries, we have chemists and druggists and in addition to lawyers, there is one solicitor and two attorneys at law. A number of types of lawyers, there is one solicitor and two attorneys at law. A number of types of surveyor also make an appearance. There is a jockey and a studgroom, John Boon, the Commander of a South Sea whaler and Richard Slann of Southtown, historical engraver to the Queen.

The decline of the woollen industry is illustrated by a sharp drop in the number of worstead weavers, only 23 from Norwich having their wills proved during this period as compared with over 120 between 1751 and 1818. Administrators of the 19th cent. Poor Law both before and after the 1834 Act are represented by two governors or principals of Seckford's Hospital, Woodbridge, Robert Fosdike whose will was proved in 1832 and Edward Loder whose will was proved in 1852. The will of Thomas Charles Rackham of Kenninghall, Master of the Guiltcross Union workhouse was proved in 1853; that of John Lucas, Master of the Thetford Union workhouse in 1854; William Charles Lownes of Norwich, Master of the workhouse had his will proved in 1854; Thomas Faulkner of Swainsthorpe, Master of the workhouse in 1856; and Thomas Johnson, Governor of Wymondham Bridewell also in 1856. Wills of William Staples of Burwell, Cambridgeshire, relieving officer and John Barnard of Worstead, Clerk to the Guardians of Tunstead and Happing Hundreds were proved in 1852 and 1853. Railway employees make their appearance for the first time and in 1852 we have the wills of James Chenery of Ipswich, railway porter and Jonathon Spurling of Bolton-Le-Moors, Lancashire, railway clerk.

Some interesting combinations of occupation occur. William Ansell of Fakenham was an auctioneer and cabinet maker, Alfred Barber of Gorleston a farmer and sailmaker, Thomas Bryant of New Buckenham a bookseller and watchmaker, William Burch of Norwich a hairdresser and jeweller, John Fiddaman of Brancaster a butcher and publican, Zachariah Finch of Smallburgh a thatcher and shopkeeper, Thomas Gooch of North Lopham an innkeeper and linen manufacturer, Edward Mayes of Norwich a vintner and printer and Robert Olby of Brandon a gunflint maker and furrier. Other occupations appear more naturally linked such as Joseph Allerton of Lowestoft, fish merchant and cooper, Samuel Ashford of Woodbridge pawnbroker and clothier, William Buckenham of Fersfield farmer and miller and Edward Cook of Norwich corn and coal merchant and livery stable keeper.

Mrs. Frostick is to be congratulated on undertaking the considerable amount of work involved in compiling this volume, which will be widely used by social and economic as well as family and local historians.

The wills, indexes and registers are held by the Norfolk Record Office, Central Library, Norwich, to whom acknowledgement of permission to publish is made and the Society is also grateful to the staff for help and advice.

JEAN KENNEDY

Diocese of Norwich

WILLS
PROVED IN THE
CONSISTORY COURT
1819-1857

LIST OF REGISTER BOOKS

1819 Le Neve
1820 Mack
1821 Dewell
1822 Sadler
1823 Tann
1824 Borrett
1825 Hayward
1826 Davy
1827 Wood
1828 Farrow
1829 Green
1830 Pettingill
1831 Hart
1832 Cooke
1833 Cubitt
1834 Lane
1835 Harrowing
1836 Smith
1837 Warren
1838 Skepper
1839 Calton
1840 Turner
1841 Traxton
1842 Canler
1843 Miles
1844 Ebbage
1845 Pedgrift
1846 Baret
1847 Broom
1848 Denny
1849 Womack
1850 Cuthbert
1851 Friar
1852 Latten
1853 Veale
1854 Day
1855 Whitty
1856 Code
1857 Youngs

WILLS PROVED IN THE CONSISTORY COURT OF NORWICH 1819-1857

	Aayton - see Hayton	
1841	Abbott, David, Witnesham, S., servant	133 Traxton
1842	Abbott, Henry, Castle Acre, N., gent.	690 Canler
1830	Abbott, John, Mellis, S.	418 Mack
1861	Abbott, John, Brandeston, S., wheelwright	406 Friar
1841	Abbott, Peter, Aylsham, N., baker	377 Traxton
1820	Abbott, Rebecca, Needham Market, S., widow	44 Mack
1847	Abbott, Stephen, Doughton, N., gent.	184 Tann
1823	Abbott, Thomas, Stoke Ash, S., yeoman	184 Tann
1830	Abbott, Thomas, Ipswich, S., yeoman	444 Pettingill
1841	Abbs, Francis, Runton, N.	336 Traxton
1855	Abbs, James, Weybourne, N., tailor	558 Whitty
1832	Abbs, John, North Walsham, N., yeoman	510 Cooke
1839	Abbs, Lucy, Hevingham, N., widow	12 Calton
1845	Abbs, Mary, Stratton St Mary, N., widow	146 Pedgrift
1832	Abbs, Richard, Runton, N., farmer	160 Cooke
1827	Abbs, Robert, Aylsham, N., yeoman	141 Wood
1833	Abbs, Stephen, Bunwell, N., farmer	7 Cubitt
1838	Abbs, Thomas, Hevingham, N., innkeeper	55 Skepper
1848	Abel, Elizabeth, East Tuddenham, N., widow	438 Denny
1836	Abel, Jeremiah, Norwich, N., butcher	260 Smith
1829	Abel, Mary Ann, Heigham, Norwich, N., widow	66 Green
1832	Abel, Matthias, Bungay, S., gent.	613 Cooke
1836	Abell, Mary, Norwich, N., spinster	207 Smith
1836	Abill, David, Norwich, N.	464 Smith
1847	Able, Robert, Norwich, N., worstead weaver	527 Broom
1821	Ablett, Amy, Bungay, S., widow	174 Dewell
1842	Ablett, Charles, Great Wenham, S.	488 Canler
1857	Ablett, John, Theberton, S., farmer	466 Youngs
1846	Ablett, Thomas, Kelsale, S., farmer	366 Baret
1841	Ablitt, Charles, Alderton, S., farmer	417 Traxton
1848	Abraham, John, Stockton, N., farmer	508 Denny
1856	Abrane, Elizabeth, Hellesdon, N.	105 Code
1831	Absolon, David, Great Yarmouth, N., parish clerk	91 Hart
1821	Adams, Ann, Diss, N.	276 Dewell
1835	Adams, Ann, Bramfield, S., widow	277 Harrowing
1844	Adams, Charles, Feltwell, N., shepherd	10 Ebbage
1833	Adams, Elizabeth, Bedfield, S., widow	182 Cubitt
1850	Adams, George, Lowestoft, S., baker	606 Cuthbert
1821	Adams, Henry, Stradbroke, S., yeoman	231 Dewell
1821	Adams, James, Ipswich, S., merchant	112 Dewell
1848	Adams, John, Hickling, N., yeoman	61 Denny
1821	Adams, Mary, Tittleshall, N.	30 Dewell
1843	Adams, Robert, Heigham, Norwich, N., formerly of Bedford	276 Miles
1851	Adams, Sarah, Burwell, C., widow	286 Friar
1846	Adams, Susanna, St. Michael at Plea, Norwich. N., widow	26 Baret
1853	Adams, Thomas, Botesdale, S., farmer	518 Veale
1829	Adams, William, Witton, N., yeoman	422 Green
1844	Adams, William, St. Gregory, Norwich, N., yeoman	47 Ebbage
1857	Adams, William Bayes, Norwich, N., gent.	616 Friar
1845	Adcock, Christopher, Little Walsingham, N., surgeon	953 Pedgrift
1838	Adcock, Edmund, Felthorpe, N., labourer	215 Skepper
1840	Adcock, Francis, Great Yarmouth, N., house carpenter	397 Turner
1844	Adcock, Haddon, Little Walsingham, N., gent.	82 Ebbage
1851	Adcock, John, Thorpe next Norwich, N.	571 Friar
1857	Adcock, John Fleming, Little Walsingham, N., surgeon	180 Youngs
1848	Adcock, Mary Sophia, Holt, N., spinster	123 Denny
1834	Adcock, Thomas, Marlesford, S., yeoman	299 Lane
1840	Adcock, William, East Walton, N., farmer	498 Turner
1832	Adderson, Edward, Saham Toney, N., labourer	355 Cooke
1848	Addison, Lydia, Great Yarmouth, N., widow	489 Denny
1820	Akerly, John, Wood Norton and Hindolveston, N., yeoman	162 Mack
1849	Alborough, Elizabeth, Aslacton, N., wife of Edward Alborough, butcher	627 Womack

1831	Alborough, Henry, Brooke, N., gardener	411 Hart
1841	Albrow, George, Long Stratton, N., innkeeper	116 Traxton
1835	Albrow, Michael, alias Rivett, Haddiscoe, N., innholder	260 Harrowing
1857	Alcock, James, Stalham, N.	223 Youngs
1845	Alcock, John, Neatishead, N.	657 Pedgrift
1836	Alcock, Robert, Shipdham, N., farmer	524 Smith
1834	Alden, Charles, Norwich, N., warper	625 Lane
1842	Alden, Edward, Norwich, N., worstead weaver	O.W. 282
1840	Alden, Jane, St. Augustines, Norwich, N., widow	59 Traxton
1824	Alderson, James, Norwich, N., plumber, glazier and painter	8 Borrett
1844	Alderson, Lydia, Halesworth, formerly of Beccles, S., widow	54 Ebbage
1825	Alderson, Mary, Hevingham, N., wife of Rev. Joseph Alderson	116 Hayward
1835	Alderton, Anthony, Holbrook, S.	330 Harrowing
1824	Alderton, Fisher, Shotley, S., farmer	261 Borrett
1850	Alderton, John, Intwood, N., labourer	298 Cuthbert
1833	Alderton, Samuel, Hoxne, S., yeoman	401 Cubitt
1852	Alderton, Susan, Intwood, N., widow	230 Latten
1821	Alderton, William, Bentley, S., farmer	258 Dewell
1856	Aldis, Francis, New Buckenham, N., carpenter	51 Code
1855	Aldis, James, Stratton St. Mary, N., schoolmaster	350 Whitty
1826	Aldis, William, Bramfield, S., gent.	238 Davy
1839	Aldiss, Mary, alias Aldous, Norwich, N., spinster	198 Calton
1842	Aldiss, Thomas, Lowestoft, S., blacksmith	738 Canler
1844	Aldous, Ann, Weybread, S., widow	513 Ebbage
1827	Aldous, Elizabeth, Stradbroke, S., spinster	331 Wood
1853	Aldous, James, Fressingfield, S., yeoman	549 Veale
1820	Aldous, John, Redenhall w. Harleston, N., carpenter	603 Mack
1847	Aldous, John, Beccles, S., potman	261 Broom
1850	Aldous, John, Redenhall w. Harleston, N., farmer	491 Cuthbert
1839	Aldous, Mary, - see Aldiss	198 Calton
1828	Aldous, Robert, Rackheath, N., farmer	102 Farrow
1847	Aldous, Robert, St. Johns Maddermarket, Norwich, N., innkeeper	629 Broom
1828	Aldous, Thomas, Wilby, S., farmer	230 Farrow
1841	Aldred, James, Morningthorpe, N., farmer	269 Traxton
1846	Aldred, James, Halesworth, S., grocer and draper	585 Baret
1841	Aldred, Sarah, Morningthorpe, N., wife of James Aldred, farmer	460 Traxton
1838	Aldred, Simon, Moulton, N., farmer	881 Skepper
1851	Aldrich, Robert, the elder, Fressingfield, S., husbandman	67 Friar
1855	Aldrich, Robert, Diss, N., grocer and draper	221 Whitty
1835	Aldrich, William, Blyford, S.	632 Harrowing
1831	Aldridge, Charles, Wilby, S., farmer	582 Hart
1829	Aldridge, James, Laxfield, S., farmer	543 Green
1834	Aldridge, Thomas, St. Martins at Palace, Norwich, N., formerly of Catton	619 Lane
1820	Alebaster, Briant, Sutton, S.	108 Mack
1823	Alefounder, William, Norwich, N., gardener	310 Tann
1840	Alexander, Elizabeth, Bury St Edmunds, S.	474 Turner
1850	Alexander, James, Great Yarmouth, N., gent.	481 Cuthbert
1848	Alexander, Joseph, Norwich, N., jeweller	572 Denny
1819	Alexander, Matilda, Ipswich, S., spinster	153 Le Neve
1855	Alexander, Robert, Burgh St Margaret, N., thatcher	682 Whitty
1837	Alexander, William, Kings Lynn, N., tailor and woollen draper	470 Warren
1854	Algar, Elizabeth, Redenhall w. Harleston, N., widow	40 Day
1839	Algar, John, Barnby, S., farmer	41 Calton
1857	Algar, John, Redenhall W. Harleston, N., cordwainer	44 Youngs
1849	Algar, Mary, Alburgh, N., wife of James Algar	384 Womack
1824	Algar, Robert, Old Buckenham, N., gent.	246 Borrett
1826	Algar, Robert, Winfarthing, N., gent.	Index only
1828	Algar, Robert, Norwich, N., tavern keeper	79 Farrow
1830	Algar, Robert, Needham, N., farmer	81 Pettingill
1839	Algar, Robert, Needham, N.	Index only
1850	Algar, Robert Fousoe, West Rudham, N., gent.	60 Cuthbert
1828	Algar, Sarah, Old Buckenham, N., wife of Robert Algar, gent.	130 Farrow
1851	Algar, William, Thorndon, S., gent.	315 Friar

1840	Alison, Esther, Halvergate, N.	Index only
1822	Allard, Elizabeth, Smallburgh, N.	316 Sadler
1841	Allard, Thomas senior, Weeting, N., coachman	244 Traxton
1820	Allcock, Ann, St Ethelred, Norwich, N., widow	93 Harrowing
1820	Allcock, Jonathan, Great Yarmouth, N.	163 Mack
1837	Allcock, John Turrell, Halesworth, S., gent.	374 Warren
1826	Allden, Richard, Bungay, S., formerly of South Elmham, S., yeoman	235 Davy
1831	Alldis, Legent, Letheringham, S., yeoman	320 Hart
1838	Alldred, Henry, Norwich, N., dyer	203 Skepper
1847	Allen, Charles, Bawdeswell, N., farmer	39 Broom
1824	Allen, Elizabeth, Thelnetham, S., widow	251 Borrett
1832	Allen, George Walter, Ovington, N., farmer	232 Coke
1819	Allen, James, Docking, N., carrier	240 Le Neve
1830	Allen, James, Swardeston, N., carpenter	187 Pettingill
1852	Allen, James Wiffen, Ipswich, S., ironfounder	319 Latten
1849	Allen, Jane, Heigham, Norwich, N., formerly of Swannington, N., widow, o.w. missing	412 Womack
1834	Allen, John, Irstead, N., labourer	713 Lane
1839	Allen, John, Ubbeston, S., farmer	565 Calton
1827	Allen, Mary, Upwell, N., widow	356 Wood
1827	Allen, Mary Ann, St Stephens, Norwich, N., spinster	464 Wood
1836	Allen, Mary Grice, Burnham Westgate, N., widow	496 Smith
1820	Allen, Richard, Norwich, N., woollen draper	592 Mack
1821	Allen, Robert, Snettisham, N., cordwainer	167 Dewell
1829	Allen, Robert, Upton, N.	435 Green
1849	Allen, Samuel, Wortham, S., farmer	392 Womack
1853	Allen, Samuel, Tuttington, N., yeoman	72 Veale
1849	Allen, Sexton, Cromer, N., weaver	171 Womack
1822	Allen, William, Mattishall, N., yeoman	99 Sadler
1829	Allen, William, Norwich, N., gent.	536 Allen
1834	Allen, William, Tuttington, N., yeoman	262 Love
1850	Allen, William, Thornham, N., mariner	18 Cuthbert
1852	Allen, William, Heigham, Norwich, N.	736 Latten
1851	Allerton, Joseph, Lowestoft, S., fish merchant and cooper	595 Friar
1846	Allesbrook, James, Worthing, N., tanner	558 Baret
1831	Allison, Ann, Billingford, N., spinster	447 Hart
1847	Allison, David Francis, Norwich, N., cutler	639 Broom
1825	Allison, Esther, Halvergate, N., widow	527 Hayward
1834	Allison, John, Field Dalling, N., shoemaker	487 Lane
1843	Allison, Philip, North Elmham, N., yeoman	341 Miles
1831	Allison, Susan, Hockwold cum Wilton, N., widow	429 Hart
1829	Allison, William, St Peter Mancroft, Norwich, N., bricklayer	175 Green
1819	Allman, Elizabeth, St Giles, Norwich, N., widow	223 Le Neve
1846	Allsop, Henrietta Ellen, Bungay, S., spinster	607 Baret
1850	Alpe, Edmund, Carbrooke, N., yeoman	271 Cuthbert
1837	Alsop, June, Cromer, N., widow, schoolmistress	590 Warren
1823	Alwood, Elizabeth, Thursford, N., widow	241 Tann
1850	Ambrose, Thomas, Stow Bardolph, N., yeoman	488 Cuthbert
1832	Ames, Abraham, Ridlington, N., miller	606 Cooke
1820	Ames, Ann, Thorpe next Norwich, N.	82 Mack
1852	Ames, Daniel, Lakenham, Norwich, N., gent.	473 Latten
1848	Ames, James Anger, Great Yarmouth, N., baker and shopkeeper	471 Denny
1825	Ames, John, Norwich, N., gardener	97 Hayward
1837	Amies, John, Trunch, N., gent.	635 Warren
1828	Amies, Joseph, Tunstead, N., farmer	80 Farrow
1832	Amies, Joseph, St Peter Mancroft, Norwich, N., publican	398 Cooke
1850	Amies, Lee, Roughton, N., farmer	354 Cuthbert
1835	Amis, Ann, Ufford, S., widow	554 Harrowing
1831	Amis, Elizabeth, Beighton, N., widow	550 Hart
1846	Amis, James the elder, Barton Turf, N., waterman	552 Baret
1826	Amis, John, Catfield, N.	207 Davy
1827	Amis, Robert, Gorleston, S., blacksmith	220 Wood
1851	Amis, Thomas, Hackford next Reepham, N., carpenter	411 Friar

1856	Amiss, Thomas, North Walsham, N., yeoman	375 Code
1820	Amond, Elizabeth, St Gregory, Norwich, N., widow of Edward Amond, late keeper of county gaol	255 Mack
1843	Amos, Hannah, Norwich, N., spinster	386 Miles
1849	Amos, Samuel, Woodbridge, S., ferryman	66 Womack
1823	Amos, William, Woodbridge, S., mariner	321 Tann
1856	Anderson, John, St Saviours, Norwich, N., tea dealer	102 Code
1821	Anderson, William, Thorpe Hamlet, N., merchant	123 Dewell
1845	Andrews, George Philip, Great Yarmouth, N., hair dresser	689 Pedgrift
1834	Andrews, James, Lavenham, S., innkeeper	522 Lave
1842	Andrews, James, Horsford, N., parish clerk	340 Canler
1847	Andrews, Jemima, Bergh Apton, N., widow	560 Broom
1827	Andrews, John, Debenham, S., horsedealer	640 Wood
1841	Andrews, John, Syderstone, N., husbandman	245 Traxton
1845	Andrews, Joseph, Kings Lynn, N., grocer	573 Pedgrift
1830	Andrews, Mary, Ipswich, S., widow	263 Pettingill
1828	Andrews, Ralph, Horsford, N.	11 Farrow
1844	Andrews, Robert, Great Yarmouth, N., yeoman	226 Ebbage
1827	Andrews, Rowland, Merton, N., farmer	308 Wood
1838	Andrews, Stephen, St Saviours, Norwich, N., gent.	713 Skepper
1838	Andrews, Thomas, Newmarket St Mary, S., baker	474 Skepper
1847	Andrews, Thomas, Hunstanton, N., labourer	176 Broom
1853	Andrews, Thomas, Kings Lynn, N., whitesmith	687 Veale
1826	Andrews, William, Sudbury, S., shopkeeper	132 Davy
1834	Andrews, William, Feltwell, N., farmer	477 Lave
1838	Andrews, William, Kings Lynn, N., millwright	425 Skepper
1845	Angell, John, Norwich, N., leather merchant	728 Pedgrift
1850	Angell, Mary, St Michael at Thorn, Norwich, N., widow	20 Cuthbert
1847	Angell, Robert, Norwich, N., gent.	56 Broom
1830	Annis, John, Norwich, N., gent.	327 Pettingill
1820	Annis, Thomas, East Dereham, N., gent.	664 Mack
1842	Annison, Edward, Hickling, N.	562 Canler
1838	Annison, Elizabeth, Norwich, N., widow	169 Skepper
1838	Anness, John, Braiseworth, S., farmer	871 Skepper
1828	Annock, Mary, East Rudham, N., widow	293 Farrow
1848	Ansell, Ann, Fakenham, N., widow	108 Denny
1827	Ansell, John, Norwich, N., plumber	133 Wood
1849	Ansell, William, Fakenham, N., auctioneer and cabinet maker	567 Womack
1848	Ansted, Diana, Lyng, N., widow	340 Denny
1827	Anthony, Joshua, Brancaster, N., yeoman	504 Wood
1823	Anthony, Mary, Kings Lynn, N., widow	178 Tann
1823	Anthony Michael, Kings Lynn, N., mariner	142 Tann
1826	Applegate, Robert, Fulmodeston, N., farmer	81 Davy
1838	Appleton, John, Hevingham, N., husbandman	594 Skepper
1842	Appleton, Samuel, Tunstead, N., shopkeeper	388 Canler
1831	Arber, John, Bunwell, C., bricklayer	48 Hart
1855	Arbon, Charles, Mendlesham, S., wheelwright and carpenter	363 Whitty
1829	Arbon, James, Great Yarmouth, N., bricklayer	399 Green
1838	Arbour, Thomas, Mundford, N., labourer	603 Skepper
1842	Archer, Ann, Heigham, Norwich, N., spinster	484 Canler
1838	Archer, John, Finborough Magna, S.	103 Skepper
1836	Archer, Samuel, Nedging, S.	396 Smith
1830	Archer, Thomas, Hopton, S., yeoman	79 Pettingill
1838	Arger, John, Kings Lynn, N., yeoman	494 Skepper
1844	Arger, William, Runton, N., husbandman	245 Ebbage
1839	Armes, Ann, Hindolveston, N.	636 Calton
1843	Armes, John, South Lynn All Saints, N., gent.	691 Miles
1855	Armes, Thomas, Holt, N., yeoman	631 Whitty
1839	Armiger, William, Wimbotsham, N., farmer	91 Calton
1832	Arms, Amy, Sutton, N., widow	563 Cooke
1842	Armstrong, Henry, Great Yarmouth, N., master mariner	746 Canler
1847	Arnold, George, St Augustines, Norwich, N.	114 Broom
1840	Arnold, James, Aslacton, N., farmer	78 Turner

1837	Arnold, John, St Margarets, Norwich, N., wine, spirit and porter merchant	613 Warren
1856	Arnold, Mary Rawling, St Augustines, Norwich, N., widow	147 Code
1839	Arnold, Roger, Aslacton, N., farmer	628 Calton
1847	Arnold, William, New Buckenham, N., yeoman	521 Broom
1856	Arnold, Sarah, Tacolneston, N., widow	97 Code
1840	Arrow, Elizabeth, Burwell, C., wife of James Arrow, dissenting minister	18 Turner
1854	Arthey, John, Lindsey, S., farmer	426 Day
1850	Artis, Elizabeth, Great Yarmouth, N., widow	483 Cuthbert
1821	Artis, John, Ipswich, S., tailor	268 Dewell
1821	Artis, John, Norwich, N., cordwainer	104 Dewell
1829	Artis, Joseph, Wrentham, S., bricklayer	401 Green
1819	Artis, Mary, Norwich, N., widow	30 Le Neve
1829	Ashby, John, Bungay, S., single man, draper and grocer	144 Green
1845	Ashford, Abel, Kenton, S., farmer	480 Pedgrift
1838	Ashford, Philip, Badingham, S., farmer	560 Skepper
1828	Ashford, Samuel, Woodbridge, S., pawnbroker and clothier	374 Farrow
1829	Ashley, Jacob, Great Yarmouth, N., joiner	397 Green
1839	Ashley, James, Harpley, N., farmer	111 Calton
1838	Ashley, John, St Clements, Norwich, N., tailor	765 Skepper
1856	Ashley, William, Harpley, N., blacksmith	624 Code
1827	Ashwell, William, Burgh, S., miller	275 Wood
1837	Asker, James Thomas, Thorpe next Norwich, N., gent.	147 Warren
1857	Asker, Jane Harriot, St Peter Mancroft, Norwich, N., widow	819 Youngs
1833	Assey, Mary, Eye, S., widow	331 Cubitt
1855	Astley, Henry Nicholas, East Barsham, N., clerk	149 Whitty
1829	Astley, Sarah Maria, East Barsham, N.	292 Green
1830	Astwick, alias Ostwick, Robert, Repps with Bastwick, N., yeoman	257 Pettingill
1832	Astwick, alias Ostwick, Thomas, Repps with Bastwick, N. formerly Norwich, farmer and coachmaker	192 Cooke
1830	Atcheson, John Shipden, Cromer, N., mariner	347 Pettingill
1837	Atherton, William, Norwich, N., gent.	275 Warren
1826	Athow, Hannah, Ipswich, S., spinster	309 Davy
1854	Athow, John, Norwich, N., gent.	46 Day
1838	Athow, Mary, Holt, N., milliner	651 Skepper
1833	Athill, John, Holt, N., cordwainer	454 Cubitt
1848	Atkin, James, St Augustines, Norwich, N., draper	68 Denny
1853	Atkin, James, Hastings, Sussex, formerly of Norwich, N., draper	77 Veale
1849	Atkins, Bartholomew, Heigham next Norwich, N., tailor	510 Womack
1848	Atkins, James, Moulton, N., farmer	224 Denny
1838	Atkins, John, Laxfield, S., farmer	484 Skepper
1841	Atkins, Samuel, Dennington, S., farmer	413 Traxton
1847	Atkins, Thomas, Strumpshaw, N., gent.	568 Broom
1833	Atkinson, Hannah, Swafield, N., widow	305 Cubitt
1841	Atkinson, John, Wrestlers Plain, Great Yarmouth, N., gent.	636 Traxton
1835	Atkinson, Maria Goldsmith, Norwich, N., widow	7 Warren
1842	Atkinson, Mary Ann, alias Bultitude, Great Yarmouth, N., widow	283 Canler
1826	Atkinson, Samuel, Ipswich, S., cutler	38 Davy
1848	Atmore, James, Attleborough, N., bricklayer	484 Denny
1853	Aufrere, George John, Ridlington, N., clerk	184 Veale
1828	August, Isaac, Sutton, N.	431 Farrow
1824	August, William, Great Yarmouth, N., carpenter	226 Borrett
1835	August, William the elder, Sloley, N., blacksmith	234 Harrowing
1844	Austin, Benjamin, Norwich, N., tailor	701 Ebbage
1851	Austin, Charles, St Martin at Oak, Norwich, N., publican	270 Friar
1846	Austin, Edward, Norwich, N., yeoman	632 Baret
1838	Austin, Jane, Honingham, N., spinster	109 Skepper
1825	Austin, John, Carleton Rode, N., cordwainer	479 Hayward
1856	Austin, Matthew, Salle, N., farmer	67 Code
1852	Austin, Owen, Swanton Abbott, N., shopkeeper	639 Latten
1837	Austin, Robert, Kerdiston, N., farmer	119 Warren
1853	Austin, Robert, Moulton, N., farmer	679 Veale

1853	Austin, Thomas, Foulsham, N., farmer	31 Veale
1851	Austin, William, Great Yarmouth, N., gent.	570 Friar
1857	Auston, Thomas, Brockdish, N., butcher	138 Youngs
1850	Avely, William, Soham, C., yeoman	5 18 Cuthbert
1839	Aves, Jeremiah, Thetford, N., waggoner	513 Calton
1842	Avey, George, Fulmodeston, N., shepherd	310 Canler
1851	Ayers, John Wigg, Lingwood, N., esquire	181 Friar
1853	Ayers, Jonathan, Lowestoft, S.	552 Veale
1832	Ayers, Robert, Great Yarmouth, N., fish merchant	292 Cooke
1853	Aylard, James, Fordham, C., carpenter	485 Veale
1829	Aylard, Martin, Kirtling, C., farmer	392 Green
1855	Ayre, Edward, South Lynn All Saints, Kings Lynn, N., milkman	293 Whitty
1836	Ayton, Martha, Thorpe Hamlet, Norwich, N., widow	15 Smith
1847	Ayton, Robert, Gissing, N., carpenter	600 Broom
1844	Ayton, Sarah, Eye, S., spinster	591 Ebbage
1850	Back, Charles, Little Snoring, N., yeoman	537 Cuthbert
1822	Back, Henry, Middleton, N., farmer	354 Sadler
1853	Backett, Isaac the elder, Kelsale, S., yeoman	609 Veale
1840	Backhouse, Joseph, Carlton, S., farmer	451 Turner
1851	Backlog, John the elder, Thetford, N., fellmonger	602 Friar
1833	Bacon, Ann, Wicklewood, N., spinster	181 Cubitt
1851	Bacon, Daniel, Hilborough, N., farmer	572 Whitty
1855	Bacon, Edmund, Norwich, N., sacking manufacturer	358 Whitty
1854	Bacon, Elizabeth, Holbrook, S., widow	189 Day
1841	Bacon, Hannah, Norwich, N., spinster	137 Traxton
1833	Bacon, John Fuller, Fritton, N., farmer	384 Cubitt
1838	Bacon, Margaret, Aylsham, N., spinster	287 Skepper
1835	Bacon, Maria, Aylsham, N.	595 Harrowing
1853	Bacon, Martha Ann, Norwich, N., spinster	312 Veale
1848	Bacon, Mildred, Marsham, N.	669 Denny
1825	Bacon, Phillis, South Creake, N widow	20 Hayward
1838	Bacon, Robert, Marsham, N., gent.	557 Skepper
1835	Bacon, Samuel, Ipswich, S., cordwainer	219 Harrowing
1825	Bacon, Sarah, Holt, N., widow	45 Hayward
1844	Bacon, Sarah, Woodbridge, S., spinster	160 Ebbage
1851	Bacon, Sarah, Great Ormesby, N., widow	502 Friar
1845	Bacon, Sophia, Norwich, N., spinster	354 Pedgrift
1839	Bacon, Thomas Custance, Norwich, N., ironmonger and iron founder	311 Calton
1851	Bacon, Thomas, Hanworth, N., farmer	593 Friar
1826	Bacon, William, Walcot, N., gent.	197 Davy
1838	Bacon, William, Crimplesham, N., farmer	830 Skepper
1847	Bacon, William, Great Yarmouth, N., tailor	526 Broom
1838	Badcock, Edmund, Deopham, N., blacksmith	288 Skepper
1840	Badcock, Thomas, Burwell, C., sedge dealer	54 Turner
1823	Badely, Samuel, Great Yarmouth, N., gent.	283 Tann
1840	Bagg, Christmas John, Shipdham, N., tailor	231 Turner
1855	Bagg, Henry, Tittleshall, N., labourer	327 Whitty
1848	Bagg, Sarah, Shipdham, N., widow	746 Denny
1834	Bagge, Grace, Stradsett Hall, N., widow	77 Lave
1843	Bagge, Henry, Arrah, East Indies, Bengal Civil Service	77 Miles
1820	Bagley, Sarah, Sproughton, S., widow	27 Mack
1831	Bailey, Anthony, Norwich, N., manufacturer, o.w. missing	570 Hart
1856	Bailey, Charles, Gaywood, N.	382 Code
1845	Bailey, Cullum, Newton St Faiths, N., farmer	160 Pedgrift
1833	Bailey, George, Wood Ditton, C., timber merchant and farmer	69 Cubitt
1851	Bailey, George, Wood Ditton, C., o.w. missing	index only
1841	Bailey, James, Thorne, N., butcher	612 Traxton
1854	Bailey, James, Breccles, N., farmer	22 Day
1857	Bailey, James, Thetford, N., labourer	516 Youngs
1848	Bailey, John, Hempnall, N.	845 Denny
1849	Bailey, John, Cheveley, C., cordwainer	43 Womack
1819	Bailey, Sarah, Croxton, N., widow	247 Le Neve
1826	Bailey, Thomas, Wood Ditton, C., farmer and woodward	50 Davy

1831	Bailey, William, Kenninghall, N., gent.	324 Hart
1832	Baine, alias Bean, Elizabeth, Bungay, S., maidservant	383 Cooke
1847	Baines, alias Crofts, Mary, Fakenham, N., spinster	383 Broom
1844	Baines, Thomas, Kings Lynn, N., gent.	359 Ebbage
1820	Baker, Ann, Stowmarket, S., widow of John Baker, blacksmith	378 Mack
1843	Baker, Ann, East Bilney, N., widow	558 Miles
1826	Baker, Anne, Hopton, S., widow	20 Davy
1825	Baker, Avis, Norwich, N., widow	236 Hayward
1841	Baker, Benjamin, Combs, S., farmer	117 Traxton
1843	Baker, Benjamin, Ipswich, S., master mariner	144 Miles
1855	Baker, Benjamin, Bungay, S., inspector of corn returns	541 Whitty
1856	Baker, Daniel, Plumstead, by Holt, N., farmer	150 Code
1841	Baker, Edmund, Earl Stonham, S., farmer	427 Traxton
1823	Baker, Elizabeth	307 Tann
1827	Baker, Elizabeth, Little Blakenham, S., widow	48 Wood
1835	Baker, Humphrey, Raydon, S., farmer	619 Harrowing
1835	Baker, Elizabeth, Acle, N., spinster	487 Harrowing
1841	Baker, Francis, Newmarket, S., gent.	382 Traxton
1845	Baker, Francis Plumer, Little Cressingham, N., clerk	290 Pedgrift
1847	Baker, George, Horning, N., yeoman	633 Broom
1848	Baker, Henry, Bunwell, N., farmer	532 Denny
1822	Baker, John, North Walsham, N., gent.	57 Sadler
1827	Baker, John, Norwich, N., boot and shoe maker	137 Wood
1834	Baker, John, Downham Market, N., wheelwright	22 Lane
1835	Baker, John the elder, Fakenham, N., yeoman	413 Harrowing
1837	Baker, John, Bungay, S., shoe maker	641 Warren
1844	Baker, John, Old Newton, S., farmer	191 Ebbage
1849	Baker, John, St Georges Tombland, Norwich, N., butcher	185 Womack
1852	Baker, John, Bintree, N., dealer	448 Latten
1825	Baker, Joshua, Gimingham, N., farmer	445 Hayward
1827	Baker, Mary, Combs near Stowmarket, S., widow	626 Wood
1842	Baker, Mary, Holm Hale, N., gentlewoman	734 Canler
1852	Baker, Mary, Middleton, N., widow	744 Latten
1829	Baker, Richard, Ipswich, S., butcher	49 Green
1822	Baker, Sarah, Norwich, N., widow	3 Sadler
1831	Baker, Sarah, Intwood, N., widow	216 Hart
1833	Baker, Sarah Ann, Higham, S., shopkeeper	150 Cubitt
1835	Baker, Simon, Bungay, S., gelder	552 Harrowing
1841	Baker, Thomas, Great Yarmouth, N., clerk	531 Traxton
1823	Baker, William, West Bradenham, N., late of Wetherden, S.	302 Tann
1827	Baker, William the elder, Great Yarmouth, N., cordwainer	144 Borrett
1827	Baker, William, Little Blakenham, S., farmer	638 Wood
1828	Baker, William, Combs, S., farmer	262 Farrow
1828	Baker, William, Wyverstone, S., farmer	252 Farrow
1842	Baker, William, Ipswich, S., gent.	522 Canler
1853	Baker, William, Combs, S., farmer	204 Veale
1856	Baker, William, Stalham, N., ironmonger	46 Code
1857	Baker, William, Tunstall, S., yeoman	500 Youngs
1825	Balders, William, Swaffham, N., cabinet maker and upholsterer	242 Hayward
1851	Balding, Francis, South Creake, N., yeoman	460 Friar
1819	Balding, Henry, Wortham, S., farmer	346 Le Neve
1827	Balding, Elizabeth, Wortham, S., wife of Henry Balding, farmer	62 Wood
1856	Balding, Mary, Marylebone, Middlesex, widow, also Barton Turf, N.	104 Code
1855	Balding, Michael, Narborough, N., carpenter	714 Whitty
1823	Baldrey, Anne, St Stephens, Norwich, N., spinster	198 Tann
1831	Baldrey, Grace, Woodbridge, S., widow	80 Hart
1851	Baldry, Charles, Heigham, Norwich, N., gardener	572 Friar
1853	Baldry, George, Rollesby, N., farmer	482 Veale
1851	Baldry, James, Kenninghall, N., husbandman	127 Friar

1853	Baldry, John the elder, Shadbrooke, S., farmer	382 Veale
1841	Baldry, Robert, Alburgh, N., farmer	577 Traxton
1838	Baldry, William, Wilby, S., farmer	426 Skepper
1845	Baldry, William, Southwood, S., gent.	677 Pedgrift
1850	Baldwin, Ann, Great Yarmouth, N., widow	147 Cuthbert
1837	Baldwin, Elizabeth, Norwich, N., widow	325 Warren
1838	Baldwin, George, Smallburgh, N., bricklayer	299 Skepper
1857	Baldwin, George, Fakenham, N., veterinary surgeon	188 Youngs
1825	Baldwin, John, Norwich, N., basket maker	76 Hayward
1850	Baldwin, Mary Ann, Norwich, N., spinster	166 Cuthbert
1820	Baldwin, Thomas, Walcot, N., farmer	91 Mack
1847	Baldwin, William, Diss, N., patten maker	201 Broom
1834	Baldy, Elizabeth, Norwich, N., spinster	53 Lane
1827	Baldy, Martha, Norwich, N., spinster	420 Wood
1820	Bale, Edmund, Wymondham, N., schoolmaster	109 Mack
1855	Bale, Edmund, East Harling, N., farmer	150 Whitty
1856	Bale, Edward, Toftrees, N., gent.	280 Code
1848	Bale, Mary, Wicklewood, N., widow	341 Denny
1843	Bale, Robert, Tibenham, N., farmer	430 Miles
1842	Bale, Simon, Tibenham, N., farmer	415 Canler
1821	Bales, Henry, Horsham St Faiths, N., shopkeeper	264 Dewell
1835	Bales, Henry, Ipswich, S., gunmaker	589 Harrowing
1857	Bales, James, Great Yarmouth, N., grocer and tea dealer	565 Youngs
1851	Bales, Samuel, Framingham Pigot, N., farmer	440 Friar
1854	Baley, Elizabeth, Woodton, N., widow	343 Day
1830	Baley, Rebecca, Great Yarmouth, N., widow	87 Pettingill
1834	Balls, Alfred, Lowestoft, S., innkeeper	517 Lane
1857	Balls, Benjamin, Norwich, N., carpenter and builder	254 Youngs
1848	Balls, Charles, North Walsham, N., grocer	389 Denny
1830	Balls, Elizabeth, Thursford, N., spinster	215 Pettingill
1842	Balls, Elzabeth, Stoven, S., widow	323 Canler
1849	Balls, Elizabeth, Metfield, S., widow	690 Womack
1856	Balls, Elizabeth, Grays Inn Lane, London	514 Code
1828	Balls, Francis, St Andrew Ilketshall, S., gent.	263 Farrow
1842	Balls, Hezekiah, Diss, N., broker and auctioneer	457 Canler
1822	Balls, James, Irstead, N., yeoman	359 Sadler
1835	Balls, James, Billingford, N.	289 Harrowing
1843	Balls, James, Norwich, N., shopkeeper	395 Miles
1848	Balls, James, Billingford, N., blacksmith	775 Denny
1824	Balls, John, Oulton, S., farmer	2 Borrett
1834	Balls, Margaret, Swaffham, N., widow	44 Lane
1848	Balls, Mary, Burnham Overy, N., spinster	302 Denny
1830	Balls, Robert, Spexhall, S., gent.	343 Pettingill
1822	Balls, Samuel, Heigham, Norwich, N., yeoman	75 Sadler
1853	Balls, Sarah, Topcroft, N.	see 1854
1854	Balls, Sarah, Topcroft, N., widow	16 Day
1851	Balls, Susan, Stow Bedon, N., widow	157 Friar
1836	Balls, Thomas, Thrandeston, S., yeoman	219 Smith
1841	Balls, Thomas, Somerleyton, S., licensed victualler	146 Traxton
1855	Balls, Thomas, Bramerton, N., farmer	373 Whitty
1840	Balls, William, Beccles, S., yeoman	597 Turner
1822	Baly, John, Hillington, N., farmer	281 Sadler
1834	Bambridge, George, Stody, N., yeoman	823 Lane
1839	Bammant, Sarah, Great Yarmouth, N., widow	678 Calton
1826	Bands, Eleanor, Reedham, N., wife of Philip Bands, farmer	283 Davy
1844	Bane, George Morris, Aylsham, N.	525 Ebbage
1834	Bane, James, Martham, N., farmer	189 Lane
1845	Bane, John Weasay, Worstead, N., baker	139 Pedgrift
1849	Bane, Matthew, Blofield, N., farmer	483 Womack
1839	Baney, Robert, Snettisham, N.	155 Calton
1857	Baney, William, Snettisham, N., saddler, collar and harness maker	567 Youngs
1835	Banham, James, Earsham, N., hempen cloth manufacturer	217 Harrowing

1839	Banham, Jonathan, Bungay, S., yeoman	164 Calton
1829	Banham, Robert, Bedingham, N., farmer	349 Green
1830	Banks, Hannah, Rougham, N., widow	299 Pettingill
1836	Banks, William, Finningham, S gent.	433 Smith
1841	Banks, William, Bury St Edmunds, S., gardener	560 Traxton
1847	Bannister, John, Eye, S., yeoman	682 Broom
1857	Banton, Susannah, Norwich, N., widow	325 Youngs
1851	Bany, George, Holme next the Sea, N., labourer	547 Friar
1856	Banyard, Charles, East Dereham, N., gent.	613 Code
1844	Banyard, Mary, Woodbridge, S., spinster	449 Ebbage
1847	Banyard, Robert, Soham, C., yeoman	546 Broom
1855	Banyer, Charlotte Sarah, Great Yarmouth, N., widow	532 Whitty
1837	Banyer, William, Worstead, N., farmer	534 Warren
1852	Banyer, William, Fakenham, N., gent.	660 Latten
1847	Barber, Alfred, Gorleston, S., farmer and sailmaker	244 Broom
1841	Barber, Benjamin, Norwich, N., gent.	176 Traxton
1837	Barber, Elizabeth, Great Yarmouth, N., widow	212 Warren
1828	Barber, George, North Pickenham, N., farmer	202 Farrow
1832	Barber, George the elder, Catfield, N., farmer	363 Cooke
1855	Barber, Georgiana, Eye, S., wife of Thomas Barber, chemist	678 Whitty
1842	Barber, James, Gorleston, S., farmer and merchant	425 Canler
1844	Barber, James, Thorpe Market, N.	363 Ebbage
1850	Barber, James Rash, Thurning, N., farmer	599 Cuthbert
1844	Barber, Jane, Newmarket All Saints, C., widow	148 Ebbage
1828	Barber, John, Foulsham, N., farmer	15 Farrow
1837	Barber, John, Great Yarmouth, N., gent.	621 Warren
1854	Barber, John, Redenhall, N., husbandman	198 Day
1856	Barber, John, Little Barningham, N., farmer	68 Code
1853	Barber, Jonathan, Shipmeadow, S., carpenter	278 Veale
1820	Barber, Robert, Great Ormesby, N., shopkeeper	537 Mack
1842	Barber, Robert, Billingford, N.	423 Canler
1848	Barber, Stephen, Burgh next Aylsham, N., yeoman	311 Denny
1825	Barber, Thomas, Potter Heigham, N., yeoman	406 Hayward
1855	Barber, Thomas, Bedingham, N., farmer	675 Whitty
1825	Barber, William, Great Yarmouth, N., master mariner	19 Hayward
1833	Barber, William, Great Yarmouth, N., milkman	490 Cubitt
1839	Barber, William, Sutton, N., gent.	418 Calton
1845	Barber, William, Belton, S., farmer	125 Pedgrift
1851	Barber, William, Redenhall with Harleston, N., miller	476 Friar
1849	Barcham, Batchelor, Lowestoft, S., boatbuilder	99 Womack
1839	Barcham, Benjamin, Sheringham, N., merchant	349 Calton
1821	Barcham, Edward, Aldeby, N., weaver	171 Dewell
1829	Barcham, John, North Walsham, N., gent.	18 Green
1846	Barcham, Mary, Aylmerton, N., widow formerly of Sheringham, N.	10 Baret
1849	Barcham, Mary, Hellington, N., widow	647 Womack
1842	Barcham, Neal Rowen, Sheringham, N., master mariner	387 Canler
1840	Barcham, William, Great Yarmouth, N., house carpenter	83 Turner
1849	Bardwell, George, Wangford, S., woodman	357 Womack
1842	Bardwell, Margaret, Mendham, N., widow	156 Canler
1853	Bardwell, Richard, Beccles, S., gent.	261 Veale
1833	Bardwell, William, Diss, N., draper	21 Cubitt
1846	Baret, Lydia, Thwaite, N., spinster	1 Baret
1829	Barham, Mary, Kenninghall, N., widow	359 Green
1838	Barham, Mary, Shelfanger, N.	278 Skepper
1821	Barham, Michael, Kenninghall, N., yeoman	226 Dewell
1834	Barham, Philip, Winfarthing, N., tailor	45 Lane
1830	Barham, Susannah, Kenninghall, N., spinster	11 Pettingill
1843	Barker, Ann Maria, Costessey, N., wife of Matthew Barker, gent.	292 Miles
1840	Barker, Charles, Thursford, N., cattle jobber	663 Turner
1845	Barker, Charles, Monk Soham, S., farmer	922 Pedgrift
1824	Barker, Christopher, Norwich, N., worstead weaver	90 Borrett

1853	Barker, Daniel, Ashfield Thorpe, S., farmer	153 Veale
1834	Barker, Elizabeth, Southtown, S., widow	151 Lane
1830	Barker, George, Bunwell, N., farmer	188 Pettingill
1854	Barker, Hannah, Redenhall, N., widow	253 Day
1842	Barker, Henry George, Norwich, N., gent.	94 Canler
1820	Barker, James, Norwich, N., gent.	557 Mack
1849	Barker, James, Blofield, N., house carpenter	212 Womack
1825	Barker, Jeremiah, St Margarets, Norwich, N., pawnbroker	326 Hayward
1829	Barker, John, Sutton, N., farmer	98 Green
1833	Barker, John, Norwich, N., gent.	465 Cubitt
1839	Barker, John, Heigham, Norwich, N., weaver	653 Calton
1842	Barker, John, Kings Lynn, N., cabinet maker	185 Canler
1846	Barker, John, Heigham, Norwich, N.	Original will 1839
1834	Barker, Joseph, Debenham, S., farmer	442 Lane
1843	Barker, Matthew, Costessey, N., farmer	288 Miles
1843	Barker, Providence, Norwich, N., widow	668 Miles
1835	Barker, Richard, Norwich, N., coal merchant	11 Harrowing
1835	Barker, Robert, Framingham Pigot, N., carpenter	120 Harrowing
1856	Barker, Robert, Norwich, N., formerly of Wramplingham, N., farmer	476 Code
1857	Barker, Robert, Yoxford, S., gent.	518 Youngs
1828	Barker, Samuel, Thwaite, N., farmer	485 Farrow
1837	Barker, Samuel, Great Yarmouth, N., gent.	83 Warren
1857	Barker, Sarah, Attleborough, N., widow	142 Youngs
1845	Barker, Smith, Swaffham, N., gent.	274 Pedgrift
1837	Barker, Susannah, St Clements, Norwich, N., widow	211 Warren
1839	Barker, Susannah, Ipswich, S., formerly of Coddenham, S., widow	154 Calton
1823	Barker, Thomas, Kenninghall, N., blacksmith	291 Tann
1829	Barker, Thomas Lincolne, Ipswich, S., gent.	451 Green
1839	Barker, Thomas, Kenninghall, N. o.w. missing	Index only
1848	Barker, Thomas, Attleborough, N., tailor	568 Denny
1825	Barker, William, Great Bealings, S., farmer	436 Hayward
1844	Barker, William, St Augustines, Norwich, N., silk winder	70 Ebbage
1831	Barlee, Charles, Framlingham, S., clerk	141 Hart
1853	Barley, William, Theberton, S., husbandman	513 Veale
1832	Barlow, Francis, Norwich, N., tavern keeper	287 Cooke
1843	Barnaby, Mary, Lowestoft, S., wife of Robert Barnaby, yeoman	487 Miles
1835	Barnaby, Robert, Lowestoft, S., carpenter	243 Harrowing
1838	Barnard, Ann, Norwich, N., single woman	509 Skepper
1845	Barnard, Elizabeth, Worstead, N., spinster	310 Pedgrift
1844	Barnard, Henry, Norwich, N., plumber and glazier	67 Ebbage
1830	Barnard, James, Great Ellingham, N., farmer	449 Pettingill
1853	Barnard, John, Worstead, N., clerk to the Guardians of the Tunstead and Happing Hundreds	664 Veale
1848	Barnard, Philip, Woodbridge, S., gent.	627 Denny
1845	Barnard, Thomas, Kings Lynn, N., lawyer	290 Pedgrift
1828	Barnard, William, Cromer, otherwise Shipden, N., gent.	50 Farrow
1828	Barnard, William, Walsham Le Willows, S., gent.	532 Farrow
1835	Barnell, William, Blundeston, S., farmer	327 Harrowing
1822	Barnes, Ann, Strumpshaw, N., spinster	246 Sadler
1844	Barnes, Bridget Maria, Thetford, N., spinster	351 Ebbage
1848	Barnes, Cecilia, Norwich, N., widow	677 Denny
1824	Barnes, Edmund, Surlingham, N., gent.	203 Borrett
1849	Barnes, Edward, Earsham, N., farmer	60 Womack
1831	Barnes, Elizabeth, Redgrave, S., widow	267 Hart
1850	Barnes, Henry, Feltwell, N., farmer	350 Cuthbert
1832	Barnes, Isaac, Pulham St Mary Magdalen, N., farmer	373 Cooke
1842	Barnes, Jane, Yoxford, S., widow	165 Canler
1843	Barnes, Jeremiah, Great Yarmouth, N., butcher	70 Miles
1856	Barnes, Jeremiah, Great Yarmouth, N., butcher	57 Code
1822	Barnes, John, Barney, N., carpenter	363 Sadler

1824	Barnes, John, Lowestoft, S., gardener	331 Borrett
1834	Barnes, John, East Dereham, N., farmer	167 Lane
1840	Barnes, John, Feltwell, N., farmer	288 Turner
1845	Barnes, John, Yoxford, S., innkeeper and farmer	529 Pedgrift
1846	Barnes, John the elder, Redlingfield, S., farmer	125 Baret
1852	Barnes, John, Norwich, N., yeoman	36 Latten
1857	Barnes, John the elder, Reedham, N., farmer	554 Youngs
1838	Barnes, Lettice, Dickleburgh, N., wife of Samuel Barnes	817 Skepper
1820	Barnes, Mary, Barney, N., single woman	380 Mack
1837	Barnes, Mary, Heydon, N., spinster	88 Warren
1837	Barnes, Mary, Little Walsingham, N., spinster	33 Warren
1843	Barnes, Mary, Great Yarmouth, N., widow	75 Miles
1856	Barnes, Mary, Great Yarmouth, N., spinster	56 Code
1830	Barnes, Michael, Bungay, S., singleman	234 Pettingill
1826	Barnes, Robert, Gazeley, S., innkeeper and millwright	60 Davy
1856	Barnes, Ruth, Sporle with Palgrave, N., spinster	633 Code
1845	Barnes, Samuel, Heydon, N., wheelwright	800 Pedgrift
1852	Barnes, Samuel, Surlingham, N., brick manufacturer	44 Latten
1856	Barnes, Samuel, Dickleburgh, N., yeoman	429 Code
1829	Barnes, Sarah, Bungay, S., single woman	22 Green
1845	Barnes, Susanna, Saham Toney, N., widow	595 Pedgrift
1831	Barnes, Thomas, Beeston St Andrew, N., esquire	O.W. 250
1844	Barnes, Thomas, Norwich, N., publican	490 Ebbage
1843	Barnes, William, Norwich, N., carpenter	367 Miles
1827	Barney, John, Skeyton, N., husbandman	680 Wood
1828	Barney, John, Norwich, N., manufacturer	438 Farrow
1845	Barney, Samuel, Skeyton, N., yeoman	932 Pedgrift
1831	Barnsdale, Alice, Bale, N., widow	427 Hart
1829	Barr, Dorothy, Norwich, N., spinster	314 Green
1854	Barratt, John, Great Yarmouth, N., cooper	571 Day
1852	Barrell, Anne, Wickham Market, S., widow	675 Latten
1835	Barrell, Elizabeth, Beccles, S., widow	293 Harrowing
1820	Barrell, Ralph, Hopton, S., yeoman	220 Mack
1829	Barrett, Charles, Lowestoft, S., mariner	521 Green
1846	Barrett, Hannah Matilda, Mattishall, N., widow	452 Baret
1856	Barrett, James, Lowestoft, S., yeoman	208 Code
1837	Barrett, John, Kings Lynn, N., master mariner	155 Warren
1845	Barrett, John, Whitwell, N., farmer	858 Pedgrift
1849	Barrett, John, Grimstone, N., yeoman	554 Womack
1857	Barrett, John, Lowestoft, S., cordwainer, sexton and bellman	417 Youngs
1819	Barrett, Randel, Great Yarmouth, N., shipmaster	172 Le Neve
1853	Barrett, Robert, Lowestoft, S., plumber and glazier	583 Veale
1846	Barrett, Samuel, Feltwell, N.	464 Baret
1840	Barrett, Simon, Holme Hale, N., carpenter	513 Turner
1849	Barrett, William, Flitcham, N., gamekeeper	586 Womack
1843	Barritt, Edward, Debenham, S.	613 Baret
1832	Barritt, John, Debenham, S., butcher	491 Cooke
1856	Barrow, Eliza, Honington, S., spinster	246 Code
1852	Barrow, Laura, Honington, S., spinster	122 Latten
1837	Barsham, Robert, Mattishall, N., worstead weaver	441 Warren
1845	Bartlett, Robert, East Harling, N., farmer	825 Pedgrift
1844	Barton, David, Southburgh, N.	624 Ebbage
1834	Barton, Henry, Downham Market, N., farmer	295 Lane
1839	Barton, James, Worlington, S., farmer	515 Calton
1843	Barton, Susan, Newmarket St Mary, S., widow	525 Miles
1847	Barton, William, Lammas, N., farmer	517 Broom
1843	Bartram, Habakkuk, Langmere, N., farmer	233 Miles
1850	Bartram, James, Southrepps, N., miller	43 Cuthbert
1833	Bartram, Simon, Filby, N., farmer	145 Cubitt
1833	Bartrum, William, Wortham, S., farmer	4 Cubitt
1822	Barwick, Anthony, Worlingham, S., late of Horning, N., clerk	233 Sadler

1827	Barwick, George, Beccles, S., gent.	482 Wood
1824	Base, William, Norwich, N., wheelwright	315 Borrett
1824	Basey, John, St Augustine, Norwich, N., weaver	294 Borrett
1832	Basey, Mary, Norwich, N., widow	227 Cooke
1846	Basey, William, Hevingham, N., broom maker	658 Baret
1833	Basham, Edmund, Colkirk, N., cordwainer	295 Cubitt
1848	Basham, Phillippa, Holt, N., widow	166 Denny
1843	Basham, Robert the elder, Northwold, N., miller	277 Miles
1847	Bass, Anna Maria, Scole, N., widow	605 Broom
1844	Bass, John, Scole, N.	107 Ebbage
1846	Bassingthwaite, Rebecca Matilda, Great Yarmouth, N., spinster	167 Baret
1856	Bassingthwaight, William, Hunworth, N., farmer	335 Code
1832	Batchelder, William Smith, Claxton, N., gent.	43 Cooke
1837	Batchelor, Ann, Norwich, N., widow	296 Warren
1846	Batchelor, Elizabeth, Beccles, S.	548 Baret
1822	Batchelor, Henry, Norwich, N., yeoman	381 Sadler
1845	Bate, Edward, Eye, S., farmer	193 Pedgrift
1851	Bate, George, Houghton, N., farmer	415 Friar
1832	Bate, Mary, Eye, S., widow	198 Cooke
1837	Bately, Elizabeth, Halvergate, N., widow	331 Warren
1832	Bately, Lionel, Halvergate, N., farmer	212 Cooke
1826	Bateman, Francis, Barney, N., yeoman	51 Davy
1834	Bateman, Thomas, Great Yarmouth, N., esquire, doctor of medicine	767 Lane
1837	Bates, Jane, Hickling, N., shopkeeper	124 Warren
1840	Bates, Mary, Marlesford, S., widow	219 Turner
1829	Bathurst, Robert, Horstead, N.	399 Green
1834	Batley, Ann, Burwell, C., widow	545 Lane
1849	Batson, Potter Dyball, Aylsham, N., butcher	116 Womack
1823	Batterham, John, Kings Lynn, N., butcher	294 Hayward
1857	Batterham, Richard, Tilney St Lawrence, N.	76 Youngs
1848	Bauley, Dennis, Stowupland, S., miller	443 Denny
1856	Bauley, Lydia, Stowupland, S., widow	510 Code
1845	Bauley, Thomas, Stowupland, S.	747 Pedgrift
1851	Bawtree, Theodora, Yelverton, N., widow	136 Friar
1839	Baxter, Elizabeth, Bury St Edmunds, S., widow	328 Calton
1825	Baxter, John, Mundham, N., farmer	224 Hayward
1829	Baxter, John, Shouldham, N., yeoman	363 Green
1847	Baxter, Nathaniel, Stowmarket, S.	164 Broom
1830	Baxter, Patience, Norwich, N., spinster	172 Pettingill
1855	Baxter, Philip, South Lynn All Saints, N., yeoman	74 Whitty
1856	Baxter, Robert, Hempnall, N., miller	171 Code
1834	Baxter, Thomas, Norwich, N., yeoman	247 Lane
1846	Baxter, William, Wrentham, S., beerhouse keeper	567 Baret
1852	Bayes, Edward, Hemblington, N., carpenter	604 Latten
1834	Bayes, Elizabeth, Ipswich, S., widow	701 Lane
1853	Bayes, Henry, Neatishead, N., farmer	192 Veale
1836	Bayes, Robert, Saxlingham Nethergate, N., yeoman	114 Smith
1827	Bayes, Thomas, Blofield, N., thatcher	361 Wood
1854	Bayes, Thomas Henry, Stiffkey, N., farmer	349 Day
1824	Bayes, William, Great Yarmouth, N., stonemason	278 Borrett
1840	Bayes, William, Wymondham, N., farmer	620 Turner
1830	Bayfield, Elizabeth, Norwich, N., widow	350 Pettingill
1825	Bayfield, John, West Winch, N., gent.	202 Davy
1828	Bayfield, Judith, North Walsham, N., spinster	298 Farrow
1855	Bayfield, Thomas Matthew, Norwich, N., yeoman	354 Whitty
1820	Bayles, John, Denham, S., farmer	469 Mack
1856	Bayles, Robert, Stradbroke, S., miller	407 Code
1857	Bayles, Thomas, Horham, S., farmer	306 Youngs
1841	Bays, Robert, Saxlingham, N., farmer	432 Traxton
1835	Beach, John, Kings Lynn, N., gent.	182 Harrowing
1820	Beadle, Thomas, Melford, S., papermaker	294 Mack
1827	Beales, Ann, Hopton, S., widow	181 Wood

1833	Beales, Rebecca, Old Buckenham, N., spinster	491 Cubitt
1819	Beales, Richard, Eye, S., butcher and farmer	306 Le Neve
1828	Beales, Richard, Neatishead, N., gent.	119 Farrow
1833	Beales, Robert, North Lopham, N., victualler and linen weaver	39 Cubitt
1843	Beales, Robert, Beccles, S., surveyor of taxes	245 Miles
1840	Beales, William, East Dereham, N., farmer	616 Turner
1840	Beales, William, Golden Square, Middlesex, pianoforte maker	90 Turner
1853	Beales, William, Thetford, N., formerly of Old Buckenham, yeoman	472 Veale
1849	Bealey, Mary, Costessey, N.	O.W. 298
1832	Beamish, Noah, Covehithe, S., husbandman	214 Cooke
1849	Beamiss, Arabella, Hilgay, N., widow	4 Womack
1832	Bean, alias Baines, Elizabeth, Bungay, S., maidservant	383 Cooke
1836	Bean, Richard, Great Yarmouth, N., coal meter	331 Smith
1828	Bean Susanna, St Georges Tombland, Norwich, N., widow	454 Farrow
1834	Beane, Benjamin, Thorpe, N., gent.	248 Lane
1837	Bear, Jonathan the elder, Beeston next Mileham, N., farmer	1 Warren
1845	Bear, Mary, Bawdeswell, N., widow	828 Pedgrift
1842	Beard, William, Stowupland, S., farmer	583 Canler
1857	Beare, Amelia, Norwich, N., spinster	236 Youngs
1831	Beare, Martha, Norwich, N., widow	576 Hart
1823	Beare, William, Norwich, boot and shoe maker	286 Tann
1831	Beart, Elizabeth, Mendlesham, S., formerly of Blo Norton, N., spinster	66 Hart
1834	Beart, Robert, Hopton, S., farmer	776 Lane
1830	Beart, William, Welney, N., farmer	98 Pettingill
1831	Beart, William, Palgrave, S.	431 Hart
1857	Beasy, Edwin, Cromer, N., carrier	74 Youngs
1823	Beatley, Matthew, Brancaster, N., husbandman	409 Tann
1852	Beatley, George, Norwich, N., hatter and hosier	237 Latten
1822	Beats, John, Tivetshall St Margaret, N., farmer	264 Sadler
1857	Beaumont, Dorothy, Norwich, N., widow	494 Youngs
1848	Beaumont, Elizabeth, Redenhall with Harleston, N., widow	644 Denny
1841	Beaumont, George, St John Sepulchre, Norwich, N., gent.	210 Traxton
1841	Beaumont, James the elder, Mendham, S., gent.	554 Traxton
1824	Beaumont, John, Ringshall, S., yeoman	154 Borrett
1824	Beaurain, John, Kings Lynn, N., gent.	304 Borrett
1845	Beavis, Henry, Stow Bardolph, N., farmer	143 Pedgrift
1823	Beavor, Ann, St Andrews, Norwich, N.	14 Tann
1841	Beazor, James, Little Walsingham, N., butcher	347 Traxton
1845	Beck, Edward Bigsley, Creeting St Mary, S., gent.	713 Pedgrift
1851	Beck, George, Hainford, N., labourer, o.w. missing	376 Friar
1855	Beck, George, Caistor Next Yarmouth, N., farmer and miller	97 Whitty
1824	Beck, Henry, Stalham, N., husbandman	106 Borrett
1838	Beck, William, Catfield, N., farmer	773 Skepper
1823	Beckerton, William, Wells next the sea, N., labourer	282 Tann
1849	Beckett, James senior, Tharston, N., yeoman	311 Womack
1835	Beckett, John, Topcroft, N., carpenter	622 Harrowing
1820	Beckett, Thomas, Stalham, N., butcher	602 Mack
1822	Beckett, Thomas, Woodton, N., yeoman	329 Sadler
1833	Beckett, William, Great Yarmouth, N., baker	366 Cubitt
1846	Beckham, Edmund, Norwich, N., cooper	554 Baret
1841	Beckham, Elizabeth, St Edmund, Norwich, N., widow	171 Traxton
1829	Beckwith, Martha, St Peter Permountergate, Norwich, N., widow	410 Green
1855	Beckwith, Thomas, Crostwight, N., clerk	696 Whitty
1843	Bedford, Martha, Norwich, N., wife of Charles Bedford, brazier	311 Miles
1851	Bedford, Mary, Great Yarmouth, N., widow	540 Friar
1855	Bedingfield, Cornelius, Westhall, S., tailor	240 Whitty
1856	Bedingfield, James, Mettingham, S., yeoman	430 Code
1840	Bedingfield, William, Denham, S., farmer	390 Turner

1821	Bedwell, James, Brandeston, S., carpenter	173 Dewell
1827	Bedwell, John, Middleton, S., blacksmith	438 Wood
1841	Bedwell, Sarah, Woodbridge, S., spinster	469 Traxton
1847	Beecroft, Ann, Lowestoft, S., widow	141 Broom
1833	Beecroft, Thomas, Debenham, S., hairdresser	361 Cubitt
1848	Beecroft, William, Lowestoft, S., butcher	678 Denny
1850	Beecroft, William, Bungay, S., innkeeper	149 Cuthbert
1827	Beeden, Thomas, Sudbourne, S., yeoman	647 Wood
1842	Beer, John, Little Waldingfield, S., carpenter	170 Canler
1850	Beer, John, Thorpe, Norwich, N., gent.	411 Cuthbert
1845	Beer, Susan, Little Waldingfield, S., widow	860 Pedgrift
1843	Beercroft, Thomas, Debenham, S.	Index only
1838	Beeson, William, Wiggenhall St Germains, N., farmer	127 Skepper
1850	Beeston, alias Gedge, John, Norwich, N., shopkeeper	220 Cuthbert
1840	Beeston, Thomas the elder, Mileham, N., farmer	305 Turner
1856	Beets, Elizabeth, Great Yarmouth, N., widow	2 Code
1850	Beets, Lydia, Downham, N.	180 Cuthbert
1834	Beevor, Arthur Brauthwayt, Norwich, N., gent.	41 Lane
1846	Beevor, Bridget, Norwich, N., widow	230 Baret
1829	Bell Benjamin, Potter Heigham, N., yeoman	58 Green
1857	Bell, Benjamin, East Ruston, N., yeoman	521 Youngs
1857	Bell, Benjamin, Foulsham, N., gent.	453 Youngs
1820	Bell, James, Norwich, N., manufacturer	O.W. 284
1837	Bell, James, Horsham St Faiths, N.	107 Warren
1838	Bell, John, Norwich, N., bricklayer	842 Skepper
1855	Bell, John, Kings Lynn, N., formerly of Shouldham, yeoman	745 Whitty
1853	Bell, Martin, Great Ryburgh, N., gent.	450 Veale
1822	Bell, Philip, Stibbard, N., innkeeper	289 Sadler
1844	Bell, Sarah, Blickling, N., widow	205 Ebbage
1832	Bell, William senior, Tivetshall St Mary, N., farmer	542 Cooke
1832	Bell William, West Walton, N., farmer	280 Cooke
1837	Bell, William, Tivetshall St Mary, N., grocer and draper	70 Warren
1829	Bellman, John, Eye, S., gent.	213 Green
1853	Bellward, William the elder, Hardley, N., innkeeper and maltster	505 Veale
1820	Bellwood, Elizabeth, Kings Lynn, N., widow	14 Mack
1836	Beloe, John, Great Yarmouth, N., gent.	556 Smith
1830	Beloe, William, Norwich, N., manufacturer	O.W. 253
1857	Beloe, William, St Clements, Norwich, N., yeoman, formerly of Wroxham, N., innkeeper	442 Youngs
1826	Belson, John, Snettisham, N.	151 Davy
1857	Belson, Miles, Snettisham, N., butcher	488 Youngs
1851	Belson, Rosetta, Acle, N., spinster	25 Friar
1848	Bemment, Joseph, Lowestoft, S., carpenter	348 Denny
1827	Bendy, Charles, Coltishall, N., surgeon	534 Wood
1843	Bendy, Susanna Avis, Coltishall, N.	448 Miles
1830	Bennington, Joseph, Framlingham, S., farmer	64 Pettingill
1857	Bennell, Nicholas, Brancaster, N., blacksmith	113 Youngs
1825	Bennell, Robert, Brancaster, N., smith	343 Hayward
1847	Bennett, Arthur, Downham Market, N., tailor and woollen draper	685 Broom
1822	Bennett, James the elder, Botesdale, S., cordwainer	203 Sadler
1835	Bennett, John, Winston, S., farmer	400 Harrowing
1837	Bennett, John, Great Yarmouth, N., linen weaver	81 Warren
1838	Bennett, John, Saham Toney, N., farmer	4 Skepper
1842	Bennett, John, Knodishall, S., yeoman	344 Canler
1848	Bennett, John, Docking, N., blacksmith	593 Denny
1832	Bennett, Joseph, Wiggenhall St Mary Magdalen, N., farmer	577 Cooke
1855	Bennett, Joseph, Whittington, Northwold, N., yeoman	691 Whitty
1830	Bennett, Martha, Debenham, S.	373 Pettingill
1840	Bennett, Rebecca, Little Brandon, N., widow	229 Turner
1857	Bennett, Rose, Docking, N.	316 Youngs

1838	Bennett, William, Norwich, N., baker	876 Skepper
1840	Bensley, Benjamin, Norwich, N.	Index only
1849	Bensley, Elizabeth, Great Yarmouth, N., widow	29 Womack
1825	Bensley, Henry, North Burlingham, N., carpenter	87 Hayward
1826	Bensley, John, Cley, N., customs surveyor	348 Davy
1846	Bensley, John, Norwich, N., carpenter	25 Baret
1857	Bensley, Margaret, Geldeston, N., widow	536 Youngs
1820	Bensley, Noah, Reedham, N., bricklayer	648 Mack
1852	Benstead, John, West Dereham, N., farmer	24 Latten
1838	Bensted, Frances, South Creake, N., widow	689 Skepper
1819	Bentfield, William, Ringsfield, S., farmer	30 Le Neve
1839	Berney, Elizabeth, Bracon Ash, N., widow	199 Calton
1848	Berney, Elizabeth, Bracon Ash, N., spinster	457 Denny
1838	Berrett, Robert, Sutton, S., farmer	692 Skepper
1834	Berry, Daniel, Thorndon, S., shoemaker	85 Lane
1833	Berry, Hannah, Norwich, N., widow	323 Cubitt
1848	Berry, James, Thrandeston, S., yeoman	552 Denny
1819	Berry, John, Upwell, C., victualler	163 Le Neve
1850	Berry, Robert, Kings Lynn, N., yeoman	246 Cuthbert
1840	Berry, William, Palgrave, S., cattle dealer	37 Turner
1840	Berwick, John, Foulsham, N., farmer	342 Turner
1824	Berwick, Mary, St Margarets, Norwich, N., widow	48 Borrett
1849	Berwick, Sarah, Bungay, S., widow	467 Womack
1850	Besfor, Mary, Surlingham, N., widow	449 Cuthbert
1844	Besfor, Robert, Pockthorpe, Norwich, N., boatbuilder	672 Ebbage
1838	Besford, Benjamin, Kerdiston, N., farmer	146 Skepper
1825	Besouth, Ann, St, Michael at Thorn, Norwich, N.	103 Hayward
1840	Bessey, James, Great Yarmouth, N., merchant	186 Turner
1821	Bethel, John, Norton, S., farmer	97 Dewell
1842	Betts, Benjamin, Scottow, N., farmer	715 Canler
1827	Betts, Charles, Old Buckenham, N., farmer	656 Wood
1844	Betts, George, Shadbrooke, S., bricklayer	143 Ebbage
1845	Betts, James, Upton, N., husbandman	39 Pedgrift
1849	Betts, James, Eye, S., clerk	569 Womack
1822	Betts, Jane, Tibbenham, N., spinster	261 Sadler
1853	Betts, John, Sloley, N., gardener	317 Veale
1845	Betts, Mary, Felthorpe, N., widow	893 Pedgrift
1849	Betts, Thomas, Stradbroke, S., bricklayer	168 Green
1849	Betts, Thomas, East Dereham, N., husbandman	50 Womack
1823	Betts, William, Blakeney, N., tailor	377 Tann
1836	Betts, William, Old Buckenham, N., farmer	261 Smith
1836	Betts, William, Tittleshall, N., farmer	43 Smith
1843	Betts, William, East Carleton, N., gardener	552 Miles
1820	Beverley, Elizabeth, Poringland, N., widow	490 Mack
1830	Beverley, Elizabeth, St Gregory, Norwich, N., spinster	443 Pettingill
1849	Beverley, Michael, Forncett St Mary, N., farmer	502 Womack
1837	Beverly, John, St Andrews, Norwich, N., gent.	722 Warren
1855	Beverly, Levi, Beccles, S., miller	732 Whitty
1848	Bexfield, John, Thorpe next Haddiscoe, N., gent.	671 Denny
1844	Bexfield, Richard, Heigham, Norwich, N., gent.	17 Ebbage
1840	Bexfield, Thomas, Thurlton, N., farmer	490 Turner
1853	Bezance, John, Great Yarmouth, N., master mariner	640 Veale
1837	Bezant, William, Mettingham, S., farmer	435 Warren
1827	Bickers, Ann, Framlingham, S.	147 Wood
1841	Bickers, Mary, Great Yarmouth, N., spinster	569 Traxton
1827	Bickmore, Thomas the elder, Copdock, S., wheelwright	528 Wood
1852	Bidwell, George, Norwich, N., innkeeper	426 Latten
1831	Bidwell, Martha, Norwich, N., widow	135 Hart
1855	Bidwell, Thomas, Trunch, N., farmer	239 Whitty
1848	Bigg, Isaac, Glemsford, S., farmer	180 Denny
1840	Bigg, John, Glemsford, S., farmer	464 Turner
1834	Bigg, Samuel, Glemsford, S., farmer	318 Lane
1823	Bilby, John, Beccles, S., yeoman	50 Tann

1849	Bilham, Benjamin, Watton, N., gardener	213 Womack
1848	Bilham, Hannah, wife of John Bilham, Norwich, N.	174 Denny
1826	Billing, George, Heigham, Norwich, N., gent.	O.W. 174
1832	Billing, John, Kings Lynn, N., victualler	573 Cooke
1838	Billing, John, Mileham, N.,	244 Skepper
1845	Billing, John, East Rudham, N., farmer	576 Pedgrift
1852	Birch, Ann, Sloley, N., widow	514 Latten
1826	Birch, William, Charsfield, S., husbandman	133 Davy
1839	Bircham, Ann, Brooke, N., spinster	231 Calton
1834	Bircham, John, Wood Dawling, N., farmer	488 Lane
1829	Bircham, Mary, Reepham, N., widow	142 Green
1849	Bircham, Thomas, Briston, N.innkeeper	409 Womack
1856	Bird, Benjamin, Stowupland, S., farmer	384 Code
1849	Bird, Candler, Cotton, S., farmer	115 Womack
1829	Bird, Dunham, Westwick, N., gamekeeper	385 Green
1841	Bird, Elizabeth, St Clements, Norwich, N., innkeeper	578 Traxton
1853	Bird, Elizabeth, Burnham Westgate, N., widow	52 Veale
1832	Bird, John, Burnham Westgate, N., butcher	539 Cooke
1839	Bird, John Thornsby, Riddlesworth, N., rector	439 Calton
1842	Bird, John, Florden, N., farmer	140 Canler
1854	Bird, John, Carlton Colville, S., yeoman	325 Day
1854	Bird, Lucy, Norwich, N., spinster	188 Day
1843	Bird, Mary, Southwold, S., widow	619 Miles
1846	Bird, Mary, Southwold, S., spinster	402 Baret
1854	Bird, Patience, Norwich, N., spinster	482 Day
1829	Bird, Sarah, Kings Lynn, N., widow	280 Green
1837	Bird, Susan, Needham Market, S., spinster	549 Warren
1826	Bird, William, Docking, N., gardener	90 Davy
1837	Bird, William, Whitton cum Thurlston, Ipswich, S., formerly of Westerfield, S., gent.	337 Warren
1854	Birt, Martha Isabella, North Walsham, N., widow	579 Day
1847	Bishop, Anna, Eye, S., spinster	478 Broom
1820	Bishop, Farmer, Mattishall, N., hairdresser, and barber	563 Mack
1853	Bishop, Hannah, Hickling, N., spinster	262 Veale
1839	Bishop, John, Eye, S., gent.	674 Calton
1850	Bishop, Joseph, Beeston Regis, N., fishdealer	589 Cuthbert
1857	Bishop, Lyas, Snettisham, N., gent.	285 Youngs
1827	Black, John, Tittleshall, N., farmer	688 Wood
1839	Black, Samuel, Great Yarmouth, N., yeoman	613 Calton
1849	Blackbon, Aaron Harter, Bungay, S., hairdresser	350 Womack
1841	Blackburn, Anthony, Southtown, Yarmouth, S., gent.	86 Traxton
1848	Blackburn, Martha, Southtown, S., widow	331 Denny
1856	Blackburn, William, Worstead, N., gardener	539 Code
1846	Blackett, Sophia, Great Yarmouth, N., widow	Index only
1845	Blade, James, Feltwell, N., grocer and draper	644 Pedgrift
1848	Blagg, Mary Ann, Great Yarmouth, N., singlewoman	675 Denny
1826	Blake, David, Norwich, N., dyer	183 Davy
1842	Blake, Dodshan, St Clements, Norwich, N., gent.	7 Canler
1845	Blake, Henry, Ipswich, S., cordwainer	328 Pedgrift
1835	Blake, Isaac, Norwich, hotpresser	369 Harrowing
1849	Blake, Sarah, Norwich, N., widow	685 Womack
1822	Blakely, Elizabeth, Norwich, N., widow	262 Sadler
1828	Blakes, John, Little Stonham, S., husbandman	17 Farrow
1827	Blakes, William, Bacton, S., thatcher	479 Wood
1855	Blancher, John, Norwich, N., bricklayer	260 Whitty
1846	Blanchflower, Benjamin, Fakenham, N., carpenter	328 Baret
1832	Blanchflower, Francis, Helhoughton, N., blacksmith	580 Cooke
1827	Blanchflower, John, Foulsham, N., yeoman	85 Wood
1839	Blanchflower, Robert, Toftrees, N., yeoman	228 Calton
1827	Blancks, John, Framingham Pigot, N., clerk	233 Wood
1855	Bland, Joshua, Wereham, N., farmer	605 Whitty
1833	Bland, Thomas, Fincham, N., carpenter	33 Cubitt
1828	Blaxall, Simon, Eyke, S., farmer	435 Farrow
1836	Blaxcell, John, Middleton, S., farmer	205 Warren

1840	Blazeby, John the elder, Norwich, N., chairmaker	399 Turner
1853	Blazeby, Martha, Norwich, N., widow	78 Veale
1821	Bleakley, Elijah, St Mary's Coslany, Norwich, N., manufacturer,	21 Dewell
1853	Bleakley, Robert, Hellesdon, N., formerly of Oxnead, N., farmer	57 Veale
1820	Bleckly, George, Ipswich, S.	429 Mack
1820	Block, Mary, Rendham, S., widow	540 Mack
1831	Block, William, St Lawrence, Ipswich, S.	92 Hart
1855	Blofeld, Robert, Fakenham, N., lime burner	330 Whitty
1820	Blofield, John, Norwich, N., gent.	21 Mack
1826	Blogg, Elizabeth, Corpusty, N., widow	7 Davy
1835	Blogg, Mary, Creeting St Olaves, S., widow	419 Harrowing
1831	Blogg, Samuel the elder, Creeting St Olaves, S., farmer	323 Hart
1852	Blogg, Samuel, Creeting St Olaves, S., farmer	817 Latten
1829	Blomefield, Frances, Norwich, N., wife of William Blomefield, cook	45 Green
1854	Blomefield, Eliza, Billingford, N., spinster	328 Day
1819	Blomfield, the Reverend Ezekiel, Redenhall with Harleston, N.	49 Le Neve
1825	Blomfield, Fanny	299 Hayward
1846	Blomfield, James, Barton Bendish, N., farmer	436 Baret
1820	Blomfield, John, Newton next Castle Acre, N., farmer	369 Mack
1832	Blomfield, John, Ashbocking, S., yeoman	582 Cooke
1841	Blomfield, John, Billingford Hall, N., farmer	668 Traxton
1844	Blomfield, John, Holt, N., glover	365 Ebbage
1845	Blomfield, Maria, Billingford, N., spinster	874 Pedgrift
1826	Blomfield, Miles, Billingford, N., yeoman	109 Davy
1832	Blomfield, Miles, Warham, N., formerly of Flitcham, farmer	184 Cooke
1856	Blomfield, Miriam, Billingford, N., spinster	361 Code
1829	Blomfield, Robert, Hemley, S., farmer	180 Veales
1848	Blomfield, Samuel, Eye, S., yeoman	318 Denny
1845	Blomfield, Sarah, Mattishall, N., widow	753 Pedgrift
1847	Blomfield, Stephen, Mendlesham, S., farm bailiff	751 Broom
1846	Blomfield, Susan, Walsham Le Willows, S., spinster	301 Baret
1833	Blomfield, Thomas, Otley, S., gent.	291 Cubitt
1841	Blomfield, William, Norwich, N., gent.	23 Traxton
1843	Blomfield, William, Great Yarmouth, N., late master mariner	523 Miles
1848	Blomfield, William, Yaxley, poulterer	472 Denny
1850	Blomfield, William, Barton Bendish, N., farmer	380 Cuthbert
1842	Bloom, Ann, Wells, N., spinster	567 Canler
1847	Bloom, Ann, Eye, S., spinster	668 Broom
1842	Bloom, George, Burwell, C., yeoman	390 Canler
1857	Bloomfield, James, St Lawrence Ilketshall, S., farmer	169 Youngs
1834	Bloomfield, Thomas, Stradbrooke, S., farmer	604 Lane
1850	Bloomfield, William, Sheringham, N., farmer	47 Cuthbert
1848	Bloss, Francis Linch, Newmarket, S., innkeeper	819 Denny
1836	Blower, John, Denver, N., carpenter	88 Smith
1853	Bloy, James, Stratton St Michael, N., formerly of Bradwell, S., gent.	494 Veale
1835	Blunderfield, Henry, Earsham, N., farmer	134 Harrowing
1835	Blunderfield, Samuel, Norwich, N., carpenter	107 Harrowing
1852	Bly, Benjamin, South Creake, N., wheelwright	831 Latten
1820	Bly, Elizabeth, Great Yarmouth, N., spinster	598 Mack
1839	Bly, Elizabeth, Yarmouth, N., widow	130 Calton
1853	Bly, George, Heacham, N., plumber and glazier	481 Veale
1837	Bly, Susannah, Great Yarmouth, N., widow	51 Warren
1820	Bly, Thomas, Great Yarmouth, N., gent.	550 Mack
1844	Blyford, Mary, Little Walsingham, N., spinster	685 Ebbage
1820	Blyth, Edward, Bircham Newton, N., singleman	319 Mack
1829	Blyth, Hannah, Norwich, N., spinster	O.W. 243
1830	Blyth, Hannah, Southrepps, N., widow	444 Pettingill
1857	Blyth, James, Felthorpe, N., farmer	574 Youngs

1837	Blyth, John, Sparham, N., tailor	591 Warren
1857	Blyth, Joseph, Norwich, N., publican	647 Youngs
1834	Blyth, Matthew, Ringland, N., wheelwright	65 Lane
1827	Blyth, Philip, Norwich, N., yeoman	552 Wood
1830	Blyth, Philip the younger, Norwich, N., weaver	161 Pettingill
1832	Blyth, Robert Burton, Burnham Westgate, N., esquire	457 Cooke
1847	Blyth, Robert, Drayton, N., carpenter	757 Broom
1838	Blyth, Samuel, Heigham, Norwich, N., plasterer	155 Skepper
1825	Blyth, Sarah, Orford, S., widow of John Blyth	341 Hayward
1855	Blyth, Timothy, Norwich, N., yeoman	118 Whitty
1845	Blyth, William, Salhouse, N., farmer	648 Pedgrift
1845	Blyth, William Dennis, Erpingham, N., farmer	437 Pedgrift
1825	Blythe, Sarah, Letheringham, S., widow	443 Hayward
1831	Boardman, Elizabeth, St Giles, Norwich, N., widow	108 Hart
1823	Boardman, John, Norwich, hatter and hosier	349 Tann
1827	Boardman, Philip, Heigham by Norwich, N.	O.W. 310
1852	Boardman, Richard Roper, Norwich, N., gent.	563 Latten
1833	Boardman, Sarah, Norwich, N., widow	13 Cubitt
1825	Boast, Robert, Norwich, N., lawyer	35 Hayward
1855	Boatwright, James, the Tuns Inn, Broome, N., publican	660 Whitty
1842	Boatwright, John, Blofield, N., farmer	727 Canler
1835	Boby, Ann, Stowmarket, S., widow	180 Harrowing
1820	Boby, John Wright, Haughley, S., gent.	479 Mack
1829	Boby, Robert, Barningham, S., gent.	90 Green
1834	Boby, William Johnson, Beccles, S.	562 Lane
1834	Bocking, Ann, Mendlesham, S., widow	609 Lane
1853	Bocking, Thomas, Norwich, N., carpenter	376 Veale
1830	Body, Benjamin, Snettisham, N., farmer	99 Pettingill
1819	Body, William, Mileham, N., husbandman	206 Le Neve
1838	Boggis, James, Felsham, S., farmer	498 Skepper
1836	Bohun, Mary Ann, Beccles, S., spinster	479 Smith
1846	Bokenham, Thomas, Southwold, S., innkeeper	418 Baret
1841	Bokenham, William, Framingham Earl, N., farmer	564 Traxton
1851	Boldero, Elizabeth, Southrepps, N., spinster	319 Friar
1821	Bolding, Elizabeth, Cley next Sea, N., widow	332 Dewell
1826	Bolton, George, Norwich, N., ironmonger	306 Davy
1854	Bolton, Rebecca, Burnham Market, N., spinster	420 Day
1832	Bolton, Samuel, Downham Market, N., butcher	574 Cooke
1836	Bolton, Uriah, Horham, S., formerly of Redlingfield, farmer	165 Smith
1857	Bond, Alice, Great Snoring, N., spinster	313 Youngs
1851	Bond, Anna Maria, Great Yarmouth, N., spinster	618 Friar
1828	Bond, Barnabas, Pulham St Mary the Virgin, N., gent.	137 Farrow
1832	Bond, George, Hacheston, S., farmer	515 Cooke
1837	Bond, Henry, Winterton, N., miller	165 Warren
1834	Bond, John, Ludham, N., farmer	340 Lane
1838	Bond, John, Gresham, N.	580 Skepper
1850	Bond, John, Cawston, N., farmer	485 Cuthbert
1852	Bond, Richard, Kirby Bedon, N., farmer	316 Latten
1847	Bond, Robert, Briston, N., clerk	237 Broom
1852	Bond, Robert, Great Yarmouth, N., gent.	317 Latten
1849	Bond, Stephen, Wickham Skeith, S., yeoman	454 Womack
1836	Bond, Thomas the elder, Little Walsingham, N., gardener	7 Smith
1847	Bond, Thomas, Thrandeston, S.	659 Broom
1848	Bond, William, Great Yarmouth, N.	330 Denny
1820	Bone, Ann, Fakenham, N., widow	234 Mack
1831	Bone, Ann, Scarning, N., farmer	218 Hart
1822	Bone, Barnard, Swaffham, N., wheelwright	80 Sadler
1847	Bone, James, Billingford, N., butcher	147 Broom
1842	Bone, Thomas, Norwich, N., baker	211 Canler
1830	Bonfellow, Susanna, Bungay, S., spinster	153 Pettingill
1849	Bonfield, William, Outwell, Isle of Ely, C., gent.	234 Womack
1840	Boniwell, William, Halesworth, S., tailor	84 Turner

1848	Bonner, Ann, Kings Lynn, N., wife of William Bonner, merchant	633 Denny
1826	Bonnet, Sarah, Caister next Yarmouth, N.	201 Davy
1833	Bonnett, John, Burnham Westgate, N.	212 Cubitt
1834	Bonney, James, Gorleston, S., fish merchant	515 Lane
1836	Bonney, Sarah, St Peter Mancroft, Norwich, N., widow	559 Smith
1835	Boom, Thomas, Great Walsingham, N., farmer and coal carter	148 Harrowing
1850	Boon, Charles, Ellingham, N., farmer	103 Cuthbert
1846	Boon, Edward, Oulton, S., husbandman	41 Baret
1853	Boon, Edward, Weston, S., farmer	617 Veale
1820	Boon, George, Benhall, S., brickmaker	235 Mack
1841	Boon, John, Ringsfield, S.	79 Traxton
1854	Boon, John, Burgh St Peter, N., commander mutine South Sea whaler	268 Day
1850	Boon, William, Burgh St Peter, N., gent.	448 Cuthbert
1837	Boorne, William, Erpingham, N., wine merchant	649 Warren
1846	Boorne, Mary, Blakeney, N., widow	626 Baret
1827	Booth, Rose, Houghton, N., widow	144 Wood
1819	Boothby, Ann, Kings Lynn, N., widow	212 Le Neve
1824	Boothby, Ann, Heacham, N., single woman	355 Borrett
1827	Bootman, John, Bridgeham, N., yeoman	70 Wood
1829	Bootwright, Henry, Wissett, S., farmer	266 Green
1842	Booty, Abigail, Norwich, N., widow	204 Canler
1847	Booty, Edward, Ipswich, S., baptist preacher	765 Broom
1820	Booty, Elizabeth, Bardwell, S., widow	219 Mack
1846	Booty, Elizabeth, Weybread, S., widow	238 Baret
1845	Booty, Hanslip, Hockwold cum Wilton, N., yeoman	585 Pedgrift
1828	Booty, James Gallaway, Binham, N., gent.	89 Farrow
1833	Booty, James, Rishangles, S, farmer	251 Cubitt
1843	Booty, James, West Lynn, N.	12 Miles
1843	Booty, John the elder, Bardwell, S gent.	662 Miles
1844	Booty, John, Horsford, N., farmer	566 Ebbage
1847	Booty, John, Dickleburgh, N., yeoman	400 Broom
1840	Booty, Susan, Hempnall, N., widow	630 Turner
1819	Bore, John, Swaffham, N., schoolmaster	285 Le Neve
1828	Borrett, Elizabeth, Dennington, S., widow	121 Farrow
1824	Borrett, Henry, Topcroft, N.	1 Borrett
1846	Borrett, Henry, Bungay, S., bachelor	514 Baret
1853	Borrett, John, Eye, S., tailor and grocer	668 Veale
1839	Borrett, Mary, Neatishead, N.	624 Calton
1852	Borrett, Mary Maria, Bungay, S., wife of William Borrett, wheelwright	877 Latten
1824	Borrett, William, Ipswich, S., shopkeeper	86 Borrett
1826	Borrett, William, Stradbroke, S., yeoman	233 Davy
1831	Borrett, William, Great Yarmouth, N., ship agent	393 Hart
1839	Borrett, William, Horham, S., yeoman	389 Calton
1854	Borrett, William, Bungay, S., wheelwright	307 Day
1857	Borrett, William, Walberswick, S., farmer	431 Youngs
1851	Borritt, Sophia, Diss, N., widow	359 Friar
1843	Borroughs, Ann, The Close, Norwich, N., widow	360 Miles
1844	Bossley, William, Southtown, Yarmouth, S., gent.	271 Ebbage
1821	Botwright, James, Laxfield, S., yeoman	99 Dewell
1847	Botwright, Jeremiah, Bungay, S., carpenter and builder	207 Broom
1850	Botwright, William, Henstead with Hulverstreet, S., cordwainer	68 Cuthbert
1844	Boughen, John, Barton Bendish, N., formerly of Fincham, N., farmer	258 Ebbage
1843	Boughey, (or Boughay), John, Trunch, N., farmer	521 Miles
1823	Boult, George, Acle, N., gent.	255 Tann
1830	Boult, George the younger, Heigham, Norwich, N., tanner	377 Pettingill
1847	Boult, Mary, Stokesby, N., widow	15 Broom
1830	Boult, William, Runham, N., farmer	243 Pettingill
1825	Boulter, Anne, Brockdish, N., spinster	202 Hayward

1857	Boulter, Joseph Luff, Norwich, N., merchants clerk	652 Youngs
1846	Boulter, Mary, Great Yarmouth, N., widow	32 Baret
1848	Boulter, Money, Great Ryburgh, N., farmer	808 Denny
1831	Boulton, James, Great Fransham, N., labourer	553 Hart
1826	Boutell, Charles, Swaffham, N., gent.	289 Davy
1848	Boutell, Thomas, Hempnall, N., farmer	569 Denny
1842	Bowell, William, North Lopham, N., farmer	87 Canler
1830	Bowen, Frances, Swaffham, N., widow	71 Pettingill
1851	Bowen, Thomas, Beeston, N., farmer	435 Friar
1856	Bower, Robert, Colchester, Essex, also Potter Heigham, N., hosier	497 Cole
1823	Bowers, Henry, Aldeburgh, S., surgeon	12 Tann
1850	Bowers, Solomon, North Pickenham, N., baker	572 Cuthbert
1842	Bowles, Barnard, St Lawrence, Norwich, N., shoeing smith	699 Canler
1855	Bowles, Edward, Great Yarmouth, N., labourer	559 Whitty
1835	Bowles, Elizabeth, Great Yarmouth, N., widow	8 Warren
1854	Bowles, James, Kings Lynn, N., corn and flour dealer	52 Day
1825	Bowles, Mary, Great Yarmouth, N., widow	72 Hayward
1837	Bowles, Mary, New Buckenham, N., wife of Richard Bowles, Wilby, N., gent.	421 Warren
1842	Bowles, Thomas, Great Yarmouth, N., publican	257 Canler
1846	Bowles, Thomas, Great Yarmouth, N., carter	219 Baret
1856	Bowman, Deborah, Great Yarmouth, N., widow	321 Code
1855	Bowman, Moses, North Tuddenham, N., labourer	580 Whitty
1849	Bowman, James, Great Yarmouth, N., carter and cow keeper	445 Womack
1840	Bowman, John, Newmarket St Mary, S., gent.	531 Turner
1841	Bowring, John, Horning, N.	567 Traxton
1823	Box, Samuel, Winterton, N., mariner and pilot	104 Tann
1828	Boyce, Barnabas, St Mary, Bungay, S., victualler	26 Farrow
1820	Boyce, Edmund, Wrentham, formerly of Blundeston, S., yeoman	272 Mack
1825	Boyce, Elizabeth Henrietta, Dunston, N.	514 Hayward
1836	Boyce, Francis, Wood Ditton, C., jockey	545 Smith
1825	Boyce, George, Norwich, N., plumber and glazier	367 Hayward
1854	Boyce, George, Upwell, C., farmer and beerseller	561 Day
1826	Boyce, John, Norwich, N., plumber and glazier	56 Davy
1822	Boyce, John, Gorleston, S., cordwainer	231 Sadler
1852	Boyce, Richard, Garboldisham, N., gent.	436 Latten
1834	Boyce, Sarah, Norwich, N., spinster	16 Lane
1821	Boyce, Thomas, Lowestoft, S., tailor and broker	143 Dewell
1834	Boyce, Thomas, Langham, N., wheelwright	165 Lane
1850	Boyce, Thomas, Repps, N., glazier	49 Cuthbert
1852	Boyd, Maria, Holt, N., widow	O.W. 256
1847	Boyden, Catherine, Beccles, S., spinster	Index Only
1853	Boyles, Samuel, Wangford, S., yeoman	242 Veale
1834	Brabbins, Henry, Thurlton, N., husbandman	183 Lane
1825	Bradbury, Amey, Ipswich, S., widow	451 Hayward
1820	Braddy, Elizabeth, Clare, S., spinster	151 Mack
1823	Bradfield, Charles, North Elmham, N., farmer	367 Tann
1841	Bradfield, Elizabeth, Great Yarmouth, N., widow	411 Traxton
1825	Bradfield, James, Great Yarmouth, N., yeoman	208 Hayward
1839	Bradfield, James, North Elmham, N., farmer	467 Calton
1822	Bradfield, John, Colton, N.	198 Sadler
1845	Bradfield, Mary, Houghton on the Hill, N., widow	355 Pedgrift
1848	Bradfield, Pleasance, Stanfield, N., spinster	231 Denny
1848	Bradfield, Robert, North Elmham, N., innkeeper	139 Denny
1847	Bradfield, Thomas, North Walsham, N., yeoman	719 Broom
1841	Bradfor, Isaac, Upton, N., husbandman	565 Traxton
1827	Bradley, Charles, Emneth, N., yeoman	166 Wood
1852	Bradley, Susannah, Great Finborough, S., widow	75 Latten
1833	Bradley, William, Melton, S., clerk	521 Cubitt
1846	Bradnum, William, Beccles, S., gardener	204 Baret
1843	Brady, Gosker, Norwich, N., plumber, glazier and painter	436 Miles
1850	Brady, Robert Watts, Kerdiston, N., farmer	585 Cuthbert
1841	Brady, William, Great Yarmouth, N., gent.	169 Traxton

1827	Braham, Robert the elder, Snape, S., farmer	233 Wood
1849	Brainsby, Elizabeth, Walpole St Peter, N., widow	86 Womack
1823	Brainsby, Thomas, Walpole St Peter, N., blacksmith	223 Tann
1855	Bramble, Edward, Catfield, N., farmer	401 Whitty
1853	Bramble, Matthew, North Walsham, N., yeoman	195 Veale
1852	Brame, John, Lowestoft, S., gent.	116 Latten
1832	Brame, Thomas, Bridgham, N., innholder	303 Cooke
1855	Branch, Edward, Seething, N., gent.	169 Whitty
1840	Brand, Jacob, Great Waldingfield, S., farmer	313 Turner
1841	Brand, John the elder, Acton, S., farmer	223 Traxton
1824	Brand, Mary, Lowestoft, S., widow	187 Borrett
1845	Brand, Mayes, Loddon, N., gent.	488 Pedgrift
1837	Brand, Thomas, Reepham, N., gent.	523 Warren
1853	Brand, William, Great Yarmouth, N., woollen draper	380 Veale
1837	Branford, Benjamin, Horningtoft, N., farmer	622 Warren
1853	Branford, Richard, Swainsthorpe, N., yeoman	74 Veale
1820	Branford, William, Caistor next Great Yarmouth, N., gent.	141 Mack
1857	Bransby, John, South Lynn All Saints, N., clerk	682 Youngs
1845	Branson, Maria, Bressingham, N., single woman	427 Pedgrift
1840	Bray, John, Norwich, N., tailor and salesman	155 Turner
1841	Bray, John Michael, Norwich, N., haberdasher and hardware dealer	92 Traxton
1838	Bray, Thomas, Diss, N., farmer	416 Skepper
1853	Brazell, George, Heigham next Norwich, N., bachelor	217 Veale
1840	Breame, William, North Elmham, N., sailor	609 Turner
1854	Brecknell, Sarah, Great Yarmouth, N., widow	448 Day
1851	Breese, Ann, Hockering, N., widow	170 Friar
1838	Breese, Chamberlayne, Weasenham All Saints, N., gardener	726 Skepper
1828	Breese, James, Saxthorpe, N., tailor	12 Farrow
1855	Breese, James, Reepham, N., gardener	135 Whitty
1845	Breese, Jane, Walsoken, N., widow	418 Pedgrift
1840	Breese, Matthew, Hackford next Reepham, N., alehouse keeper	217 Turner
1847	Breese, Mary, Lakenham, N., spinster	520 Broom
1831	Breeze, Elizabeth, Great Yarmouth, N., wife of Simon Breeze, mariner	389 Hart
1831	Breeze, Robert, Great Yarmouth, N., sergeant at Mace	180 Hart
1836	Breeze, William, Great Yarmouth, N., hairdresser	11 Smith
1821	Brereton, Elizabeth, Norwich, N., collar and harness maker	133 Dewell
1830	Brereton, Elizabeth, Brinton, N., widow	321 Pettingill
1853	Brereton, Margretta, Cromer, N., spinster	142 Veale
1826	Brereton, Mary, Thorpe Hamlet, Norwich, N., widow	128 Davy
1841	Brett, Benjamin, Cawston, N., wheelwright	256 Traxton
1844	Brett, Charlotte, Little Walsingham, N., widow	681 Ebbage
1840	Brett, Elizabeth, Southrepps, N., single woman	73 Turner
1844	Brett, Henry, Saxthorpe, N., farmer	358 Ebbage
1836	Brett, James, Wrentham, S., gent.	302 Smith
1834	Brett, John, Norwich, N., gent.	732 Lane
1847	Brett, John, Thetford, N., tailor	662 Broom
1854	Brett, Robert, Shelland, S., blacksmith	573 Day
1837	Brett, Thomas, Norwich, N., tailor	564 Warren
1840	Brewen, Ann, East Harling, N., widow	123 Turner
1837	Brewen, Francis, East Harling, N., upholsterer	399 Warren
1848	Brewster, Ann, Starston, N., wife of Richard Brewster, farmer	844 Denny
1855	Brewster, John, Lowestoft, S., gent.	298 Whitty
1842	Briant, Harriet, Bungay, S., widow	146 Canler
1828	Briant, Philip, Mettingham, S., farmer	491 Farrow
1846	Bridge, John, Norwich, N., tailor	665 Baret
1836	Bridgeman, John, Burwell, C., farmer	151 Smith
1853	Bridges, Caroline, Seething, N., widow	399 Veale
1834	Bridges, Isaac, Norwich, N., plasterer	486 Lane
1835	Bridges, John, Framlingham, S., blacksmith	72 Harrowing

1849	Bridges, William, Laxfield, S., farmer, corn and seed merchant	521 Womack
1850	Briggs, Ann, Brooke, N., spinster	408 Cuthbert
1819	Briggs, James, Brandon Parva, N., labourer	208 Le Neve
1827	Briggs, James, Norwich, N., waterman	622 Wood
1853	Briggs, John, Great Yarmouth, N., ship master	387 Veale
1839	Briggs, Mary, Mickfield, S., widow	394 Calton
1852	Briggs, Thomas the elder, Kelsale, S., yeoman	396 Latten
1831	Briggs, William Duke, Howe, N., farmer	69 Hart
1852	Brigham, Emma, St Johns Sepulchre, Norwich, N., spinster	214 Latten
1834	Brigham, John the younger, Brooke, N., gent.	27 Lane
1845	Brigham, John, Brockdish Hall, N., farmer	965 Pedgrift
1833	Brightman, William, Great Yarmouth, N., gent.	53 Cubitt
1839	Brightman, William, Great Yarmouth, N.	Index only, o. w. missing
1829	Brighton, Alexander, Ipswich, S., hawker	106 Green
1835	Brighton, Ann, Downham Market, N. widow	445 Harrowing
1825	Brighton, John, Carlton Rode, N., grocer	371 Hayward
1840	Brighton, Sarah, Wingfield, S., widow	47 Turner
1853	Brighton, Taylor, Metfield, S., gent.	219 Veale
1819	Brighton, William, Downham Market, N., victualler	237 Le Neve
1820	Bringloe, Porter, Hingham, N., surgeon	526 Mack
1850	Bristow, Amy, Gorleston, S., widow	124 Cuthbert
1848	Bristow, Katey, otherwise Catherine, Gorleston, S., widow	437 Denny
1850	Bristow, William the elder, Great Yarmouth, N., gent.	224 Cuthbert
1842	Britten, Thomas, Downham Market, N., yeoman	285 Canler
1855	Broadbent, Sarah, Kings Lynn, N., formerly of South Lynn All Saints, widow	92 Whitty
1845	Broadbent, Thomas, West Lynn, N., corn merchant	367 Pedgrift
1852	Broadway, Edward, Kings Lynn, N., bricklayer	246 Latten
1857	Brock, Anne, Norwich, N., spinster	117 Youngs
1836	Brock, James, Great Yarmouth, N., master mariner	482 Smith
1854	Brock, Joseph, Reedham, N., gardener	440 Day
1851	Brock, Philip, Saxlingham, N., gent.	498 Friar
1853	Brock, Robert, Thorndon, S., farmer	33 Veale
1824	Brock, Roger, Mendham, N., millwright	275 Borrett
1847	Brock, Samuel, Great Dunham, N., bricklayer	456 Broom
1847	Brock, Sarah, Saxlingham, N., wife of Philip Brock, shopkeeper	88 Broom
1820	Brock, William, Great Dunham, N., bricklayer	355 Mack
1844	Bromehead, John Nowill, Lincoln, L. gent.	319 Ebbage
1844	Bromehead, John May, Lincoln, L. gent.	314 Ebbage
1841	Bromiley, Mary, Little Bolton, Lancaster, spinster	518 Traxton
1844	Bromiley, Mary, Bolton Le Moors	Index only
1839	Bromley, Thomas, Bildeston, S., farmer	222 Calton
1839	Bronwin, William Reeve, Hunston, S.	331 Calton
1849	Brookbank, John, East Dereham, N., farmer	623 Womack
1827	Brookbank, Mary, Great Yarmouth, N., widow	457 Wood
1829	Brooke, Ann, Thetford, N., spinster	552 Green
1827	Brooke, Henry Dyson, Thetford, N., innkeeper	501 Wood
1819	Brooke, James, Thetford, N., gent.	303 Le Neve
1837	Brooke, James, Gooderstone, N., farmer	31 Warren
1820	Brooke, John Henry, Norwich, N., hot presser	516 Mack
1839	Brooke, Mary, Norwich, N., widow	109 Calton
1835	Brooke, William, Garboldisham, N., yeoman	128 Harrowing
1837	Brooks, Eleanor, North Walsham, N., spinster	445 Warren
1829	Brooks, Elizabeth, Kings Lynn, N., widow	274 Green
1823	Brooks, George, Exning, S., farmer	4 Tann
1823	Brooks, George, Saxmundham, S., carpenter	405 Tann
1843	Brooks, James, Oulton, N., farmer	106 Miles
1826	Brooks, John, Kings Lynn, N., wheelwright	263 Davy
1855	Brooks, John, St Martin at Palace, Norwich, N., carpenter and builder	749 Whitty
1851	Brooks, Jonathan, St Michael at Thorn, Norwich, N., innkeeper	527 Friar

1855	Brooks, Mary, Brooke, N., wife of Bransby Brooks, gent.	548 Whitty
1839	Brooks, William, Norwich, N., leather cutter	194 Calton
1845	Brooks, William, Ipswich, S., gent.	23 Pedgrift
1855	Brooks, William, Norwich, N., carpenter	192 Whitty
1847	Broom, Eliza, Mendham, N., single woman	1 Broom
1845	Broom, Hannah, Banningham, N., widow	422 Pedgrift
1831	Broom, John, Pakefield, S., customs officer	417 Hart
1833	Broom, John, Clopton, S., yeoman	299 Cubitt
1847	Broome, Elizabeth, Norwich, N., widow, formerly of Ashmanhaugh, N.	298 Broom
1852	Broome, Richard, Horsham St Faiths, N., pork butcher	854 Latten
1838	Broughton, Robert the younger, Holt, N., shopkeeper	58 Skepper
1843	Browes, Catherine, Denton, N., widow	590 Miles
1845	Browes, Hannah, Burgh St Peter, N., spinster	571 Pedgrift
1820	Brown, Ann, Hempnall, N., spinster	202 Mack
1852	Brown, Ann, Blofield, N., wife of William Brown, yeoman	709 Latten
1842	Brown, Blomfield, Gressenhall, N., farmer	389 Canler
1855	Brown, Catherine Ann, Norwich, N., wife of James Brown, clerk	71 Whitty
1845	Brown, Davis, Marham, N., farmer	639 Pedgrift
1837	Brown, Deborah, Westleton, S., widow	356 Warren
1842	Brown, Deborah, Great Yarmouth, N., widow	291 Canler
1843	Brown, Edmund, Coddenham, S., blacksmith	66 Miles
1855	Brown, Elizabeth, Burnham Market, N., spinster	2 Whitty
1857	Brown, Elizabeth, Hanworth, N., widow, formerly of Kings Lynn, N.	518 Youngs
1844	Brown, Emma, Burnham Market, N., spinster	542 Ebbage
1849	Brown, Frances, Ipswich, S., widow	92 Womack
1832	Brown, George, Woodbridge, S., cordwainer	41 Cooke
1845	Brown, Henry, Kings Lynn, N., yeoman	95 Pedgrift
1856	Brown, Henry, Great Yarmouth, N., fish salesman	562 Code
1828	Brown, James, Upton, N., bricklayer	396 Farrow
1839	Brown, James, Homersfield, S.	92 Calton
1823	Brown, John, Great Yarmouth, N., gent.	237 Tann
1832	Brown, John, Loddon, N., gent.	325 Cooke
1837	Brown, John, Wretton, N., farmer	743 Warren
1843	Brown, John, Saxtead, S., farmer	302 Miles
1845	Brown, John, Redenhall with Harleston, N., watchmaker	855 Pedgrift
1853	Brown, John, Erpingham, N., maltster and brewer	37 Veale
1857	Brown, John, Norwich, N., baker	6 Youngs
1832	Brown, Joseph, St Nicholas, South Elmham, S., farmer	200 Cooke
1851	Brown, Maria, Aylsham, N., spinster	232 Friar
1830	Brown, Mary, Stockton, N., wife of John Brown, gent.	137 Pettingill
1852	Brown, Mary Ann, Kings Lynn, N., spinster	655 Latten
1837	Brown, Robert, Wiggenhall St Germains, N., victualler	406 Warren
1845	Brown, Samuel, Great Yarmouth, N., ironmonger	765 Pedgrift
1826	Brown, Sarah, Mattishall, N., widow	19 Davy
1847	Brown, Susanna, Norwich, N., spinster	707 Broom
1819	Brown, Thomas, St Lawrence, Ilketshall, S., gent.	231 Le Neve
1828	Brown, Thomas, Norwich, N., printer	252 Farrow
1828	Brown, William, St Johns Sepulchre, Norwich, N., butcher	275 Farrow
1829	Brown, William, Blaxhall, S., cordwainer	160 Green
1834	Brown, William, Marlesford, S., clerk	120 Lane
1835	Brown, William, Dillington next East Dereham, N., farmer	254 Harrowing
1842	Brown, William, St Lawrence, Norwich, N., shoe maker	582 Canler
1845	Brown, William, Soham, C., turfman	42 Pedgrift
1847	Brown, William, Exning, S., farmer	775 Broom
1855	Brown, William, Soham, C., turfman	646 Whitty
1830	Brown, Zackariah, Upwell, N., tailor	438 Pettingill
1837	Browne, Anne, Hethersett, N., widow	309 Warren
1840	Browne, Charles, All Saints, Norwich, N., clerk	411 Turner
1855	Browne, Charles, Forncett St Peter, N., farmer	306 Whitty
1828	Browne, Christopher, Ashwellthorpe, N., yeoman	319 Farrow
1855	Browne, Edmund, Norwich, N., printer and publican	147 Whitty

1827	Browne, Edward, Norwich, N., carpenter	321 Wood
1828	Browne, Elizabeth, Langley, N., widow	229 Farrow
1832	Browne, Elizabeth, Heigham, Norwich, N., widow	216 Cooke
1832	Browne, Elizabeth, Lowestoft, S., widow	207 Cooke
1849	Browne, Elizabeth, Kings Lynn, N., spinster	359 Womack
1851	Browne, Elizabeth, Saxlingham Nethergate, N., single woman	433 Friar
1844	Browne, Frances, Elsing Hall, N., widow	75 Ebbage
1853	Browne, James Eaton, Norwich, N., baker	138 Veale
1827	Browne, John, Hardwick, N., farmer and cowleech	64 Wood
1855	Browne, John, Bungay, S., organist	585 Whitty
1843	Browne, Mark, Heigham, Norwich, N., yeoman	403 Miles
1853	Browne, Martha, Great Yarmouth, N., widow	81 Veale
1847	Browne, Mary, Heacham, N., wife of Robert Browne, tailor	810 Broom
1853	Browne, Peter, Norwich, N., gent.	452 Veale
1857	Browne, Robert, Winterton, N., mariner	59 Youngs
1830	Browne, Rose, Bungay, S., widow	147 Pettingill
1847	Browne, Sarah, Great Yarmouth, N., spinster	811 Broom
1835	Browne, Simon, Tacolnestone, N., weaver	579 Harrowing
1824	Browne, Spencer B. Proved at Boyton, S.	310 Borrett
1820	Browne, Tabez, Stowmarket, S., pastor of the Baptist Church	99 Mack
1825	Browne, Thomas, Wendling, N., late of Beeston, farmer	300 Hayward
1827	Browne, Thomas Haddon, Ludham, N.	60 Wood
1834	Browne, William, Hales, N., blacksmith and general shopkeeper	170 Lane
1853	Browne, William the elder, Blofield, N., yeoman	172 Veale
1826	Brownfield, James, Norwich, N.	144 Davy
1837	Browning, Benjamin, Limpenhoe, N., yeoman	736 Warren
1844	Browning, John, Palgrave, S., farmer	373 Ebbage
1820	Browning, Mary, Setchey, N., widow	168 Mack
1834	Browning, William, Hoxne, S., butcher	408 Lane
1838	Browning, William, Garboldisham, N.	306 Skepper
1845	Brownlee, James, Weeting, N., gardener	659 Pedgrift
1820	Bruce, Thomas, Shimpling, S., blacksmith	83 Mack
1819	Brundell, Benjamin, Tunstead, N., cordwainer	161 Le Neve
1836	Brundell, John, Lakenham, Norwich, N., bricklayer	69 Smith
1834	Brundell, William, Norwich, N., shopkeeper	707 Lane
1820	Brundley, Davey, Braiseworth, S., farmer	372 Mack
1828	Brunning, John, Great Yarmouth, N., victualler	258 Farrow
1839	Brunning, Mary, Great Yarmouth, N., widow	570 Calton
1845	Brunning, William, Bedingham, N., yeoman	700 Pedgrift
1836	Brunton, William, Mattishall, N., surgeon	533 Smith
1839	Brunton, William, Weasenham All Saints, N., innkeeper and blacksmith	168 Calton
1820	Brunton, Joseph, Fakenham, N., schoolmaster	233 Mack
1821	Bruton, Susanna, Fakenham, N., widow	33 Dewell
1856	Bryan, Mary, Norwich, N., widow	172 Code
1834	Bryant, James, Mendham, S., farmer	122 Lane
1827	Bryant, John Brinkley, Stradbroke, S.	99 Wood
1853	Bryant, Robert Willoughby, Mellis, S., draper	111 Veale
1831	Bryant, Thomas, New Buckenham, N., bookseller and watchmaker	22 Hart
1853	Buck, Benjamin, Ellingham, N., carpenter	595 Veale
1837	Buck, George Harrison, Norwich, N., saddler	384 Warren
1845	Buck, James, Hindringham, N., farmer	715 Pedgrift
1848	Buck, James, Denton, N., farmer	446 Denny
1824	Buck, John the elder, Burnham Westgate, N., flour seller and baker	14 Borrett
1828	Buck, John, Westleton, S., farmer	326 Farrow
1844	Buck, Joseph Smith, East Dereham, N., schoolmaster	496 Ebbage
1857	Buck, Mary, Heigham next Norwich, N., widow	767 Youngs
1852	Buck, Peter, Norwich, N., schoolmaster	595 Latten
1853	Buck, Richard, Hedenham, N., farmer	589 Veale
1838	Buck, Robert, Ellingham, N., farmer	123 Skepper
1840	Buck, Robert, Stow Bardolph, N., brickmaker	290 Turner

1850	Buck, Robert, Little Thornham, S., farmer	422 Cuthbert
1827	Buck, Thomas, Cockley Cley, N., farmer	575 Wood
1834	Buck, Timothy Bond, Beccles, S., fishmonger	826 Lane
1851	Buck, William, Fincham, N., farmer	131 Friar
1840	Buckenham, Daniel, Gorleston, S., gent., formerly of the army	264 Turner
1819	Buckenham, John, Saint Clements, Norwich, N., plumber and glazier	96 Le Neve
1841	Buckenham, John the elder, North Lopham, N, farmer	531 Traxton
1840	Buckenham, Joseph, West Dereham, N.	568 Turner
1831	Buckenham, Richard, Shouldham, N., labourer	493 Hart
1843	Buckenham, William, Fersfield, N., farmer and miller	366 Miles
1838	Buckingham, Henry, Charsfield, S., farmer	411 Skepper
1853	Buckingham, Margaret, Diss, N., widow	704 Veale
1831	Buckingham, Robert, Framlingham, S., farmer	365 Hart
1847	Buckingham, Timothy, Diss, N., farmer and innkeeper	296 Broom
1852	Buckle, Henry, Roydon, N., shopkeeper	273 Latten
1843	Budds, William, Great Yarmouth, N., sailmaker and fish curer	493 Miles
1838	Bugden, John, Skeyton, N., farmer	864 Skepper
1852	Bugden, William, Skeyton, N., carpenter	232 Latten
1847	Bugg, John, South Walsham St Mary, N., saddler and harness maker	770 Broom
1856	Bugg, Mary Ann, Coltishall, N., schoolmistress	560 Code
1823	Bull, Abraham the elder, Bungay, S., bricklayer	52 Tann
1840	Bull, David, Wetherden, S., farmer	533 Turner
1838	Bull, Elizabeth, Stowmarket, S., widow	271 Skepper
1843	Bull, Lydia, Great Yarmouth, N., widow	178 Miles
1843	Bull, James, Norwich, N., labourer	273 Miles
1823	Bull, Joseph, North Runcton, N., yeoman	299 Tann
1856	Bullar, Noah, Peasenhall, S.	485 Code
1842	Bullard, Susan, Barnham Broom, N., spinster	39 Canler
1850	Bullard, Samuel, Norwich, N., gardener	234 Cuthbert
1855	Bullard, Samuel, Oulton, S., small farmer	626 Whitty
1855	Bullen, John, Newton Flotman, N., bricklayer	53 Whitty
1831	Bullen, Robert, Swanton Novers, N.	411 Hart
1844	Bullen, Robert, Blakeney, N., carrier	136 Ebbage
1844	Bullent, Henry, Great Yarmouth, N., hackney - man	391 Ebbage
1841	Bulley, Ann, Great Yarmouth, N., widow	461 Traxton
1830	Bulley, Charles, Blofield, N., cordwainer	196 Pettingill
1840	Bulley, John, Blofield, N., shoemaker	565 Turner
1840	Bullimore, Richard, Honing, N., farmer	566 Turner
1843	Bullimore, William Mark, East Dereham, N., shopkeeper	684 Miles
1853	Bullin, Joseph, Kings Lynn, N., master mariner	239 Veale
1847	Bulling, Edward, Tilney St Lawrence, N., miller	489 Broom
1845	Bulling, Frances, Warham, N., spinster	919 Pedgrift
1857	Bullman, John, Wicken, C., schoolmaster	133 Youngs
1819	Bullock, Frances, Pulham St Mary Magdalen, N.	214 Le Neve
1857	Bullock, George, Beccles, S., miller	501 Youngs
1827	Bullock, John, Walsham Le Willows, S., gent.	182 Wood
1820	Bullock, Lydia, Fakenham, N., widow	181 Mack
1850	Bultitude, Ferris, Ellingham, N., farmer	567 Cuthbert
1856	Bultitude, John Fairweather, Aldeby, N., farmer	673 Code
1842	Bultitude, Mary Ann, - see Atkinson	283 Canler
1828	Bultitude, William, Somerleyton, S., farrier	288 Farrow
1839	Bulton, Robert, Garboldisham, N.	229 Calton
1831	Bulwer, Augustine, Heydon, N., clerk	534 Hart
1841	Bulwer, James, Aylsham, N., gent.	425 Traxton
1841	Bulwer, Mary, Cley next Sea, N., widow	160 Traxton
1827	Bulwer, Thomas, Wood Dalling, N., gent.	693 Wood
1849	Bummer, Mary, Kings Lynn, N., widow	686 Womack
1853	Bumpstead, Edmund, Great Yarmouth, N., yeoman	18 Veale
1830	Bumpstead, John, Stradbroke, S., farmer	149 Pettingill
1853	Bumstead, George, Palgrave, S., baker and grocer	584 Veale
1855	Bunkell, John, Great Yarmouth, N., gardener	55 Whitty

1830	Bunn, John, Thornham, N., yeoman	256 Pettingill
1819	Bunn, Stephen, Worstead, N., farmer	312 Le Neve
1825	Bunn, Thomas the elder, Gunthorpe, N., gardener	495 Hayward
1820	Bunn, William, Hedenham, N., yeoman	170 Mack
1851	Bunn, Ann, Great Yarmouth, N.	O.W. 263
1848	Bunn, Charles, Ellingham, N., servant	184 Denny
1840	Bunn, Elizabeth, Stratton St Mary, N., single woman	488 Turner
1846	Bunn, George, Felmingham, N., yeoman	130 Baret
1840	Bunn, Hannah, Fundenhall, N., spinster	234 Turner
1855	Bunn, John Phillips, Kenninghall, N., farmer	442 Whitty
1852	Bunn, Richard, Weston, N., farmer	481 Latten
1837	Bunn, Thomas Read, Great Yarmouth, N., coal meter	333 Warren
1838	Bunn, William, Beeston, N., farmer	652 Skepper
1838	Bunn, Zachariah, Norwich, N., gent.	190 Skepper
1831	Bunnett, Simon, Matlask, N., yeoman	170 Hart
1844	Bunnett, Samuel, Shipdham, N., druggist	276 Ebbage
1849	Bunting, Ann, Feltwell, N., spinster	595 Ebbage
1824	Bunting, James, Norwich, N., alehouse keeper	23 Borrett
1844	Bunting, John, St Marys Norwich, N., manufacturer	528 Ebbage
1853	Bunting, Robert, Heacham, N., yeoman	188 Veale
1841	Bunting, Thomas, Thornham, N., butcher	586 Traxton
1847	Bunton, John, Litcham, N., innkeeper	269 Broom
1834	Bunyan, Robert, Kings Lynn, N., tinplate worker	117 Lane
1838	Burbage, John, Ipswich, S., hosier	322 Skepper
1835	Burch, James the younger, Kings Lynn, N., tailor	288 Harrowing
1827	Burch, Thomas, Bildeston, S., wheelwright	554 Wood
1829	Burch, William, Norwich, N., hairdresser and jeweller	501 Green
1839	Burcham, Ann, Stowmarket, S., widow	237 Calton
1824	Burcham, Henry, Fersfield, N., farmer	379 Borrett
1824	Burcham, John, Fersfield, N., yeoman	281 Borrett
1837	Burcham, Richard, Gissing, N.	254 Warren
1840	Burcham, Robert, South Lopham, N., bachelor	125 Turner
1843	Burcham, Robert, Bintree, N., yeoman	627 Miles
1842	Burcham, Thomas, South Lopham, N., farmer	682 Canler
1838	Burdett, Margaret, Norwich, N., spinster	303 Skepper
1852	Burges, James, Gorleston, S., carpenter	141 Latten
1850	Burgess, Ann, Northwold, N.	352 Cuthbert
1838	Burgess, James, Northwold, N., labourer	395 Skepper
1855	Burgess, James, Tivetshall St Mary, N., innkeeper	313 Whitty
1838	Burgess, John, Bungay, S., paper maker	706 Skepper
1846	Burgess, Mary Ann, Pulham St Mary the Virgin, N., widow	574 Baret
1837	Burgess, Michael, Cley next Sea, N., yeoman	257 Warren
1841	Burgess, Robert, Dagworth, S., yeoman	332 Traxton
1827	Burgess, Thomas, Wenhaston, S., yeoman	253 Wood
1841	Burgess, Thomas, Northwold, N., yeoman	58 Traxton
1851	Burgess, Thomas, Northwold, N., labourer	607 Friar
1857	Burgess, Thomas, Wood Dalling, N., farmer	67 Youngs
1829	Burgis, Hannah, Foulsham, N., widow	220 Green
1840	Burgis, Richard, Docking, N., gent.	532 Turner
1851	Burgis, Richard, Docking, N., farmer	308 Friar
1851	Burley, Hannah, Wells next the Sea, N., widow	256 Friar
1857	Burley, John, Theberton, S., gent.	711 Youngs
1848	Burman, James, Great Yarmouth, N., cork cutter	97 Denny
1850	Burman, James, Isle of Man, formerly of Diss, N., surgeon and apothecary	501 Cuthbert
1834	Burnett, Thomas senior, Bungay, S., late miller and baker	586 Lane
1821	Burney, Joseph, Stalham, N., clerk	274 Dewell
1855	Burrell, Ann, Blaxhall, S., widow	578 Whitty
1841	Burrell, Frances, Ingworth, N., widow	216 Traxton
1846	Burrell, Francis, Norwich, N., worstead weaver	463 Baret
1834	Burrell, James, Terrington St Johns, N., farmer	583 Lane
1826	Burrell, John, Letheringsett, N., clerk	52 Davy
1844	Burrell, John, Coltishall, N., innkeeper	408 Ebbage
1857	Burrell, Matthew, Brinton, N., farmer	216 Youngs

1833	Burrell, Mary, Holt, N., widow	502 Cubitt
1840	Burrell, Stephen, South Lopham, N., farmer	182 Turner
1827	Burrell, Thomas, Sternfield, S., carpenter	671 Wood
1833	Burrell, William, Flitcham, N., farmer	393 Cubitt
1847	Burrell, William, Fakenham, N., ironmonger	129 Broom
1827	Burroughs, Ann, Burfield Hall, Wymondham, N., widow	383 Wood
1828	Burroughs, Ann, Heigham next Norwich, N., widow	175 Farrow
1832	Burroughs, Charles, New Buckenham, N., o.w. missing	587 Cooke
1846	Burroughs, Elizabeth, Great Yarmouth N., widow	115 Baret
1838	Burroughs, Mary, East Dereham, N., spinster	326 Skepper
1828	Burroughs, Stephen, Heigham, Norwich, N.	54 Farrow
1822	Burroughes, Randall Proctor, Wymondham, N., esquire	122 Sadler
1826	Burrows, Elizabeth, North Elmham, N., widow	125 Davy
1857	Burrows, Francis, Norwich, N., pensioner	404 Youngs
1838	Burrows, Jane, Kings Lynn, N.	7 Skepper
1838	Burrows, Jemmia, Norwich, N., spinster	51 Skepper
1838	Burrows, Mary, Beachamwell, N., widow	455 Skepper
1850	Burrows, Rebecca, Heigham, Norwich, N., spinster	355 Cuthbert
1838	Burrows, Robert, Stoke Holy Cross, N., farmer	95 Skepper
1847	Burrows, Richard, Clopton, S., farmer	173 Broom
1857	Burrows, Samuel, Bawdsey, S., yeoman	751 Youngs
1855	Burrows, William, Alburgh, N., shopkeeper	653 Whitty
1822	Burt, Jane, Combs, S., spinster	203 Sadler
1845	Burton, Charles, Ipswich, S., attorney at law	230 Pedgrift
1849	Burton, Charlotte, South Walsham St Mary, N., widow	495 Womack
1853	Burton, Clement, Caister next Great Yarmouth, N., yeoman	425 Veale
1857	Burton, Edward, Claxton, N., farmer	251 Youngs
1854	Burton, Elizabeth, North Walsham, N., widow	270 Day
1827	Burton, Elizabeth, Coltishall, N., spinster	557 Wood
1847	Burton, Gent, St Stephens, Norwich, N., yeoman	355 Broom
1830	Burton, George, Norwich, N., currier	227 Pettingill
1849	Burton, George, Gorleston, S., gent.	15 Womack
1838	Burton, Henry, Great Yarmouth, N., mariner	724 Skepper
1831	Burton, John, Burlingham, N, farmer	462 Hart
1833	Burton, John, Norwich, N., innkeeper	381 Cubitt
1843	Burton, John, St Simon and St Jude, Norwich, N., victualler	529 Miles
1845	Burton, Joseph, Hackford next Reepham, N., butcher	566 Pedgrft
1833	Burton, Mary Ann, Claxton, N., spinster	244 Cubitt
1838	Burton, Robert, Stalham, N., merchant	26 Skepper
1852	Burton, Susan, Kings Lynn, N., widow	342 Latten
1842	Burton, Walter, Colkirk, N., blacksmith	217 Canler
1840	Burton, William, Wreningham, N., farmer	209 Turner
1857	Burton, William Otley, Wreningham, N.	577 Youngs
1841	Burtsal, Robert, Bungay, S., miller	104 Traxton
1824	Burtsal, Susanna, Bungay, S., widow	320 Borrett
1847	Burwood, Henry the elder, Southwold, S., gent.	40 Broom
1841	Burwood. John, Hollesley, S., gent.	7 Traxton
1846	Buscall, Edmund, Little Walsingham, N., farmer	190 Baret
1851	Buscall, Elizabeth, Necton, N., widow	468 Friar
1855	Buscall, John, Swaffham, N., gent.	574 Whitty
1855	Bush, Edward, Great Yarmouth, N., gardener	429 Whitty
1832	Bush, Elizabeth, Great Yarmouth, N., widow	506 Cooke
1853	Bush, Francis, Norwich, N., dyer	468 Veale
1849	Bush, Henry, Burnham Overy, N., innkeeper and mariner	111 Womack
1847	Bush, alias Cox, Joseph, Terrington St Johns, N., miller	165 Broom
1827	Bush, William, Yaxham, N., farmer	512 Wood
1840	Bushell, John, St Georges Tombland, Norwich, N., innkeeper	12 Turner
1831	Bushell, Richard, Great Hockering, N., general shopkeeper	275 Hart
1839	Bussey, John, Blofield, N., yeoman	432 Calton
1853	Bussey, Sarah, Thorpe next Norwich, N., widow	493 Veale
1852	Butcher, Benjamin, Great Yarmouth, N., mariner	551 Latten
1847	Butcher, Edward, Campsey Ash, S., farmer	357 Broom
1853	Butcher, Edward, Bungay, S., merchant	402 Veale
1823	Butcher, James, Assington, S., broom maker	374 Tann

1837	Butcher, James, Norwich, N., wine, spirit and porter merchant	14 Warren
1856	Butcher, James, Kirstead, N., farmer	59 Code
1840	Butcher, John, Burnt Fen, Soham, C., bailiff	349 Turner
1856	Butcher, John, Weybread, S., coachman	504 Code
1846	Butcher, May, Bungay, S., spinster	323 Baret
1836	Butcher, Matthew, Lowestoft, S., fisherman	17 Smith
1823	Butcher, Robert, Burgh, S., gent.	134 Tann
1843	Butcher, Samuel, Debenham, S., ratcatcher	612 Miles
1841	Butcher, Sarah, Lowestoft, S.	123 Traxton
1840	Butcher, William, Lowestoft, S., bird preserver	286 Turner
1857	Butler, John, Aylsham, N., bachelor	114 Youngs
1837	Butler, Robert, Houghton next Walsingham, N., farmer	529 Warren
1857	Butler, Sarah, Gorleston, S., shopkeeper	827 Youngs
1819	Butler, Thomas, Brandon, S., shoemaker	219 Le Neve
1841	Butler, William, Thorpe, Norwich, N., weaver	75 Traxton
1844	Butler, William, Tilney All Saints, N., farmer	596 Ebbage
1855	Butler, William, Barney, N., farmer	63 Whitty
1834	Butter, Christmas, Shouldham, N., yeoman	163 Lane
1837	Butterfield, Susanna, Bassingham, N., widow	204 Warren
1832	Butterick, Edmund, Wiggenhall St Mary Magdalen, N., farmer	385 Cooke
1855	Butters, Ellen, West Dereham, N., widow	537 Whitty
1851	Buttifant, John Stolworthy, Norwich, N., millwright	133 Friar
1830	Buttifant, Josiah, Norwich, N., hairdresser	205 Pettingill
1846	Buttifant, March, Rackheath, N., yeoman	131 Baret
1848	Buttifant, Tamazin Sarah, Norwich, N., haberdasher	735 Denny
1847	Buttitude, Frances, Needham, N., widow	670 Broom
1844	Buttivant, Mary, Norwich, N., widow	390 Ebbage
1839	Buttolph, John, Saham Toney, N.	669 Calton
1832	Button, James, Bramford, S., farmer	299 Cooke
1838	Button, Jonathan, Capel St Andrew, S., farmer	594 Skepper
1847	Button, Ephraim, Denton, N., miller	305 Broom
1846	Button, George, St Andrew Ilketshall, S., yeoman	647 Baret
1841	Button, John Harrison, Laxfield, S., yeoman	286 Traxton
1852	Button, Joseph, Sutton, S., butcher and farmer	462 Latten
1838	Button, alias Howard, William, Monk Soham, S., farmer	745 Skepper
1848	Button, William, Nayland, S., tanner	209 Denny
1843	Buxton, John, Lenwade, N., harness maker	159 Miles
1848	Buxton, Lydia, Wacton, N., widow	553 Denny
1852	Buxton, Mary, Norwich, N., widow	431 Latten
1826	Buxton, Robert, Wortwell, N., blacksmith·	39 Davy
1835	Buxton, Robert, Walton, N., gent.	307 Harrowing
1839	Buxton, Sarah Maria, Northrepps, N., spinster	552 Calton
1839	Bydell, John, Skeyton, N., farmer	361 Calton
1844	Bye, Stephen, Newmarket All Saints, C., bricklayer and builder	704 Ebbage
1857	Bye, William, Soham, C., gardener	409 Youngs
1821	Bygrave, John, Hickling, N., farmer, formerly Sutton, N., miller	142 Dewell
1822	Bygrave, Mary, Sutton, N., spinster	247 Sadler
1855	Cable, John, Capel St Andrew, S., wood ranger	131 Whitty
1846	Cack, Thomas, Woolpit, S., plumber, glazier and painter	523 Baret
1841	Cadge, Michael, Hoveton St John, N., miller and farmer	348 Traxton
1844	Cadge, Thomas, Barton Turf, N., miller	176 Ebbage
1857	Cadge, Thomas, Burston, N., farmer	328 Youngs
1846	Cadge, William, Swanton Abbott, N.	302 Baret
1848	Cadman, Mary, Fordham, C., spinster	295 Denny
1855	Cady, Samuel, Spexhall, S.	499 Whitty
1819	Cage, William, Hoxne, S., blacksmith	282 Le Neve
1838	Caley, Stephen, Forncett St Mary, N., thatcher, carpenter, and farmer	805 Skepper
1836	Callow, Abraham, Ludham, N.	86 Smith
1820	Callow, Edward, Norwich, N., warehouseman	O.W. 285
1822	Callow, John, Wymondham, N., yeoman	199 Sadler
1855	Callow, John, Lowestoft, S., gent.	O.W. 345
1833	Callow, Michael, Northrepps, N., farmer and butcher	402 Cubitt

1847	Calthorpe, Charlotte, Ipswich, S., singlewoman, see No. 341 - 1862	133 Broom
1842	Calthorpe, Robert, Bedingfield, S., farmer	641 Canler
1820	Calthorpe, William, Norwich, N., gent.	240 Mack
1839	Calton, James, Hinderclay, S., farmer	1 Calton
1835	Calton, Thomas, Bressingham, N., farmer	126 Harrowing
1830	Calver, Frances, Diss, N., widow	230 Pettingill
1846	Calver, George, Wenhaston, S., yeoman	160 Baret
1830	Calver, Hannah, Woodbridge, S., widow	445 Pettingill
1842	Calver, Henry, St James South Elmham, S., butcher	267 Canler
1835	Calver, Samuel the elder, Ellingham, N.	330 Harrowing
1840	Calver, Samuel, Banham, N., gent.	236 Turner
1836	Calver, Thomas Betts, Diss, N., auctioneer	358 Smith
1854	Calver, William, Yoxford, S., stonemason	565 Day
1857	Cambridge, William, South Runcton, N., farmer	149 Youngs
1850	Camell, Charles, Thwaite, S., farmer	250 Cuthbert
1820	Camell, George, Thwaite, S., farmer	322 Mack
1854	Camell, Lois, Ditchingham, N., widow	378 Day
1850	Camp, William, Wicklewood, N., gent.	256 Cuthbert
1835	Campling, Edward, Salhouse, N., farmer	34 Harrowing
1857	Campling, James, Thornham Magna, S., innkeeper	428 Youngs
1827	Campling, Joseph, Heigham, Norwich, N.	200 Wood
1845	Campling, Quartana, Salhouse, N., widow	633 Pedgrift
1857	Campling, alias Ranier, Susanna, Great Yarmouth, N., widow	386 Youngs
1840	Campling, William, Great Witchingham, N., yeoman	424 Turner
1828	Candler, Mary, Gorleston, S., widow	257 Farrow
1842	Candler, Stephen, Mutford, S., farmer	117 Canler
1845	Candy, William, Scole, N., tailor and woollen draper	33 Pedgrift
1856	Canfor, Ellis, Aylsham, N., basket maker	602 Code
1846	Canham, James, Ubbeston, S., farmer	450 Baret
1855	Canham, Peter, Wymondham, N., carpenter and joiner	323 Whitty
1840	Canham, Thomas, Cheveley, C., yeoman	160 Turner
1857	Canler, Edward, Stoke Ash, S., farmer	547 Youngs
1842	Canler, Elizabeth, Denham, S., widow	1 Canler
1855	Canler, George, Cotton, S., farmer	38 Whitty
1822	Canler, Thomas, Wetherden, S., farmer	161 Sadler
1821	Canler, William, Thornham Magna, S., miller	118 Dewell
1823	Cann, James, Norwich	99 Tann
1820	Cann, Robert, Mundford, N., farmer	252 Mack
1839	Cann, Stephen, Botesdale, S., yeoman	300 Calton
1854	Cannell, Ann, Norwich, N., widow	386 Day
1826	Cannell, Isaac, Cringleford, N., farmer	74 Davy
1840	Cannell, Mary, Keswick, N.	113 Turner
1824	Cannell, Sarah, Keswick, N., widow	82 Borrett
1846	Cannon, Benjamin, Hempstead, N.	559 Baret
1831	Cantrell, Richard, Salle, N., formerly of Morton, N., farmer	38 Hart
1852	Capon, Curtis, Rishangles, S., farmer	O.W. 359
1819	Capon, Elizabeth Eleanor, Bradfield, S., widow	Index only
1820	Capon, John, Great Yarmouth, N., gent.	68 Mack
1822	Capon, John, Dennington, S., yeoman	201 Sadler
1857	Capon, John Baldry, Thornham Magna, S., grocer, draper and general shopkeeper	527 Youngs
1847	Capon, Stephen, Bramfield, S., yeoman	673 Broom
1847	Capon, William, Occold, S., farmer	541 Broom
1836	Capp, Robert, Brandon, S., warrener	9 Smith
1853	Capps, John, Lowestoft, S., beachman	42 Veale
1834	Capps, Joseph, Benacre, S., innkeeper	564 Lane
1849	Capps, Samuel, Lowestoft, S., fish merchant	290 Womack
1844	Capps, William, Lowestoft, S., fisherman	204 Ebbage
1827	Card, Ann, Redenhall with Harleston, N., widow	O.W. 306
1845	Carey, William Hilton, Wells next the Sea, N., cordwainer	866 Pedgrift
1830	Carley, James, Metfield, S., farmer	283 Pettingill
1828	Carley, Jonathan, Thetford, N., gent.	236 Farrow

1844	Carlos, James, Frostenden, S., clerk	254 Ebbage
1849	Carman, Mary, Little Fransham, N., widow	654 Womack
1832	Carman, Richard, St Michael Coslany, Norwich, shopkeeper and dealer in grocery	277 Cooke
1840	Carpenter, Last Dring, Dunston, N., farmer	429 Turner
1822	Carpenter, John, Redenhall with Harleston, N., late of Ipswich, S., draper	172 Sadler
1836	Carpenter, Robert, St Martins at Oak, Norwich, N.	307 Smith
1823	Carpenter, William, Toft Monks, N., esquire	147 Tann
1820	Carr, Ann, Woodbridge, S., spinster	533 Mack
1856	Carr, Ephraim, Alby, N., carpenter	55 Code
1842	Carr, George, Bergh Apton, N., yeoman	141 Canler
1833	Carr, John, East Dereham, N., tailor and draper	290 Cubitt
1834	Carr, John, Woodbridge, S., cordwainer	207 Lane
1819	Carr, Susanna, Happisburgh, N., spinster	119 Le Neve
1835	Carr, William, Norwich, N., tavernkeeper	147 Harrowing
1857	Carrall, Roger, Great Yarmouth, N., toy merchant, formerly of Hull, Yorks	250 Youngs
1849	Carrier, John, Ormesby St Margaret, N., yeoman	251 Womack
1851	Carrier, Mary, Great Yarmouth, N., widow	586 Friar
1848	Carrington, Elizabeth, Walton, S., widow	781 Denny
1831	Carrington, James, Mileham, N., farmer	191 Hart
1856	Carrington, Thomas, Great Walsingham, N., labourer	379 Code
1822	Carrington, William, Walton, S., tailor	411 Sadler
1847	Carsey, Francis, Norwich, N.	234 Broom
1830	Carter, Christopher, Swafield, N., yeoman	300 Skepper
1833	Carter, Christopher, Wiggenhall St Germains, N., gent.	229 Cubitt
1852	Carter, Christopher, Wiggenhall St Germains, N., esquire	174 Latten
1849	Carter, Daniel the elder, Wretton, N., thatcher	469 Womack
1850	Carter, Edward Nicholson, East Dereham, N., plumber and glazier	42 Cuthbert
1854	Carter, Elizabeth, Norwich, N., spinster	591 Day
1828	Carter, Francis, Northrepps, N., shoemaker	287 Farrow
1835	Carter, George, Heacham, N., farmer	238 Harrowing
1830	Carter, Henry, Norwich, surgeon	O.W. 83
1835	Carter, Henry, Litcham, N., gent.	203 Harrowing
1819	Carter, John, Brockdish, N., husbandman	236 Le Neve
1827	Carter, John, Brancaster, N., schoolmaster	478 Wood
1843	Carter, John, Ipswich, S., esquire	148 Miles
1838	Carter, Joseph Chamberlin, Eaton, Norwich, N., merchant and manufacturer	163 Skepper
1845	Carter, Richard, Ipswich, S., baker	351 Pedgrift
1849	Carter, Richard, East Dereham, N., veterinary surgeon	164 Womack
1843	Carter, Robert, Royal Hospital Haslar, acting gunner	94 Miles
1845	Carter, Robert, South Town, S., corn merchant	653 Pedgrift
1845	Carter, Rose, Little Framingham, N., shopkeeper	252 Pedgrift
1832	Carter, Samuel, Fersfield, N., clerk	301 Cooke
1845	Carter, Sarah, Gayton, N., widow	71 Pedgrift
1851	Carter, Susan, East Dereham, N., widow	432 Friar
1824	Carter, Thomas, Wereham, N., farmer	134 Borrett
1832	Carter, Thomas, Great Yarmouth, N., master to sea	341 Cooke
1835	Carter, William, Hoxne, S., farmer	470 Harrowing
1850	Carter, William Henry, Great Yarmouth, N., mariner	172 Cuthbert
1826	Cartermould, Mary, Outwell, N., widow	219 Davy
1821	Carthew, Morden, Mattishall, N., clerk	O.W. 143
1849	Carvell, James, West Newton, N., gamekeeper, o.w. missing	282 Womack
1834	Carver, Ann, Norwich, N., widow	617 Lane
1824	Carver, Daniel, Norwich, N.	O.W. 177
1827	Carver, Elah Thomas, Ranworth, N., farmer	562 Wood
1838	Carver, Mary, Norwich, N., widow	52 Skepper
1848	Carver, Mary, Langley, N., widow	218 Denny
1838	Carver, Susan, Stratton St Mary, N., widow	768 Skepper
1855	Carver, Thomas, Heigham, Norwich, N., printer	674 Whitty

1829	Cary, Elizabeth, Weston, N., widow	102 Green
1847	Cary, Thomas Wolsey, South Lynn All Saints, N., gent.	590 Broom
1825	Casburn, Jonathan, Burwell, C., farmer	106 Hayward
1854	Case, Charles, Toftrees, N., gent.	123 Day
1838	Casebow, Richard, Downham Market, N., yeoman	841 Skepper
1835	Cassidy, James Nugent., Upwell, C.	70 Harrowing
1853	Castell, Charles, Monk Soham, S., husbandman	192 Veale
1832	Caston, John, Ipswich, S., shipowner and master mariner	33 Cooke
1842	Catchpole, Andrew, Charsfield, S., farrier	232 Canler
1833	Catchpole, George, Mickfield, S., farmer	190 Cubitt
1853	Catchpole, John, Kessingland, S., fisherman	691 Veale
1835	Catchpole, William, Melford, S., carpenter and joiner	250 Harrowing
1855	Cater, William Christmas, Upton, N., labourer	569 Whitty
1856	Cater, William, St Stephens, Norwich, N., yeoman	424 Code
1848	Cates, John, Barnham, S., yeoman	293 Denny
1838	Cates, Mary, Bury St Edmunds, S., spinster	283 Skepper
1857	Cates, Robert, Fakenham, N., gent.	684 Youngs
1855	Catlin, Thomas, Butley Abbey, S., farmer	736 Whitty
1854	Catling, Elizabeth, Fressingfield, S., spinster	17 Day
1838	Catling, Maria, Wingfield, S., spinster	491 Skepper
1837	Catling, William, West Walton, N.	417 Warren
1831	Cattell, William, South Town, Yarmouth, S., master mariner	362 Hart
1848	Cattermole, Frances, Bungay, S., widow	557 Denny
1823	Cattermole, James, Thelnetham, S., farmer	143 Tann
1856	Cattermole, James, Diss, N., husbandman	508 Code
1840	Cattermole, John, Pulham St Mary the Virgin, N., farmer	103 Turner
1857	Cattermole, Richard the elder, Bungay, S., painter, plumber and glazier	434 Youngs
1851	Catton, Elizabeth, Thetford, N, widow	252 Friar
1829	Catton, John, Shipdham, N., baker	456 Green
1839	Catton, William, St Benedicts, Norwich, N., baker	140 Calton
1843	Catton, William, Shipdham, N., gent.	404 Miles
1850	Catton, William, Thetford, N., yeoman	30 Cuthbert
1835	Caulke, Elizabeth, North Walsham, N., spinster	557 Harrowing
1820	Cave, William, Kings Lynn, N., carpenter	253 Mack
1828	Cavell, Corry the elder, Bawdsey, S., gent.	165 Farrow
1825	Cavell, Mary, Theberton, S., widow	365 Hayward
1832	Cavell, Nathaniel Page, Theberton, S., formerly of Claxton, E., farmer	594 Cooke
1854	Cavendish, Thomas, Eaton, Norwich, N., gent.	137 Day
1839	Cawdron, Charles, St Mary Coslany, Norwich, N., whitesmith	381 Calton
1819	Cawston, John, Banningham, N., tailor	276 Le Neve
1824	Cawston, William, Boxford, S., gent.	56 Borrett
1854	Chadd, Hannah, Kings Lynn, N., widow	222 Day
1844	Chadwick, George, Dersingham, N., yeoman	479 Ebbage
1856	Chadwick, John, Cromer, N., saddler	305 Code
1831	Chalker, James the elder, Aldeby, N., gent.	98 Hart
1844	Chalker, James, Aldeby, N., gent.	625 Ebbage
1856	Chalker, William the elder, Bungay, S., sheriffs officer	355 Code
1831	Challis, James, Thetford, N., yeoman	163 Hart
1832	Challis, John senior, Norwich, N.	421 Cooke
1836	Challiss, Benjamin, Downham Market, N., blacksmith	329 Smith
1844	Chalmers, David, Great Yarmouth, N., draper and tea dealer	176 Ebbage
1827	Chalton, George, Stow Bardolph, N.	393 Wood
1827	Chamberlain, Charles, Norwich, N., grocer	428 Wood
1830	Chamberlain, Frances, Norwich, N., widow	416 Pettingill
1840	Chamberlain, Joseph, Ipswich, S., apothecary	93 Turner
1835	Chamberlain, Maria, Norwich, spinster	221 Harrowing
1826	Chamberlain, Mary, Kempstone, N., wife of William Chamberlain, farmer	259 Davy
1847	Chamberlain, Moses, Kings Lynn, N., yeoman	740 Broom
1845	Chamberlain, Richard, Needham, N., husbandman	881 Pedgrift
1838	Chamberlain, Sarah, Norwich, N., formerly of Hethersett, widow	60 Skepper

1853	Chamberlain, Sarah, Norwich, N., formerly of Trowse Newton, N., widow	465 Veale
1857	Chamberlain, Thomas, Kempstone, N., farmer	477 Youngs
1825	Chamberlain, William, North Elmham, N., gent.	160 Hayward
1837	Chamberlin, James, Lowestoft, S., fish merchant	401 Warren
1852	Chamberlin, Matthew, Hoveton St John, N., farmer	435 Latten
1826	Chamberlin, Mary, Sheringham, N., single woman	5 Davy
1820	Chambers, Anna, Colkirk, N., widow	O.W. 286
1829	Chambers, Edmund, Wacton, N., farmer	131 Green
1856	Chambers, Henry, Norwich, N., yeoman	267 Code
1827	Chambers, James, St James, South Elmham, S., yeoman	487 Wood
1848	Chambers, John Snr, Cranwich, N., formerly of Thetford, farmer	813 Denny
1826	Chambers, Richard, Thetford, N., farmer	266 Davy
1843	Chambers, Samuel senior, St James, South Elmham, S., farmer	390 Miles
1857	Chambers, Samuel, Lowestoft, S., hairdresser	201 Youngs
1837	Chambers, Sarah, Lowestoft, S., widow	24 Warren
1827	Chambers, William, Starston, N., farmer	258 Wood
1848	Chambers, William, Lowestoft, S., yeoman	57 Denny
1852	Chandler, John, Middleton, S., farmer	366 Latten
1841	Chandler, Robert, Shipdham, N.	409 Traxton
1848	Chaney, John, Pulham St Mary the Virgin, N., husbandman	663 Denny
1855	Chaney, William, Hemsby, N., husbandman	658 Whitty
1834	Channing, Edward, Somersham, S., innholder	791 Lane
1843	Chapham, Mary, Weybread, S., widow	723 Miles
1834	Chaplain, Susannah, Yarmouth, N., widow	230 Lane
1848	Chaplin, Charles, Geldeston, N., carpenter	213 Denny
1825	Chaplin, Edward, Belaugh, N., farmer	369 Hayward
1856	Chaplin, Edward, Beccles, S., farmer	376 Cole
1857	Chaplin, George, Thetford, N., miller	595 Youngs
1822	Chaplin, John, Great Yarmouth, N., yeoman	318 Sadler
1851	Chaplin, John, North Elmham, N., formerly of Stibbard, N., farmer	453 Friar
1843	Chaplin, Louisa, Geldeston, N., spinster	489 Miles
1837	Chaplin, Mary Anne, Cley next the Sea, N.	185 Warren
1849	Chaplin, Meshack, Great Finborough, S., farmer	636 Womack
1819	Chaplin, Thomas, Guist, N., maltster and farmer	197 Le Neve
1839	Chaplin, William the elder, Geldeston, N., carpenter	170 Calton
1826	Chapling, Frances, North Elmham, N., widow	162 Davy
1852	Chaplyn, Edmund, Palgrave, S., farmer	661 Latten
1852	Chapman, Adam, North Delph, Upwell, N., carpenter and millwright	292 Latten
1822	Chapman, Benjamin, St Peter, Thetford, N.	250 Sadler
1847	Chapman, Charles, St Marys Newmarket, S., auctioneer and appraiser	592 Broom
1857	Chapman, Charles, Bungay, S., linen weaver	493 Youngs
1827	Chapman, Dixie, Mildenhall, S., yeoman	473 Wood
1829	Chapman, Elizabeth, Cromer, N., widow	485 Green
1843	Chapman, Elizabeth, Newmarket, S., widow	332 Miles
1831	Chapman, James, Walton, S., gent.	205 Hart
1843	Chapman, Jane, Kings Lynn, N., widow	262 Miles
1833	Chapman, John, Mundford, N., farrier	O.W. 229
1850	Chapman, John, Ashwellthorpe, N., farmer and shoemaker	425 Cuthbert
1856	Chapman, John, Great Yarmouth, N., gent.	111 Code
1821	Chapman, Lionel, Badingham, S., farmer	53 Dewell
1856	Chapman, Lydia, Sproughton, S., single woman	623 Code
1850	Chapman, Manning, Coddenham, S., farmer	396 Cuthbert
1840	Chapman, Mary Ann, Ixworth, S., spinster	O.W. 263
1820	Chapman, Paul Taylor, Hanworth, carpenter	454 Mack
1852	Chapman, Philip, Swannington, N., shopkeeper	496 Latten
1854	Chapman, Richard the elder, Earsham, N., publican	308 Day
1842	Chapman, Robert, Great Yarmouth, N., cowkeeper	290 Canler
1843	Chapman, Robert, Great Yarmouth, N., yeoman	340 Miles
1823	Chapman, Samuel, Norwich, gent.	385 Tann
1834	Chapman, Samuel, Hemingstone, S.	40 Lane
1820	Chapman, Thomas, Chippenham, C., gent.	455 Mack
1823	Chapman, Thomas, Pulham St Mary Magdalen, N., farmer	331 Tann

1846	Chapman, Thomas, Hunstanton, N., cordwainer	254 Baret
1837	Chapman, William, Southwold, S., yeoman	194 Warren
1845	Chapman, William, Scole, N., yeoman	565 Pedgrift
1850	Chapman, William, Downham Market, N., gent.	556 Cuthbert
1856	Chapman, William, New Buckenham, N., carpenter	424 Code
1855	Chappell, Lucy Elizabeth, Fressingfield, S., schoolmistress	620 Whitty
1849	Chappell, Samuel the elder, Redenhall with Harleston, N., whitesmith	223 Womack
1854	Charlton, Joel, Wimbotsham, N., alehouse keeper	333 Day
1856	Chase, Harriet, Fressingfield, S., spinster	183 Code
1824	Chase, John, Dilham, N.	120 Borrett
1854	Chase, Mary, Great Yarmouth, N.	55 Day
1856	Chase, Mary Ann, Stradbroke, S., spinster	179 Code
1842	Chase, Robert the elder, Wissett, S., farmer	590 Canler
1839	Chase, William, Metfield, S., farmer	451 Calton
1846	Chase, William, Shadbrooke, S., yeoman	665 Baret
1834	Chastney, Sophia Maria, Lower Sheringham, N., wife of Thomas Chastney, carpenter	766 Lane
1856	Chaston, Daniel, Lowestoft, S., draper	249 Code
1852	Chaston, Mary, St Margarets South Elmham, S., widow	274 Latten
1855	Chaston, Mary Ann, East Dereham, N., widow	604 Whitty
1827	Cheatle, Richard, Holt, N., gent.	281 Wood
1819	Chenery, Catherine, Brandeston, S., widow	262 Le Neve
1824	Chenery, Charles, Wilby, S., farmer	250 Borrett
1852	Chenery, Elizabeth, Norwich, N., widow	752 Latten
1852	Chenery, James, Ipswich, S., railway porter	315 Latten
1849	Chenery, John, Bedingfield, S., farmer	330 Womack
1844	Chenery, Maria Anna, Eye, S., spinster	569 Ebbage
1853	Chenery, Thomas, Norwich, N., wool - comb maker	327 Veale
1831	Chenery, William, Syleham, S., labourer	197 Hart
1845	Chenery, William, Witton, N., machine maker	833 Pedgrift
1838	Chesnut, Elizabeth, Swaffham, N., spinster	486 Skepper
1837	Chester, Benjamin, Norwich, N., coachmaker	322 Warren
1844	Chester, Elizabeth, Westwick, N., widow	699 Ebbage
1835	Chester, Francis, Norwich, N., yeoman	382 Harrowing
1843	Chester, William, Reedham, N., brickmaker	193 Miles
1837	Cheston, Constantine, Little Plumstead, N., yeoman	563 Warren
1851	Cheston, Dudley Locke, Bungay, S., widow	494 Friar
1827	Cheston, Elizabeth, Mellis, S., widow	627 Wood
1826	Chettleburgh, Daniel, Norwich, N., saddler and harness maker	301 Davy
1839	Chettleburgh, Edward, Morningthorpe, N., farmer	43 Calton
1828	Chettleburgh, Harrison, Norwich, N., gent.	426 Farrow
1824	Chettleburgh, James, Great Yarmouth, N., publican	66 Borrett
1851	Chettleburgh, Robert, Bixley, N., groom	320 Friar
1854	Child, Elizabeth, East Tuddenham, N., widow	186 Day
1857	Child, Enoch Littlewood, Wymondham, N., brewers clerk	27 Youngs
1851	Child, Esther, Hillborough, N., widow	189 Friar
1824	Child, James, Norwich, N., serving man	340 Borrett
1825	Child, John, East Tuddenham, N., farmer	408 Hayward
1836	Child, John, Great Yarmouth, N., whitesmith	372 Smith
1843	Child, John, Stanhoe, N., yeoman	79 Miles
1826	Childerhouse, John, Rockland All Saints, N., yeoman	112 Davy
1832	Chilvers, James, Bedingfield, S., farmer	602 Cooke
1856	Chilvers, John, Walsoken, N., yeoman	386 Code
1848	Chilvers, Mary, Bedingfield, S., widow	43 Denny
1833	Chilvers, Samuel, Tottington, N., carpenter	482 Cubitt
1835	Chilvers, William, Wiggenhall St Mary Magdalen, N., labourer	535 Harrowing
1854	Chinery, Charles, Beccles, S., gent.	357 Day
1833	Chinery, John, Bungay, S., hatter	523 Cubitt
1842	Chipperfield, Sarah, St Julian, Norwich, N.	145 Canler
1838	Chisnall, Richard, Stutton, S., wheelwright	874 Skepper
1842	Chittleburgh, Tabitha, Great Yarmouth, N., widow	360 Canler
1854	Chittock, James, Norwich, N., gent.	12 Day

1856	Chitton, John, Pakefield, S., labourer	10 Code
1856	Chives, Robert, Soham, C., farmer	437 Code
1819	Choat, Christopher, Ipswich, S., cordwainer	279 Le Neve
1842	Choat, Lucy, Ipswich, S., spinster	21 Canler
1826	Christian, Thomas, St Andrews, Norwich, N., gent.	349 Davy
1825	Christie, John the elder, Ipswich, S., pawnbroker	470 Hayward
1845	Christmas, Edward, East Dereham, N., yeoman	515 Pedgrift
1829	Christmas, James, East Dereham, N., gent.	511 Green
1841	Christmas, James, Gressenhall, N., farmer and beer seller	342 Traxton
1836	Christmas, John, Rollesby, N., gent.	55 Smith
1837	Christmas, Mary, East Dereham, N., spinster	39 Warren
1852	Christmas, Mary, Norwich, N., widow	365 Latten
1851	Christmas, Susanna Waters, Edgefield, N., widow	481 Friar
1819	Christopher, Ellis, Thetford, N., widow	104 Le Neve
1857	Chubbock, Thomas, Swannington, N., innkeeper	505 Youngs
1826	Church, Adelaide, Great Yarmouth, N., widow	30 Davy
1854	Church, Edward Forster, Great Yarmouth, N., schoolmaster	156 Day
1833	Church, Hannah, Caister next Yarmouth, N., widow	387 Cubitt
1839	Church, John, Eye, S., broker and shoemaker	58 Calton
1846	Church, John, Hickling, N., marshman	573 Baret
1846	Church, Maria, Swaffham, N., spinster	266 Baret
1845	Churchill, William, Ipswich, S., labourer	767 Pedgrift
1838	Churchman, Elizabeth, St Michael Coslany, Norwich, N., widow	285 Skepper
1834	Churchman, John, Norwich, N., worstead weaver	511 Lane
1836	Churchman, Robert, Trimley St Mary, S., yeoman	6 Smith
1837	Churchman, Thomas, Kings Lynn, N., carpenter	688 Warren
1855	Churchyard, Henry, Ufford, S., gent.	145 Whitty
1855	Churchyard, Isaac, Wickham Market, S., veterinary surgeon	604 Whitty
1851	Churchyard, James, Wantisden, S., farmer and farrier	383 Friar
1840	Churchyard, Lydia, Fressingfield, S., widow	562 Turner
1824	Churchyard, Sarah, Besthorpe, N., spinster	359 Borrett
1841	Churchyard, William, Eye, S., publican	384 Traxton
1843	Churlish, Joseph, Earsham, N., labourer	269 Miles
1857	Clabburn, Catharine, Thorpe, Norwich, N., widow	138 You
1849	Clabburn, Charles, Norwich, N., yeoman	249 Womack
1820	Clabburn, Robert, Lakenham, Norwich, N., yeoman	214 Mack
1837	Clabon, Elizabeth, Great Yarmouth, N., widow	O.W. 342
1833	Clackson, Studd, Ipswich, S., yeoman	168 Cubitt
1836	Clamp, Charles, Newmarket, S., currier	287 Smith
1855	Clamp, Robert, Harpley, N., carrier	748 Whitty
1845	Clare, Michael, Great Yarmouth, N., master mariner	971 Pedgrift
1855	Clark, Benjamin, Fordham, C., shoemaker	533 Whitty
1841	Clark, Caroline, Bodham, N., widow	450 Traxton
1827	Clark, Edmund, Aldborough, N., farmer	329 Wood
1820	Clark, George, Seething, N., dealer in stock	634 Mack
1825	Clark, Isaac, Butley, S., blacksmith	449 Hayward
1820	Clark, James, Brandon, S., hairdresser	65 Mack
1835	Clark, alias Mace, James	415 Harrowing
1849	Clark, James, St John de Sepulchre, Norwich, N., labourer	253 Womack
1822	Clark, John, Saxmundham, S., fellmonger	429 Sadler
1823	Clark, John, Kings Lynn, N., gent.	262 Tann
1824	Clark, John, Upwell, C., farmer and grazier	307 Borrett
1832	Clark, John, Burwell, C., yeoman	19 Cooke
1842	Clark, John, Newmarket, S., innkeeper	605 Canler
1844	Clark, Margaret, Worstead, N., widow	219 Ebbage
1842	Clark, Mary, Ludham, N., widow	30 Canler
1834	Clark, Richard, Worstead, N., baptist minister	788 Lane
1854	Clark, Richard, Wingfield, S., husbandman	287 Day
1836	Clark, Robert John, Ludham, N., butcher	509 Smith
1845	Clark, Robert, Shottesham St Mary, N., blacksmith	181 Pedgrift
1819	Clark, Samuel, late of Hull, Yorks. Benhall, S., gent.	38 Le Neve
1829	Clark, Sarah, Great Yarmouth, N., widow	433 Green

1819	Clark, Thomas, Wetheringsett cum Brockford, S., carpenter	118 Le Neve
1841	Clark, William, Great Yarmouth, N., shopkeeper	525 Traxton
1841	Clark, John, Shipdham, N., carpenter	2 Traxton
1845	Clark, William, Kings Lynn, N., innkeeper	199 Pedgrift
1857	Clarke, Charles, Henstead, S., clerk	112 Youngs
1852	Clarke, Edmund, Upton, N., parish clerk	607 Latten
1833	Clarke, Elizabeth, Methwold, N., widow	131 Cubitt
1842	Clarke, Elizabeth, Saxthorpe, N.	492 Canler
1848	Clarke, Hannah, St Georges Colegate, Norwich, N., wife of John Clarke, manufacturer	254 Denny
1825	Clarke, Henry, Beccles, S., yeoman	31 Hayward
1852	Clarke, Henry, Fressingfield, S., farmer	266 Latten
1854	Clarke, Henry, St Gregorys, Norwich, N., plane maker	339 Day
1825	Clarke, Hester, Acle, N., widow	112 Hayward
1839	Clarke, James, Norwich, N., yeoman	583 Calton
1844	Clarke, James, Worlingworth, S., farmer	679 Ebbage
1845	Clarke, James, Norwich, N., cordwainer	973 Pedgrift
1849	Clarke, Jeremiah, Bungay, S., hatter	592 Womack
1827	Clarke, John, St Martin at Oak, Norwich, N., formerly of Tottington, N., shopkeeper	333 Wood
1829	Clarke, John, Acle, N., gent.	423 Green
1835	Clarke, John, Fressingfield, S., farmer	339 Harrowing
1835	Clarke, John Spilman, Lowestoft, S., shipwright	294 Harrowing
1838	Clarke, John, Haughley, S., gent.	5 Skepper
1849	Clarke, John, Great Yarmouth, N., gent.	365 Womack
1855	Clarke, John, Thorpe next Norwich, N., tailor	Index only
1856	Clarke, John, Limpenhoe, N., shopkeeper	457 Code
1827	Clarke, Joseph, Thursford, N., yeoman	400 Wood
1842	Clarke, Martha, Lowestoft, S., widow	373 Canler
1845	Clarke, Martha, Soham, C., widow	605 Pedgrift
1830	Clarke, Mary, Ipswich, S., widow	413 Pettingill
1836	Clarke, Mary, Magdalen St, Norwich, N, widow	49 Smith
1846	Clarke, Mary, Carbrooke, N., widow	96 Baret
1852	Clarke, Mary, Mellis, S., spinster	453 Latten
1829	Clarke, Nicholas, Great Snoring, N., millwright	513 Green
1849	Clarke, Osborne, Benacre, S., farmer	385 Womack
1842	Clarke, Philip William, Bergh Apton, N., farmer	683 Canler
1855	Clarke, Robert, Fundenhall, N., labourer	59 Whitty
1855	Clarke, Samuel, St Clements, Norwich, N., city missionary	633 Whitty
1850	Clarke, Sarah, Tuddenham, S., spinster	158 Cuthbert
1842	Clarke, Susanna, Shipdham, N., widow	278 Canler
1820	Clarke, Thomas, Wiggenhall St Mary Magdalen, N., farmer	591 Mack
1827	Clarke, Thomas, Marlingford, N., husbandman	606 Wood
1834	Clarke, Thomas, Earsham, N., miller	421 Lane
1839	Clarke, Thomas, Thorpe Market, N., gent.	405 Lane
1846	Clarke, Thomas, Beeston Regis, N., carpenter	655 Baret
1820	Clarke, William, Thetford, N., yeoman	244 Mack
1821	Clarke, William, South Elmham St Cross, S., farrier	252 Dewell
1831	Clarke, William, Great Snoring, N., carpenter	337 Hart
1831	Clarke, William, Southtown, Yarmouth, S., gent.	506 Hart
1834	Clarke, William, Kenton, S., farmer	711 Lane
1835	Clarke, William the elder, Hethersett, N., farmer	161 Harrowing
1837	Clarke, William	706 Warren
1838	Clarke, William, Thetford, N., carrier	392 Skepper
1845	Clarke, William, South Lynn All Saints, Kings Lynn, N., gardener	153 Pedgrift
1854	Clarke, William, Rollesby, N., yeoman	435 Day
1854	Clarke, William, Thetford, S., gent.	497 Day
1857	Clarke, William, Needham Market, S., gent.	605 Youngs
1845	Clarkson, Ezekiel Studd, Ipswich, S., cabinet maker	135 Pedgrift
1837	Claxton, Edmund, Beeston next Mileham, N., jobber	589 Warren
1831	Claxton, Henry Nuttal, Belton, S., wheelwright	386 Hart
1857	Claxton, Joseph, Burnham Westgate, N., tailor	352 Youngs

1839	Claxton, Mary, Burnham Westgate, N., widow	133 Calton
1829	Claxton, Sarah, Great Yarmouth, N., widow	263 Green
1850	Claxton, Sarah, Morningthorpe, N., spinster	145 Cuthbert
1850	Claxton, Susan, Heigham, Norwich, N., spinster	133 Cuthbert
1838	Claxton, William, Beeston cum Bittering, N., jobber	321 Skepper
1839	Claxton, William, Hethersett, N., yeoman	585 Calton
1820	Clayton, John, Sibton Park, S., esquire	260 Mack
1831	Clayton, John, Norwich, N.	513 Hart
1847	Clayton, Rebecca, Norwich, N., spinster	522 Broom
1853	Clayton, Thomas, East Dereham, N., gent.	453 Veale
1831	Clemas, Mary Ann, Great Yarmouth, N., widow	134 Hart
1845	Clemence, Martha, Debenham, S., spinster	166 Pedgrift
1845	Clemence, William, Debenham, S., yeoman	167 Pedgrift
1839	Clement, James, Norwich, N., whitening maker	575 Calton
1851	Clements, James, Soham, C., yeoman	239 Friar
1822	Clements, John, Thetford, N., gardener	55 Sadler
1840	Clements, John Read, Great Yarmouth, N., master mariner	74 Turner
1853	Clements, John, Norwich, N., weaver	141 Veale
1851	Clements, Phoebe, Norwich, N., widow	549 Friar
1832	Clements, Valentine, Great Yarmouth, N., cabinet maker	426 Cooke
1852	Clements, William, Norwich, N., carpenter and publican	447 Latten
1838	Cleveland, James, Brampton, S., farmer and innkeeper	125 Skepper
1845	Cleveland, John, Gillingham, N., innkeeper	416 Pedgrift
1840	Cleveland, Simon, Earsham, N., farmer	569 Turner
1848	Cleveland, Robert, Lowestoft, S., mariner	735 Denny
1841	Cliff, William, Newmarket, S., yeoman	11 Traxton
1845	Cliffen, John, Whissonsett, N., labourer	649 Pedgrift
1837	Clifton, James, New Buckenham, N., blacksmith	708 Warren
1855	Climenson, Joseph, Welney, N., farmer	630 Whitty
1844	Climenson, Thomas, Upwell, N., farmer	22 Ebbage
1845	Climpson, John, Marsham, N., farmer formerly of Hevingham	202 Pedgrift
1846	Clipperton, John, Smallburgh, N., smith	168 Baret
1840	Clipperton, Thomas, Burgh next Aylsham, N., labourer	308 Turner
1838	Clouting, John, Eye, S., music master	520 Skepper
1852	Clouting, Samuel, Kelsale, S., gent.	627 Latten
1857	Clover, Thomas, Colby, N., farmer	247 Youngs
1833	Clubbe, Charles the elder, Hoxne, S., gent.	160 Cubitt
1821	Clubbe, George, Ipswich, S., yeoman	6 Dewell
1847	Clutten, Joseph, Dennington, S., farmer	324 Broom
1842	Clutten, William, Earsham, N., farmer	317 Canler
1857	Clutton, Anne, Bungay St Mary, S., widow	22 Youngs
1851	Coalman, Isaac, Thorpe, Norwich, N., builder	266 Friar
1828	Coalman, John Rising, Norwich, N., bricklayer	18 Farrow
1839	Coates, John the elder, Methwold, N., cordwainer	250 Calton
1846	Coates, John Robinson, Methwold, N.	636 Baret
1849	Coats, William, Thetford, N., carpenter and joiner	563 Womack
1835	Cobb, Ann, Garboldisham, N., widow	135 Harrowing
1851	Cobb, Edward, Terrington St Clements, N.	508 Friar
1850	Cobb, Frank Orttewell, Mellis, S., yeoman	535 Cuthbert
1820	Cobb, George, North Lopham, N., farmer	280 Mack
1819	Cobb, John, Great Yarmouth, N., cordwainer	67 Le Neve
1846	Cobb, John, Ormesby St Michael, N., farmer	654 Baret
1853	Cobb, John Jermy, Thetford, N.	523 Veale
1828	Cobb, Martin, Stoke Ash, S., farmer	295 Farrow
1849	Cobb, Michael, Gislingham, S., miller	334 Womack
1849	Cobb, Robert, Kings Lynn, N., carpenter	72 Womack
1827	Cobb, William, Norwich, N., gent.	669 Wood
1847	Cobb, William, Wroxham, N., carpenter	97 Broom
1848	Cobb, William, Bradwell, S., farmer	250 Denny
1836	Coble, Mary, Diss, N., widow	395 Smith
1845	Cock, Elizabeth, Great Yarmouth, N., widow	466 Pedgrift
1855	Cock, Jeremiah the elder, Mendham, S., farmer	609 Whitty
1853	Cock, John, Heigham, Norwich, N., baker	24 Veale
1839	Cock, Thomas, Mundesley, N., blacksmith	610 Calton

1855	Cock, Thomas, Diss, N.	332 Whitty
1838	Cock, William, North Runcton, N., farmer	662 Skepper
1844	Cockerele, Samuel, Peasenhall, N., butcher	215 Ebbage
1842	Cockerell, John, Freethorpe, N., farmer	O.W. 284
1848	Cockerill, Nathaniel, Great Fransham, N., farming steward	281 Denny
1845	Cockrill, Benjamin, Earl Stonham, S., farmer	744 Pedgrift
1845	Cockrill, Samuel, Coddenham, S., cordwainer	256 Pedgrift
1855	Cocks, Francis, Shipdham, N., farmer	411 Whitty
1821	Cocks, John, Framingham, N., late of Norwich, yeoman	342 Dewell
1854	Cocksedge, Martha, Norwich, N., widow	530 Day
1848	Codd, Mary, Thorpe next Norwich, N., widow	807 Denny
1841	Codd, Stockdell, Haughley, S.	108 Traxton
1821	Coddenham, James, Lyng, N., weaver	166 Dewell
1856	Code, William, Burgh St Margaret, N., farmer	1 Code
1822	Codling, John, Cranwich, N., innholder	213 Sadler
1857	Codling, William, Bungay, S., shoemaker	222 Youngs
1832	Codman, William, Little Walsingham, N., plumber and glazier	278 Code
1852	Coe, Ann, Rougham, N., widow	738 Latten
1827	Coe, Charles, Thornham Parva, S.	136 Wood
1843	Coe, Dye, Rougham, N., yeoman	681 Miles
1840	Coe, George, Alpheton, S., farmer	413 Turner
1828	Coe, James, Binham, N.	208 Farrow
1853	Coe, James, Field Dalling, N., yeoman	636 Veale
1856	Coe, John, Gissing, N.	630 Code
1856	Coe, Joseph, Edgefield, N., yeoman	569 Code
1827	Coe, Lydia, Woodbridge, S., wife of Moses Coe, carpenter	337 Wood
1845	Coe, Ruth Ann, Norwich, N., spinster	654 Pedgrift
1852	Coe, William, Tilney All Saints, formerly of Walpole St Peter, N., farmer	644 Latten
1836	Cogman, Benjamin, Norwich, N., baker	401 Smith
1835	Cogman, Harriett, Norwich, N., widow	341 Harrowing
1828	Coke, Jacob, Yaxham, N., late of London	O.W. 233
1855	Coker, Charles, Watlington, N., farmer	615 Whitty
1842	Coker, Fuller senior, Shipdham, N.	762 Canler
1847	Coker, James, Fakenham, N., blacksmith	320 Broom
1856	Coker, James the elder, Little Walsingham, N., yeoman	362 Code
1820	Colby, James, St Georges Colegate, Norwich, N., shoemaker	557 Mack
1820	Colchester, Samuel, Creeting All Saints, S., farmer	653 Mack
1856	Coldwell, Phoebe, Norwich, N., widow	268 Code
1845	Cole, Ann, New Catton, Norwich, N., widow	764 Pedgrift
1848	Cole, Ann, Norwich, N., widow	304 Davy
1840	Cole, Elizabeth, Eaton, Norwich, N., widow	607 Turner
1820	Cole, James, Cringleford, N.	293 Mack
1832	Cole, James, Loddon, N., gent.	62 Cooke
1846	Cole, James, Bath, formerly of Thetford, N., gent.	616 Baret
1848	Cole, James, Morningthorpe, N., farmer	680 Denny
1841	Cole, John, N., gent.	12 Traxton
1842	Cole, John, Brockford, S., farmer	219 Canler
1845	Cole, John, Dickleburgh, N., yeoman	475 Pedgrift
1848	Cole, John, St Clements, Ipswich, S., merchant	658 Denny
1849	Cole, John, Bawburgh, N., wheelwright and blacksmith	642 Womack
1853	Cole, John, North Tuddenham, N., gent.	Index only
1856	Cole, John, Worstead, N., husbandman	371 Code
1856	Cole, Joseph, Hevingham, N., farm servant	328 Code
1839	Cole, Peter Smyth, Sculthorpe, N., gent.	656 Calton
1848	Cole, Philip, Weston, S., farmer	24 Denny
1820	Cole, Susan, Orford, S., blacksmith	451 Mack
1833	Cole, Thomasin, Skeyton, N., widow	180 Cubitt
1838	Cole, William, Catton, Norwich, N., gent.	851 Skepper
1845	Cole, William, Little Cornard, S., bailiff	307 Pedgrift
1822	Coleby, Charles, Starston, N., farmer	412 Sadler
1831	Coleby, Charles, Roughton, N., schoolmaster	230 Hart
1819	Coleby, Edmund, Starston, N., farmer	297 Le Neve
1833	Coleby, Elizabeth, Starston, N., wife of John Coleby, farmer	124 Cubitt

1820	Coleby, John, Dickleburgh, N., linen weaver	509 Mack
1833	Coleby, John, Starston, N., farmer	123 Cubitt
1834	Coleman, Abraham, New Buckenham, N., labourer	232 Lane
1848	Coleman, Betsy, Antingham, N., widow	560 Denny
1849	Coleman, Edmund, Great Yarmouth, N., mast and block maker	24 Womack
1835	Coleman, George, Norwich, N., linen draper	46 Harrowing
1845	Coleman, George, Bunwell, N., thatcher	811 Pedgrift
1840	Coleman, James the younger, Scarning, N., farmer and cattle dealer	19 Turner
1850	Coleman, Jeremiah, Gressenhall, N.	613 Cuthbert
1826	Coleman, John, Brockdish, N., esquire	154 Davy
1834	Coleman, John, Bergh Apton, N., late of Ashby, bricklayer	237 Lane
1839	Coleman, John, Norwich, N., labourer	625 Calton
1856	Coleman, John, Weybread, S., husbandman	8 Code
1845	Coleman, Nathan, East Dereham, N., blacksmith	805 Pedgrift
1839	Coleman, Ruth Charlotte, Norwich, N., widow	681 Calton
1828	Coleman, Samuel, Norwich, N., builder	529 Farrow
1825	Colk, John, Bacton, N., farmer	277 Hayward
1831	Colk, Thomas, North Walsham, N., gent.	589 Hart
1822	Colkett, William Samuel, Norwich, N., manufacturer	190 Sadler
1841	Collett, Ann, Great Yarmouth, N., formerly of Halesworth, S., widow	368 Traxton
1835	Collett, Job Arnold, Ipswich, S., baker	333 Harrowing
1837	Collett, Mary, Fakenham, N., widow	265 Warren
1832	Collett, Phillis, Dunwich, S., widow	345 Cooke
1825	Collett, William, Swanton Morley, N., clerk	418 Hayward
1828	Collier, George, Ipswich, S., innholder	471 Farrow
1841	Collin, Michael, Soham, C., yeoman	372 Traxton
1851	Collin, William, Kirtling, C., farmer	99 Friar
1848	Collings, John Maris, Bacton, N., farmer	373 Denny
1825	Collings, Henry, Wilby, S.	383 Hayward
1854	Collings, Mary, Ipswich, S.	584 Day
1829	Collins, John, Great Yarmouth, N., yeoman	14 Green
1835	Collins, John, East Wretham, N., labourer	292 Harrowing
1844	Collins, Joseph, Sudbury, S., manufacturer	547 Ebbage
1838	Collins, Mary, St Michael Coslany, Norwich, N.	867 Skepper
1836	Collins, Thomas, Bucklesham, S., labourer	311 Smith
1856	Collins, Thomas, Mellis, S., farmer	174 Code
1844	Collins, William, Halvergate, N., yeoman	587 Ebbage
1829	Colls, Ann, Worstead, N., widow	510 Green
1844	Colls, John, Rushall, N., bricklayer	485 Ebbage
1819	Colls, Sarah, Swaffham, N., widow	158 Le Neve
1819	Colls, Thomas, Guist, N., yeoman	170 Le Neve
1838	Colman, Francis Ensor, Bildeston, S., innkeeper	75 Skepper
1841	Colman, Henry, Forncett St Peter, N., farmer	542 Traxton
1830	Colman, Joseph, Briningham, N., shepherd	261 Pettingill
1850	Colman, Thomas, Norwich, N., tailor and draper	38 Cuthbert
1823	Colman, William, Ashwellthorpe, N., farmer	167 Tann
1851	Colson, Charles, Stowmarket, S., blacksmith	597 Friar
1850	Colthorp, Charles, Framsden, S., farmer	496 Cuthbert
1821	Columbine, Paul, Little Plumstead, N., doctor of divinity	340 Dewell
1825	Comer, Isaac, Castle Acre, N., brickmaker	O.W. 215
1855	Comer, John, Bunwell, N.	381 Whitty
1836	Comer, Paul, Ingham, N., yeoman	355 Smith
1848	Comer, William, Lyng, N., farmer	685 Denny
1855	Conder, Martha, Ipswich, S., widow	672 Whitty
1836	Condor, Mary Foster, Wymondham, N., widow	351 Smith
1849	Cone, James, Whatfield, S., farmer	41 Womack
1854	Cone, Robert, Lowestoft, S., fisherman	447 Day
1832	Constable, Charles, Methwold, N., yeoman	525 Cooke
1835	Constable, George, Dickleburgh, N., yeoman	441 Harrowing
1847	Constable, John, Methwold, N., carpenter	495 Broom
1847	Constable, Joseph, Feltwell, N., innkeeper	12 Broom
1827	Constable, William Phillips, Methwold, N., yeoman	392 Wood
1841	Constable, William, Southery, N., farmer	618 Traxton

1846	Conyers, Elizabeth, Great Yarmouth, N., widow	180 Baret
1841	Conyers, James, Great Yarmouth, N., gent.	673 Traxton
1833	Cook, Amos, Walton, S.	489 Cubitt
1822	Cook, Charles the elder, Swefling, S., farmer	347 Sadler
1822	Cook, Charles, Wissett, S., blacksmith	288 Sadler
1836	Cook, Charles	334 Smith
1838	Cook, Edward, Ovington, N.	832 Skepper
1852	Cook, Edward, St Mary Coslany, Norwich, N., corn and coal merchant and livery stable keeper	849 Latten
1852	Cook, Elizabeth, Thorpe, Norwich, N., spinster	669 Latten
1830	Cook, George, Marsham, N., brickmaker	73 Pettingill
1822	Cook, James, Woolverstone, S., gardener	341 Sadler
1835	Cook, James, Lower Sheringham, N., fisherman	188 Harrowing
1819	Cook, John, Bedingfield, S., yeoman	277 Le Neve
1836	Cook, John, Yarmouth, N., master mariner	333 Smith
1846	Cook, John, Lowestoft, S., fisherman	74 Baret
1834	Cook, Joseph, Whitton, S., farmer	188 Lane
1847	Cook, Joseph, Scottow, N., gardener	583 Broom
1821	Cook, Mary, Norwich, N., single woman	216 Dewell
1839	Cook, Noah the elder, Rickinghall Superior, S., farmer	532 Calton
1840	Cook, Robert, Norwich, N., whitesmith	31 Turner
1840	Cook, Samuel, Lowestoft, S., baker	94 Turner
1830	Cook, Stephen, Brome, S., gent.	91 Pettingill
1832	Cook, Thomas, Ovington, N., farmer	557 Cooke
1852	Cook, Thomas, Aylsham, N., esquire	798 Latten
1820	Cook, William, Brundish, S., miller	303 Mack
1820	Cook, William, Lyng, N., yeoman	271 Mack
1829	Cook, William, Mundesley, N., coastwaiter of His Majestys customs	198 Green
1845	Cook, William Charles, Thelnetham, S., farmer	254 Pedgrift
1849	Cook, William, Wilby, S., shoemaker	531 Womack
1855	Cook, William the elder, Lowestoft, S., fisherman	542 Whitty
1856	Cook, William, Lowestoft, S., mariner	112 Code
1857	Cook, William Barnard, Aylsham, N., yeoman	385 Youngs
1857	Cook, William, Lowestoft, S., gent.	616 Youngs
1831	Cooke, Corbett, Cley next the Sea, N., merchant	449 Hart
1843	Cooke, Elizabeth, Bergh Apton, N., widow	301 Miles
1826	Cooke, Frances, Bergh Apton, N., spinster	232 Davy
1826	Cooke, Grimwood, Botesdale, S., butcher	105 Davy
1830	Cooke, Henry, Stalham, N., farmer	423 Pettingill
1836	Cooke, John, Felmingham, N., yeoman	548 Smith
1840	Cooke, John, Bungay Uplands, S., farmer	263 Turner
1855	Cooke, Maria, Brome, S., spinster	534 Whitty
1834	Cooke, Samuel, Stalham, N., miller and farmer	801 Lane
1832	Cooke, Thomas, St Faiths Lane, Norwich, N., widower	1 Cooke
1826	Cooke, William, Thornage, N., farmer	337 Davy
1841	Cooke, William, Norwich, N., gent.	516 Traxton
1836	Coole, Chad Nurse, St Peter Mancroft, Norwich, N., shopkeeper	448 Smith
1826	Cooper, Ann, Ipswich, S., spinster	320 Davy
1857	Cooper, Ann, Leiston, S., spinster	681 Youngs
1846	Cooper, Arthur, Mendham, N., farmer	479 Baret
1819	Cooper, Ashley, Hilgay, N., farmer	87 Le Neve
1846	Cooper, Betsey, Great Glemham, S., wife of William Cooper, farmer	645 Baret
1821	Cooper, Blyford, North Walsham, N., innkeeper	183 Dewell
1853	Cooper, Bridgett, Earsham, N., spinster	193 Veale
1850	Cooper, Charles, Norwich, N.	O.W. 294
1822	Cooper, Daniel, Tivetshall St Mary, N., gent.	398 Sadler
1840	Cooper, David, Langham, N., farmer	500 Turner
1841	Cooper, Edward, Homersfield, S., carpenter	289 Traxton
1836	Cooper, Elizabeth, Kettlebaston, S., wife of Joseph Cooper, farmer	558 Smith
1846	Cooper, Elizabeth, Hollesley, S., innholder	31 Baret
1854	Cooper, Elizabeth, Stowupland, S., widow	452 Day

1852	Cooper, George, Rendlesham, S., farmer	185 Latten
1834	Cooper, James, Butley, S., yeoman	414 Lane
1838	Cooper, James, Blaxhall, S., farmer	510 Skepper
1839	Cooper, James, Nedging, S., yeoman	428 Calton
1840	Cooper, James, Hopton, S., blacksmith	2 Turner
1845	Cooper, James, Heveningham, S., gent.	533 Pedgrift
1824	Cooper, John, Great Yarmouth, N., innkeeper	172 Borrett
1834	Cooper, John the younger, Topcroft, N., farmer	841 Lane
1835	Cooper, John, Knapton, N., farmer	113 Harrowing
1838	Cooper, John, Ashwellthorpe, N., weaver	105 Skepper
1841	Cooper, John, Matlaske, N., cordwainer	507 Traxton
1843	Cooper, John, Hilgay, N., farmer	95 Miles
1843	Cooper, John, Rattlesden, S., farmer	63 Miles
1844	Cooper, John, Braiseworth, S., farmer	149 Ebbage
1845	Cooper, John, Exning, S., shepherd	729 Pedgrift
1846	Cooper, John, Bedingham, N., farmer	197 Baret
1849	Cooper, John, North Elmham, N., yeoman	245 Womack
1852	Cooper, John, Henstead, S., farmer	516 Latten
1857	Cooper, Jonathan, Ringshall, S., yeoman	740 Youngs
1856	Cooper, Joseph, Little Wenham, S.	106 Code
1820	Cooper, Judith, Belton, S., widow	258 Mack
1849	Cooper, Margaret, Southwold, S., widow	22 Womack
1857	Cooper, Margaret, Gaywood Hospital, N.	726 Youngs
1855	Cooper, Maria, Framlingham, S., spinster	139 Whitty
1829	Cooper, Mary, Great Yarmouth, N., spinster	344 Green
1835	Cooper, Mary, Long Melford, S., widow	492 Harrowing
1852	Cooper, Matthew, Scoulton, N.	654 Latten
1820	Cooper, Richard, Kings Lynn, N., mariner	244 Mack
1841	Cooper, Sarah, West Winch, N., widow	474 Traxton
1831	Cooper, Thomas, Kings Lynn, N., linen draper	524 Hart
1836	Cooper, Thomas, South Elmham, St. Cross, S., farmer	310 Smith
1839	Cooper, Thomas, Stowupland, S., gent.	60 Calton
1839	Cooper, Thomas, Tasburgh, N., blacksmith	204 Calton
1845	Cooper, Thomas, Gunton, S., farmer	423 Pedgrift
1855	Cooper, Thomas, South Town, Little Yarmouth, S., miller	251 Whitty
1826	Cooper, William, Kings Lynn, N., ironmonger	360 Davy
1827	Cooper, William, Kessingland, S., farmer	261 Wood
1834	Cooper, William, Cawston, N., blacksmith	787 Lane
1840	Cooper, William, Butley, S., farmer	48 Turner
1842	Cooper, William Thompson, Norwich, N., gent.	536 Canler
1845	Cooper, William, Lowestoft, S., carter	211 Pedgrift
1848	Cooper, William, Ormsby St Margaret, N., farmer	198 Denny
1832	Coote, Isaac, Sudbury, S., carpenter	428 Cooke
1841	Copemam, Edward, Little Melton, N.	653 Traxton
1851	Copeman, James the elder, Beccles, S., yeoman	112 Friar
1832	Copeman, Katherine, Aylsham, N., widow	569 Cooke
1843	Copeman, Mary, Thurgarten, N., wife of Edward James Copeman, formerly of Coltishall, gent.	447 Miles
1832	Copeman, Robert, Itteringham, N., gent.	513 Cooke
1834	Copeman, Susanna, St Giles, Norwich, N., widow	676 Lane
1845	Copeman, William, Wiggenhall St Germains, N., farmer	410 Pedgrift
1845	Copland, Pooley, Hempton, N., yeoman, formerly of Wells next the Sea	854 Pedgrift
1854	Copling, Richard, Weybourne, N., shopkeeper	533 Day
1856	Copperwheat, John, St Swithins, Norwich, N., pensioner	333 Code
1823	Coppin, David, Norwich	379 Tann
1837	Coppin, James, South Lynn, N., formerly of Norwich, plumber and glazier	138 Warren
1845	Coppin, James, South Lynn, N.	Index only
1832	Coppin, Selth, Norwich, N., gent.	170 Cooke
1850	Copping, Ann, Rickinghall Superior, S., single woman	361 Cuthbert
1819	Copping, Edward, Hardwick, N., chief constable	145 Le Neve
1853	Copping, Elizabeth, Wilby, S., widow	708 Veale
1854	Copping, John, Barnham Broom, N., shopkeeper	118 Day

1830	Copping, Rebecca, Norwich, N., spinster	249 Pettingill
1852	Corbould, Elizabeth, Norwich, N., widow	137 Latten
1851	Corbyn, Hartwell, Halesworth, S., tailor	316 Friar
1841	Cordell, John, Weybread, S., yeoman	247 Traxton
1826	Corder, John, Polstead, S., farmer	177 Davy
1832	Cordingley, William, Ipswich, S., shipbuilder	181 Cooke
1848	Cordy, Christopher, Hoxne, S., farmer	718 Denny
1847	Cork, Edward, Swaffham, N., linen draper	794 Broom
1830	Cork, Robert, Wendling, N., yeoman	169 Pettingill
1835	Cork, William, Bradfield, N., carpenter	28 Harrowing
1845	Cork, William, Heigham, Norwich, N., gent.	885 Pedgrift
1841	Corneby, Mary, Topcroft, N., widow	471 Traxton
1827	Cornell, Deborah, New Buckenham, N., widow	636 Wood
1823	Cornell, John, Carleton Rode, N., farmer	389 Tann
1825	Cornell, John, Westhorpe, S., yeoman	69 Hayward
1827	Cornell, John, Haverhill, S., labourer	376 Wood
1843	Corner, Samuel Theobald, Debenham, S., yeoman	62 Miles
1834	Cornish, Benjamin, Bungay, S., farmer	690 Lane
1852	Cornish, Elizabeth, Fakenham, N., widow	847 Latten
1847	Cornish, John, Fakenham, N., brazier	494 Broom
1833	Cornish, Robinson, Knapton, N., carpenter and wheelwright	307 Cubitt
1819	Corsbie, Benjamin, St Martin at Oak, Norwich, N., innholder	220 Le Neve
1826	Corston, Robert, Thornham, N., mariner	326 Davy
1843	Corston, William, Holborn, London, formerly of Fincham, N.	322 Miles
1841	Cory, Esther, Great Yarmouth, N., widow	364 Traxton
1837	Cory, James, Reepham, N., baker	552 Warren
1837	Cossey, Francis, Horham, S., farmer	772 Warren
1838	Cossey, John, Norwich, N, gent.	257 Skepper
1820	Cossey, Thomas, Norwich, N., yeoman	209 Mack
1848	Cossey, William, Norwich, N., wool counter	581 Denny
1846	Cottingham, Lionel, Shadingfield, S., gent.	312 Baret
1829	Cotton, John, Wingfield, S., gent.	200 Green
1837	Cotton, Robert Rix, Kings Lynn, N., auctioneer, O.W. missing	710 Warren
1841	Cotton, Robert Rix, Kings Lynn, N., auctioneer	13 Traxton
1827	Cotton, Sophia, Great Yarmouth, N.	580 Wood
1833	Cottrell, George, Hoe, N., labourer	360 Cubitt
1822	Coulson, Ralph, Norwich, N., gent.	194 Sadler
1834	Couperthwaite, Mary, Ipswich, S.	519 Lane
1829	Courtnall, James, Beccles, S., tailor	301 Green
1822	Cousens, John, Polstead, S., farmer	170 Sadler
1823	Cousings, John, Rockland All Saints, N., cordwainer	376 Tann
1853	Cousins, James, Emneth, N., farmer	250 Veale
1831	Cousins, William, Stoke by Nayland, S., yeoman	195 Hart
1840	Couzens, Abigail, Holme next the Sea, N., widow	127 Turner
1838	Couzens, Henry, Sporle with Palgrave, N., carpenter	725 Skepper
1825	Covel, Sarah, Bildeston, S., widow	482 Hayward
1825	Covell, Jonas, Bungay, S., miller	480 Hayward
1857	Covell, Mary, Soham, C., widow	817 Youngs
1823	Coward, Michael Godman, Swaffham, N., upholsterer	47 Tann
1849	Cowell, John, Fleggburgh, N., blacksmith	8 Womack
1839	Cowles, John, Wetheringsett, S., farmer	128 Calton
1824	Cowles, Richard, Attleborough, N., yeoman	152 Borrett
1852	Cowles, Samuel, Blundeston, S., gardener	206 Latten
1846	Cowper, Thomas, Downham, N., carpenter and joiner	274 Baret
1850	Cox, John, Sheringham, N., fisherman	419 Cuthbert
1847	Cox, alias Bush, Joseph, Terrington St Johns, N., miller	165 Broom
1842	Cox, William, Kings Lynn, N.	617 Canler
1834	Coxford, James, North Elmham, N., yeoman	631 Lane
1855	Coxford, John, Norwich, N., gent.	679 Whitty
1843	Coxton, Henry, Thorpe, Norwich, N., yeoman	435 Miles
1829	Cozens, Jeremiah, Buxton Lodge, N., farmer	217 Green
1834	Cozens, Lydia, Downham Market, N., widow	379 Lane
1827	Crabb, Clement, Downham Market, N., innholder	18 Wood

1853	Crabb, Robert, Tilney All Saints, N., farmer	266 Veale
1857	Crabbe, Honor, Freethorpe, N., spinster	349 Youngs
1832	Cracknell, Benjamin, Laxfield, S., farmer	527 Cooke
1844	Cracknell, Benjamin, Denham, S., farmer	172 Ebbage
1823	Cracknell, Charles, Bedingfield, S., farmer	327 Tann
1849	Cracknell, Charles, Redlingfield, S., farmer	335 Womack
1850	Cracknell, Charles, Gislingham, S., farmer	346 Cuthbert
1843	Cracknell, George, Redlingfield, S., farmer	538 Miles
1844	Cracknell, George the elder, Redlingfield, S., farmer	613 Ebbage
1846	Cracknell, George, Redlingfield, S., farmer	522 Baret
1830	Cracknell, James, Charsfield, S., farmer	138 Pettingill
1847	Cracknell, James, Scole, N., innkeeper and farmer	745 Broom
1847	Cracknell, John, Stradbroke, S., farmer	713 Broom
1857	Cracknell, John, Redgrave, S., formerly of Botesdale, cordwainer	9 Youngs
1845	Cracknell, Latham, Redlingfield, S., formerly of Stonham, S., farmer	681 Pedgrift
1857	Cracknell, Phillis, Hoxne, S., widow	158 Youngs
1835	Cracknell, Richard, Hoxne, S., grocer and linen draper	14 Harrowing
1839	Cracknell, Sarah, St James South Elmham, N., wife of Thomas Cracknell, gent.	645 Calton
1848	Cracknell, Thomas, Wilby, S., farmer	396 Denny
1854	Cracknell, Thomas, Redlingfield, S., farmer	589 Day
1851	Crampton, Amery, West Lynn St Peters, N., gent.	469 Friar
1828	Crane, John, Great Yarmouth, N., blacksmith	57 Farrow
1854	Crane, John, Saxmundham, S., baker	518 Day
1828	Crane, Joseph, Blofield, N., blacksmith	476 Farrow
1843	Crane, Martin, Catfield, N.	599 Miles
1844	Crane, Mary, St Stephens, Norwich, N., widow	409 Ebbage
1855	Crane, Neville, Filby, N., gardener	377 Whitty
1849	Crane, Robert Howse, Great Yarmouth, N., whitesmith	121 Womack
1821	Crane, Thomas, Kings Lynn, N., wine porter	30 Dewell
1822	Cranefield, Corba, Sheringham, N., land surveyor	321 Sadler
1822	Cranness, Elizabeth, Wymondham, N., wife of William Cranness, carpenter	393 Sadler
1826	Cranstone, Mary, Great Yarmouth, N., widow	282 Davy
1839	Craske, Elizabeth, Alderton, S., formerly of Creeting All Saints, S., widow	623 Calton
1840	Craske, Elizabeth, Heigham, Norwich, N., widow	161 Turner
1830	Craske, Peter, Norwich, N., cordwainer	125 Pettingill
1845	Craske, Robert, Great Yarmouth, N., coal meter	622 Pedgrift
1836	Creak, Elizabeth, Nayland, S., spinster	405 Smith
1841	Creak, Jonathon, Outwell, C., farmer	633 Traxton
1829	Creake, William, Kings Lynn, N., gent.	156 Green
1833	Creanfield, James, Holt, N., yeoman	96 Cubitt
1834	Creanfield, Margaret Ann, Holt, N., widow	410 Lane
1829	Creasy, James, Monk Soham, S., farmer	215 Green
1837	Creasy, James, Barking, S., farmer	517 Warren
1822	Creed, Matthew, Norwich, N., weaver	293 Sadler
1820	Cremer, John, Gimingham, N., esquire	543 Mack
1852	Crick, James, Soham, C., innkeeper	165 Latten
1822	Crick, Sarah, Norwich, N., widow	181 Sadler
1857	Crickmay, John, Beccles, S., postmaster	412 Youngs
1838	Crickmay, Mary Ann Dorothy Susannah, Southwark, Surrey, wife of Charles Crickmay	627 Skepper
1820	Crickmay, Rachel, Yarmouth, N., and Lowestoft, S., widow	350 Mack
1851	Crickmay, Samuel, Rushmere, S., baker	222 Friar
1852	Crickmay, Thomas, Southtown, Yarmouth, S., gent.	321 Latten
1855	Crickmer, Charlotte, Wymondham, N., wife of John Crickmer, farmer	615 Whitty
1850	Crickmer, Susan, Heigham, Norwich, N., widow	324 Cuthbert
1846	Crighton, Samuel, Great Glenham, S.	314 Baret
1833	Crisp, Amos, Brandon, S., yeoman	357 Cubitt
1835	Crisp, Ann, Little Glemham, S., single woman	426 Harrowing

1853	Crisp, Catherine, Great Yarmouth, N., yeoman	642 Veale
1834	Crisp, Fortunatus, Great Yarmouth, N., plumber, glazier and painter	523 Lane
1843	Crisp, Jane, South Lynn All Saints, N., widow	227 Miles
1826	Crisp, John, Chediston, S., farmer	91 Davey
1829	Crisp, John, Chedgrave, N., gent.	328 Green
1832	Crisp, John, Badingham, S., shoemaker	528 Cooke
1842	Crisp, Samuel, Frostenden, S., esquire	625 Canler
1833	Crisp, Sarah, Beccles, S., widow	493 Cubitt
1825	Crisp, Susanna, Redenhall with Harleston, N., widow	167 Hayward
1854	Crispe, John, West Bilney, N., farmer	329 Day
1845	Critoph, Mary Ann, Roughton, N.	128 Pedgrift
1824	Crockley, Edward, Pensthorpe, N., labourer	7 Borrett
1857	Crofts, Dinah, Cley next the Sea, N., widow	450 Youngs
1847	Crofts, alias Baines, Mary, Fakenham, N., spinster	383 Broom
1834	Crofts, Thomas, Blakeney, N., gent.	419 Lane
1847	Crome, Samuel, Kings Lynn, N., coal merchant	48 Broom
1833	Crome, William, Horsford, N., yeoman	403 Cubitt
1838	Crompton, Elizabeth, Cranworth, N., wife of Rev. Thomas Crompton, clerk	681 Skepper
1829	Crook, William, Norwich, N., silk merchant	406 Green
1852	Crooks, Jonathan, Ringshall, S., parish clerk	422 Latten
1842	Cross, James Helsdon, Overstrand, N., farmer	279 Canler
1835	Cross, John, Bungay, S., corporal in H.M. 12th Regiment of Lancers	560 Harrowing
1835	Cross, John, Sibton, S., farmer	530 Harrowing
1842	Cross, Judith, Bungay, S., widow	632 Canler
1842	Cross, Maria, Bungay, S.	569 Canler
1829	Cross, Roberts, Great Yarmouth, N., schoolmaster	68 Green
1853	Cross, Samuel, Wantisden, S., farmer	49 Veale
1820	Cross, Sarah, Little Finborough, S., widow	85 Mack
1848	Cross, Thomas, Newmarket, S., hostler	296 Denny
1838	Cross, William, Scottow and North Walsham, N., farmer and butcher	728 Skepper
1839	Cross, William, Newmarket, S., ironmonger	299 Calton
1851	Cross, William the elder, Bungay, S., cordwainer	339 Friar
1853	Crossley, James, Covent Garden, Middlesex, brush maker	515 Veale
1837	Crosswell, Thomas, Great Yarmouth, N., labourer	108 Warren
1834	Crow, Charles, Great Yarmouth, N., cabinet maker	6 Lane
1826	Crow, John Hammond, Great Yarmouth, N., gent.	369 Dent
1850	Crow, Thomas, Metton, N., labourer	214 Cuthbert
1830	Crowe, John, Northrepps, N., labourer	2 Pettingill
1836	Crowe, John, Cratfield, S., gent.	438 Smith
1839	Crowe, John the younger, Catfield, N., gent.	486 Calton
1842	Crowe, John, Catfield, N., gent.	672 Canler
1854	Crowe, Martha Maria, Runton, N., widow	534 Day
1848	Crowe, Peter, Mendlesham, S., wheelwright	269 Denny
1845	Crowe, Robert, Ranworth, N., yeoman	778 Pedgrift
1821	Crowe, Spicer, Norwich, plumber, painter and glazier	1 Dewell
1830	Crowe, Sophia, Shottesham, N.	427 Pettingill
1836	Crowe, Thomas, Bungay, S., yeoman	265 Smith
1824	Crowe, William, Norwich, N., painter	309 Borrett
1825	Crowe, William, Swanton Abbott, N., farmer	36 Hayward
1855	Crowfoot, Elizabeth, Kessingland, S., widow	243 Whitty
1850	Crowfoot, John, Norwich, N., yeoman	490 Cuthbert
1853	Crowfoot, John Sibel, Kessingland, S., gent.	345 Veale
1841	Crowther, Samuel, Great Yarmouth, N., gent.	459 Traxton
1834	Cruso, Edmund, Norwich, N., surgeon	17 Lane
1847	Crutwell, Richard, Spexhall, S., rector	414 Broom
1830	Cubitt, Benjamin, St Mary, Norwich, N., wool comber	374 Pettingill
1849	Cubitt, Bridget, Southrepps, N., widow	583 Womack
1850	Cubitt, alias Page, Cubitt, Burgh next Aylsham, N.	375 Cuthbert
1821	Cubitt, Elizabeth, Ludham, N., widow	277 Dewell
1837	Cubitt, Hannah, Tunstead, N., spinster	61 Warren
1849	Cubitt, Horatio, Beeston St Lawrence, N., farmer	87 Womack

1827	Cubitt, James, Lessingham, N., gent., o.w. missing	686 Wood
1853	Cubitt, James, Sheringham, N., farmer	629 Veale
1828	Cubitt, Jane, Norwich, N., widow	422 Farrow
1820	Cubitt, John, Aldborough, N., farmer	408 Mack
1842	Cubitt, John, Southrepps, N., clerk	61 Canler
1850	Cubitt, John Pye, Hevingham, N., farmer	42 Cuthbert
1828	Cubitt, Mary Ann, Witton, N., wife of Thomas Cubitt, farmer	129 Farrow
1852	Cubitt, Robert, Brundall, N.	142 Latten
1833	Cubitt, Samuel, Brumstead, N., farmer	1 Cubitt
1824	Cubitt, William, Bacton, N., farmer	192 Borrett
1841	Cudbard, William, Norwich, N., machine maker	260 Traxton
1839	Cuddon, Alban, Loddon, N., basket maker	391 Calton
1828	Cuddon, James, Layham, S., farmer	341 Farrow
1822	Cufaude, John the elder, St Edmunds, Norwich, N., gent.	328 Sadler
1833	Culham, Frances, Wilby, S., widow	448 Cubitt
1824	Culham, Lydia, Orford, S., widow	158 Borrett
1849	Culham, Robert, Iken, S., farmer	316 Womack
1857	Culham, Thomas, Mettingham, S., yeoman	538 Youngs
1849	Cullen, Margaret, Tilney St Lawrence, N., widow	315 Womack
1834	Culley, Elizabeth, Bacton, N., widow	290 Lane
1849	Culley, Henry, Brandeston, N., gent.	299 Womack
1822	Culley, John, Norwich, N., gent.	14 Sadler
1819	Culley, Richard, North Walsham, N., gent.	287 Le Neve
1819	Culley, Samuel, Ludham, N., gent.	339 Le Neve
1823	Culley, Sarah, North Walsham, N., widow	227 Tann
1843	Culling, Charles, Salhouse, N., farmer	423 Miles
1827	Cullingham, James the elder, Lowestoft, S., mariner	335 Wood
1838	Cullingham, James, Lowestoft, S., pilot	213 Skepper
1836	Cullingham, John, Lowestoft, S., pilot	335 Smith
1833	Cullington, Elizabeth, Norwich, N., widow	25 Cubitt
1834	Cullum, Jeremiah, Alderton, S., miller	135 Lane
1854	Cullum, William, Thornham Magna, S., shoemaker	10 Day
1838	Cullyer, John, Heigham, Norwich, N., coachsmith	446 Skepper
1853	Culpeper, Edmund, Ormesby St Michael, N., gent.	25 Veale
1831	Culyer, Samuel, Norwich, N., victualler	77 Hart
1833	Culyer, Samuel, St Clements, Norwich, N., innkeeper	258 Cubitt
1838	Culyer, Samuel, Norwich, N., cordwainer	69 Skepper
1849	Culyer, William, Mattishall, N., farmer, o.w. missing	599 Womack
1845	Cumpston, John, Kings Lynn, N., coachman	237 Pedgrift
1853	Cunnell, Joseph, Leiston, S., yeoman	454 Veale
1851	Cunningham, Ann, Wilby, S., formerly of Bramfield, widow	574 Friar
1850	Cunningham, Esther, Kessingland, S., widow	258 Cuthbert
1836	Cunningham, James, St Peters South Elmham, S., farmer	249 Smith
1819	Cunningham, Jonathan, Banham, N., farmer	164 Le Neve
1822	Cunningham, Thomas, Kessingland, S., farmer	48 Sadler
1834	Cunningham, Thomas, Pulham St Mary the Virgin, N., farmer	159 Lane
1835	Cunningham, William, Barnham Broom, N., labourer	259 Harrowing
1838	Cupper, Barker, Wingfield, S., husbandman	92 Skepper
1835	Cupper, Esther, Norwich, N., widow	253 Harrowing
1832	Cupper, Rebecca, Withersdale, S., wife of John Cupper, yeoman	187 Cooke
1828	Cupper, William, Norwich, N., worstead weaver	161 Farrow
1857	Cupper, William, Yaxley, S., gent., formerly of Framlingham	546 Youngs
1840	Curl, George, Swannington, N., farmer	254 Turner
1847	Curll, John, Beeston with Bittering, N., husbandman	586 Broom
1823	Curll, Richard the elder, Swannington, N., gent.	76 Tann
1834	Curll, Richard, Swannington, N., farmer	785 Lane
1825	Curll, Sarah, Swannington, N.	56 Hayward
1834	Curll, Sarah, Norwich, N., spinster	593 Lane
1848	Currey, Mary, Norwich, N.	216 Denny
1834	Currey, Robert, Brandon, S., yeoman	739 Lane
1831	Currey, William, Lakenheath, S., yeoman	78 Hart
1827	Currie, William, Kings Lynn, N., gent.	402 Wood
1844	Curry, Ann, Feltwell, N.	581 Ebbage
1853	Curson, Edward, Denver, N., farmer	282 Veale

1851	Curson, James, Stibbard, N., formerly of Little Ryburgh, N., farmer	300 Friar
1851	Curson, Jeremiah, Morley St Botolph, N., farmer	530 Friar
1842	Curson, John, Ashill, N., yeoman	72 Canler
1850	Curson, John, Palgrave, S., innkeeper, formerly of Deopham, N., farmer	152 Cuthbert
1840	Curson, Robert, Kings Lynn, N., master mariner	409 Turner
1840	Curson, Thomas, Little Walsingham, N., general shopkeeper	297 Turner
1832	Curties, Mary, Wormegay, N., widow	185 Cooke
1820	Curtis, Ann, Gayton, N., widow	416 Mack
1837	Curtis, Ann, Halesworth, S., widow	89 Warren
1846	Curtis, Edward, Thornage, N., yeoman	O.W. 258
1831	Curtis, Henry, Hoveton St John, N., farmer	41 Hart
1850	Curtis, James, Cromer, N., blacksmith	39 Cuthbert
1833	Curtis, John, Aldeburgh, S., tailor and draper	505 Cubitt
1837	Curtis, John, Burgh, N., farmer	122 Warren
1857	Curtis, Maria, Hoveton St John, N., wife of Thomas Curtis, farmer	192 Youngs
1846	Curtis, Robert, Docking, N., bricklayer	178 Baret
1847	Curtis, Robert, Barton Turf, N., carpenter	323 Broom
1857	Curtis, Robert, Northrepps, N., gamekeeper	141 Youngs
1835	Curtis, William, Cromer, N., blacksmith	90 Harrowing
1825	Curtis, William, Barningham, N., late of Caston, farmer	235 Hayward
1851	Curtis, William, Hingham, N., shoemaker	413 Friar
1837	Cusande, John, Halesworth, S., gent.	282 Warren
1850	Cushing, Elizabeth, Norwich, N., widow	591 Cuthbert
1857	Cushing, James, Heigham, Norwich, N., shoemaker	343 Youngs
1830	Cushing, Jane, Shipdham, N., spinster	248 Pettingill
1829	Cushing, Mark, Fakenham, N., carrier	363 Green
1835	Cushion, Joseph, Southrepps, N., gardener	473 Harrowing
1848	Cushion, Samuel, Worstead, N., farmer	452 Denny
1857	Cushion, William, Reymerstone, N., farmer	293 Youngs
1837	Custance, Ann, St Georges, Colegate, Norwich, N., spinster	45 Warren
1842	Custance, Martha, Gimingham, N.	O.W. 283
1852	Cuthbert, James, North Creake, N., miller	865 Latten
1850	Cuthbert, Thomas, Letheringham, S., farmer	1 Cuthbert
1829	Cutting, Frances, Halesworth, S., spinster	325 Green
1831	Cutting, John, Southtown, Yarmouth, S., formerly of Toft Monks, N., farmer	395 Hart
1842	Cutting, John, Redenhall with Harleston, N., gent.	59 Canler
1849	Cutting, John, Bacton, S., farmer	285 Womack
1849	Cutting, Philip, Swilland, S., farmer	119 Womack
1820	Cutting, Thomas, Bramford, S., butcher	38 Mack
1855	Cutting, William, Aylsham, N., innkeeper	186 Whitty
1855	Cuttris, John, Norwich, N., butcher	703 Whitty
1839	Dabnaham, Maria Hull, Gorleston, S., spinster	240 Calton
1848	Dabnaham, Maria, Gorleston, S., spinster	443 Denny
1850	Dabson, Robert, Norwich, N., shuttle maker	303 Cuthbert
1843	Dacheux, Peter Lewis, Kings Lynn, N., clerk	397 Miles
1850	Dack, John, Hevingham, N., cordwainer	308 Cuthbert
1852	Dack, Paul, East Dereham, N., grocer and draper	163 Latten
1840	Dade, Edward, Wrentham, S., carpenter	114 Turner
1833	Dade, Hester, Great Yarmouth, N., widow	O.W. 230
1846	Dade, Jonathon, Wacton, N., labourer	211 Baret
1832	Dade, John, Swefling, S., farmer	27 Cooke
1842	Dade, Mary, Thetford, N., spinster	O.W. 285
1848	Dady, David, Shottesham, N., yeoman	113 Denny
1834	Dady, George, Norwich, N., wine and spirit merchant	655 Lane
1831	Dagless, Elizabeth, Fakenham, N., widow	167 Hart
1852	Dagless, Thomas, Bodham, N., blacksmith and farmer	414 Latten
1843	Daines, George, Mettingham, S., wheelwright	613 Miles
1822	Daines, James, Buxton, N., yeoman	409 Sadler
1850	Daines, Mary, Sibton, S., spinster	439 Cuthbert
1834	Dains, Isaac, Tibbenham, N., carpenter	577 Lane

1852	Dains, Robert, Mettingham, S, farmer	707 Latten
1843	Dains, William, Great Yarmouth, N., mariner	480 Miles
1855	Dalby, James, Ipswich, S., gent.	60 Whitty
1823	Dale, Charles, Norwich, N., lawyer	363 Tann
1842	Dale, Daniel, Ipswich, S., bricklayer	757 Canler
1839	Dale, Henry Edward, Kelsale, S., farmer	571 Calton
1826	Dale, James the elder, Ipswich, S., ship caulker	24 Davy
1820	Dale, John Smith, Norwich, N., hairdresser	414 Mack
1822	Dale, Robert, Thorpe next Norwich, N., carpenter	109 Sadler
1845	Dale, Sarah, Bentley, S., widow	482 Pedgrift
1832	Dale, William, Norwich, N., woolcomber	493 Cooke
1833	Dallinger, Charles Chenery, Wilby, S., farmer	231 Cubitt
1847	Dams, John, Downham Market, N., innkeeper	485 Broom
1840	Danby, Hannah, Burwell, C., widow	584 Turner
1853	Danby, Mary, Soham, C., widow	488 Veale
1831	Daniel, Elizabeth, Dersingham, N., widow	21 Hart
1829	Daniel, John Stanhawe Watts, Dillington, N., esquire	150 Green
1842	Daniel, Richard, Stokesby, N., gent.	131 Canler
1848	Daniel, Robert, Falkenham, S., gent.	798 Denny
1848	Daniel, William, South Creake, N.	Index only
1846	Daniells, Ann, St Peter Mancroft, Norwich, N., widow	669 Baret
1857	Daniels, John, Seething, N., farmer	70 Youngs
1849	Daniels, Robert, Framingham Pigot, N., farmer and market gardener	272 Womack
1851	Daniels, Sophia, Rendham, S., widow	507 Friar
1857	Daniels, Thomas, Swanton Abbott, N., blacksmith	262 Youngs
1823	Dann, James, Denton, N.	340 Tann
1828	Dann, Mary, Mendham or Redenhall, N., widow	419 Farrow
1855	Dann, Mary Ann, Norwich, N., widow	129 Whitty
1839	Dann,William, Shadingfield, S., yeoman	479 Calton
1839	Danson, Thomas, Salhouse, N., yeoman	531 Calton
1840	Darborough, William, Snettisham, N., farmer	157 Turner
1835	Darby, Charlotte, Lowestoft, S., widow	279 Harrowing
1841	Darby, Edward, Suffield, N., gent.	383 Traxton
1843	Darby, Edward, Bungay, S., wheelwright	82 Miles
1843	Darby, Elizabeth, Helmingham, S., widow	167 Miles
1846	Darby, Elizabeth, Diss, N., widow	116 Baret
1830	Darby, John, Bungay, S., coal merchant	368 Pettingill
1846	Darby, John Wareyn, Framlingham, S., clerk	622 Baret
1842	Dark, Robert, North Creake, N., farmer	304 Canler
1822	Darkin, George, Norwich, N., yeoman	340 Sadler
1833	Darkin, Robert, Heigham, Norwich, N., gent.	63 Cubitt
1836	Darkins, John, Castle Acre, N., bricklayer	220 Smith
1852	Darnell, John, Redgrave, S., farmer	834 Latten
1831	Darnell, William, Redgrave, S., farmer	473 Hart
1835	Darnton, Jemima Mary, Yoxford, S.	496 Harrowing
1831	Darseley, William, Ashill, N., victualler	90 Hart
1851	Davey, Abraham, Ludham, N., bricklayer	311 Friar
1845	Davey, Daniel, Heigham, Norwich, N., stone mason	600 Pedgrift
1835	Davey, Elizabeth, Norwich, N., spinster	491 Harrowing
1850	Davey, Elizabeth, Bressingham, N., spinster	328 Cuthbert
1855	Davey, Elizabeth, Heigham next Norwich, N., widow	716 Whitty
1834	Davey, Henry, Saxthorpe, N., lieut. in Royal Navy	O.W. 352
1852	Davey, James, East Carlton, N. carpenter and farmer	408 Latten
1841	Davey, John, Upton, N., husbandman	213 Traxton
1848	Davey, John, Beeston next Mileham, N., gent.	313 Denny
1854	Davey, Joseph, Great Yarmouth, N., accountant	62 Day
1820	Davey, Richard, Great Ryburgh, N., yeoman	179 Mack
1856	Davey, Sarah, Norwich, N., widow	262 Code
1824	Davey, Thomas, Aldborough, N., late of Saxthorpe, yeoman	213 Borrett
1835	Davey, William the elder, Old Buckenham, N., farmer	286 Harrowing
1827	David, Elizabeth, St Georges Colegate, Norwich, N., widow	514 Wood
1841	David, William Heron, Heigham, Norwich, N., gent.	281 Traxton
1836	Davidson, George, Snape, S., yeoman	550 Smith

1850	Davidson, Hannah, Hackford next Reepham, N., spinster	3 Cubitt
1853	Davie, Ann, Great Yarmouth, N., widow	222 Veale
1827	Daville, John, Grimston, N., gent.	174 Wood
1853	Davis, James, Norwich, N., gent.	395 Veale
1824	Davison, Daniel, Swanton Abbott, N., cotton weaver	9 Borrett
1825	Davison, John, St Clements, Norwich, N., formerly of St Luke, Middlesex	156 Hayward
1847	Davy, Ann, Norwich, N., widow	688 Broom
1829	Davy, Augustine, Heacham, N.	260 Green
1827	Davy, Christopher, Rackheath, N., farmer	54 Wood
1824	Davy, John, Diss, N., late of Bressingham, farmer	131 Borrett
1845	Davy, John, Norwich, N., gent.	47 Pedgrift
1848	Davy, John, Holt, N.	Index only
1857	Davy, Jonathan, Thornage, N., farmer	529 Youngs
1838	Davy, Mary, St Georges Colegate, Norwich, N.	159 Skepper
1844	Davy, Robert the elder, Banham, N., cordwainer	269 Ebbage
1830	Davy, Sarah, Wells next the Sea, N., widow	10 Pettingill
1826	Davy, Thomas, New Buckenham, N., cooper	1 Davy
1834	Davy, Thomas, Norwich, N., liquor merchant	210 Lane
1824	Davy, William, Caister by Yarmouth, N., miller	43 Borrett
1826	Davy, William, Little Hautbois, N., clerk	352 Davy
1837	Davy, William, Shadbrooke, S., farmer	691 Warren
1852	Davy, William, Kings Lynn, N., gaoler	465 Latten
1843	Daw, John, Trunch, N.	O.W. 261
1841	Daw, Robert, Snettisham, N., farmer	410 Traxton
1845	Dawes, Elizabeth, Kings Lynn, N., widow	456 Pedgrift
1857	Dawes, Larrance, Wreningham, N., farmer	61 Youngs
1846	Daws, James, Wreningham, N., farmer	576 Baret
1842	Daws, Thomas, St John Maddermarket, Norwich, carpenter	707 Canler
1852	Dawson, George, South Shields, Co. Durham, flour merchant	204 Latten
1838	Dawson, Henry, Great Yarmouth, N.	493 Skepper
1820	Dawson, John, Foxley, N., farmer	642 Mack
1833	Dawson, John, Kings Lynn, N., baker	395 Cubitt
1834	Dawson, John, Kings Lynn, N., baker	1 Lane
1850	Dawson, Margaret, Norwich, N., widow	326 Cuthbert
1822	Dawson, Peter, Norwich, N., yeoman	311 Sadler
1847	Dawson, Ruth, Gorleston, S., widow	34 Broom
1830	Dawson, Samuel, Great Yarmouth, N., baker	5 Pettingill
1835	Dawson, Thomas, Gorleston, S., pilot	629 Harrowing
1824	Dawson, William, Horsey, N.	119 Borrett
1838	Dawson, William, Neatishead, N., labourer	102 Skepper
1825	Day, Ann, Rollesby, N., widow	29 Hayward
1847	Day, Ann, Swanton Morley, N., widow	162 Broom
1838	Day, Elizabeth, Bungay, S., widow	714 Skepper
1835	Day, George, Clopton, S., yeoman	263 Harrowing
1833	Day, Griggs, Wreningham, N., shopkeeper	498 Cubitt
1832	Day, Isaac, Elmsett, S.yeoman	206 Cooke
1832	Day, Jacob, Upton, N., yeoman	238 Mack
1846	Day, Jacob, Upton, N.	Index only
1838	Day, Rev. Jeremiah Ives, Yelverton, N., clerk	221 Skepper
1840	Day, John, Upton, N., farmer	606 Turner
1849	Day, John, Upwell, C., farmer	537 Womack
1850	Day, John, Rollesby, N., farmer	121 Cuthbert
1837	Day, Joseph the elder, Eye, S., carpenter and joiner, wheelwright and pumpmaker	234 Warren
1848	Day, Joseph, Upwell, Isle of Ely, farmer	676 Denny
1856	Day, Joseph, Eye, S., carpenter and wheelwright	471 Code
1854	Day, Kerridge, Dennington, S., coal dealer	152 Day
1848	Day, Mary, Catton, N., wife of James Day, esquire	101 Denny
1849	Day, Peter, Ixworth Thorpe, S., farmer	416 Womack
1834	Day, Piddock, Norwich, N., planemaker	672 Lane
1819	Day, Richard, Norwich, N., clerk	126 Le Neve
1835	Day, Robert the elder, Wreningham, N., farmer	69 Harrowing
1826	Day, Samuel, Newmarket, N., carrier	116 Davy

1854	Day, Sarah, Norwich, N., widow	1 Day
1826	Day, Thomas, Upton, N., farmer	129 Davy
1837	Day, Thomas, Swanton Morley, N., farmer	333 Warren
1848	Day, Thomas, Upton, N., yeoman	128 Denny
1848	Day, Thomas, Upwell, N.	699 Denny
1850	Daynes, Francis, Swanton Morley, N., miller	379 Cuthbert
1857	Deacon, Harriet, Norwich, N., spinster	461 Youngs
1823	Deacon, Samuel Story, Norwich, surgeon	346 Tann
1846	Dean, James, Great Yarmouth, N., gas fitter	646 Baret
1843	Dearing, George, Norwich, N., hairdresser	433 Miles
1836	Dearing, William, butler to the Bishop of Norwich	574 Smith
1822	Dearn, Margaret, Stalham, N., spinster	356 Sadler
1857	Dearnes, William, Thornham, N., mariner	710 Youngs
1822	Dearsley, Amy, Cowling, S., spinster	227 Sadler
1827	Dearsley, John, East Bergholt, S., farmer	256 Wood
1844	Death, Francis, Gazeley, S., farmer and miller	344 Ebbage
1831	Debenham, Amy, North Elmham, N., widow	225 Hart
1838	Debenham, Dan, Ovington, N., farmer	789 Skepper
1837	Debenham, Edward, Rickinghall Inferior, S. shopkeeper	603 Warren
1837	Debenham, Elizabeth, East Dereham, N., widow	380 Warren
1831	Debenham, Henry, Rickinghall Superior, S., innholder	407 Hart
1831	De Benne, John Stephen, North Walsham, N., shopkeeper	165 Hart
1823	Debenne, Thomas, North Walsham, N., gent.	107 Tann
1820	Debney, Ann, Tunstall, S., widow of Thomas Debney	570 Mack
1826	De Carle, James, Ipswich, S., stone mason	84 Davy
1834	De Carle, Rebekah, Ipswich, S., widow	401 Lane
1829	De Carle, Robert the younger, Norwich, N., stone and marble mason	533 Green
1843	De Caux, Lucas, Lakenham, Norwich, N., innkeeper	588 Miles
1841	De Caux, William, St John Maddermarket, Norwich, cabinet maker and upholsterer	95 Traxton
1857	Deeks, Charles, Hingham, N., yeoman	319 Youngs
1854	De Grube, Mary, East Dereham, N., widow	82 Day
1823	Delph, Dinah, Norwich, widow	290 Tann
1845	Delf, Rhoda, Denton, N., shopkeeper	420 Pedgrift
1831	Delf, William the elder, Topcroft, N., farmer	198 Hart
1841	Delph, William, Soham, C., gardener	373 Traxton
1837	Denham, Samuel, Eye, S.	214 Warren
1851	Dennant, John, Halesworth, S., dissenting minister	213 Friar
1830	Dennes, William, Wiggenhall St Marys, N., gent.	405 Pettingill
1847	Denney, Joshua the elder, Roughton, N., farmer	418 Broom
1845	Denney, Samuel, Southolt, S., parish clerk	130 Pedgrift
1844	Dennis, Edward, Litcham, N., baker	495 Ebbage
1819	Dennis, James, West Dereham, N., farmer	101 Le Neve
1820	Dennis, John, Felmingham, N., blacksmith	422 Mack
1830	Dennis, Robert, East Runton, N., labourer	208 Pettingill
1826	Denny, Catharine, Eye, S., spinster	217 Davy
1856	Denny, Elizabeth, Norton Subcourse, N., spinster	220 Code
1835	Denny, James William, Bungay, S., liquor merchant	240 Harrowing
1846	Denny, Joseph, Great Yarmouth, N., boatman and public house keeper	218 Baret
1848	Denny, Martin, Roughton, N., grocer	1 Denny
1839	Denny, Samuel, Walpole, S., farmer	332 Calton
1855	Denny, Stephen, Heckingham, N., gent.	467 Whitty
1819	Denny, Susannah, Lowestoft, S., widow	51 Le Neve
1834	Denny, Thomas, Beccles, S, fishmonger	595 Lane
1848	Denny, William, Bungay, S., farmer	116 Denny
1852	Denny, Thomas William, Coddenham, S., gent.	268 Latten
1846	Dent, Matthew, Ludham, N.	486 Baret
1841	Dent, Thomas Howlett, North Elmham, N., postmaster and registrar	278 Traxton
1829	Dent, William, Thetford, N., yeoman	523 Green
1835	Denton, James, Strumpshaw, N., husbandman	281 Harrowing

1840	Denton, James, Surlingham, N., cordwainer	612 Turner
1840	Denton, Jane, Wymondham, N., spinster	336 Turner
1839	Denton, John, Hopton, S., farmer	359 Calton
1830	Denton, Mary, Norwich, N., widow	209 Pettingill
1820	Derisley, Elizabeth, Thetford, N., widow	34 Mack
1848	Derisley, John, Mileham, N., farmer	417 Denny
1857	Derry, Alice, South Lynn All Saints, Kings Lynn, N., widow	159 Youngs
1844	Desborough, James, Wiggenhall St Germains, N., farmer	469 Ebbage
1828	De Vear, John, Norwich, N., gent.	35 Farrow
1852	Devereux, Benjamin the elder, Alburgh, N., farmer	782 Latten
1845	Devereux, Edmund the elder, Norwich, N., plumber, glazier and house painter	173 Pedgrift
1834	Devereux, William the elder, Norwich, N., plumber, glazier and house painter	568 Lane
1851	Devereux, William, St Georges Colegate, Norwich, N. plumber glazier and painter	622 Friar
1848	Dew, Barbara, Kettleston, N., widow	701 Denny
1832	Dew, John, Swanton Novers, N., gent.	406 Cooke
1831	Dew, Richard, Swanton Novers, N., farmer	607 Hart
1857	Dew, Robert, Reepham Moor, N., dealer	169 Youngs
1821	Dewell, Margaret, Copdock, S., widow	1 Dewell
1842	Dewhurst, Thomas, Kings Lynn, N., yeoman	662 Canler
1827	Dewing, Edward, Guist, N., esquire	250 Wood
1832	Dewing, Edward, Raynham, N., clergyman	319 Cooke
1829	Dewing, Mary Ann, Weasenham, N., spinster	371 Green
1843	Dewing, Sarah, St Georges Colegate, Norwich, N., widow	500 Miles
1837	Dexter, Elizabeth, Rockland St Peter, N., widow	351 Warren
1830	Dexter, William, Rockland St Peter, N., bricklayer	389 Pettingill
1845	Diball, John, Great Yarmouth, N., carpenter and builder	771 Pedgrift
1827	Dible, William, Kings Lynn, N., broker	380 Wood
1831	Dick, William, Great Yarmouth, N., gent.	532 Hart
1825	Dickens, Mark Hildesley, East Dereham, N.	263 Hayward
1819	Dickerson, Joseph, Finningham, S., yeoman	229 Le Neve
1853	Dickerson, Sophia, Needham Market, S., widow	381 Veale
1825	Dickinson, Sarah, Norwich, N., spinster	112 Hayward
1849	Digby, Joseph, Smallburgh, N., waterman	628 Womack
1839	Digby, Matthew, Cley next the Sea, N., yeoman	277 Calton
1850	Diggens, Edmund King, Ashbocking, S., yeoman	59 Cuthbert
1831	Diggens, James, Hackford next Reepham, N., yeoman	566 Hart
1824	Diggins, Samuel, Gaywood, N., alehouse keeper	353 Borrett
1830	Diggon, Nicholas, Thetford, N., currier	132 Pettingill
1856	Diggons, John, Rockland St Mary, N., gent.	461 Cuthbert
1849	Diggons, Thomas, Kings Lynn, N., alehouse keeper	504 Womack
1845	Ding, Hannah, Great Yarmouth, N., widow	289 Pedgrift
1852	Dingle, Catherine Theresa, Cley next the Sea, N., widow	832 Latten
1842	Ditcham, James, Sea Palling, N., farmer	307 Canler
1852	Diver, Eleanor, Great Yarmouth, N., wife of Richard Diver, gent.	610 Latten
1855	Diver, Richard, Great Yarmouth, N., gent.	355 Whitty
1827	Dix, Ann, Halesworth, S., widow	398 Wood
1831	Dix, Francis, Fundenhall, N., farmer	478 Hart
1847	Dix, James, Tivetshall St Mary, N., farmer	686 Broom
1854	Dix, Joseph, Dunwich, S., farmer, and merchant	245 Day
1828	Dix, Matthew, Stibbard, N.	294 Farrow
1828	Dix, Richard, Smallburgh, N., surgeon	468 Farrow
1843	Dix, Robert, Dickleburgh, N., farmer	305 Miles
1855	Dix, Robert, Northrepps, N., farmer	510 Whitty
1855	Dix, Sturley, Docking, N.	635 Whitty
1836	Dixon, Ann, South Pickenham, N., widow	345 Smith
1838	Dixon, Elizabeth, Norwich, N., widow	74 Skepper
1849	Dixon, George, Bungay, S., farmer	464 Womack
1836	Dixon, Joseph, Yarmouth, N., customs officer	19 Smith
1850	Dixon, Mary Dorothy, Norwich, N., widow	511 Cuthbert
1856	Dixon, Robert, East Ruston, N., farmer	413 Code

1853	Dixon, Samuel, Heigham, Norwich, N.	615 Veale
1828	Dixon, Thomas, Great Yarmouth, N., yeoman	494 Farrow
1820	Dixson, Edmund, Burnham Westgate, N., yeoman	387 Mack
1834	Dobbs, John, North Walsham, N., bricklayer	710 Lane
1841	Dobson, George, Kings Lynn, N, gent.	397 Traxton
1842	Dobson, Isaac, Kings Lynn, N., plumber and glazier	6 Canler
1822	Dobson, James, Norwich, N., carpenter	290 Sadler
1854	Dobson. Jane, Aylsham, N., spinster	192 Day
1821	Dobson, Mary, Barton Turf, N., spinster	215 Dewell
1827	Dobson, Richard, Barton Turf, N., farmer	O.W. 306
1841	Dobson, William, Heigham, Norwich, N., formerly of Hindolveston, N., farmer	261 Traxton
1842	Dodd, David, St Margarets Ilketshall, S., farmer	516 Canler
1836	Dodd, John Beck, New Buckenham, N., druggist	120 Smith
1849	Dodman, George, Gressenhall, N., innkeeper	75 Womack
1823	Dodman, Martin, Thornham, N., farmer	137 Tann
1852	Dodman, Robert Thompson, Heigham, Norwich, N., reed maker	474 Latten
1832	Dodshon, Robert, Diss, N., surgeon and apothecary	91 Cooke
1834	Doe, John, Bury St Edmunds, S., broker	239 Lane
1853	Doe, John, Denton, N., yeoman	565 Veale
1824	Doe, Robert, Bradestone, N., farmer	149 Borrett
1834	Doe, Thomas, Wattisfield, S., miller	141 Lane
1848	Doggett, Ann, Burnham Westgate, N., spinster	271 Denny
1842	Doggett, Thomas, Mellis, S., farmer	552 Canler
1844	Doman, George, Norwich, N., stonemason	201 Ebbage
1848	Dordery, William the elder, Mendham, N., farmer	53 Denny
1824	Dotheredge, William, Aylsham, N., collar maker	373 Borrett
1845	Dotheridge, Robert, St Michaels Coslany, Norwich, N. brewer	807 Pedgrift
1829	Doughton, Mary, Bungay, S., spinster	218 Green
1833	Doughty, Benjamin, Coltishall, N., butcher	325 Cubitt
1827	Doughty, James, Darsham, S., formerly of London, widower	700 Wood
1844	Doughty, Robert, Norwich, N., gent.	10 Ebbage
1822	Doughty, Thomas, Coltishall, N., butcher	207 Sadler
1852	Douglas, Thomas, Great Yarmouth, N., gent.	11 Latten
1854	Dove, Daniel, Redgrave, S., yeoman	122 Day
1835	Dove, Elizabeth, Ipswich, S., widow	334 Harrowing
1844	Dove, John, Hinderclay, S., yeoman	340 Ebbage
1831	Dove, Susannah, Orford, S., spinster	419 Hart
1847	Dowell, William Smith, Kings Lynn, N., formerly of Sunderland, Co. Durham, master mariner	3 Broom
1857	Dowling, Alice, Lowestoft, S., wife of John Dowling, land agent	578 Youngs
1827	Dowling, Jeremiah, Redenhall with Harleston, N., yeoman	449 Wood
1830	Downes, James, Norwich, N., servant to Messieurs Booth, Theobald and Booth, manufacturers	224 Pettingill
1853	Downes, William, Great Ellingham, N.	516 Veale
1845	Downing, Edward, Litcham, N., farmer	275 Pedgrift
1822	Downing, Elizabeth, Norwich, N., widow	243 Sadler
1831	Downing, Henry, Great Yarmouth, N., house carpenter	397 Hart
1834	Downing, John, Raveningham, N., farmer	603 Lane
1827	Downing, Sarah, Wrentham, S., widow	346 Wood
1851	Downing, William, Norwich, N., carpenter	130 Friar
1849	Downs, William, Tivetshall St Margaret, N., farmer	O.W. 299
1845	Dowsing, James, Shadbrooke, S., husbandman and farmer	196 Pedgrift
1855	Dowson, Elizabeth, Ditchingham, N., widow	108 Whitty
1826	Dowson, James, St John Timberhill, Norwich, N., cordwainer	299 Davy
1846	Dowson, Susanna, Geldeston, N., widow	437 Baret
1848	Doy, Charles, Barnby, S.	127 Denny
1825	D'Piza, Anne Maria, Caston, N., schoolmistress	358 Hayward
1837	Drake, Edmund, South Lopham, N., yeoman	278 Warren
1819	Drake, Eleanor, Great Yarmouth, N., widow	121 Le Neve
1845	Drake, George, Fersfield, N., farmer	627 Pedgrift
1856	Drake, Hannah, Fritton, N., wife of Daniel Drake, Esquire	449 Code

1852	Drake, James, Great Yarmouth, N., wheelwright	869 Latten
1837	Drake, John, Cranworth, N., farmer	97 Warren
1825	Drake, Maria, Wood Dalling, N., widow	158 Hayward
1857	Drake, Robert, Thetford, N., ostler	413 Youngs
1849	Drake, Sarah, Norwich, N., widow	180 Womack
1820	Drake, Thomas, Lessingham, N., carpenter and wheelwright	21 Mack
1825	Drake, Thomas, Stow Bardolph, N., farmer	148 Hayward
1854	Drake, William, Newton Flotman, N., farmer	313 Day
1831	Drane, Charles, Kirby Bedon, N., farmer	456 Hart
1850	Drane, James, Dickleburgh, N., yeoman	125 Cuthbert
1854	Drane, James the elder, Hargham, N., farmer	125 Day
1825	Drane, John, Langmere, N., farmer	452 Hayward
1838	Drane, Thomas, Thelnetham, S., yeoman	261 Skepper
1821	Drane, William, Fakenham, N., yeoman	154 Dewell
1835	Draper, Ann, Oulton, S., widow	497 Harrowing
1830	Draper, Elizabeth, Great Yarmouth, N., widow	141 Pettingill
1829	Draper, John, Great Yarmouth, N., formerly of North Walsham, wheelwright	136 Green
1838	Draper, John, Ditchingham, N., farmer	792 Skepper
1840	Draper, John, Great Yarmouth, N., butcher	442 Turner
1855	Draper, John, Ditchingham, N., farmer	65 Whitty
1846	Drayton, James, St Marys, Newmarket, S.	365 Baret
1845	Drew, James, Docking, N., breeches maker	687 Pedgrift
1820	Drew, Sarah, Easton, N., widow	646 Mack
1837	Drew, Sarah, Little Walsingham, N., formerly of Weasenham, spinster	200 Warren
1827	Drew, William, North Runcton, N., clerk	71 Wood
1850	Drewell, Edmund, Norwich, N., warehouseman	427 Cuthbert
1852	Drewell, Robert, alias Warner, Fakenham, N., yeoman	662 Latten
1843	Drewmilk, William, Brockdish, N., postman	428 Miles
1844	Dring, George, Norwich, N., gent.	389 Ebbage
1820	Dring, John, Norwich, N., baker	498 Mack
1853	Driver, Elizabeth, Holt, N., spinster	359 Veale
1849	Driver, Samuel, Wiveton, N., farmer	306 Womack
1857	Driver, William, Bungay, S., innkeeper	172 Youngs
1850	Drory, Daniel, Hevingham, N., yeoman	498 Cuthbert
1845	Drozier, Edward, Holt, N., chemist and druggist	579 Pedgrift
1835	Drozier, Thomas, Holt, N., gent.	21 Harrowing
1819	Druery, Mary, Norwich, N., spinster	263 Le Neve
1850	Druery, Thomas, Little Walsingham, N., draper	357 Cuthbert
1836	Drury, Sarah, Oxborough N.	330 Smith
1824	Duck, William, Ludham, N., blacksmith	155 Borrett
1823	Ducker, Catharine, North Walsham, N., widow	318 Tann
1823	Ducker, Daniel, Swanton Abbott, N., farmer	18 Tann
1819	Ducker, David, North Walsham, N., tailor	275 Le Neve
1826	Ducker, Thomas	25 Davy
1845	Duffield, Elizabeth, Woodbridge, S., spinster	519 Pedgrift
1857	Duffield, George, Norwich, N., grocer	310 Youngs
1840	Duffield, John the elder, Old Buckenham, N., yeoman	75 Turner
1850	Duffield, Martha, Itteringham, N., widow	212 Cuthbert
1856	Duffield, Mary Ann, Heacham, N., widow	567 Code
1855	Duffield, Thomas, Heacham, N., farmer	410 Whitty
1827	Duffield, William, Tottenhill, N., farmer	655 Wood
1824	Duffin, Joseph, Hardley, N., yeoman	334 Borrett
1836	Dunger, William, Great Dunham, N., farmer	201 Smith
1828	Dunham, John, Hackford next Reepham, N., yeoman	487 Farrow
1833	Dunn, Ann, Burwell, C., widow	379 Cubitt
1855	Dunn, George, Alderton, S., shoemaker	609 Whitty
1829	Dunn, James, Norwich, N., gent.	445 Green
1830	Dunn, James, Preston, S., rector	112 Pettingill
1849	Dunnell, David, Fritton Hall, S., ship owner	564 Womack
1820	Dunnett, James, Hedenham, N., gardener	448 Mack
1849	Dunnett, Richard, St Lawrence Ilketshall, S., yeoman	493 Womack
1827	Dunning, John, Swaffham, N., coachmaker	417 Wood

1840	Dunning, Thomasina, St Benedicts, Norwich, N., spinster	611 Turner
1833	Dunt, Elizabeth, Tasburgh, N., widow	318 Cubitt
1838	Dunt, John, Topcroft, N., grocer	663 Skepper
1845	Dunt, Richard, Great Witchingham, N., farmer and carpenter	634 Pedgrift
1841	Dunt, Samuel, Foulsham, N., farmer	201 Traxton
1823	Dunthorne, John, Dennington, S., grocer	64 Tann
1827	Dunton, John, Holme Hale, N., farmer	66 Wood
1836	Dunton, Susanna, Sporle, N., widow	377 Smith
1822	Durant, Robert Boult, Great Yarmouth, N.	362 Sadler
1843	Durant, William Dobson, Gorleston, S., gent.	246 Miles
1832	Durham, Jane, Mendlesham, S., spinster	50 Cooke
1831	Durham, Robert, Mickfield, S., yeoman	262 Hart
1829	Durrant, Abraham, Ipswich, S.	130 Green
1828	Durrant, Ann, Heigham, Norwich, N.	87 Farrow
1823	Durrant, Bridget, Swanton Abbott, N., spinster	245 Tann
1830	Durrant, Edward, St Peters South Elmham, S., farmer	420 Pettingill
1857	Durrant, Elizabeth, Blaxhall, S.	148 Youngs
1850	Durrant, George, Great Yarmouth, N., silversmith	232 Cuthbert
1853	Durrant, Humphrey, St Peters South Elmham, S., farmer	134 Veale
1820	Durrant, Isaac, Sternfield, S., farmer	336 Mack
1831	Durrant, James, Burgh St Peters, N., labourer	500 Hart
1847	Durrant, James, Caister next Great Yarmouth, N., wheelwright	267 Broom
1837	Durrant, Jeremiah, Eye, S., carter	369 Warren
1826	Durrant, John, Woodbridge, S., harness maker	342 Davy
1834	Durrant, John, Kessingland, S., carpenter	23 Lane
1855	Durrant, John, Holme Hale, N., shopkeeper	499 Whitty
1846	Durrant, Samuel, Dennington, S., miller	598 Baret
1857	Durrant, Samuel, Sutton, N., farmer	470 Youngs
1827	Durrant, Thomas, Hickling, N., farmer	503 Wood
1832	Durrant, William, Burgh St Peters, N., bachelor	165 Cooke
1834	Durrant, William, Lound, S.	590 Lane
1840	Durrant, William, Brumstead, N., gent.	113 Turner
1842	Durrant, William, Billockby, N., farmer	196 Canler
1847	Durrant, William, Hickling, N., farmer	4 Broom
1854	Durrant, William Henry, Norwich, N., gent.	79 Day
1852	Durrell, John, Colby, N., farmer and shopkeeper	441 Latten
1855	Durrell, Joseph, Hanworth, N., schoolmaster	624 Whitty
1841	Durrell, Pleasant, Woodbridge, S., spinster	472 Traxton
1823	Durrell, Robert, Woodbridge, S., fruiterer	144 Tann
1830	Dutchman, James, East Dereham, N., gent.	435 Pettingill
1839	Dutt, William, Ditchingham, N., coachman	490 Calton
1855	Dybal, James, Overstrand, N.	621 Whitty
1826	Dyball, Ann, Bungay, S., widow	316 Davy
1842	Dyball, Benjamin, Sutton, N.	244 Canler
1854	Dyball, Elizabeth, Worstead, N., spinster	538 Day
1823	Dyball, James, Sheringham, N., farmer	297 Tann
1850	Dyball, Mary Ann, Worstead, N., formerly of Westminster, spinster	439 Cuthbert
1834	Dyball, Robert, North Walsham, N.	51 Lane
1853	Dyball, William, Bungay, S., gent.	290 Veale
1839	Dye, Alice, Castle Acre, N., spinster	440 Calton
1848	Dye, Charles James Nichols, Great Yarmouth, N., gent.	423 Denny
1847	Dye, Elizabeth, East Winch, N., wife of Samuel Dye, farmer	22 Broom
1850	Dye, Elizabeth, Wymondham, N., spinster	535 Cuthbert
1847	Dye, George, Syleham, S., miller	435 Broom
1820	Dye, Isaac, Norwich, N., grocer	403 Mack
1837	Dye, James, Norwich, N., fishmonger	163 Warren
1842	Dye, John, Marham, N., farmer	326 Canler
1846	Dye, John, Pentney, N., farmer	610 Baret
1837	Dye, Mary, Norwich, N., widow and fishmonger	327 Warren
1837	Dye, Mary, Heigham, Norwich, N., widow	550 Warren
1841	Dye, Phillis, Great Yarmouth, N., widow	294 Traxton
1833	Dye, Robert, Hemblington, N., yeoman	39 Cubitt
1838	Dye, Robert, Foulsham, N., carter	269 Skepper

1841	Dye, Robert, Great Yarmouth, N., cordwainer	295 Traxton
1855	Dye, Robert, Swanton Novers, N., farmer	546 Whitty
1856	Dye, Robert, East Winch, N., farmer	90 Code
1833	Dye, Stephen, Hardingham, N., farmer	190 Cubitt
1834	Dye, Susanna, Norwich, N., widow	O.W. 353
1834	Dye, William, Kirby Cane, N., gent.	489 Lane
1856	Dye, William, Norwich, N., tailor	204 Code
1849	Dyer, Ann, Bury St Edmunds, S., widow	557 Womack
1819	Dyer, Thomas, Bures St Mary, S., farmer	23 Le Neve
1840	Dyer, William Edward, Norwich, N., cane worker	195 Turner
1854	Dyerson, Ann, Swaffham, N., spinster	379 Day
1838	Dykes, Philip, Beccles, S., esquire	667 Skepper
1828	Dymes, John, Norwich, N., yeoman	324 Farrow
1850	Dynes, Harriet, Wimbotsham, N., widow	508 Cuthbert
1827	Dynes, Henry, Stoke Ferry, N., miller	320 Wood
1833	Dyson, John, Syleham, S., gent.	185 Cubitt
1835	Eade, Charles, Metfield, S., clerk	530 Harrowing
1820	Eade, Jeremiah, Blythburgh, S., innholder	207 Mack
1845	Eade, Thomas French, Eye, S., clerk	438 Pedgrift
1836	Eagle, Henry, Thetford, N.	211 Smith
1847	Eagle, John, Badingham, S., farmer	236 Broom
1851	Eagle, Thomas, Fakenham, N., yeoman	452 Friar
1828	Eaglen, Mary, Besthorpe, N., spinster	533 Farrow
1838	Eagling, Thomas, Wymondham, N., farmer	208 Skepper
1855	Earl, Judith, Southrepps, N., widow	83 Whitty
1835	Earl, Lydia, Norwich, N., spinster	178 Harrowing
1823	Earle, James, Mundesley, N., farmer	363 Tann
1832	Earle, James, Calthorpe, N., yeoman	357 Cooke
1833	Earle, Samuel, St Stephens, Norwich, N., innholder	471 Cubitt
1847	Earthey, Thomas, Stowmarket, S., farrier	423 Broom
1834	East, Joseph, The Crown, Southgates, Lynn, N., victualler	75 Lane
1846	Eastall, Samuel, Mendlesham, S., farmer	98 Baret
1833	Eastall, William, Wereham, N., miller and baker	126 Cubitt
1850	Eastaugh, Elizabeth, Heckingham, N., spinster	118 Cuthbert
1857	Eastaugh, Mary, Beccles, S., widow	757 Youngs
1840	Eastaugh, Samuel, Fakenham, N., preacher of the Gospel	46 Turner
1822	Eastaugh, William, Cookley, formerly Bramfield, S. innholder	265 Sadler
1857	Easter, John, Sutton, S., bailiff	53 Youngs
1835	Easter, Mary, Woodbridge, S., widow	568 Harrowing
1833	Eastgate, Elizabeth, Feltwell, N., widow	224 Cubitt
1857	Eastgate, Susan, Swaffham, N., spinster	90 Youngs
1855	Easthaugh, Jonathon Darby, Heckingham, N., farmer	238 Whitty
1852	Eastick, John, Gorleston, S., mariner	116 Latten
1845	Eastlaugh, Catherine, Fakenham, N., widow	496 Pedgrift
1820	Eastwell, Christian, Wicken, C., widow	353 Mack
1845	Eastwell, William, Burwell, C., carpenter and beer-seller	823 Pedgrift
1836	Easy, William the elder, Walberswick, S.	195 Smith
1844	Eaton, Rhoda, Gislingham, S., widow	531 Ebbage
1856	Ebbage, Francis, Bungay St Mary, S., builder	396 Code
1837	Ebbage, John, Ipswich, S., gent.	705 Warren
1844	Ebbage, Lydia, Halesworth, S., spinster	1 Ebbage
1851	Ebbage, Robert the elder, Bungay, S., gent.	331 Friar
1832	Ebbage, Samuel, Halesworth, S., farmer	329 Cooke
1824	Ebbetts, Daniel, Rippon Hall, Hevingham, N., farmer	34 Borrett
1850	Ebbetts, John, Great Witchingham, N., gent.	477 Cuthbert
1830	Ebbetts, Sarah, Hellesdon, N., widow	128 Pettingill
1844	Ebbs, Jeremiah, Gillingham, N., gardener	536 Ebbage
1836	Ebbs, Thomas, Mutford, S., gent.	157 Smith
1857	Ebdale, Richard, South Creake, N., shepherd	79 Youngs
1855	Ebden, Elizabeth, Fressingfield, S., widow	70 Whitty
1845	Ecclestone, Stehen Bately, Upton, N., gent.	915 Pedgrift
1840	Ecclestone, William, Billockby, N., gent.	331 Turner
1839	Edgar, Edmund, Great Finborough, S., farmer	482 Calton

1856	Edgar, Edward, Soham, C., farmer	434 Code
1837	Edgar, Elizabeth Katherine, Ipswich, S., spinster	132 Warren
1843	Edge, Hannah, Long Stratton, N., widow	391 Miles
1856	Edge, James, Downham Market, N., carpenter	142 Code
1843	Edmonds, Henry, Newton next Castleacre, N., husbandman	484 Miles
1857	Edmunds, Martha, Lowestoft, S., widow	823 Youngs
1845	Edwards, Anna Maria, Shouldham, N.	127 Pedgrift
1823	Edwards, Edmund, St Saviours, Norwich, N., gardener	O.W. 177
1832	Edwards, Edward, Gosbeck, S., gent.	377 Cooke
1823	Edwards, Elizabeth, Norwich, widow	65 Tann
1826	Edwards, Elizabeth, St Saviour, Norwich, N., widow	29 Davy
1835	Edwards, Ernest, Ipswich, S., linen draper	603 Harrowing
1845	Edwards, Hannah, Homersfield, S., widow	12 Pedgrift
1856	Edwards, Harriet, Downham Market, N., spinster	331 Code
1819	Edwards, James, Alburgh, N., carpenter	216 Le Neve
1830	Edwards, James, Norwich, N., watchmaker	175 Pettingill
1837	Edwards, James, Newmarket St Mary, S., training groom	782 Warren
1840	Edwards, James, Bruisyard, S., farmer	435 Turner
1819	Edwards, Jane, Wickham Market, S., widow	133 Le Neve
1838	Edwards, Japhet the elder, Metfield, S., farmer	390 Skepper
1830	Edwards, John, Coltishall, N., baker	389 Pettingill
1831	Edwards, John, Norwich, N., carpenter	237 Hart
1839	Edwards, John, Beccles, S., yeoman	258 Calton
1847	Edwards, John, St Peter Permountergate, Norwich, N. innkeeper	480 Broom
1851	Edwards, John Francis, Runcton Holme, N., clerk	303 Friar
1849	Edwards, Judith, Shimpling, N., wife of Benjamin Edwards, farmer	322 Womack
1856	Edwards, Maria, Bedingfield, S., spinster	O.W. 281
1823	Edwards, Mary, Alburgh, N., widow	284 Tann
1825	Edwards, Mary, Newmarket, S., late of Chevely, C., spinster	98 Hayward
1834	Edwards, Mary, St Georges Tombland, N., widow	O.W. 354
1841	Edwards, Mary, Wolterton, N., widow	515 Canler
1831	Edwards, Robert, Cheveley, C., yeoman	285 Hart
1832	Edwards, Robert, Fordham, C., baker	511 Cooke
1838	Edwards, Robert, Starston, N., farmer	163 Skepper
1845	Edwards, Robert, Great Yarmouth, N., coal meter	624 Pedgrift
1834	Edwards, Samuel, Norwich, N., shopkeeper	368 Lane
1853	Edwards, Sarah, Needham, N., wife of Alfred Edwards, farmer	556 Veale
1833	Edwards, Thomas, Ipswich, S., whitesmith	113 Cubitt
1842	Edwards, Thomas, Brockford, S., gent.	313 Canler
1854	Edwards, Thomas, Norwich, N., city treasurer	43 Day
1825	Edwards, William, Framlingham, S., gent.	227 Hayward
1827	Edwards, William, Oakley, S., farmer	357 Wood
1842	Edwards, William, Cawston, N., schoolmaster	332 Canler
1847	Edwards, William, Shouldham, N., farmer	814 Broom
1852	Edwards, William, Norwich, N., baker	730 Latten
1824	Edwick, Joseph, Nedging, S., farmer	71 Borrett
1839	Egar, Samuel, Upwell, N., grocer and draper	541 Calton
1855	Eggleton, Thomas, Stibbard, N., sweep	667 Whitty
1828	Eglington, Ann, Hackford, N., late of Kerdiston, N., widow	467 Farrow
1853	Eglington, Ann, Norwich, N., widow	108 Veale
1823	Eglington, John, Terrington St Johns, N., farmer	414 Tann
1849	Eglington, John, Diss, N., tailor	697 Womack
1849	Eglington, John, Kerdiston, N., farmer	697 Womack
1849	Eglington, John, Kerdiston, N., farmer	184 Womack
1828	Eglington, Richard, Norwich, N., gent.	307 Farrow
1819	Eglington, Samuel, Stibbard, N., husbandman	323 Le Neve
1845	Eglington, Samuel, Pockthorpe, Norwich, N., carpenter and shopkeeper	96 Pedgrift
1827	Eke, Mary, St Stephens, Norwich, spinster	O.W. 309
1820	Eke, Peter, Wood Dalling, N., yeoman	4 Mack
1832	Elba, John, Burnham Norton, N., warrener	432 Cooke

1856 Elbey, James, Wells next the Sea, N., groom 504 Code
1843 Eldear, Ann, Great Yarmouth, N., spinster 252 Miles
1844 Elden, Hannah, Aylsham, N., widow O.W. 283
1820 Elden, John, Calthorpe, N., blacksmith 435 Mack
1841 Eldred, Hannah, Occold, S. 76 Traxton
1829 Eldred, John, Shipdham, Cromer, N., gent. 111 Green
1835 Eldred, Mary, Norwich, N., widow 255 Harrowing
1857 Eldred, William, Occold, S., farmer 49 Youngs
1820 Eldrid, Daniel, Upwell, C., yeoman 370 Mack
1836 Elennor, William, Badwell Ash, S., labourer 357 Smith
1855 Elgar, Charles, Gateley, N., farmer 635 Whitty
1833 Elgar, Edmund, Barney, N., cooper 280 Cubitt
1837 Elgar, Isaac, Barney, N., cooper 499 Warren
1843 Elgar, John Riseborough, Binham, N., farmer 236 Miles
1821 Elgar, Robert, Wells next the Sea, N., shopkeeper 239 Dewell
1834 Elis, Anne, Kings Lynn, N., widow 166 Lane
1824 Eller, Susanna, Great Yarmouth, N., widow 198 Borrett
1821 Ellis, Edward John, Whitwell, N., gent. 49 Dewell
1823 Ellis, Elizabeth, Diss, N., wife of Robert Ellis, farmer 402 Tann
1828 Ellis, Henry, Edgefield, N., yeoman 56 Farrow
1846 Ellis, Henry, Blofield, N., labourer 202 Baret
1822 Ellis, John, Henstead with Hulver Street, S., labourer 378 Sadler
1836 Ellis, John, Somerleyton, S. 543 Smith
1839 Ellis, John, Old Buckenham, N., farrier 345 Calton
1850 Ellis, John, Necton, N., labourer 325 Cuthbert
1835 Ellis, Martha, Holt, N., widow 20 Harrowing
1829 Ellis, Mary, Southrepps, N., widow 170 Green
1832 Ellis, Richard, Shelfanger, N., farmer 547 Green
1832 Ellis, Robert, Hevingham, N., yeoman 359 Cooke
1849 Ellis, Samuel, Norwich, N., baker 680 Womack
1851 Ellis, Susanna, Norwich, N., widow 100 Friar
1819 Ellis, Thomas, Diss, N., farmer 36 Le Neve
1834 Ellis, Thomas, Thornage, N., formerly of Cley
next the Sea, gent. 336 Lane
1837 Ellis, William, Kings Lynn, N., shopkeeper 407 Warren
1840 Ellis, William, Little Barningham, N., gent. 109 Turner
1854 Ellis, William, Burston, N., farmer 160 Day
1830 Ellinet, Mary, Norwich, N., spinster 32 Pettingill
1833 Ellingham, Samuel, Blofield, N., glazier 108 Cubitt
1838 Ellington, Leonard, Mildenhall, S., gardener 364 Skepper
1845 Ellinor, John, Blo Norton, N., yeoman 459 Pedgrift
1830 Elliot, James William, Norwich, N., watch maker 31 Pettingill
1851 Elliot, Robert, Norwich, N., currier and leather cutter 260 Friar
1840 Elliott, Ann, Stowupland, N., spinster 151 Turner
1834 Elliott, John Faircloth, Fakenham, N., corn inspector 458 Lane
1852 Elliott, Joseph, Barking, S., farmer 567 Latten
1853 Elliott, Martha, Briston, N., widow 573 Veale
1838 Elliott, Thomas, Kings Lynn, N., yeoman 141 Skepper
1850 Elliott, William, Roydon, N., farmer 601 Cuthbert
1821 Eliston, Nice, Great Thornham, S., farmer 120 Dewell
1850 Ellsworth, Elizabeth, Snettisham, N., spinster 293 Cuthbert
1836 Elmer, Elizabeth, Reepham, N., widow 404 Smith
1840 Elmer, James, Great Witchingham, N., gent. 430 Turner
1831 Elmer, John, North Delph, Upwell, N., farmer 212 Hart
1839 Elmer, John, North Delph, Upwell, N., farmer 99 Calton
1853 Elmer, William, Watlington, N., cattle dealer 690 Veale
1838 Elsden, John, Kings Lynn, N., yeoman 170 Skepper
1832 Elsden, Robert, Kersey, S., miller 474 Cooke
1827 Elsden, William, Needham Market, S., gent. 533 Wood
1825 Elsey, Richard, Downham Market, N., gent. 215 Hayward
1848 Elvin, Elizabeth, Hoxne, S., widow 766 Denny
1832 Elvin, John, Hoxne, S., farmer 471 Cooke
1820 Elvin, Robert, Laxfield, S., labourer 351 Mack
1855 Elvish, William, Norwich, N., innkeeper 339 Whitty

1832	Elwin, Joseph, Loddon, N., yeoman	259 Cooke
1832	Elwin, Mary, Loddon, N., spinster	258 Cooke
1850	Ely, Mary, Great Yarmouth, N., widow	550 Cuthbert
1857	Ely, Robert, Norwich, N., shopkeeper and broker	75 Youngs
1839	Emans, Mary, Burwell, C., spinster	283 Calton
1827	Emeny, Eleanor, Framsden, S., widow	340 Wood
1829	Emeris, Joanna, Weston, N., wife of Robert Emeris, farmer	48 Green
1852	Emerson, Edward, Gaywood, N., gent.	243 Latten
1845	Emerson, James, Worlingworth, S., farmer	408 Pedgrift
1847	Emerson, Robert, Holme Hale, N., gent.	784 Broom
1854	Emerson, William Charles, Shipdham, N., surgeon	517 Day
1825	Emery, Daniel, St Georges, Colegate, Norwich, publican	445 Hayward
1832	Emery, Eleanor, Kings Lynn, N., widow	296 Cooke
1824	Emery, James, Fulmodeston w. Croxton, N., farmer	239 Borrett
1849	Emery, James, Northrepps, N., farmer	415 Womack
1827	Emery, John, Stody, N., gent.	371 Wood
1823	Emery, Joseph, Norwich, carpenter	48 Tann
1852	Emery, Sarah, Holt, N., widow	625 Latten
1855	Emery, Thomas, Stibbard, N., gent.	634 Whitty
1820	Emms, George, Great Yarmouth, N., tailor	296 Mack
1852	Emms, Henry, Foulsham, N., veterinary surgeon	377 Latten
1853	Emms, James, Great Yarmouth, N., baker	112 Veale
1849	Emms, Samuel, Swanton Morley, N., yeoman	590 Womack
1850	Empson, Robert, Palling, N., farmer	64 Cuthbert
1845	Enefer, Martin, Stowmarket, S.	417 Pedgrift
1824	England, George, Acle, N., cordwainer	110 Borrett
1855	England, Mary, Aylsham, N., spinster	669 Whitty
1837	England, Robert, Acle, N.	661 Warren
1841	England, Robert, Surlingham, N., farmer	280 Traxton
1826	England, Sarah, Neatishead, N., spinster	260 Davy
1828	England, Stephen, Binham, N.	329 Farrow
1829	England, William, Foulsham, N.	532 Green
1848	Engledew, Francis, Horstead, N., blacksmith, o.w. missing	183 Denny
1857	Engledow, Edward, Gaywood, N., innkeeper	378 Youngs
1827	English, Dorothy, Kings Lynn, N., widow	342 Wood
1847	English, Mary, Norwich, N., widow	816 Broom
1842	English, Robert, Stow Bardolph, N., labourer	248 Canler
1836	English, William, Stokesby, N., husbandman	84 Smith
1855	Estaugh, Enoch, Saxmundham, S., farmer	658 Whitty
1825	Etheridge, Mary, Fakenham, N., widow	102 Hayward
1854	Etheridge, Mary Ann, Thorpe Hamlet, N., spinster	178 Day
1819	Etheridge, Thomas, Sibton, N., gent.	34 Le Neve
1832	Etheridge, Thomas, Fressingfield, S., gent.	72 Cooke
1836	Ethersey, Richard, Ipswich, S., yeoman	462 Smith
1838	Etteredge, Mary, Attleborough, N., spinster	811 Skepper
1819	Evans, James, Hemblington, N., cordwainer	142 Le Neve
1849	Evans, James, Blofield, N.	596 Womack
1833	Evans, Mary, Hemblington, N., widow	278 Cubitt
1855	Evans, Robert, Fressingfield, S., farmer	87 Whitty
1839	Evans, Sarah, Fressingfield, S., widow	160 Calton
1852	Evans, Susanna, Saxmundham, S., widow	128 Latten
1830	Evans, Thomas Burdett, Gorleston, S., customs officer	325 Pettingill
1830	Evans, Thomas Browne, Heigham, Norwich, N., esquire	100 Pettingill
1835	Evens, Hannah, Woodbridge, S., single woman	608 Harrowing
1831	Everet, Francis Wright the elder, Stowmarket, S., gent.	129 Hart
1849	Everett, George, Swaffham, N., formerly of Barnsbury Park, Middlesex, plumber and painter	456 Womack
1852	Everett, George, Diss, N.	332 Latten
1842	Everett, Harriett Freeman, Snape, S., spinster	334 Canler
1834	Everett, John Row, Snape, S., carpenter	516 Lane
1843	Everett, John, Swefling, S., farmer	666 Miles
1855	Everett, John, Brooke, N., yeoman	602 Whitty
1855	Everett, Sarah, East Harling, N., widow	398 Whitty
1847	Everett, William, Norwich, N., woolstapler	Index only

1844	Everitt, George, Lowestoft, S., brewer	342 Ebbage
1853	Everitt, Jane, Caister by Yarmouth, N., widow	213 Veale
1841	Everson, Robert, Brockford, S., farmer	391 Traxton
1847	Everson, William, Hainford, N., carpenter and builder	313 Broom
1844	Evetts, Thomas Ember, Kings Lynn, N., confectioner	390 Ebbage
1839	Ewing, Elizabeth, Norwich, N., widow	469 Calton
1841	Ewing, Elizabeth, Horsford, N., widow	134 Traxton
1854	Ewing, Stephen, Newton St Faiths, N., miller	8 Day
1843	Fab, Luke, alias Gotts, Aylsham, N., miller formerly of Great Ryburgh, N.	318 Miles
1830	Fabb, Mary, Norwich, N., widow	107 Pettingill
1844	Fabb, Richard, Hemsby, N., farmer	109 Ebbage
1855	Fabb, Richard, Runham, N., gent.	684 Whitty
1825	Fabrum, Swan, Merton, N., yeoman	205 Hayward
1820	Failes, James, Upwell, N., farmer and grazier	52 Mack
1838	Fair, Charles, Norwich, N., gent.	112 Skepper
1834	Faircliff, Ann, Burwell, C., single woman	50 Lane
1833	Faircliff, Mary, Burwell, C., spinster	68 Cubitt
1824	Faircliff, William, Burwell, C., yeoman	273 Borrett
1832	Faircloth, Robert the elder, East Barsham, N., farmer	429 Cooke
1830	Fairweather, John the elder, Weybread, S., farmer	393 Pettingill
1831	Fairweather, John, Southtown, Yarmouth, S., gent.	363 Hart
1838	Fairweather, John, Heigham, N., gent.	199 Skepper
1837	Fairweather, William, Ditchingham, N., gent.	315 Warren
1825	Fake, John, Wortham, S., wheelwright	351 Hayward
1832	Fake, Thomas, Wortham, S., carpenter	177 Cooke
1849	Farman, Bartholomew, North Tuddenham, N. miller and shopkeeper	208 Womack
1852	Farman, Henry, Great Yarmouth, N., innkeeper	678 Latten
1850	Farman, John, Freethorpe, N., thatcher	500 Cuthbert
1835	Farman, Robert, Salhouse, N., thatcher	168 Harrowing
1849	Farman, Robert, Oulton, S., farmer	76 Womack
1848	Farman, Samuel, East Dereham, N., painter	271 Denny
1838	Farman, William, Salhouse, N., cordwainer	54 Skepper
1853	Farmelo, Thomas, Ditchingham, N., yeoman	396 Veale
1837	Farrant, Joseph, Kings Lynn, N., blacksmith	687 Warren
1849	Farrer, John, Lowestoft, S., gent.	538 Womack
1830	Farrer, Samuel, Great Yarmouth, N., gent.	398 Pettingill
1840	Farrer, Samuel, Lowestoft, S., gent.	120 Turner
1819	Farrer, Thomas, Winston, S., yeoman	169 Le Neve
1828	Farrett, John, Lowestoft, S., pilot	8 Farrow
1827	Farrington, David, Pulham St Mary Magdalen, N., bachelor	616 Wood
1831	Farron, Hannah, South Walsham, N., widow	75 Hart
1851	Farrow, Adam, Suffield, N., farmer	551 Friar
1844	Farrow, Barnabas, Bale, N.	43 Ebbage
1853	Farrow, Bilby, Wingfield, S., farmer	667 Veale
1849	Farrow, Elizabeth, Hopton, S., wife of James Farrow, house carpenter	63 Womack
1850	Farrow, James, North Elmham, N., bricklayer	76 Cuthbert
1830	Farrow, John, Hunworth, N., horse farrier and cow leech	172 Pettingill
1838	Farrow, John, Great Yarmouth, N., gent.	177 Skepper
1828	Farrow, Martha, Norwich, N., widow	1 Farrow
1833	Farrow, Mary, Fulmodeston, N., widow	486 Cubitt
1849	Farrow, May, Somerleyton, S., wheelwright	240 Womack
1852	Farrow, Rebecca, Thetford, N., spinster	105 Latten
1845	Farrow, Robert, Shadbrooke, S., miller	581 Pedgrift
1850	Farrow, Sarah, Coney Weston, S., spinster	282 Cuthbert
1857	Farrow, Stephen, Raveningham, N., farmer	777 Youngs
1821	Farrow, Thomas, Diss, N., gent.	137 Dewell
1851	Farrow, Thomas, Foulsham, N., innkeeper	337 Friar
1825	Farrow, William, Aylmerton, N., gent.	498 Hayward
1841	Farrow, William, Shelton, N., farmer	150 Traxton

1854	Farrow, William, Gisleham, S., gardener	86 Day
1834	Faukener, Mary, Hilgay, N., widow	339 Lane
1849	Faulke, Elizabeth, Norwich, N., widow	242 Womack
1850	Faulke, Robert, Norwich, N., tallow chandler	99 Cuthbert
1837	Faulkner, Thomas, Bracon Ash, N., gent.	670 Warren
1856	Faulkner, Thomas, Swainsthorpe, N., master of the workhouse	470 Code
1845	Fawn, John, Upwell, N., farmer	286 Pedgrift
1840	Fayer, Robert the younger, Kings Lynn, N., fisherman	15 Turner
1837	Fayerman, Ann, Brancaster, N., formerly of Swaffham, widow	35 Warren
1836	Fayerman, Robert Smith, Swaffman, N., esquire	48 Smith
1829	Fayers, David, Great Bricett, S., farmer	496 Green
1841	Fayers, George, Battisford, S., shopkeeper	629 Traxton
1855	Fayers, Margaret, Snettisham, N., widow	157 Whitty
1848	Fayers, Robert Septimus, Bildeston, S., carpenter	7 Denny
1825	Fayers, Samuel the elder, Bildeston, S., farmer	148 Hayward
1847	Fear, John, Great Yarmouth, N., gent.	635 Broom
1821	Fearman, William, Upton, N., thatcher	130 Dewell
1850	Feek, John Townley, Great Yarmouth, N., baker	127 Cuthbert
1820	Felby, William, Wickham Market, S., wheelwright	453 Mack
1831	Felmingham, William the elder, Acle, N., bricklayer	409 Hart
1846	Felmingham, William Smith, Denton, N., farmer	79 Baret
1844	Felstead, George, Norwich, N., shawl weaver	38 Ebbage
1854	Feltham, George Thomas, Great Yarmouth, N., shoemaker	334 Day
1848	Feltham, James, Great Yarmouth, N., boot and shoemaker	823 Denny
1848	Feltham, Thomas, Tibbenham, N., shopkeeper	653 Denny
1847	Felton, John, Hedenham, N., gent.	488 Broom
1854	Felton, Sarah, Cringleford, N., widow	199 Day
1835	Feltwell, John, Gaywood, N., farmer	100 Harrowing
1841	Fendick, Charles the elder, Castle Acre, N., shoemaker	222 Traxton
1846	Fendick, Isaac, Narford, N., gamekeeper	670 Baret
1845	Fendick, Sarah, Castle Acre, N.	910 Pedgrift
1824	Fendick, William, Little Cressingham, N., wheelwright	371 Borrett
1841	Fenn, Anthony, Fordham, C., farmer	463 Traxton
1848	Fenn, George, Beccles, S., nurseryman	25 Denny
1819	Fenn, John, Blofield, N., yeoman	329 Le Neve
1840	Fenn, John, Gillingham, N.	398 Turner
1828	Fenn, Robert, Horstead, N., yeoman	361 Farrow
1827	Fenn, Samuel, Combs, S., farmer	272 Wood
1857	Fenn, William, Norwich, N., gent.	422 Youngs
1849	Fennell, Henry, Hoxne, S., farmer	481 Womack
1837	Fennell, Lititia, Aldeburgh, S., formerly of Chelsea, Middlesex, widow	O.W. 344
1828	Fennell, Thomas, St Andrews, Norwich, N.	492 Farrow
1851	Fenton, John Lockwood, Northwold, N., glover	548 Friar
1826	Fenton, Mary, Coddenham, S., spinster	261 Davy
1854	Fenton, Paul William, Heigham, Norwich, N., printer	112 Day
1834	Fenton, Philip, Friston, S., gent.	374 Lane
1835	Ferra, Mary, Pulham St Mary the Virgin, N., widow	343 Harrowing
1845	Ferrier, John, Great Yarmouth, N., gent.	162 Pedgrift
1844	Ficklin, Mary Russell, Bracondale, Norwich, N., widow	261 Ebbage
1846	Fickling, Robert the elder, Norwich, N., gent.	505 Baret
1851	Fiddaman, John, Brancaster, N., butcher and publican	269 Friar
1828	Fiddeman, Samuel, Norwich, N., worstead weaver	214 Farrow
1834	Fiddymont, Samuel, Topcroft, N., farmer	817 Lane
1844	Fidgett, James, Foulsham, N., currier	464 Ebbage
1849	Fidgett, John, Fakenham, N., currier	692 Womack
1819	Field, Edward, Woodbridge, S., farmer	108 Le Neve
1827	Field, Hannah, Fressingfield, S., spinster	109 Wood
1848	Field, Sarah, Sheringham, N., widow	171 Denny
1846	Field, William, Mickfield, S., farmer	17 Baret
1837	Fielde, John, Aylsham, N., millwright	774 Warren
1825	Fielding, James, Ellingham Parva, N., cooper	159 Hayward
1857	Filbee, John, Caston, N., gent.	634 Youngs
1829	Filbee, William, Shipdham, formerly of Foulden, N, farmer	378 Green

1837	Filbey, Mary Melicent, Fakenham, N.	802 Warren
1844	Filby, Elizabeth, Thrandeston, S., widow	599 Ebbage
1852	Fill, Sarah, Great Yarmouth, N., widow	748 Latten
1824	Finch, Frederick, St Matthew, Ipswich, S., cooper	20 Borrett
1836	Finch, James, Bildeston, S., bricklayer	3 Smith
1843	Finch, John, Great Yarmouth, N., cowkeeper	682 Miles
1839	Finch, Joseph, Burwell, C., farmer	239 Calton
1850	Finch, Mary Ann, East Dereham, N., widow	395 Cuthbert
1819	Finch, Robert, Ipswich, S., cooper	71 Le Neve
1850	Finch, Zachariah, Smallburgh, N., thatcher and shopkeeper	233 Cuthbert
1857	Fincham, Harriett, Diss, N., spinster	390 Youngs
1856	Fincham, James, Diss, N., gent.	174 Code
1837	Fincham, Mary, Norwich, N., singlewoman	608 Warren
1839	Fincham, Sophia, Diss, N., widow	267 Calton
1842	Fincham, William, Tivetshall St Margaret, N.	372 Canler
1827	Fincham, Zachariah, Diss, N.	517 Wood
1848	Firman, John, Soham, C., blacksmith	367 Denny
1847	Firth, Ann, Norwich, N., widow	588 Broom
1839	Firth, Lucy Rosalind Procter, Crostwick, N., spinster	321 Calton
1839	Fish, Eleanor, Beccles, S., widow	284 Calton
1857	Fish, Hellena, Great Yarmouth, N., widow	452 Youngs
1852	Fish, James, Nacton, S.	510 Latten
1855	Fish, Sarah, Carlton St Peter, N., widow	134 Whitty
1857	Fish, Simon, Southtown, Little Yarmouth, S., gent.	65 Youngs
1848	Fisher, Ann, Boxtead, Essex, widow	227 Denny
1840	Fisher, Clare the elder, Wramplingham, N., farmer	59 Turner
1832	Fisher, David, East Dereham, N., formerly of Cambridge, S., gent.	529 Cooke
1828	Fisher, Elizabeth, Kings Lynn, N., widow	170 Farrow
1820	Fisher, John, Pentney, N., shopkeeper	420 Mack
1824	Fisher, John, Walsham Le Willows, S., farmer	160 Borrett
1829	Fisher, John, Grimston, N., grocer and draper	323 Green
1829	Fisher, John, Stonham Aspall, S., yeoman	427 Green
1839	Fisher, John, Worlingham, S., yeoman	556 Calton
1840	Fisher, John, Athelington, S., farmer	554 Turner
1840	Fisher, John the elder, Woodbridge, S., baker	651 Turner
1846	Fisher, John, Norwich, N., brickmaker	543 Baret
1825	Fisher, Matthew, Fincham, N., labourer	521 Hayward
1839	Fisher, Michael, Terrington St Clements, N., farmer	158 Calton
1849	Fisher, Money, North Elmham, N., gent.	666 Womack
1829	Fisher, Robert, Woodbridge, S., baker	535 Green
1851	Fisher, Robert, Field Dalling, N., farmer	60 Friar
1856	Fisher, Samuel, Norwich, N., stonemason	542 Code
1853	Fisher, Sarah, Redenhall with Harleston, N., singlewoman	354 Veale
1832	Fisher, Thomas, Stratton St Mary, N., butcher	543 Cooke
1837	Fisher, Thomas, Norwich, N., dissenting minister	216 Warren
1840	Fisher, Thomas, Carleton Rode, N., wheelwright	302 Turner
1846	Fisher, William, Terrington St Clements, N., farmer	110 Baret
1845	Fisk, Anthony, Ellingham, N., farmer	621 Pedgrift
1834	Fisk, John, Lowestoft, S.	386 Lane
1823	Fisk, Joseph, Holton, S., farmer	94 Tann
1850	Fisk, Samuel, Wrentham, S., beer seller	143 Cuthbert
1828	Fisk, William, Westwick, N., basket maker	25 Farrow
1836	Fisk, William, Lowestoft, S., mariner	162 Smith
1848	Fisk, William, Hulverstreet with Henstead, S., farmer	830 Denny
1824	Fiske, George, Dunkestone, S., gent.	316 Borrett
1852	Fiske, George, Starston, N., farmer	410 Latten
1822	Fiske, Helen, Stowmarket, S., spinster	85 Sadler
1855	Fiske, Samuel Rampley, Stanton, S., farmer	8 Whitty
1844	Fison, James, Thetford, N., merchant	413 Ebbage
1845	Fitch, Thomas, Hazelwood, S., farmer	205 Pedgrift
1827	Fitch, William, Catton, N., yeoman	303 Wood
1822	Fitt, Amy, Coltishall, N., widow	327 Sadler
1838	Fitt, Ann, Norwich, N., single woman	66 Skepper

1830	Fitt, Gemelia, Wood Dalling, N., widow	443 Pettingill
1825	Fitt, John, Norwich, N., publican	40 Hayward
1829	Flack, John, Earl Stonham, S., innholder	508 Green
1851	Flack, Nathan, Thetford, N., miller	474 Friar
1820	Flacke, Samuel, Hindolveston, N., farmer	433 Mack
1828	Flaherty, Edmond, Norwich, N., butcher	367 Farrow
1856	Flanagan, Timothy, Wimbotsham, N., gent.	26 Code
1837	Flatman, Henry, Redgrave, S., yeoman	547 Warren
1831	Flatman, Robert, Great Yarmouth, N., carpenter	572 Hart
1828	Flatt, Hayhow, Methwold, N.	87 Farrow
1838	Flatt, John, Denver, N., farmer	279 Skepper
1834	Flatt, Sarah, Broome, N., housekeeper	518 Lane
1854	Flatt, Susan, Northwold, N., widow	237 Day
1843	Flatt, Thomas, Tunstall, S., farmer	43 Miles
1820	Flatt, William senior, Methwold Hithe, N., farmer	245 Mack
1846	Flatt, William, Methwold, N., farmer	329 Baret
1850	Flatt, William, Saxmundham, S., grocer and draper	260 Cuthbert
1856	Flatt, William, Methwold, N., farmer	317 Code
1847	Flaxman, Elizabeth, Heigham, Norwich	72 Broom
1853	Flaxman, Henry, Woodbridge, S., innholder	70 Veale
1823	Flaxman, Mary, Potter Heigham, N., widow	70 Tann
1857	Flaxman, Robert, Worstead, N., farmer	822 Youngs
1846	Flaxman, William, Haddiscoe, N., yeoman	392 Baret
1853	Fleet, Ann the elder, Thetford, N., widow	564 Veale
1823	Fleet, Jonathan, Tivetshall St Mary, N., farmer	158 Tann
1841	Flegg, Elizabeth, Kings Lynn, N., widow	599 Traxton
1835	Fleming, Elizabeth, Southtown, Yarmouth, S., widow	398 Harrowing
1834	Fleming, Francis, Great Snoring, N., widow	324 Lane
1823	Fleming, John, Great Snoring, N., esquire	289 Tann
1829	Fleming, John, Huntingfield, S., yeoman	52 Green
1834	Fletcher, Lawrence, Eyke, S., miller	304 Lane
1833	Fletcher, Rebecca, Great Yarmouth, N., widow	71 Cubitt
1840	Fletcher, Susan, Botesdale, S.	241 Turner
1834	Flick, Samuel the elder, Wickham Market, S. saddler and harness maker	143 Lane
1822	Flint, James, Ketteringham, N., shopkeeper	243 Sadler
1819	Flint, John, Freethorpe, N., husbandman	314 Le Neve
1838	Flint, Sarah, Hempnall, N.	198 Skepper
1841	Flogdell, Joseph, Gissing, N., farmer	174 Traxton
1845	Flood, Dorothy, Sparham, N.	353 Pedgrift
1855	Flood, Edmund, Fincham, N., collar maker	673 Whitty
1837	Flood, Ellen, Ringstead, N., spinster	352 Warren
1847	Flood, Henry, Great Dunham, N., carpenter	660 Broom
1852	Flood, John, Great Fransham, N., gent.	850 Latten
1833	Flood, Nicholas, Foulsham, N., yeoman	103 Cubitt
1847	Flood, Robert, East Rudham, N., cordwainer	446 Broom
1844	Flood, Sabra, Great Dunham, N., wife of Henry Flood, carpenter	313 Ebbage
1835	Flory, Thomas the elder, Witnesham, S., farmer	456 Harrowing
1856	Flowerday, Joshua, Somerleyton, S., miller	143 Code
1848	Flowerdew, Lydia, Stowmarket, S., widow	759 Denny
1853	Flowerdew, John, Wortham, S., yeoman	400 Veale
1829	Flowerdew, Richard, Redgrave, S., gent.	413 Green
1849	Flowerdew, Susan, Coltishall, N., spinster, formerly of Norwich	385 Womack
1853	Foley, Andrew, Great Yarmouth, N., out pensioner of H.M. Royal Hospital, Greenwich	264 Veale
1844	Folkard, Ann, Redenhall with Harleston, N., widow	229 Ebbage
1850	Folkard, William, Lowestoft, S., pilot	603 Cuthbert
1857	Folker, Elizabeth, Hethersett, N., widow	542 Youngs
1833	Folker, John, Burnham Westgate, N., yeoman	371 Cubitt
1822	Folmingham, John, Hempnall, N., husbandman	362 Sadler
1853	Folthorp, Joseph the elder, Methwold, S., butcher	355 Veale
1840	Foote, Mary, Bury St Edmunds, S., spinster	418 Turner

1849	Forby, Ann, Sparham, N., widow	23 Womack
1857	Forby, John, Tittleshall, N., farmer	370 Youngs
1826	Forby, Joshua, Whissonsett, N., miller	290 Davy
1837	Forby, Michael Mitchell, Godwick Hall, N., farmer	185 Warren
1826	Forby, Robert, Fincham, N., clerk	O.W. 175
1833	Forby, Thomas, North Runcton, N., farmer	184 Cubitt
1835	Forby, William, Tittleshall, N., farmer	537 Harrowing
1847	Ford, Ann, Ludham, N., widow	405 Broom
1839	Ford, George, Palgrave, S., carpenter and joiner	303 Calton
1829	Ford, James, Edgefield, N., yeoman	174 Green
1829	Ford, James, Happisburgh, N., miller	135 Green
1851	Ford, Job, Bacton, S., farmer and miller	153 Friar
1838	Ford, Samuel, Elmsett, S., farmer	866 Skepper
1851	Ford, Thomas, Palgrave, S., carpenter	621 Friar
1825	Ford, William, Dickleburgh, N., labourer	464 Hayward
1849	Forder, Isaac, Great Yarmouth, N., cornmeter	102 Womack
1834	Forder, Joanna, Chedgrave, N., spinster	274 Lane
1856	Forder, Joseph, Aldeby, N.	274 Code
1857	Forder, Joseph, Great Yarmouth, N., cornmeter	342 Youngs
1830	Forder, William, Chedgrave, N., yeoman	418 Pettingill
1845	Fordham, Elizabeth, Soham, C., wife of John Fordham, cordwainer	608 Pedgrift
1835	Fordham, Thomas, Blo Norton, N., farmer	428 Harrowing
1826	Fordham, Zachariah, Blo Norton, N., husbandman	288 Davy
1850	Foreman, Benjamin, Great Yarmouth, N., miller and flour seller	24 Cuthbert
1853	Foreman, James, Wickham Market, S., innkeeper	423 Veale
1851	Foreman, Mary, Kessingland, S., widow	619 Friar
1845	Foreman, Richard, Stradishall, S., formerly of Cheveley, C., and Great Bradley, S., yeoman	44 Pedgrift
1850	Foreman, Samuel, Great Yarmouth, N., master mariner	327 Cuthbert
1829	Foreman, Thomas, Halesworth, S., innkeeper	197 Green
1828	Foreman, William, Stow Bardolph, N., yeoman	10 Farrow
1828	Foreshaw, Elizabeth, Kings Lynn, N., widow	449 Farrow
1820	Forsdick, John, Needham Market, S., maltster	412 Mack
1826	Forster, Edward, Grimston, N., bricklayer	171 Davy
1833	Forster, John, Brandon, S., blacksmith	426 Cubitt
1837	Forster, John, Great Yarmouth, N., clerk	O.W. 343
1849	Forster, John, Horstead, N., innkeeper	356 Womack
1825	Forster, Mary, Norwich, N., spinster	276 Hayward
1838	Forster, Samuel, Cookley, S.	389 Skepper
1825	Forster, William, North Walsham, N., gent.	57 Hayward
1819	Forster, Sarah, Norwich, N., widow	266 Le Neve
1853	Fortin, William, Swaffham, N., gent.	292 Veale
1854	Fosdick, Mary, Sporle, N., widow, formerly of Litcham	464 Day
1832	Fosdike, Robert, Woodbridge, S., governer of Seckfords Almshouse	89 Cooke
1854	Foster, William the elder, Kessingland, S., farmer	442 Day
1850	Foulger, John, Colton, N., yeoman	343 Cuthbert
1851	Foulger, Mary, Redenhall with Harleston, N., widow	225 Friar
1850	Foulger, Rebecca, Croxton, N., widow	294 Cuthbert
1851	Foulger, Samuel, New Buckenham, N., yeoman	4 Friar
1845	Foulger, Susan, Norwich, N., servant	690 Pedgrift
1822	Foulsham, James, Old Buckenham, N.	96 Sadler
1827	Foulsham, John, Wymondham, N., shoemaker	637 Wood
1833	Foulsham, John, Westleton, S., butcher	363 Cubitt
1847	Foulsham, William, Norwich, N., farmer formerly of Loddon	759 Broom
1838	Fountain, Ann, Heigham next Norwich, N., widow	45 Skepper
1855	Fountain, Henry, Norwich, N., brewer	453 Whitty
1828	Fountain, Martin, Norwich, N., builder	115 Farrow
1835	Fowell, Henry, Ipswich, S., wine merchant	99 Harrowing
1825	Fowell, Mary, Thorpe next Norwich, N., widow	78 Hayward
1820	Fowell, Richard, Thetford, N., gent.	605 Mack
1849	Fowell, William, Thetford, N., carpenter	552 Womack

1845	Fowler, Elizabeth, Great Yarmouth, N., spinster	135 Pedgrift
1834	Fowler, John, Limpenhoe, N., farmer	623 Lane
1847	Fowler, Mary, Lakenham, N.	Registered in D and C peculiar
1838	Fowler, Samuel, Beighton, N., farmer	359 Skepper
1856	Fowler, Sarah, Swainsthorpe, N., widow	275 Code
1839	Fowler, Susan, Great Yarmouth, N., spinster	571 Calton
1825	Fowler, Thomas, North Runcton, N., farmer	151 Hayward
1847	Fowlser, Robert, Needham, N., farmer	389 Broom
1843	Fox, Ann, Felthorpe, N., spinster	711 Miles
1849	Fox, Charles, Hempnall, N., grocer and draper	689 Womack
1852	Fox, Charlotte Vertue, Norwich, N., wife of Denny Fox, schoolmaster	234 Latten
1834	Fox, Elizabeth, St Giles, Norwich, N., single woman	459 Lane
1834	Fox, Esther Ann, Norwich, N., widow	176 Lane
1856	Fox, Francis, Hoveton St John, N., bricklayer	359 Code
1831	Fox, Hannah, Horstead, N., single woman	67 Hart
1841	Fox, Henry George, St Peter Permountergate, Norwich, N., cooper	376 Traxton
1840	Fox, James, Winfarthing, N., linen weaver	5 Turner
1845	Fox, John, Barton Mills, S., clerk	434 Pedgrift
1849	Fox, John, Wymondham, N., cordwainer	425 Womack
1838	Fox, Martha, Reepham, N., widow	396 Skepper
1820	Fox, Mary, Swardeston, N., late of Norwich, N., widow	410 Mack
1839	Fox, Mary, Brockford, S., widow, innkeeper	677 Calton
1845	Fox, Mary, Norwich, N., widow	968 Pedgrift
1845	Fox, Samuel, Binham, N., carpenter	53 Pedgrift
1855	Fox, Thomas Barnes, Banham, N., yeoman	436 Whitty
1835	Fox, William, Cromer, N., lapidary	318 Harrowing
1855	Fox, William, Whinburgh, N., farmer	490 Whitty
1832	Foyster, Ann, Northwold, N., widow	213 Cooke
1845	Foyster, John the elder, St Margarets Ilketshall, S., yeoman	218 Pedgrift
1820	Francis, Alice, Kings Lynn, N., widow	25 Mack
1839	Francis, Charles, Kings Lynn, N., carpenter	459 Calton
1854	Francis, George, Great Yarmouth, N., ropemaker	252 Day
1853	Francis, Samuel, Norwich, N., manufacturer	303 Veale
1847	Francis, Stephen, Cotton, S., husbandman	742 Broom
1820	Francis, Thomas, Tuttington, N., yeoman	49 Mack
1836	Francis, Thomas, Barton Turf, N., carpenter	238 Smith
1838	Francis, Thomas Cubitt, Foulsham, N., esquire	357 Skepper
1846	Francis, Thomas, Wicklewood, N., labourer	530 Baret
1842	Frankland, Elizabeth, Kirby Bedon, N., spinster	628 Canler
1851	Frankland, James, Reepham, N., formerly of Holt, gent.	9 Friar
1848	Franklin, John, Southtown, S., baker	4 Denny
1850	Franklin, Robert, Reepham, N.	412 Cuthbert
1832	Franklin, William, East Dereham, N., farmer	316 Cooke
1849	Franklin, William, Woodton, N., gent.	508 Womack
1857	Frankling, Felix, Stiffkey, N., miller and baker	397 Youngs
1837	Frankling, Francis, Buxton, N., stock jobber	329 Warren
1819	Franks, Peter, Stoke Ferry, N., gent.	238 Le Neve
1847	Fransham, Robert, Great Yarmouth, N., gardener	202 Broom
1827	Frarey, John, Lessingham, N., farmer	398 Wood
1840	Frary, Sarah, Dilham, N., wife of John Frary, husbandman	28 Turner
1825	Frary, William Oxley, North Walsham, N., late of Knapton, N., gent.	168 Hayward
1825	Free, William, Fordley, S., farmer	484 Hayward
1829	Freeman, Alice, Lowestoft, S., wife of Edward Freeman, gent.	430 Green
1819	Freeman, Ann, Shadingfield, S., widow	16 Le Neve
1847	Freeman, Edward, Southwold, S., gent.	188 Broom
1823	Freeman, Jeremiah, Norwich, carver and gilder	191 Tann
1831	Freeman, John, Kings Lynn, N., officer of H.M. Customs	14 Hart
1834	Freeman, John, Swanton Morley, N., gent.	462 Lane

1853	Freeman, Joseph Haywood, Thorpe next Norwich, N., formerly of Norwich, gent.	569 Veale
1828	Freeman, Mary, Blofield, N., widow	412 Farrow
1843	Freeman, Mary, Wicklewood, N.	O.W. 262
1827	Freeman, Rodwell, Great Yarmouth, N., tailor	51 Wood
1828	Freeman, Sarah, Doughtys Hospital, St Georges Colegate, Norwich, N., widow	450 Farrow
1823	Freeman, Thomas, Swanton Abbott, N., farmer	111 Tann
1827	Freeman, Thomas, Little Glenham, S., land agent	440 Wood
1849	Freeman, Thomas the elder, Henham, S., land agent	258 Womack
1832	Freeman, William, Norwich, N., gilder	14 Cooke
1823	Freestone, Anthony, St Margarets South Elmham, S., gent.	267 Tann
1844	French, Henry the elder, St Gregory, Sudbury, S., brewer	196 Ebbage
1850	French, John, Drayton, N., yeoman	156 Cuthbert
1832	French, Mary, Great Yarmouth, N., widow	469 Cooke
1825	French, Robert, Horsford, N., alehouse keeper	403 Hayward
1836	French, William, St Martins at Palace, Norwich, N.	537 Smith
1857	Freston, George, Hempnall, shopkeeper	790 Youngs
1841	Fretwell, John, West Dereham, N., farmer	505 Traxton
1830	Fretwell, William, West Dereham, N., farmer	323 Pettingill
1845	Frever, Sophia, Framlingham, S., widow of John Frever	O.W. 406
1856	Frewer, Ann, Westhorpe, S., widow	507 Code
1851	Friar, Henry, Toft Monks, N., labourer	1 Friar
1848	Friston, Judith, Hinton, S., widow	574 Denny
1835	Froggate, Sarah, Holbrook, S., widow	56 Harrowing
1820	Fromow, Ann, Norwich, N., widow	393 Mack
1825	Fromow, James Ludlam, Horsham St Faiths, N., farmer	254 Hayward
1857	Fromow, William, Norwich, N., chemist and druggist	37 Youngs
1844	Frosdick, William, Surlingham, N.	595 Ebbage
1837	Frost, Benjamin, Scole, N., stonemason and bricklayer	362 Warren
1829	Frost, Catharine, Thornham, N., widow	321 Green
1820	Frost, Edward, Scarning, N., farmer	129 Mack
1837	Frost, Edward, Redgrave, S., yeoman	500 Warren
1842	Frost, Elizabeth, Norwich, N., spinster	302 Canler
1852	Frost, Hannah, Docking, N., widow	360 Latten
1835	Frost, James Henry, Norwich, N.	160 Harrowing
1830	Frost, John, Beeston next Mileham, N., shopkeeper	375 Pettingill
1834	Frost, John, Potter Heigham, N.	600 Lane
1841	Frost, Joseph Blunden, Sudbury, S., grocer	419 Traxton
1828	Frost, Josop, Horsford, N.	12 Farrow
1842	Frost, Mark, Barrow, S., blacksmith	237 Canler
1830	Frost, Mary, Brancaster, N., widow	134 Pettingill
1841	Frost, Mary, Norwich, N., linen draper	89 Traxton
1843	Frost, Mary, Redgrave, S., widow	107 Miles
1823	Frost, Robert the younger, North Walsham, N., farmer	266 Tann
1837	Frost, Robert, South Lopham, N., hemp dresser	240 Warren
1839	Frost, Robert, Dersingham, N., blacksmith	471 Calton
1857	Frost, Robert, Norwich, N., draper and stay maker	73 Youngs
1848	Frost, Samuel, Kings Lynn, N., yeoman	780 Denny
1828	Frost, Thomas, Brancaster, N., yeoman	497 Farrow
1827	Frost, William, Wickhambrook, S., farmer	246 Wood
1837	Frostick, Sarah, Banningham, N., widow	378 Warren
1834	Fruer, John, Framlingham, S., builder	348 Lane
1852	Fryer, James, Wereham, N., wheelwright and machine maker	558 Latten
1839	Fryer, John, Stratton St Mary, N., farmer	316 Calton
1848	Fryer, John Thomas, Morningthorpe, N., farmer	594 Denny
1845	Fryer, Henry, Westleton, S., patten maker	790 Pedgrift
1849	Fryer, Thomas, Great Yarmouth, N., wheelwright	396 Womack
1846	Fulcher, Henry, Diss, N., farmer	315 Baret
1829	Fulcher, Jane, Finningham, S., spinster	60 Green
1843	Fulcher, John, Heigham, Norwich, N., harness maker	715 Miles
1853	Fulcher, John, Combs, S.	438 Veale
1853	Fulcher, Joseph, Great Yarmouth	271 Veale

1846	Fulcher, Mary Ann, Norwich, N., wife of James Fulcher, currier	388 Baret
1856	Fulcher, Robert William, Norwich, N.	22 Code
1828	Fulcher, Samuel, Brinton, N., yeoman	427 Farrow
1838	Fulcher, Samuel Barnard, Great Yarmouth, N., cooper	65 Skepper
1847	Fulcher, Samuel, Norwich, N., yeoman	761 Broom
1854	Fulcher, Stephen, Norwich, N., millwright	531 Day
1853	Fulcher, William, Thorpe next Norwich, N., millwright	68 Veale
1827	Fuller, Ann, Great Yarmouth, N., spinster	642 Wood
1821	Fuller, Christopher, Downham Market, N., cordwainer	108 Dewell
1820	Fuller, Daniel, Pulham St Mary Magdalen, N., farmer	485 Mack
1849	Fuller, Elizabeth, Beccles, S., spinster	207 Womack
1851	Fuller, Elizabeth, Raveningham, N., wife of John Fuller, farmer	109 Friar
1851	Fuller, Elizabeth, Wicken, C., widow	281 Friar
1855	Fuller, George, Thetford, N., butcher	269 Whitty
1857	Fuller, James, Calthorpe, N., yeoman	O.W. 337
1824	Fuller, John, Swaffham, N., upholsterer	81 Borrett
1824	Fuller, John, Woodbridge, S., bricklayer	264 Borrett
1837	Fuller, Joseph, Stow Bedon, N., labourer	255 Warren
1845	Fuller, Luther, Chelmondiston, S., farmer	332 Pedgrift
1842	Fuller, Lydia, Gaywood, N., publican	598 Canler
1821	Fuller, Richard, Gresham, N., cordwainer	196 Dewell
1839	Fuller, Robert, Northwold, N., yeoman	685 Calton
1845	Fuller, Robert, Royden Cottage, N., gardener	478 Pedgrift
1851	Fuller, Robert, Norwich, N., yeoman	575 Friar
1823	Fuller, Samuel, St Benedict, Norwich, worstead weaver	34 Tann
1830	Fuller, Samuel, Orford, S., brewer and innholder	109 Pettingill
1845	Fuller, Sarah, Norwich, N., wife of James Fuller, tea dealer	898 Pedgrift
1849	Fuller, Susanna, Fakenham, N., wife of Benjamin Fuller, carpenter	40 Womack
1835	Fuller, Thomas, Feltwell, N., shopkeeper	23 Harrowing
1836	Fuller, Thomas, Dukes Head, West Rudham, N.	329 Smith
1843	Fuller, Thomas, South Lopham, N., shoemaker	534 Miles
1825	Furbank, Richard, Burwell, C., yeoman	353 Hayward
1843	Furniss, John, Great Yarmouth, N., mariner	37 Miles
1855	Futter, Ann Maria, Thorpe, N., widow	456 Whitty
1821	Futter, Robert, South Burlingham, N., farmer	8 Dewell
1824	Futter, Robert, South Burlingham, N., farmer	101 Borrett
1841	Futter, William, Long Stratton, N.	279 Traxton
1821	Fysh, Thomas, City of London, late West Lynn St Peters, N., gent.	269 Dewell
1842	Fyson, Susan, Fordham, C., spinster	443 Canler
1852	Fyson, Richard, Fordham, C., farmer	132 Latten
1853	Fyson, Richard, Wickhambrook, S., grocer	46 Veale
1842	Fyson, William, Exning, S., gent.	274 Canler
1847	Gage, Greenacre, Crown Inn, Pentney, N., publican	59 Broom
1843	Gage, Sarah, Mellis, S., widow	282 Miles
1834	Gagg, Joseph, Thorpe Market, N., yeoman	554 Lane
1829	Gale, John, Hempnall, N., cordwainer	447 Green
1854	Galer, William, Mutford, S., carpenter	585 Day
1841	Gales, Henry, Tunstead, N., yeoman	656 Traxton
1844	Gall, John, Framlingham, S., yeoman	56 Ebbage
1828	Gall, Sarah, Easton, S., widow	392 Farrow
1838	Gallant, Charles, alias Hewke, Hackford next Reepham, N., draper	814 Skepper
1851	Gallant, William, Hackford next Reepham, N., yeoman	272 Friar
1855	Galpine, James, Stradbroke, S., dissenting minister	495 Whitty
1850	Gammage, John, Woodbridge, S., baker	377 Cuthbert
1835	Gant, Robert, Ormesby St Margaret, N., farmer	494 Harrowing
1845	Gapp, Charlotte, Hingham, N., spinster	542 Pedgrift
1834	Gapp, Christopher, Hingham, N., farmer	525 Lane
1841	Gapp, Susanna, Norwich, N., widow	129 Traxton

1820	Gardener, John, Saint Clements, Norwich and Belaugh, N., husbandman	47 Mack
1848	Gardener, John, Stuston, S., farmer	660 Denny
1838	Gardiner, Broome, alias Jeremiah Leeds	
1833	Gardiner, John, Great Ryburgh, N., farmer	121 Cubitt
1856	Gardiner, Rebecca, Shelton, N., widow	466 Code
1847	Gardiner, William, Fornham St Martin, S., gent.	246 Broom
1836	Gardner, Francis the younger, Kings Lynn, N., gent.	300 Smith
1850	Gardner, John, Tivetshall St Mary, N., farmer	147 Cuthbert
1827	Gardner, Thomas, South Lopham, N., shopkeeper	395 Wood
1835	Gardner, Thomas, Kings Lynn, N., butcher	529 Harrowing
1854	Gardner, William, Kings Lynn, N., publican	192 Day
1837	Garman, Richard, Kings Lynn, N., hairdresser	478 Warren
1853	Garman, Richard, Kings Lynn, N., victualler	57 Veale
1852	Garner, Ann, Thetford, N., widow	252 Latten
1824	Garner, John, Great Hockham, N., yeoman	312 Borrett
1843	Garner, William, Tilney St Lawrence, N., yeoman	384 Miles
1828	Garnett, Mary, Great Thornham, S., widow	448 Farrow
1851	Garnham, Harriet, Thurton, N., spinster	330 Friar
1845	Garnham, James, Helmingham, S., farmer	662 Pedgrift
1820	Garnham, John, Earl Stonham, S., farmer	441 Mack
1848	Garnham, John, Thurton, N., farmer	186 Denny
1834	Garnham, Robert, Thetford, N., bricklayer	181 Lane
1840	Garnham, Robert, South Lopham, N., farmer	4 Turner
1836	Garnham, Sarah, Thetford, N.	547 Smith
1855	Garnham, Stephen, Needham Market, S., yeoman	183 Whitty
1850	Garnham, William, Thurton, N., farmer	280 Cuthbert
1830	Garrad, Thomas, Roughton, N., farmer	229 Pettingill
1851	Garrard, Ann, Walberswick, S., widow	598 Friar
1840	Garrard, Bazillai, Palgrave, S., farmer	287 Turner
1834	Garrard, Charles, Beccles, S., wheelwright	228 Lane
1855	Garrard, Dinah, Diss, N., widow	665 Whitty
1845	Garrard, John, Aldeburgh, S., maltster	319 Pedgrift
1857	Garrard, John, Hempnall, N., blacksmith	576 Youngs
1851	Garrard, Thomas, Norwich, N., tripe dresser	39 Friar
1840	Garreard, John, Norwich, N., yeoman	266 Turner
1832	Garred, John, Great Yarmouth, N., shipmaster	209 Cooke
1820	Garrett, William, Kettleburgh Hall, S., gent.	284 Mack
1844	Garrett, William, Ludham, N.	458 Ebbage
1831	Garrod, Ann, Beccles, S., spinster	394 Hart
1839	Garrod, Catherine, Ipswich, S., spinster	688 Calton
1844	Garrod, Elizabeth, Roughton, N., widow	194 Ebbage
1840	Garrod, John, Great Yarmouth, N.	Index only
1852	Garrod, John Blackmur, Beccles, S., currier	750 Latten
1838	Garrod, Lydia, Tattingstone, S., widow	659 Skepper
1842	Garrod, Thomas, Bredfield, S., farmer	736 Canler
1844	Garwood, George, Hempstead, N., farmer	674 Ebbage
1833	Garwood, Humphrey, Hempstead, N., farmer	376 Cubitt
1825	Garwood, James, St Clements, Norwich, carpenter	431 Hayward
1855	Garwood, James, Haddiscoe, N., farmer	564 Whitty
1834	Garwood, John the elder, Thurlton, N., farmer	272 Lane
1843	Garwood, John, West Lexham, N., farmer	449 Miles
1828	Garwood, Thomas, Great Yarmouth, N., gent.	252 Farrow
1836	Garwood, Thomas the elder, Lowestoft, S., mariner	561 Smith
1841	Garwood, Thomas Bly, Great Yarmouth, N., merchant	467 Traxton
1854	Garwood, Thomas Fryer, Great Yarmouth, N., gent.	282 Day
1823	Garwood, William, Costessey, N., baker and shopkeeper	378 Tann
1854	Garwood, William Edward, Great Yarmouth, N., baker and confectioner	63 Day
1854	Garwood, William, Rumburgh, S., farmer	60 Day
1856	Garwood, William, Hardingham, N., farmer	337 Code
1824	Gaskin, John, Mattishall, N., carpenter	13 Borrett
1830	Gates, Elizabeth, Thetford, N., widow	284 Pettingill
1848	Gates, Mary, East Harling, N., widow	182 Denny

1834	Gathercole, Flora, Tofts, N., widow	636 Lane
1845	Gathercole, James, Little Cressingham, N., farmer	617 Pedgrift
1853	Gathercole, James, Upwell, N., butcher	249 Veale
1856	Gathercole, Susan, Brighton, Sussex, single woman, also Hilborough, N.	222 Code
1820	Gathercole, Thomas, Shipdham, N., blacksmith	667 Mack
1854	Gay, Elizabeth, Norwich, N., widow	580 Day
1820	Gay, John, Aldborough, N., late of Neatishead, farmer	226 Mack
1852	Gay, John Johnson, Aldborough, N., esquire	718 Latten
1834	Gay, Richard, Norwich, N., basket maker	O.W. 355
1855	Gay, Robert, Oulton, N., yeoman	263 Whitty
1837	Gay, Sarah, Aylsham, N., widow	128 Warren
1830	Gay, Thomas, St Peter Mancroft, Norwich, N., basket maker	108 Pettingill
1855	Gayfer, Samuel, Walberswick, S., brewer and merchant	368 Whitty
1854	Gayfer, Thomas, Costessey, N.	11 Day
1847	Gayford, Denis, Croxton, N., farmer	678 Broom
1846	Gayford, John, Southwold, S., ship owner and brick maker	425 Baret
1855	Gayford, John, Croxton, N., farmer	446 Whitty
1840	Gaze, Edward, Beccles, S., hairdresser	485 Turner
1828	Gaze, Elizabeth, Norwich, N., widow	201 Farrow
1849	Gaze, Jeremiah, Great Hautbois, N., innkeeper	286 Womack
1823	Gaze, John, Happisburgh, N., sadler	406 Tann
1832	Gaze, John, Lammas, N., tanner	268 Cooke
1827	Gaze, Joseph, East Ruston, N.	539 Wood
1822	Gaze, Samuel, Stalham, N., yeoman	324 Sadler
1833	Gaze, Samuel, St Peter Hungate, Norwich, N., millwright	340 Cubitt
1848	Gaze, Sarah Lightfoot, Norwich, N., spinster	81 Denny
1822	Gaze, Thomas, Paston, N., gent.	301 Sadler
1839	Geagen, Stephen, Burnham Westgate, N., yeoman	34 Calton
1842	Geagen, William, Sparham, N., innkeeper	26 Canler
1852	Gedge, Adam, Great Yarmouth, N., yeoman	12 Latten
1839	Gedge, Alice, Great Yarmouth, N., single woman	503 Calton
1850	Gedge, alias Beeston, John, Norwich, N., shopkeeper	220 Cuthbert
1820	Gedge, Elizabeth, Honing, N., widow	314 Mack
1857	Gedge, Fanny, Great Yarmouth, N., widow	528 Youngs
1837	Gedge, John, Great Yarmouth, N., labourer	486 Warren
1850	Gedge, alias Beeston, John, Norwich, N., shopkeeper	220 Cuthbert
1852	Gedge, Samuel, Great Yarmouth, N., carpenter	172 Latten
1842	Gedney, George, Mendham, S., gent.	654 Canler
1849	Gedny, James, Southtown, Little Yarmouth, S., esquire	36 Womack
1848	Gedny, Robert Howlet, Gorleston, S., wine merchant	288 Denny
1844	Gedye, Sarah, Ludham, N.	O.W. 122
1823	Geldart, Joseph the elder, Norwich, wine merchant	157 Tann
1852	Genery, Robert the elder, Halesworth, S., yeoman	520 Latten
1833	Gent, John, Surlingham, N., farmer	26 Cubitt
1853	Gent, Lucy, Beccles, S., spinster	263 Veale
1827	Gent, Richard, North Cove, S., farmer	75 Wood
1852	Gent, Richard, Beccles, S., gent.	612 Latten
1846	Gent, Robert, North Cove, S., farmer	432 Baret
1837	Gentleman, George, Thwaite, N., linen weaver	16 Warren
1847	George, Henry the elder, Potter Heigham, N.	392 Broom
1849	George, James, Lingwood, N., wheelwright	410 Womack
1831	George, John, Lingwood, N., farmer	277 Hart
1849	George, John, Cratfield, S.	31 Womack
1853	George, Johnson, Oulton, S., miller	331 Veale
1842	George, Martin the younger, Halesworth, S., maltster	32 Canler
1847	George, Mary Ann, Stepney, Middlesex, o.w. missing	52 Broom
1845	George, Rebecca, Whissonsett, N., spinster	358 Pedgrift
1847	George, Richard, Somerleyton, S., farmer	643 Broom
1848	George, Thomas, Bergh Apton, N., farmer and cattle dealer	187 Denny
1848	George, Thomas, Great Yarmouth, N., master mariner	204 Denny
1828	George, William, Saxmundham, S., gent.	61 Farrow
1838	George, William, Beccles, S., butcher	430 Skepper

1839	George, William, Norwich, N., carman	197 Calton
1843	George, William, Shipdham, N., carpenter	274 Miles
1848	George, William, Strumpshaw, N., farmer	290 Denny
1824	Gibbon, Elizabeth, Bungay, S., widow of Jonathan Gibbon, gent.	72 Borrett
1820	Gibbon, William, Broome, N., bricklayer	295 Mack
1831	Gibbon, Wilson, Thorndon, S., farmer	169 Hart
1856	Gibbs, Charles, Coltishall, N., publican	666 Code
1855	Gibbs, Edmund, Potter Heigham, N., farmer	427 Whitty
1827	Gibbs, Elizabeth, Great Ryburgh, N.	605 Wood
1848	Gibbs, Honor, Great Yarmouth, N., spinster	486 Denny
1828	Gibbs, John, Hickling, N., farmer	84 Farrow
1847	Gibbs, Philip, Hickling, N., gent.	442 Broom
1836	Gibbs, Thomas, Hemsby, N., farmer	273 Smith
1849	Gibson, Harriet, Wickham Market, S., spinster	684 Womack
1855	Gibson, John, Norwich, N., carter	35 Whitty
1851	Gibson, Samuel, Thorpe next Norwich, N., farmer	342 Friar
1819	Gibson, William, Norwich, N.	O.W. 176
1825	Giddens, William, Walpole St Peter, N., farmer	175 Hayward
1838	Gidney, John, Great yarmouth, N., sailmaker	834 Skepper
1853	Gidney, Richard, Norwich, N., gent., formerly straw hat manufacturer	218 Veale
1840	Gifford, Joseph, Thetford, N., wine and spirit merchant	O.W. 264
1856	Gilbert, Anna, Gayton, N., wife of Rev. Arthur Gilbert, clerk	201 Code
1842	Gilbert, Charles, Moulton, N., farmer	530 Canler
1852	Gilbert, James, Norwich, N.	341 Latten
1853	Gilbert, James, Cromer, N., ordinance conductor	103 Veale
1823	Gilbert, John, Gissing, N., gent.	199 Tann
1846	Gilbert, Thomas, Beccles, S., coachbuilder	371 Baret
1832	Gilbert, William Henry, Cantley, N., gent.	134 Cooke
1822	Gilden, Henry, Neatishead, N., yeoman	303 Sadler
1842	Gilding, Edmund, Little Fransham, N., farmer	649 Canler
1849	Gilding, Elizabeth, Little Fransham, N., widow	187 Womack
1853	Giles, George, Great Yarmouth, N., gent.	234 Veale
1856	Giles, George, Great Yarmouth, N., gent.	601 Code
1833	Giles, William, Great Yarmouth, N., merchant	54 Cubitt
1857	Gilham, Hannah, Great Yarmouth, N., spinster	652 Youngs
1831	Gilham, Jonathan, Great Yarmouth, N., pastry cook	504 Hart
1832	Gilham, Robert, Hevingham, N., farmer	24 Cooke
1834	Gilham, Stephen, Trimingham, N., farmer	687 Lane
1844	Gill, James Carver, Norwich, N., cabinet maker	137 Ebbage
1854	Gill, William Brooke, Wood Norton, N., gent.	53 Day
1822	Gillam, Robert, North Walsham, N., yeoman	195 Sadler
1848	Gillett, Cyrus, Halvergate, N., gent.	785 Denny
1822	Gillett, John, Halvergate, N., gent.	123 Sadler
1843	Gillett, William, Halvergate, N., gent.	700 Miles
1857	Gillings, John Manclarke, Gorleston, S., shipwright	86 Youngs
1827	Gillings, Mary, Stonham Parva, S., widow	588 Wood
1828	Gillman, Rebecca, St Andrews, Norwich, N., spinster	O.W. 234
1830	Gills, Charles, Norwich, N., grocer	179 Pettingill
1842	Gilman, John, Norwich, N., gent.	419 Canler
1856	Gilman, Samuel, Dickleburgh, N., yeoman	549 Code
1849	Gilpin, Bernard, Burnham Westgate, N., clerk	193 Womack
1838	Gilson, Alice, Walsham Le Willows, S., spinster	269 Skepper
1852	Gimbert, Eleanor, Kings Lynn, N., widow	193 Latten
1825	Girdlestone, John Lang, Beccles, N., clerk	O.W. 213
1836	Girdlestone, John, Earsham, N., tailor	417 Smith
1828	Girdlestone, Lucy, Earsham, N., wife of John Girdlestone, tailor	312 Farrow
1832	Girdlestone, Mary Ann, Cley next the Sea, N., widow	202 Cooke
1853	Girdlestone, Mary, Rainthorpe, N., widow	525 Veale
1832	Girdlestone, Theophilus, Baconsthorpe and Bodham, N., rector	362 Cooke
1836	Girling, Benjamin, Wrentham, S., cooper	539 Smith

1852	Girling, Benjamin, Wrentham, S., gent.	118 Latten
1832	Girling, Daniel, Debenham, S., carpenter	21 Cooke
1843	Girling Edward, Spexhall, S., gent.	210 Miles
1842	Girling, Elizabeth, Little Melton, N., widow	531 Canler
1850	Girling, Elizabeth, Norwich, N., spinster	599 Cuthbert
1852	Girling, Henry, Knodishall Hall, S., farmer	221 Latten
1832	Girling, John Andrews, Foulsham, N., gent.	368 Cooke
1845	Girling, John the younger, Paston, N., gent.	694 Pedgrift
1838	Girling, Robert, Woodbridge, S., tailor	267 Skepper
1852	Girling, Samuel, Stradbroke, S., farmer	574 Latten
1829	Girling, Sarah, Ashmanhaugh, N., wife of Henry Girling, farmer	342 Green
1845	Girling, Thomas, St Lawrence Ilketshall, S., farmer	664 Pedgrift
1831	Girling, William, Henstead, S., yeoman	106 Hart
1836	Girling, William, Norwich, N., yeoman	567 Smith
1837	Girling, William, Framingham Pigot, N., formerly of Blofield, N., carpenter	503 Warren
1845	Girling, William, Worlingworth, S., farmer	206 Pedgrift
1849	Girling, William Thomas, Gun Lane, Norwich, N., boat builder	48 Womack
1853	Girling, William, Peasenhall, S., auctioneer	695 Veale
1845	Girlington, John, Bawdeswell, N., yeoman	200 Pedgrift
1838	Girt, John, Naughton, S., bachelor	785 Skepper
1847	Gissing, Samuel, Woodbridge, S., surgeon	73 Broom
1850	Gissing, Samuel, Bacton, S., gent.	455 Cuthbert
1819	Gissing, William, Woodbridge, S., carpenter	190 Le Neve
1827	Gittos, John, Burwell, C., innkeeper	386 Wood
1848	Gladden, James, St Saviours, Norwich, N., collar and harness maker	362 Denny
1853	Gladwell, John, Combs, S., sexton	436 Veale
1829	Glandfield, Ann, East Bergholt, S., widow	387 Green
1840	Glanfield, John, Winfarthing, N., yeoman	525 Turner
1851	Glassock, George, Downham Market, N., saddler and harness maker	158 Friar
1846	Glassock, Sarah Ann, Kings Lynn, N., wife of Edmund Joseph Glassock, tailor	196 Baret
1839	Glasspoole, Thomas, Blundeston, S., gent.	443 Calton
1842	Glasswel, Richard, Syderstone, N., wheelwright	652 Canler
1824	Gleed, Ellis, Dickleburgh, N., farmer	205 Borrett
1836	Gleed, Mary, Wymondham, N., widow	553 Smith
1822	Glover, Catherine, Tatterford, N., spinster	79 Sadler
1820	Glover, James, Carleton Rode, N., yeoman	48 Mack
1853	Goate, John, Stoke Ferry, N., gent., o.w. missing	534 Veale
1855	Goate, John, Stoke Ferry, N., cordwainer	247 Whitty
1839	Gobbett, Daniel, Halesworth, S., tailor and woollen draper	607 Calton
1825	Godbold, James, Aldeby, N., yeoman	368 Hayward
1830	Godbold, Jonathan, Ipswich, S., shipbuilder	439 Pettingill
1832	Godbold, Mary, Stowupland, S., widow	346 Cooke
1838	Goddard, Bridget, Barnham, S., widow	281 Skepper
1830	Goddard, Elizabeth, Ipswich, N., widow	272 Pettingill
1851	Goddard, Elizabeth Field, Woodbridge, S.	132 Friar
1835	Goddard, Godfrey, Great Yarmouth, N., whitesmith	6 Harrowing
1856	Goddard, Jane, Walsham Le Willows, S., spinster	279 Code
1839	Goddard, Jesse, Wortham, S., bricklayer	426 Calton
1838	Goddard, Joseph, Yaxley, S., carrier	888 Skepper
1824	Goddard, Mary, Kings Lynn, N., widow	385 Borrett
1841	Goddard, Robert, Ipswich, S., gent.	395 Traxton
1838	Goddard, Samuel, Norwich, N., manufacturer	443 Skepper
1843	Goddard, Samuel, Hardley, N., farmer	360 Miles
1848	Goddard, Thomas, East Harling, N., farmer	173 Denny
1847	Godfrey, Elizabeth, North Elmham, N., widow	O.W. 310
1841	Godfrey, Mary, Great Yarmouth, N., widow	466 Traxton
1837	Godfrey, Simon Gray, Thetford, N., boatbuilder	700 Warren
1850	Goff, Jonathan Johnson, Wrentham, S., merchant	207 Cuthbert

1844	Goffin, Thomas, Belton, S., yeoman	594 Ebbage
1857	Goffin, William, Blundeston, S., wheelwright	402 Youngs
1848	Goggs, Charles, Redenhall with Harleston, N., saddler	646 Denny
1846	Goggs, William, Fakenham, N., glazier	106 Baret
1847	Gogle, Henry, Cley next the Sea, N., innkeeper	379 Broom
1853	Golden, John, Colby, N., yeoman	175 Veale
1855	Golder, Robert Christmas, Norwich, N., weaver	50 Whitty
1824	Goldfinch, Samuel, Brandon, S.	41 Borrett
1820	Goldfinch, Stephen, Brandon, S., yeoman	O.W. 266
1845	Golding, Helen, Woodbridge, S., spinster	397 Pedgrift
1828	Golding, Lawrence, Oulton, N., farmer	82 Farrow
1835	Goldsbrow, Luke, Soham, C., tailor	236 Harrowing
1819	Goldsbury, Elizabeth, residing in Dallinghoo, S., wife of John Goldsbury of Aldeburgh, S.	174 Le Neve
1819	Goldsbury, John, Dallinghoo, S.	281 Le Neve
1851	Goldsmith, Benjamin, Beccles, S., bricklayer	584 Friar
1852	Goldsmith, Edward, Southwold, S., coal merchant	264 Latten
1857	Goldsmith, Henry the elder, Diss, N., gardener	359 Youngs
1845	Goldsmith, Jeremiah, Cretingham, S., husbandman	317 Pedgrift
1823	Goldsmith, John, Corpusty, N.	407 Tann
1850	Goldsmith, John, Mattishall, N., farmer	170 Cuthbert
1851	Goldsmith, Mary, Beccles, S., wife of Robert Goldsmith, yeoman	528 Friar
1851	Goldsmith, Samuel, Corpusty, N., miller	96 Friar
1828	Goldsmith, Thomas, Corpusty, N., farmer	63 Farrow
1855	Goldsmith, Thomas, All Saints, Norwich, N., tailor	594 Whitty
1837	Goldsmith, William, Norwich, N., carpenter	614 Warren
1857	Goldson, James Smyth, East Dereham, N., gent.	7 Youngs
1842	Goldson, Margaret, East Dereham, N., widow	398 Canler
1837	Goldspring, Christopher, Hindringham, N., yeoman	345 Warren
1822	Gooch, Ann, Swafield, N., spinster	260 Sadler
1857	Gooch, Benjamin, Ashwellthorpe, N.	107 Youngs
1853	Gooch, Eliza, North Lopham, N., widow	467 Veale
1849	Gooch, Elizabeth, Beccles, S., widow	273 Womack
1833	Gooch, James, Ashwellthorpe, N., woodman	196 Cubitt
1847	Gooch, James, East Dereham, N., esquire	607 Broom
1826	Gooch, John, Saxmundham, S., yeoman	340 Davy
1829	Gooch, John, Beccles, S., yeoman	531 Green
1841	Gooch, John, Old Newton, S., farmer	42 Traxton
1846	Gooch, John, Woodton, N., esquire	195 Baret
1850	Gooch, John, Woodton, N., blacksmith	315 Cuthbert
1856	Gooch, John, Hevingham, N., farmer	551 Code
1819	Gooch, Mary, Norwich, N., wife of James Gooch, saddler	14 Le Neve
1846	Gooch, Patience, Freethorpe, N., grocer	46 Baret
1857	Gooch, Phoebe, Woodton, N., widow	39 Youngs
1828	Gooch, Sarah, Beccles, S., spinster	463 Farrow
1851	Gooch, Sarah, New Catton, Norwich, N., formerly of Wroxham, N.	236 Friar
1852	Gooch, Thomas, North Lopham, N., innkeeper and linen manufacturer	331 Latten
1825	Gooch, William, Freethorpe, N., carpenter	264 Hayward
1837	Good, Charles, Roydon, N., farmer	276 Warren
1831	Gooda, Thomas Matthew, Southtown, Yarmouth, S., blacksmith	242 Hart
1841	Gooda, Thomas, Great Yarmouth, N., gent.	494 Traxton
1823	Goodale, Michael, South Runcton, N., gent.	35 Tann
1839	Goodans, Stephen, Necton, N., yeoman	360 Calton
1846	Goodens, Mary, Great Yarmouth, N., widow	296 Baret
1840	Gooderham, Ann, Eye, S., wife of James Gooderham, farmer	653 Turner
1848	Gooderham, James the elder, Eye, S., farmer	99 Denny
1826	Gooderham, William, Diss, N., yeoman	343 Davy
1843	Gooderham, William, Diss, N.	Index only
1834	Gooding, John, Ipswich, S., gent.	64 Lane
1847	Gooding, John, Debenham, S., bricklayer	381 Broom
1852	Gooding, John, Ipswich, S., yeoman	261 Latten

1836	Gooding, Richard, Ipswich, S., brickmaker	507 Smith
1827	Gooding, William, Playford, S., farmer	678 Wood
1852	Gooding, William, Debenham, S., bricklayer	23 Latten
1840	Goodisson, Thomas, Newmarket St Mary, S., gent.	347 Turner
1857	Goodisson, Thomas, Newmarket	Index only
1819	Goodman, Samuel, Hepworth, S., miller	207 Le Neve
1825	Goodman, William, Fulmodeston, N., bricklayer	101 Hayward
1838	Goodrick, Robert, Swaffham, N.	359 Skepper
1833	Goodrich, Richard, Aldeby, N., formerly of Thurlton, N., yeoman	46 Cubitt
1840	Goodrich, William, Fordham, C., maltster and farmer	170 Turner
1834	Goodrum, John, Forncett St Peter, N., farmer	216 Lane
1856	Goodson, John, Terrington St Clements, N., fisherman	574 Code
1849	Goodson, Robert, Burgh next Aylsham, N.	391 Womack
1829	Goodson, Thomas Shave, Palgrave, S., yeoman	62 Green
1848	Goodswen, James, Pulham St Mary Magdalen, N., gent.	366 Denny
1852	Goodswen, James, Stratton St Michael, N., miller	53 Latten
1845	Goodswen, John, Pulham, N.	186 Pedgrift
1841	Goodwin, Betsy, Cookley, S., spinster	181 Traxton
1822	Goodwin, Elizabeth, Woodbridge, S., spinster	415 Sadler
1845	Goodwin, Elizabeth, Woodbridge, S., widow	325 Pedgrift
1846	Goodwin, John, Wortwell, N., farmer	447 Baret
1819	Goodwin, Leonard, South Lynn All Saints, Kings Lynn, N., bricklayer	76 Le Neve
1835	Goodwin, Philip, Earsham, N., yeoman	96 Harrowing
1837	Goodwin, Richard, Fakenham, N., gent.	54 Warren
1850	Goodwin, Thomas the elder, Westleton, S., thatcher	329 Cuthbert
1834	Goodwin, William, Hevingham, N., cow-leech and farrier	475 Lane
1849	Goodwyn, Catherine, Fakenham, N., spinster	471 Womack
1829	Goodwyn, Sophia, Framlingham, S., Spinster	352 Green
1834	Goold, George, Swaffham, N.	449 Lane
1834	Goold, Jeremiah, Hevingham, N., formerly of Great Fransham, N., gent.	191 Lane
1824	Goold, Philip, Palgrave, S., smith	267 Borrett
1820	Goose, Alexander, Hempnall, N., jobber	242 Mack
1838	Goose, Frances, Norwich, N., wife of Robert Goose, builder	606 Skepper
1847	Goose, John, Great Yarmouth, N., yeoman	571 Broom
1848	Goose, John, St Augustines, Norwich, N., coachmaker	737 Denny
1823	Goose, Robert, Skeyton, N., yeoman	366 Tann
1829	Goose, Robert the elder, Horsham St Faiths, N., farmer	402 Green
1848	Goose, Robert, Ashwellthorpe, N., gent.	737 Denny
1844	Goose, William, Norwich, N., tailor	493 Ebbage
1834	Goram, Elizabeth, Norwich, N., wife of Robert Goram, worstead weaver	598 Lane
1852	Goram, James, Buxhall, S., farmer	74 Latten
1831	Gordon, William, Saxlingham, N., clerk	11 Hart
1839	Gore, John, Hockwold cum Wilton, N., yeoman	110 Calton
1825	Goskar, Ann, Kings Lynn, N., widow	147 Hayward
1825	Goskar, Thomas, Kings Lynn, N., gent.	93 Hayward
1849	Gosling, Jeremiah, Crowfield, S., farmer	606 Womack
1838	Gosling, John the elder, Boxford, S., miller	645 Skepper
1832	Gosling, Jonathan, Fressingfield, S., farmer	317 Cooke
1849	Gosling, Joseph, Ipswich, S., cordwainer	450 Womack
1840	Gosnold, Frances, Swaffham, N.	329 Turner
1824	Goss, John, Ipswich, S., grocer	350 Borrett
1837	Goss, John, Catfield, N.	643 Warren
1853	Goss, Joseph, Denver, N., gent.	273 Veale
1822	Goss, Mary Ann, Potter Heigham, N., wife of John Goss, husbandman	343 Sadler
1856	Gostling, Elizabeth, Castle Acre, N., widow	501 Code
1820	Gostling, Francis, Diss, N., clock and watchmaker	59 Mack
1843	Gotts, Luke, alias Fab	318 Miles
1833	Gotts, Thomas, Norwich, N., yeoman	109 Cubitt

1827	Goulder, Christopher, Woodbastwick, N., farmer	198 Wood
1835	Goulder, Christopher, Hoveton St Peter, N., farmer	265 Harrowing
1855	Goulder, Christopher, New Houghton, N., farmer	681 Whitty
1844	Gouldin, William, Outwell, N., gent.	116 Ebbage
1835	Goulding, Robert, Lowestoft, S., mariner	468 Harrowing
1832	Goulson, Thomas, Fakenham, N., innkeeper	585 Cooke
1836	Goult, James, Newbourn, S., yeoman	316 Smith
1821	Goulty, Thomasine, Norwich, N., widow	111 Dewell
1838	Gourlay, David, Great Yarmouth, N., gent.	442 Skepper
1857	Gourlay, Joyce, Great Yarmouth, N., spinster	511 Youngs
1852	Gourlay, Susanna, Great Yarmouth, N., widow	336 Latten
1834	Gow, John, Ipswich, S., cabinet maker	207 Lane
1848	Goward, Francis, Brandon Parva, N., husbandman	284 Denny
1832	Goward, Henry, St Martins at Palace, Norwich, shopkeeper and brushmaker	Cooke 151
1819	Goward, John, Neatishead, N., farmer	324 Le Neve
1833	Goward, Susanna, Tasburgh, N., spinster	525 Cubitt
1834	Goward, Thomas, Barnham Broom, N., dauber	709 Lane
1838	Goward, Thomas, Tasburgh, N., farmer	749 Skepper
1852	Goward, William, Elsing, N., farmer	768 Latten
1857	Goward, William, Elsing, N., yeoman	812 Youngs
1831	Gowen, Abraham, Langley, N., marshman	138 Hart
1848	Gowen, Ann, Runham, N., widow	470 Denny
1847	Gowen, Isaac, Runham, N., marsh farmer	240 Broom
1837	Gowen, Robert, Wingfield, S., farmer	769 Warren
1821	Gowen, Samuel, Langley, N., marshman	80 Dewell
1854	Gowen, Thomas Love, Coslany, Norwich, N., shopkeeper	466 Day
1855	Gower, Amy, Barsham, S., widow	407 Whitty
1842	Gower, James, Shelton, N., farmer	543 Canler
1843	Gower, John, Flixton, S., farmer	258 Miles
1828	Gower, Thomas the elder, St Andrews Ilketshall, S., yeoman	502 Farrow
1848	Gower, Zachariah, Barsham, S., gent.	380 Denny
1854	Gowers, Robert, Fressingfield, S., farmer	103 Day
1836	Gowing, Abigail, Debenham, S., formerly of Winston, S.	367 Smith
1844	Gowing, Elizabeth, Eye, S., widow	582 Ebbage
1848	Gowing, George, Hellesdon, Norwich, N., farmer	689 Denny
1836	Gowing, John Lead, Lowestoft, S., ropemaker	O.W. 34
1856	Gowing, Mary Ann, Dickleburgh, N., widow	557 Code
1841	Gowing, Thomas, Pulham St Mary Magdalen, N., yeoman	50 Traxton
1842	Grand, John, Mattishall, N., yeoman	225 Canler
1830	Grant, Alexander, Beccles, S., gardener	56 Pettingill
1820	Grant, John, Hoxne, S., collar maker	26 Mack
1837	Grant, Robert, Swaffham, N.	91 Warren
1830	Grant, William the elder, Great Yarmouth, N., mariner	204 Pettingill
1849	Grapes, Jane, Potter Heigham, N., widow	73 Womack
1856	Grapes, Simon, Potter Heigham, N., yeoman	168 Code
1841	Grapes, William, Horning, N., thatcher	149 Traxton
1843	Grapes, William, Potter Heigham, N.	689 Miles
1834	Grave, George, Ludham, N., gent, formerly of Great Yarmouth	O.W. 356
1839	Grave, William, Great Yarmouth, N., merchant and sail maker	27 Calton
1853	Gravener, Sarah, Stratton Strawless, N., widow	178 Veale
1825	Graver, George Copland, South Creake, N., gent.	51 Hayward
1831	Graver, John, Happisburgh, N.	10 Hart
1825	Graver, Mary, Norwich, N., widow	67 Hayward
1845	Graver, Thomas, Hindringham, N., carpenter	589 Pedgrift
1819	Graves, James, Norwich, N., gent.	O.W. 178
1847	Gravlin, Sarah, Field Dalling, N., wife of Thomas Gravlin	286 Broom
1836	Gary, David, Kings Lynn, N., wine cooper	99 Smith
1830	Gray, Mary, Hackford, N., widow	242 Pettingill
1847	Gray, Mary, Rendlesham, S., domestic servant	51 Broom
1851	Gray, Phoebe, Norwich, N., wife of William Holden Gray, timber merchant	346 Friar
1828	Gray, Samuel, Bungay, S., yeoman	408 Farrow
1846	Gray, Thomas, Great Yarmouth, N., brazier	673 Baret

1824	Greata, Robert, Newmarket St Mary, S., tailor and draper	97 Borrett
1823	Greavener, Adam, Stalham, N., blacksmith	169 Tann
1842	Green, Ann, Naughton, S., widow	20 Canler
1857	Green, Ann, Ellough, S., widow	624 Youngs
1829	Green, Charles, Burnham Norton, N., shepherd	69 Green
1857	Green, Charles, Burgh Castle, S., clerk	O.W. 335
1829	Green, Daniel, Potter Heigham, N., farmer	1 Green
1853	Green, Edward, Burgh St Margaret, N., wheelwright	377 Veale
1828	Green, Elizabeth, Panxworth, N., widow	455 Farrow
1833	Green, Elizabeth, Sudbury, S., spinster	487 Cubitt
1835	Green, Elizabeth, Hainford, N., innkeeper	549 Harrowing
1857	Green, Elizabeth, Downham Market, N., widow	811 Youngs
1849	Green, George, Thetford, N., gent.	638 Womack
1840	Green, James, Heigham, N., gardener	615 Turner
1849	Green, Jeffrey Hammond, Norwich, N., tailor	492 Womack
1825	Green, John, Ormesby St Margaret, N., harness maker	239 Hayward
1825	Green, John, South Town, Little Yarmouth, S., merchant	323 Hayward
1833	Green, John, Winterton, N., yeoman	460 Cubitt
1834	Green, John, Shipdham, N., gent.	451 Lane
1839	Green, John, Hevingham, N., farmer	221 Calton
1844	Green, John, Necton, N., baker	89 Ebbage
1845	Green, John the elder, Overstrand, N., fisherman	357 Pedgrift
1855	Green, John, Kenninghall, N., farmer	506 Whitty
1841	Green, Jonathan, Burwell, C., publican	28 Traxton
1830	Green, Margaret Darby, Sutton Hall, Bradfield Combust, S., wife of William Green, gent.	265 Pettingill
1820	Green, Mary, West Debenham, N., spinster	77 Mack
1851	Green, Mary, Clare, S., widow	72 Friar
1856	Green, Matthew, Rumburgh, S., wheelwright	580 Code
1841	Green, Robert, St Georges Colegate, Norwich, N., yeoman	515 Traxton
1846	Green, Robert, Hapton, N.	81 Baret
1848	Green, Robert, East Rudham, N., labourer	615 Denny
1848	Green, Robert, Hapton, N., farmer	728 Denny
1851	Green, Susanna, Heigham, Norwich, N., widow	543 Friar
1822	Green, William, Potter Heigham, N., farmer	82 Sadler
1828	Green, William, Beccles, S., waterman	407 Farrow
1835	Green, William, Lowestoft, S., mariner	592 Harrowing
1844	Green, William, Beetley, N., farmer	454 Ebbage
1847	Green, William, Attleborough, N., innkeeper	183 Broom
1853	Green, William, Ellough, S., farmer	334 Veale
1837	Greenacre, Robert, East Dereham, N., nurseryman	794 Warren
1842	Greenacre, Robert, Gresham, N.	168 Canler
1851	Greenard, George the elder, Horham, S., farmer	26 Friar
1829	Greene, Philip, West Bradenham, N., farmer	411 Green
1857	Greenfield, Elizabeth, Norwich, N., spinster	434 Youngs
1852	Greenfield, Samuel, Norwich, N., gardener	657 Latten
1835	Greenfield, Thomas, St Martins at Palace, Norwich, N., chandler	436 Harrowing
1856	Greengrass, John, Ashill, N., gent.	79 Code
1841	Greensmith, Robert the elder, Catfield, N., farmer	232 Traxton
1827	Greeves, Sarah, Horsford, N., widow	489 Wood
1824	Greeves, Thomas, Horsford, N., farmer	377 Borrett
1845	Gregory, Augustus, Wells next the Sea, N., cordwainer	959 Pedgrift
1834	Gregory, John, Norwich, N., gardener	706 Lane
1835	Greve, John, Thornage, N., carpenter	82 Harrowing
1830	Grice, Joseph, Lound, S., carpenter	365 Pettingill
1855	Grice, Lee Frederic, Framingham Pigot, N., farmer	719 Whitty
1841	Grice, Sarah, Palling, N., single woman	115 Traxton
1855	Grice, William, Palling, N., shoemaker	524 Whitty
1849	Gridley, Henry, Burnham Westgate, N., gent.	81 Womack
1829	Griffen, Benjamin, Lingwood, N., yeoman	315 Green
1837	Griffin, Mary, Norwich, N., widow	63 Warren
1855	Griffin, William, Norwich, N., builder	733 Whitty
1845	Griffiths, John Robert, Norwich, N., planemaker	57 Pedgrift

1833	Griggs, Dorothy, Needham Market, S., widow	64 Cubitt
1856	Grimes, Thomas, Norwich, N., baker	490 Code
1848	Grimes, William, Hintlesham, S., yeoman	712 Denny
1848	Grimmer, Benjamin, Winterton, N., yeoman	194 Denny
1819	Grimmer, Robert the elder, Hockwold cum Wilton, N., farmer	178 Le Neve
1837	Grimmer, Robert, Hockwold cum Wilton, N., farmer	765 Warren
1845	Grimmer, Robert, Honing, N., farmer	943 Pedgrift
1851	Grimmer, Sarah, Walsoken, N., widow	356 Friar
1857	Grimsby, Mary Nicholas, Stowmarket, S., spinster	585 Youngs
1834	Grimson, John, Norwich, N., publican	844 Lane
1856	Grimson, William, Rockland, N., cordwainer	314 Code
1832	Grimwade, George, Whatfield, S., farmer	274 Cooke
1841	Grimwade, John, Mendlesham, S., farmer	293 Traxton
1836	Grimwood, John, Hemingstone, S., farmer	468 Smith
1841	Grimwood, Sarah, Hemingstone, S., widow	3 Traxton
1848	Grimwood, Thomas, Woodbridge, S., timber merchant	9 Denny
1834	Grinling, John, Norwich, N., gent. formerly of Laxfield, S., maltster	849 Lane
1833	Grinling, Mary, Norwich, N., widow	423 Cubitt
1823	Grinling, William senior, Stradbroke, S., farmer	72 Tann
1850	Grinling, William, Laxfield, S., maltster and gent. farmer	403 Cuthbert
1846	Grissings, George, Kenninghall, N., husbandman	80 Baret
1820	Grix, Stephen, Hevingham, N., yeoman	519 Mack
1844	Groom, Roger, Old Newton, S., farmer	370 Ebbage
1849	Groome, Edward, Great Yarmouth, N., labourer	101 Womack
1839	Groome, Elizabeth, Flixton, S., widow	581 Calton
1826	Gross, Nathaniel, Glemsford, S., gent.	44 Davy
1836	Gross, Samuel, Pettistree, S., gent.	437 Smith
1836	Grout, Frances, Ashmanhaugh, N., widow	O.W. 232
1825	Grout, John, Ashmanhaugh, N., collar maker	O.W. 212
1846	Grove, Henry, Wells next the Sea, N.	340 Baret
1830	Grove, John, Castle Acre, N., shopkeeper	322 Pettingill
1841	Grubb, John, Sudbury, S., formerly of Clonnel, Ireland	399 Traxton
1856	Grymes, Elizabeth, Horning, N., widow	475 Code
1857	Grymes, Francis Barnabas, Bradfield, N., farmer	108 Youngs
1821	Gudgeon, Elizabeth, St Gregory, Norwich, N., widow	136 Dewell
1835	Gudgeon, Thomas, Norwich, N., plumber and glazier	325 Harrowing
1826	Guild, Robert, Pakefield, S., farmer	224 Davy
1841	Gunn, William, Smallburgh, N., clerk	203 Traxton
1840	Gunnell, Mary, Great Yarmouth, N., formerly of Halesworth, S., widow	369 Turner
1838	Gunton, Ann, Loddon, N., widow	57 Skepper
1828	Gunton, Francis, Weasenham St Peter, N., gent.	227 Farrow
1821	Gunton, Gabriel, Great Yarmouth, N., herring curer	161 Dewell
1832	Gunton, James, Gaywood, N., fellmonger	271 Cooke
1845	Gunton, Louisa, Aylsham, N., widow	19 Pedgrift
1828	Gunton, Samuel, St Swithin, Norwich, N.	360 Farrow
1845	Gunton, Samuel Charles, New Buckenham, N., wine merchant	537 Pedgrift
1849	Gunton, Samuel Charles, New Buckenham, N., wine merchant	430 Womack
1820	Gunton, William, Crimplesham, N., gardener	590 Mack
1828	Gurling, John Fisher, Norwich, N., millwright	284 Farrow
1830	Gurney, Richard, Norwich, N., innholder	241 Pettingill
1822	Gurney, Samuel, Norwich, N., publican	119 Sadler
1842	Gutteridge, Edmund, Bale and Field Dalling, N.	260 Canler
1824	Guy, Sarah, Caister by Yarmouth, N., widow	318 Borrett
1837	Guyett, Thomas, Saxlingham Nethergate, N., carpenter	109 Warren
1841	Guymer, Thomas, Strumpshaw, N., shoemaker	28 Traxton
1846	Guymer, William, Stibbard, N., farmer	164 Baret
1856	Guyton, Robert, Belton, S., farmer	570 Code
1840	Gymer, Richard, Wroxham, N., carpenter	380 Turner
1829	Habberton, Elizabeth, Redenhall with Harleston, N., widow	446 Green
1845	Habberton, John, Stibbard, N., wheelwright	32 Pedgrift
1855	Habberton, Samuel Tuffs, Fakenham, N., saddler and harness maker	680 Whitty

1822	Hacon, Dennis, Tunstead, N., gent.	25 Sadler
1845	Hacon, Elizabeth, St Marys, Norwich, N., widow	787 Pedgrift
1845	Hacon, James, Great Yarmouth, N., baker	601 Pedgrift
1851	Haddock, William, Rickinghall Superior, S., clerk	219 Friar
1852	Haddon, William, Repps, N., yeoman	476 Latten
1847	Hadingham, John, Southwold, S., farmer	771 Broom
1827	Hadingham, William, St Andrews Ilketshall, S., farmer	269 Wood
1847	Hadley, John, Wells next the Sea, N., cordwainer	744 Broom
1820	Hadley, Martha, Ipswich, S., widow	122 Mack
1845	Hadman, John, Worlingham, S., farmer	315 Pedgrift
1835	Hagg, Edward, Norwich, N., cutler	272 Harrowing
1829	Hagger, Samuel, Needham Market, S., husbandman	391 Green
1845	Hagon, Ann, Kings Lynn, N., widow	123 Pedgrift
1844	Hagon, John, Kings Lynn, N., carpenter	39 Ebbage
1821	Hague, John, Little Walsingham, N., gent.	163 Dewell
1832	Hail, John, Earl Stonham, S., carpenter	508 Cooke
1824	Haill, Benington, Ipswich, S.	85 Borrett
1852	Haill, James, Ipswich, S., auctioneer	389 Latten
1833	Hales, Phebe, Great Yarmouth, N., widow	288 Cubitt
1834	Hales, John, Stokesby, N., shoemaker	26 Lane
1837	Hales, John, Hopton, S., yeoman	767 Warren
1856	Hales, John, Burgh St Margaret, N., yeoman	564 Code
1845	Hales, William, West Somerton, N., husbandman	820 Pedgrift
1851	Hales, William, Norwich, N., bachelor	37 Friar
1840	Halfnight, Rebecca, Gorleston, S., widow	511 Turner
1834	Hall, Benjamin, Warham, N., alehouse keeper	278 Lane
1849	Hall, George, Gayton Thorpe, N., farmer and innkeeper	497 Womack
1843	Hall, Henry, Norwich, N, gent.	669 Miles
1850	Hall, Isabella, Kings Lynn, N., widow	120 Cuthbert
1835	Hall, Jacob the elder, Geldeston, N., farmer	545 Harrowing
1834	Hall, James, Lingwood, N., yeoman	439 Lane
1844	Hall, Jane, Shipdham, N., widow	246 Ebbage
1829	Hall, John the elder, Monk Soham, S., farmer	481 Green
1834	Hall, John, Westhall, S., farmer	508 Lane
1838	Hall, John, Great Yarmouth, N., cordwainer	178 Skepper
1850	Hall, John King the younger, Wiggenhall St Mary Magdalen, N., farmer	574 Cuthbert
1851	Hall, John King, Wiggenhall St Peters, N., farmer	417 Friar
1853	Hall, John, St Johns Ilketshall, S., farmer	268 Veale
1854	Hall, John, Southwold, S., yeoman	288 Day
1857	Hall, Maria, Wiggenhall St Peters, N., widow	441 Youngs
1832	Hall, Mary, Norwich, N., spinster	427 Cooke
1831	Hall, Robert, Gatesend, Tatterford, N., cordwainer	508 Hart
1852	Hall, Robert, Norwich, N., coal merchant	641 Latten
1856	Hall, Robert, Lowestoft, S., carpenter	409 Code
1848	Hall, Susanna, Great Yarmouth, N., widow	771 Denny
1840	Hall, Thomas, Beccles, S., boot and shoemaker	68 Turner
1838	Hall, William, Great Yarmouth, N., victualler	219 Skepper
1845	Hall, William, Norwich, N., pawnbroker	962 Pedgrift
1850	Hall, William, Great Yarmouth, N., master mariner	310 Cuthbert
1856	Hallock, Robert, Hautbois, Great, N., cabinet maker and publican	629 Code
1827	Hallowell, Samuel, Tilney St Lawrence, N.	156 Wood
1828	Hallox, James sen., Hitcham, S., labourer	4 Farrow
1840	Halls, Avis, Gipping, S., widow	414 Turner
1855	Halls, Pearl, Leiston, S., butcher	219 Whitty
1846	Halls, Robert, Alpington, N., farmer	186 Baret
1834	Halls, Samuel, Beck Row, Mildenhall, S., yeoman	151 Lane
1830	Halls, William the younger, Norwich, N., cabinet maker	459 Pettingill
1825	Hamblin, John, Ispwich, S., gent.	74 Hayward
1849	Hambling, Herbert, Snape, S., farmer	377 Womack
1820	Hambling, John, Snape, S., farmer	248 Mack
1833	Hambling, Samuel, St Andrews, Ilketshall, S., blacksmith	117 Cubitt
1822	Hambling, William, Ilketshall St Andrew, S. tailor, draper and grocer	143 Sadler

1842	Hamby, Elizabeth, Rendham, S., spinster	117 Canler
1845	Hamby, Henry, Orford, S., widower	169 Pedgrift
1827	Hamby, Thomas, Orford, S., peruke maker	O.W. 308
1851	Hamerton, Eizabeth, Great Witchingham, N., widow	405 Friar
1826	Hammond, Ann, Rishangles, S., widow	118 Davy
1833	Hammond, Ann, South Lynn All Saints, N., widow	463 Cubitt
1834	Hammond, Catherine, Terrington St Clements, N., wife of Richard Hammond, farmer	616 Lane
1827	Hammond, Elizabeth, Leziate, N., widow	412 Wood
1828	Hammond, Elizabeth, Norwich, N.widow	16 Farrow
1857	Hammond, Elizabeth, Pakefield, S., wife of Jonathan Hammond, labourer	562 Youngs
1841	Hammond, Frances, Occold, S., widow	197 Traxton
1840	Hammond, George, Norwich, N., husbandman	1 Turner
1845	Hammond, Henry, Thorndon, S., farmer	440 Pedgrift
1846	Hammond, Henry, Belton, S., gent.	515 Baret
1830	Hammond, alias Kingsbury, Hester, Bungay, S., widow	387 Pettingill
1848	Hammond, James, Wetherden, S., farmer	769 Denny
1855	Hammond, James, Occold, S., farmer	649 Whitty
1827	Hammond, John, Stratton Strawless, N., husbandman	89 Wood
1830	Hammond, John, Occold, S., farmer	223 Pettingill
1838	Hammond, John the elder, Saxlingham, N., blacksmith and farrier	808 Skepper
1839	Hammond, John, Belton, S., farmer	597 Calton
1834	Hammond, Margaret, Woodbridge, S., widow	301 Lane
1821	Hammond, Maria, Holme next Sea, N., widow	177 Dewell
1847	Hammond, Mary, Thorpe next Norwich, N., widow	235 Broom
1834	Hammond, Philip, Kings Lynn, N., machine maker	591 Lane
1847	Hammond, Reuben Hasel the younger, Gayton, N., yeoman	808 Broom
1847	Hammond, Reuben Hasel, Gayton, N., publican	810 Broom
1833	Hammond, Richard, Great Yarmouth, N., liquor merchant	265 Cubitt
1852	Hammond, Robert, Redenhall with Harleston, N., carpenter	852 Latten
1852	Hammond, Robert, Wiveton, N., farmer	556 Latten
1821	Hammond, Thomas, Norwich, N., hostler	178 Dewell
1827	Hammond, Thomas, Hedenham, N., butcher	111 Wood
1849	Hammond, Thomas, Great Yarmouth, N., merchant and ballast master	255 Womack
1831	Hammond, William, Rishangles, S., miller	223 Hart
1853	Hammond, William, Earsham, N., farmer	559 Veale
1833	Hammond, Alice, Docking, N., spinster	110 Cubitt
1844	Hamond, Henry, Wells next the Sea, N., butcher	201 Ebbage
1831	Hamond, Robert, Swaffham, N., clerk	297 Hart
1825	Hampp, John Christopher, Norwich, N., merchant	229 Hayward
1834	Handcock, John, Thetford, N., baker	33 Lane
1848	Handcock, John Alphonzo, Thetford, N., baker	167 Denny
1835	Handley, Edward, South Town, Yarmouth, S., gent.	500 Harrowing
1853	Hannant, Benjamin, Dilham, N., yeoman	500 Veale
1831	Hannant, Henry, Barsham, S., formerly Ellingham, N., miller	189 Hart
1828	Hannant, Richard, Suffield, N., yeoman	124 Farrow
1833	Hannant, Richard, Dilham, N., yeoman	31 Cubitt
1826	Hannant, Susanna, Worstead, N., widow	121 Davy
1842	Hannant, Thomas, Rockland St Peter, N., formerly of Hingham, N., farmer	109 Canler
	Hannock - see Annock	
1854	Hansey, Samuel, Bungay, S., carter	51 Day
1832	Hanton, James, Stowmarket, S., merchant	31 Cooke
1845	Hanwell, Elizabeth, Kings Lynn, N., spinster	376 Pedgrift
1854	Hanwell, John, Norwich, N., Wesleyan minister	356 Day
1856	Hanwell, Mary, Norwich, N., widow	159 Code
1839	Hanworth, George the elder, Norwich, N., glover	333 Calton
1824	Harbert, William, Great Yarmouth, N., yeoman	272 Borrett
1825	Harbord, Christopher the elder, Catfield, N., labourer	405 Hayward
1839	Harbord, Christopher, Catfield, N.	305 Calton

1846	Harbord, Robert the elder, Walcot, N., blacksmith	309 Baret
1852	Harbord, Robert the younger, Walcot, N., blacksmith and shopkeeper	427 Latten
1824	Harbord, Thomas, Hemsby, N., farmer	215 Borrett
1833	Harbord, William, Catfield, N., blacksmith	498 Cubitt
1833	Harbord, William, Great Yarmouth, N., house carpenter	144 Cubitt
1840	Harbour, John, Leiston, S., yeoman	634 Turner
1845	Harby, Ann, Great Yarmouth, N.	652 Pedgrift
1837	Harcourt, Ann Maria, Norwich, N., wife of William Harcourt, gent.	396 Warren
1853	Harcourt, Elizabeth, Southtown, S., widow	579 Veale
1838	Hardesty, Elizabeth, Southrepps, N., spinster	8 Skepper
1853	Hardesty, John, St Georges Colegate, Norwich, N., grocer	655 Veale
1831	Hardiman, John, Norwich, N., gent.	510 Hart
1827	Harding, William, Lakenheath, S., yeoman	564 Wood
1838	Hardingham, Christopher, Runcton, N., labourer	758 Skepper
1852	Hardingham, Esther, Runton, N., widow	503 Latten
1827	Hardingham, Josias, St Martin at Palace, Norwich, N.	59 Wood
1831	Hardwick, John, Flowton, S., farmer	153 Hart
1834	Hardy, Ann, Great Yarmouth, N., widow	82 Lane
1836	Hardy, Charles, Morton, N., cordwainer	447 Smith
1851	Hardy, Daniel, Norwich, N.	47 Friar
1850	Hardy, Elizabeth Neal, Swaffham, N.	371 Cuthbert
1835	Hardy, George, Thorpe, N., gent.	242 Harrowing
1839	Hardy, Isaac, Swaffham, N., plumber and glazier	649 Calton
1822	Hardy, Jacob, Pulham St Mary the Virgin, N., farmer	238 Sadler
1851	Hardy, James, Weston, N., yeoman	69 Friar
1853	Hardy, James, Norwich, N., plasterer	201 Veale
1833	Hardy, John, Honingham, N., bricklayer	369 Cubitt
1842	Hardy, John, Swaffham, N., brickmaker	493 Canler
1868	Hardy, John, South Lynn All Saints, N., gent.	368 Skepper
1847	Hardy, Mary, Letheringsett, N., widow	475 Broom
1835	Hardy, Sarah, Carlton Rode, N., widow	337 Harrowing
1829	Hardy, William, Newton St Faiths, N., gent.	540 Green
1837	Hardy, William, East Dereham, N., publican	680 Warren
1841	Hardy, William, Carleton Rode, N., farmer	125 Traxton
1854	Hardy, William, Swaffham, N., miller	575 Day
1855	Hardyment, Phoebe Mace, Carbrooke, N., wife of Thomas Mace Hardyment, farmer	262 Whitty
1834	Hare, Richard, Ipswich, S., gent.	102 Lane
1855	Hargrave, William, Salhouse, N., farmer	654 Whitty
1838	Harley, Dan Warner, Tothill, Haughley, S., formerly of Strand London, musical instrument maker	549 Skepper
1842	Harley, Reuben, Burwell, C., farmer	751 Canler
1848	Harling, Lucy, Ludham, N., spinster	453 Denny
1853	Harman, Charles, Gressenhall, N., nurseryman	710 Veale
1836	Harman, Deborah, Mendham, N., spinster	143 Smith
1852	Harman, James, Great Bittering, N., nurseryman	146 Latten
1829	Harman, Joseph, Easton, N., farmer	163 Green
1819	Harman, Margaret, Great Yarmouth, N., widow	11 Le Neve
1856	Harman, Seppings Watson, Gressenhall, N., nurseryman	566 Code
1831	Harman, Thomas, Great Ryburgh, N., farmer	494 Hart
1845	Harmer, Benjamin, Blofield, N., husbandman	90 Pedgrift
1831	Harmer, Elizabeth, Bury St Edmunds, S., spinster	380 Hart
1847	Harmer, Elizabeth, Briningham, N., widow	752 Broom
1840	Harmer, Hannah, Potter Heigham, N., widow	8 Turner
1854	Harmer, Helena, Beccles, S., widow	55 Day
1835	Harmer, John, Potter Heigham, N.	472 Harrowing
1840	Harmer, William, Beccles, S., gardener	344 Turner
1846	Harmer, William, Norwich, N., coal merchant	656 Baret
1832	Harnton, Benjamin, Great Yarmouth, N., baker	601 Cooke
1835	Harnwell, Robert, Bressingham, N., farmer	526 Harrowing
1834	Harper, Ann, Horsham St Faiths, N., widow	637 Lane
1854	Harper, George, Norwich, N., chemist and druggist	552 Day

1826	Harper, John, Horsham St Faiths, N., carpenter	97 Davy
1828	Harper, John, Norwich, N., hosier	479 Farrow
1847	Harper, John, Norwich, N., gent.	704 Broom
1854	Harper, John, West Rudham, N., farmer	299 Day
1854	Harper, Nathaniel, West Rudham, N., wheelwright and farmer	479 Day
1828	Harper, William, Wenhaston, S., farmer	234 Farrow
1835	Harpham, Isaac, Middleton, N., farmer	3 Harrowing
1846	Harpley, John, Stoke Ferry, N., gent.	241 Baret
1823	Harpley, Mary, Norwich, spinster	20 Tann
1821	Harriman, William, Aylsham, N., glover and breeches maker	28 Dewell
1839	Harrington, Richard, Woodbridge, S., tailor	253 Calton
1838	Harris, Benjamin, Ludham, N., carpenter and joiner	119 Skepper
1845	Harris, Benjamin, Ludham, N.	Index only
1839	Harris, James, Horsford, N., farmer	38 Calton
1831	Harris, Jemima, Great Yarmouth, N.	201 Hart
1830	Harris, Mary, Kings Lynn, N., widow	278 Pettingill
1856	Harris, Mary Ann, Hackford next Reepham, N., spinster	606 Code
1823	Harris, Sarah, Theberton, S., spinster	359 Tann
1843	Harris, Sarah, Gorleston, S., widow	170 Miles
1830	Harris, Susanna, Sutton, N., widow	356 Pettingill
1857	Harris, Thomas, Downham Market, N., innkeeper	91 Youngs
1823	Harris, William, Southrepps, N., gent.	230 Tann
1840	Harris, William, Belstead, S., farmer	662 Turner
1853	Harris, William, West Lynn, N., gent.	424 Veale
1857	Harrison, Ann, Great Yarmouth, N., spinster	389 Youngs
1832	Harrison, Benjamin, Caister, N., husbandman	503 Cooke
1851	Harrison, Charles Joseph, Ipswich, S.	590 Friar
1840	Harrison, Edmund, Upton, N., farmer	96 Turner
1828	Harrison, Elizabeth, Barney, N., widow	195 Farrow
1829	Harrison, Isaac, Norwich, N., shopkeeper	325 Green
1842	Harrison, James, St Saviour, Norwich, N., carpenter	79 Canler
1836	Harrison, John, Eye, S., millwright	303 Smith
1843	Harrison, John, Forncett St Mary, N., farm bailiff	11 Miles
1853	Harrison, John, Weston, N., thatcher	228 Veale
1856	Harrison, John, Swaffham, N., farmer	519 Code
1855	Harrison, Margaret, Barney, N., spinster	334 Whitty
1820	Harrison, Mary, Norwich, N., spinster	572 Mack
1838	Harrison, Mary, Gaywood, N., widow	728 Skepper
1852	Harrison, Mary, Norwich, N., widow	605 Latten
1838	Harrison, Philip, Stiffkey, N., labourer	440 Skepper
1829	Harrison, Robert the elder, Ludham, N.	499 Green
1839	Harrison, Robert, All Saints, Norwich, N., publican	97 Calton
1846	Harrison, Robert, Norwich, N., wharfinger	228 Baret
1843	Harrison, Samuel, St Stephens, Norwich, N., baker	718 Miles
1837	Harrison, Thomas, Cromer, N., innkeeper	552 Warren
1841	Harrison, Thomas, Beeston cum Bittering, N., shepherd	80 Traxton
1857	Harrison, Thomas, Walberswick, S., clerk	603 Youngs
1820	Harrison, William, Great Yarmouth, N., grocer	346 Mack
1840	Harrison, William, Hackford next Reepham, N., labourer	126 Turner
1848	Harrison, William, Acle, N., gent.	428 Denny
1835	Harrold, William, Hardingham, N., yeoman	241 Harrowing
1835	Harrowing, Alice, Litcham, N., formerly Norwich, spinster	1 Harrowing
1850	Hart, Henry, Redenhall with Harleston, N., gent.	52 Cuthbert
1821	Hart John, Larling, N., miller	83 Dewell
1851	Hart, John, Braisworth, S.	2 Friar
1855	Hart, Joseph, Redgrave, S., organ builder	158 Whitty
1834	Hart Mary, Harkstead, S., widow	209 Lane
1856	Hart, Nathaniel, Palgrave, S., farmer	558 Code
1831	Hart, Phillip, Norwich, N., gent.	1 Hart
1854	Hart, Rebecca, Braiseworth, S., widow	21 Day
1827	Hart, Sarah, Nedging, S., single woman	704 Wood
1827	Hart, Thomas, Tharston, N., farmer	187 Wood
1848	Hart, Thomas, Kings Lynn, N., innkeeper	760 Denny

1854	Hart, Thomas Woodrow, Norwich, N., ironmonger	297 Day
1827	Hart, Wiliam, East Dereham, N., gent.	243 Wood
1842	Hartcup, Thomas Wilson, Bildeston, S., gent.	124 Canler
1837	Hartt, Robert, Billingford, N.	721 Warren
1855	Hartt, Thomas, Bawburgh, N., farmer	643 Whitty
1830	Hartt, Wiliam, Swaffham, N., farmer	203 Pettingill
1832	Harvey, Ann, Thorpe, N., widow	422 Cooke
1850	Harvey, Charles, Bungay, S., millwright	136 Cuthbert
1855	Harvey, Charles, Hackford next Reepham, N., blacksmith	64 Whitty
1856	Harvey, Esther, East Dereham, N., spinster	671 Code
1845	Harvey, Henry Charles, Wacton, N., farmer	545 Pedgrift
1845	Harvey, Jacob, Castle Acre, N., shopkeeper	916 Pedgrift
1832	Harvey, James, St Peter Mancroft, Norwich, N., formerly City of London, millwright	484 Cooke
1837	Harvey, John, Smallburgh, N.	719 Warren
1842	Harvey, John, Norwich, N., straw hat maker	496 Canler
1847	Harvey, John, Pulham St Mary the Virgin, N., farmer	287 Broom
1840	Harvey, Robert Blake, Wymondham, N., farmer and brickmaker	196 Turner
1842	Harvey, Robert, Aylsham, N., carver and gilder	228 Canler
1827	Harvey, Sarah, Great Yarmouth, N., widow	574 Wood
1821	Harvey, Stephen, Kenninghall, N., farmer	93 Dewell
1838	Harvey, Thomas, Holt, N., yeoman	312 Skepper
1842	Harvey, Thomas the elder, Ashwellthorpe, N., farmer	103 Canler
1856	Harvey, Thomas, Alburgh, N., farmer	667 Code
1842	Harvey, William, East Ruston, N., blacksmith	721 Canler
1845	Harvey, William, Ormesby St Margaret, N., labourer	656 Pedgrift
1821	Harwin, Ann, Hingham, N., widow	141 Dewell
1851	Hase, Elizabeth, Saxthorpe, N., widow	541 Friar
1832	Haslewood, John, Norwich, N., seed merchant	540 Cooke
1836	Haslewood, Samuel, Little Waldingfield, S., farmer	87 Smith
1838	Hastead, John, Kenninghall, N., farmer	644 Skepper
1842	Hastings, Diana, Costessey, N., widow	371 Canler
1841	Hastings, Francis, Costessey, N., gardener	320 Traxton
1827	Hastings, James, Pentney, N., farmer	405 Wood
1838	Hastings, James, South Creake, N., publican	623 Skepper
1841	Hastings, John Watson, West Winch, N., gardener	231 Traxton
1842	Hatcher, Ann, Great Ellingham, N., wife of Charles Hatcher, dissenting minister	331 Canler
1845	Hatcher, Jeremiah, Darsham, S., yeoman	836 Pedgrift
1851	Hatcher, Susanna, Norwich, N., widow	238 Friar
1852	Hatten, Nelson, Stowmarket, S., gent.	758 Latten
1850	Havers, Charles, Norwich, N., carpenter	20 Cuthbert
1826	Haward, John, Earl Soham, S., plumber and glazier	135 Davy
1830	Haward, John, Ipswich, S., fruiterer	78 Pettingill
1833	Haward, Samuel, Wrentham, S., flour merchant	263 Cubitt
1828	Haward, William, Bungay, S., yeoman	496 Farrow
1838	Haward, William, alias Button, alias Howard, Monk Soham, S., farmer	745 Skepper
1852	Haward, William, Farnham, S., gent.	769 Latten
1847	Hawes, Henry, Buxton, N., saddle and harness maker	665 Broom
1845	Hawes, James the elder, St Margarets South Elmham, S., carpenter	792 Pedgrift
1837	Hawes, John Chaplin the elder, Nayland, S., farmer	411 Warren
1849	Hawes, John, Kings Lynn, N., yeoman	250 Womack
1854	Hawes, John, Fakenham, N., draper	269 Day
1852	Hawes, Richard, Athelington, S., farmer	766 Latten
1819	Hawes, William, Wicken, C., farmer	60 Le Neve
1847	Hawke, Edward, Norwich, N.	O.W. 312
1846	Hawke, Phoebe, Beccles, S., widow	176 Baret
1824	Hawke, Thomas, Norwich, millwright	128 Borrett
1834	Hawkes, William, Mulbarton, N., blacksmith	485 Lane
1850	Hawkins, Martha the elder, Norwich, N., widow	292 Cuthbert
1852	Hawkins, Thomas, Upwell, N., innholder	505 Latten
1854	Hawks, John, Runhall, N., farmer	195 Day

1840	Hawks, William, Framingham Pigot, N., farmer	528 Turner
1820	Haws, Ann, Kings Lynn, N., widow	417 Mack
1822	Haws, Edward, Dersingham, N., yeoman	20 Sadler
1824	Haws, William, Gissing, N., farmer	218 Borrett
1840	Haws, William, Gissing, N., farmer	164 Turner
1832	Haycock, Robert, Norwich, N., formerly of Wells next the Sea	344 Cooke
1832	Haydon, Thomas, Ditchingham, N., yeoman	311 Cooke
1831	Haylett, Michael, Norwich, N., gent.	452 Hart
1834	Haylett, Richard, Coltishall, N., gardener	3 Lane
1837	Hayn, Robert, Brancaster, N., lodging house keeper	766 Warren
1847	Hayne, John, Felmingham, N., gent.	Index only
1845	Haynes, Dorothy, Great Yarmouth, N., wife of Thomas Haynes, cabinet maker	492 Pedgrift
1857	Haythorpe, Charles, St Gregory, Norwich, N., bricklayer	756 Youngs
1835	Haythorpe, William, Little Walsingham, N., carpenter	43 Harrowing
1843	Hayton, James, Acle, N.	13 Miles
1825	Hayton, Susanna, Norwich, N., spinster	274 Hayward
1837	Hayton, William, Norwich, N., gent.	115 Warren
1825	Hayward, Elizabeth, Melford, S., widow	335 Hayward
1828	Hayward, Henry, Thorndon, S., farmer	379 Farrow
1839	Hayward, Henry, alias Howard, Great Yarmouth, N., victualler	256 Calton
1838	Hayward, James, Frettenham, N., farmer	665 Skepper
1825	Hayward, John, Thorndon, S., gent.	1 Hayward
1844	Hayward, John the elder, Ipswich, S., gent.	231 Ebbage
1849	Hayward, John, Thorndon All Saints, S., gent.	362 Womack
1857	Hayward, John, Thorndon, S., gent.	426 Youngs
1819	Hayward, Mary, Wetheringsett, S., spinster	151 Le Neve
1840	Hayward, Mary, Thorndon, S., wife of Lionel Hayward, farmer and shopkeeper	129 Turner
1838	Hayward, Robert, Beccles, S., cooper	450 Skepper
1839	Hayward, Thomas, Easton, S., cordwainer	254 Calton
1825	Hayward, William, Battisford, S., farmer	401 Hayward
1832	Hayward, William, Gillingham, N., gent.	6 Cooke
1833	Hayward, William Hylton, Mutford, S., farmer	506 Cubitt
1857	Hayward, William, Swefling, S., blacksmith	394 Youngs
1825	Haywood, Ephraim, Redenhall with Harleston, N.	199 Hayward
1837	Hazell, James, Ashby, N., farmer	60 Warren
1831	Head, Benjamin, Ipswich, S., labourer	268 Hart
1837	Heald, Henry, Norwich, N., gardener	92 Warren
1854	Heap, William, Norwich, N., earthenware seller	355 Day
1840	Hearn, Daniel, Groton, S., gardener	658 Turner
1825	Heasell, Mary, Norwich, N., spinster	147 Hayward
1837	Heaslup, William, Tunstead, N., yeoman	9 Warren
1826	Heasman, Elizabeth, Norwich, N., widow	212 Davy
1824	Heath, Martha, Hemblington, N., spinster	O.W. 176
1852	Heath, William, Theberton, S., carpenter	303 Latten
1843	Hedgeman, Richard, St Georges Tombland, Norwich, N.	193 Miles
1826	Hedgeman, William, Norwich, N., carpenter	179 Davy
1850	Hedges, William, Coltishall, N., excise supervisor	464 Cuthbert
1847	Hedley, Mary, Kings Lynn, N., widow	570 Broom
1824	Heffer, George, Framlingham, S., farmer	189 Borrett
1837	Hellen, Benjamin, Beccles, S., umbrella maker	637 Warren
1850	Hellen, James, Kirkley, S., carpenter	398 Cuthbert
1857	Helsdon, Benjamin, Antingham, N farmer	335 Youngs
1832	Helsdon, Henry, Antingham, N., farmer	208 Cooke
1827	Hembling, William, Topcroft, N., formerly of Ditchingham, yeoman	608 Wood
1841	Henderson, Thomas, Wells, N., mariner	612 Traxton
1853	Hendry, John, Fakenham, N., basket maker	660 Veale
1821	Henley, John, Redenhall with Harleston, N.	306 Dewell
1834	Henley, Martha, North Runcton, N., widow	668 Lane
1842	Henry, Robert, Upton with Fishley, N., labourer	339 Canler

1834	Hepworth, Mary, North Walsham, N., widow	622 Lane
1853	Herbert, Daniel, Eye, S., innkeeper	439 Veale
1850	Herbert, John, Eye, S., tailor	159 Cuthbert
1849	Herne, James, Hautbois, N., farmer	293 Womack
1839	Herne, Robert, Hethersett, N., blacksmith	156 Calton
1835	Hermitage, Emma, Great Yarmouth, N., spinster	42 Harrowing
1825	Herod, Thomas, North Creake, N., farmer	518 Hayward
1842	Herring, John, Norwich, N., esquire	617 Canler
1856	Herring, Maria, St John Sepulchre, Norwich, N., spinster	124 Code
1856	Herring, William, St Giles, Norwich, N., esquire	411 Code
1835	Herringsham, Joseph, Downham Market, N., yeoman	57 Harrowing
1838	Herrington, Benjamin, Southwold, S., mariner	173 Skepper
1854	Herrod, Robert, Great Yarmouth, N., house carpenter	101 Day
1856	Heugh, Faith, Heacham, N., widow	38 Code
1854	Heugh, John, Brancaster, N., farmer and miller	100 Day
1838	Hewen, Henry, Methwold, N., farmer	160 Skepper
1844	Hewen, William, Methwold, N., farmer	73 Ebbage
1821	Hewet, Martha, New Buckenham, N., widow	273 Dewell
1839	Hewett, Robert, Barton Turf, N., fisherman	78 Calton
1844	Hewett, William, St Marys, Norwich, N., slay maker	428 Ebbage
1854	Hewett, William, Horsham St Faiths, N., labourer	304 Day
1854	Hewitt, Ann, Southrepps, N., widow	568 Day
1835	Hewitt, Bridget, Cromer, N., widow	569 Harrowing
1843	Hewitt, Hephzibiah Ann, Great Yarmouth, N., widow	478 Miles
1847	Hewitt, James, Southrepps, N., yeoman	492 Broom
1847	Hewitt, John, South Burlingham, N., gent.	630 Broom
1854	Hewitt, John, Antingham, N., farmer	70 Day
1831	Hewitt, Martha, East Tuddenham, N., widow	522 Hart
1838	Hewitt, Mary, Aylsham, N., widow	478 Skepper
1826	Hewitt, Samuel the younger, Cantley, N., cattle dealer	240 Davy
1845	Hewitt, Samuel, Beighton, N., farmer	540 Pedgrift
1845	Hewitt, Samuel, Buckenham, N., yeoman	223 Pedgrift
1827	Hewitt, Thomas, Downham Market, N., miller	603 Wood
1820	Hewitt, William, Stalham, N., farmer	425 Mack
1821	Hewitt, William, Alburgh, N., schoolmaster	153 Dewell
1838	Hewke, Charles Gallant, alias Gallant, Hackford next Reepham, N., draper	814 Skepper
1844	Hewke, Elizabeth, Hackford next Reepham, n. widow	382 Ebbage
1850	Hewke, Mary, Blakeney, N., widow	61 Cuthbert
1841	Hey, Ann, East Dereham, N., spinster	O.W. 307
1829	Heyhoe, Charles, Yaxham, N., gent	545 Green
1846	Hickleton, William, South Town, S., yeoman	349 Baret
1828	Hickling, Benjamin, Horsham St Faiths, N., farmer	363 Farrow
1824	Hicks, Elizabeth, Milden, S., widow	287 Borrett
1856	Hicks, Elizabeth, St Michael at Thorn, Norwich, N., widow	426 Code
1829	Hicks, John Raby, Caston, N., gent.	O.W. 240
1830	Hicks, John, Erpingham, N.	O.W. 249
1837	Hicks, John senior, Hickling, N.	271 Warren
1851	Hicks, Mary, Lowestoft, S., widow	551 Friar
1855	Hicks, Mary Baxfield, Great Yarmouth, N., spinster	672 Whitty
1848	Hicks, William, Lowestoft, S., plumber and glazier	70 Denny
1831	Higgin, Richard, Loddon, N., tailor	179 Hart
1830	High, Christopher, Horsford, N., farmer	415 Pettingill
1844	High, James Castle Acre, N., yeoman	81 Ebbage
1822	High, Peter, Norwich, N., baker	385 Sadler
1842	High, Samuel, St George, Norwich, N., stonemason	620 Canler
1828	High, Thomas, Little Plumstead, N.	46 Farrow
1841	High, Thomas, Little Plumstead, N., farmer	169 Traxton
1846	High, William, East Lexham, N., bricklayer	105 Baret
1849	High, William, Lowestoft, S.	Index only
1849	Higham, Thomas, Bramfield, S., gent.	687 Womack
1836	Hilden, Robert, South Lynn All Saints, N., yeoman	53 Smith
1825	Hildyard, Anne, Stowmarket, S., widow	344 Hayward
1839	Hill, Elizabeth, Lowestoft, S., widow	550 Calton

1857	Hill, Fanny, Shipdham, N., widow	688 Youngs
1852	Hill, Francis, Ipswich, S., farmer	387 Latten
1856	Hill, Henry, Heigham, Norwich, N., ironmonger	193 Code
1852	Hill, James, Easton, S., gardener	190 Latten
1839	Hill, Jesse, Easton, S., farmer	322 Calton
1826	Hill, John, St Cuthbert, Thetford, N., grocer and draper	26 Davy
1844	Hill, John senior, St Marys Plain, Norwich, N., grocer	404 Ebbage
1845	Hill, John, Ipswich, S., gent.	363 Pedgrift
1845	Hill, John, Tilney St Lawrence, N., yeoman	592 Pedgrift
1827	Hill, Jonathan Cook, Ufford, S., gardener	57 Wood
1822	Hill, Richard, Norwich, N., dyer	255 Sadler
1830	Hill, William, Hevingham, N., shopkeeper	264 Pettingill
1846	Hill, William, St Martin at Oak, Norwich, N., gent.	400 Baret
1857	Hill, William, Thorpe next Norwich, N., gent.	697 Youngs
1845	Hilling, William, Sibton, S., farmer	457 Pedgrift
1845	Hills, Eden, Soham, C., farmer	428 Pedgrift
1844	Hills, George the elder, Burwell, C., blacksmith	555 Ebbage
1829	Hillyard, Samuel, Kings Lynn, N., oil and colour man	467 Green
1836	Hilton, William, Little Peasenhall, S., farmer	518 Smith
1855	Hinchley, William, Palgrave, S., yeoman	614 Whitty
1855	Hind, (Hinds), Mark, Norwich, N., hairdresser	307 Whitty
1845	Hind, Sarah, North Tuddenham, N.	479 Pedgrift
1857	Hinde, Ephraim the elder, Norwich, N., gent.	698 Youngs
1847	Hindes, Edmund, Norwich, N., rope maker	651 Broom
1841	Hindes, Sarah, Sudbury, S., widow	193 Traxton
1836	Hindry, Robert, Great Yarmouth, N., earthenwareman	196 Smith
1849	Hines, Jacob, Fersfield, N., yeoman	389 Womack
1839	Hines, Joseph, St Martins Lane, Middlesex, gent.	605 Calton
1842	Hinnall, Benjamin, Weston Market, S., yeoman	265 Canler
1853	Hinnell, Ann, Bury St Edmunds, S., widow	219 Veale
1837	Hinsby, Mary, Swaffham, N., widow	714 Warren
1827	Hinsley, Mary, Geldeston, N., widow	643 Wood
1843	Hipkin, Samuel, Snettisham, N., innkeeper	478 Miles
1849	Hipkin, Thomas, Honingham, N., farmer	189 Womack
1833	Hipperson, John, Elsing, N., gent.	510 Cubitt
1845	Hipperson, Thomas, Hempnall, N., farmer	56 Pedgrift
1850	Hisby, John, North Delph, Upwell, N., labourer	467 Cuthbert
1840	Hitcham, John, Wrentham, S.	O.W. 267
1850	Hitchcock, Lydia, Norwich, N., wife of John Hitchcock, house steward	74 Cuthbert
1824	Hitchen, John, St Augustines, Norwich, haymaker	325 Borrett
1841	Hitchen, Thomas, Norwich, N., dyer, now of Cambridge, gent.	56 Traxton
1845	Hobart, Henry, Brancaster, N., mariner	215 Pedgrift
1819	Hobart, John, Hemblington, N., husbandman	274 Le Neve
1827	Hobart, John, Bildeston, S., schoolmaster	334 Wood
1840	Hobart, Robert, Norwich, N., carpenter	638 Turner
1850	Hobbs, Mary, Soham, C., widow	215 Cuthbert
1825	Hobrough, Robert, Great Yarmouth, N., book binder	342 Hayward
1847	Hockley, Charles, Great Yarmouth, N., bricklayer	82 Broom
1831	Hoddy, William, Bildestone, S.	133 Hart
1827	Hodson, John, Upwell, N., gent.	537 Wood
1831	Hogg, Henry, Wormegay, N., gent.	356 Hart
1846	Hogg, James, Great Thornham, S., yeoman	185 Baret
1829	Hogg, John Shipden, Cromer, N., yeoman	380 Green
1833	Hogg, John, Redgrave, S., farmer	176 Cubitt
1844	Hogg, Joseph, Aylsham, N., esquire	628 Ebbage
1852	Hoggard, John, Wetheringsett, S.	425 Latten
1819	Holbourn, Ann, Upwell, N., widow of late William Holbourn, blacksmith	107 Le Neve
1847	Holden, Catherine, South Lynn All Saints, N., widow	45 Broom
1847	Holden, Michael, Holbrook, S.	94 Broom
1849	Holding, Alice, Docking, N., widow	68 Womack
1834	Holding, Gilbert, Burnham Overy, N., publican	4 Lane

1838	Holditch, Mary, Kings Lynn, N., wife of George Holditch, pilot master	347 Skepper
1830	Holland, Anthony, St Michaels, South Elmham, S., farmer	18 Pettingill
1850	Holland, Benjamin, Hickling, N., farmer	71 Cuthbert
1852	Holland, Caroline Rachel, Gisleham, S., widow	322 Latten
1832	Holland, Charles Carr, Great Yarmouth, N., corn factor	471 Cooke
1819	Holland, Elizabeth, Great Bircham, N., spinster	199 Le Neve
1843	Holland, George, Great Yarmouth, N., gent.	138 Miles
1845	Holland, John, Stradbroke, S., glazier	748 Pedgrift
1820	Holland, Margaret, Norwich, N., widow	379 Mack
1847	Holland, Margaret, Southtown, Yarmouth, S., widow	386 Broom
1855	Holland, Richard, Yarmouth, N., master mariner	43 Whitty
1839	Holland, Robert, Ringsfield, S., farmer	616 Calton
1845	Holland, Susan, Cheveley, C., wife of Joseph Holland, baker	120 Pedgrift
1828	Holland, Thomas, Snettisham, N., farmer	482 Farrow
1842	Holland, Thomas, Newmarket, C., saddler	608 Canler
1831	Holland, William, Horningtoft, N., farmer	591 Hart
1838	Holland, William Henry, Newmarket All Saints, C., saddler	863 Skepper
1847	Holland, William, Stradbroke, S., glazier	279 Broom
1856	Holliday, Elizabeth, Great Yarmouth, N., spinster	336 Code
1841	Hollingdale, John, Bungay, S.	195 Traxton
1835	Hollis, William the elder, Thurne with Obey, N.	228 Harrowing
1819	Holman, Francis, Yaxham, N., yeoman	265 Le Neve
1822	Holme, Mary, Newmarket, S., widow	434 Sadler
1821	Holmes, Charles, Palgrave, S., gardener	O.W. 144
1840	Holmes, Christopher, Norwich, N., manufacturer	579 Turner
1823	Holmes, John, Tivetshall St Mary, N., gent.	339 Tann
1825	Holmes, John, Gimingham, N., farmer	523 Hayward
1854	Holmes, John, South Creake, N., bricklayer	340 Day
1839	Holmes, Maria Ann, Kings Lynn, N., spinster	469 Calton
1850	Holmes, Mary Ann, Norwich, N., widow	188 Cuthbert
1843	Holmes, Robert, Tivetshall St Mary, N., gent.	34 Miles
1854	Holmes, Samuel, Ellough, S., farmer	499 Day
1848	Holmes, Thomas, Great Yarmouth, N., gent.	811 Denny
1836	Holmes, William, Kings Lynn, N., broker	209 Smith
1853	Holmes, William, Drayton, N., yeoman	22 Veale
1849	Holsworth, Robert the elder, Earsham, N., bricklayer	614 Womack
1848	Holt, Frances, Gorleston, S., widow	555 Denny
1842	Holt, John, Great Yarmouth, N., master mariner	634 Canler
1827	Holt, Sarah, Gorleston, S., widow	583 Wood
1857	Holtaway, William Henry, St John Maddermarket, Norwich, N., shoemaker	552 Youngs
1850	Homes, Robert, St Stephens, Norwich, N., shoemaker	100 Cuthbert
1843	Hommsley, Thomas, Norwich, N., gardener	267 Miles
1836	Honeywood, Jacob Frazer, Norwich, N., bricklayer	459 Smith
1852	Honeywood, Jacob Frazer, Norwich, N., cordwainer	238 Latten
1848	Hood, John, Lound, S., labourer	666 Denny
1852	Hood, William, Brockford, S., wheelwright and blacksmith	298 Latten
1856	Hook Hannah, Worlingham, S., formerly of Great Yarmouth, N., widow	571 Code
1855	Hook, Harriet Custance, Great Yarmouth, N., widow	626 Whitty
1857	Hook James, Wood Dalling, N., yeoman	244 Youngs
1837	Hook, John, Wickmere, N farmer	743 Warren
1826	Hooke, Francis, Drayton, N., yeoman	255 Davy
1832	Hooks, John, Thornham, N labourer	588 Cooke
1848	Hooton, Robert, Upwell, N., yeoman	494 Denny
1852	Hopkin, James, Fincham, N., bricklayer	244 Latten
1834	Hopkin, Mary, Methwold, N., widow	20 Lane
1844	Hopkins, Susanna, Alburgh, N., widow	220 Ebbage
1852	Hopley, Hannah, Great Yarmouth, N., formerly of London, widow	240 Latten
1856	Hopps, Hannah, Norwich, N., widow	93 Code
1851	Hopson, James, Beetley, N.	O.W. 263

1851	Hopson, James, Norwich, N., bricklayer	25 Friar
1834	Hopson, William, Beetley, N., farmer	256 Lane
1827	Horne, Francis, Norwich, N., confectioner	8 Wood
1822	Horne, Mary, Pulham St Mary Magdalen, N., spinster	276 Sadler
1843	Horne, Richard, Bungay, S., yeoman	270 Miles
1846	Horne, Robert, Shelfanger, N.	40 Baret
1829	Horner, Francis, Calthorpe, N., cooper	40 Green
1835	Horner, Francis, Blofield, N., watchmaker	241 Harrowing
1824	Horner, William, Blofield, N., farmer	53 Borrett
1823	Horrex, John, Methwold, N., gent.	235 Tann
1852	Horsley, Matthew Coats, Downham Market, N.	312 Latten
1839	Horsley, Wacey Richard, Fakenham, N., whitesmith	622 Calton
1847	Horstead, Thomas, St Giles, Norwich, N., yeoman	319 Broom
1823	Horth, James, Norton Subcourse, N., farmer	345 Tann
1846	Horth, James, Norton Subcourse, N., farmer	76 Baret
1833	Hostler, James, Redenhall with Harleston, N., gardener	344 Cubitt
1855	Hotblack, John the elder, Norwich, N., gent.	525 Whitty
1827	Hotson, John, Belaugh, N., waterman	43 Wood
1834	Hotson, Mary, Stratton St Mary, N., widow	574 Lane
1832	Houchen, John the elder, Wereham, N., gent.	592 Cooke
1819	Houchin, Jeremiah, Stowmarket, yeoman	Index only
1839	Houghton, Francis Reathall, Shipmeadow, S., farmer	342 Calton
1845	Houghton, Sarah, Great Yarmouth, N., widow	466 Pedgrift
1828	Houghton, Thomas, Great Yarmouth, N.	4 Farrow
1845	Houke, John, Great Ellingham, N., leather cutter	570 Pedgrift
1830	Household, John, Hilgay, N., farmer	221 Pettingill
1837	Hovell, John, Ringshall, S., farmer	686 Warren
1821	Hovell, William, Martlesham, S., wheelwright	299 Dewell
1852	How, Richard, Knoddishall, S., yeoman	362 Latten
1846	Howard, Amelia, Wenhaston, S., widow	17 Baret
1857	Howard, Amy, Hethersett, N., widow	198 Youngs
1853	Howard, Ann, Hockering, N., widow	29 Veale
1824	Howard, Benjamin, Neatishead, N., farmer	340 Borrett
1838	Howard, David, Hellesdon, N., farmer	355 Skepper
1843	Howard, Dennis, Colkirk, N., carpenter	565 Miles
1852	Howard, Dennis, Norwich, N., gent.	330 Latten
1819	Howard, Elizabeth, Brandon, S., single woman	224 Le Neve
1839	Howard, Henry, alias Hayward	256 Calton
1844	Howard, James Henry, Norwich, N., dealer	669 Ebbage
1850	Howard, James, Norwich, N., weaver	196 Cuthbert
1827	Howard, John, Norwich, N., gent.	239 Wood
1841	Howard, John, Norwich, N., butcher	521 Traxton
1842	Howard, John, Halvergate, N., marsh farmer	264 Canler
1845	Howard, John, Great Yarmouth, N., butcher	702 Pedgrift
1857	Howard, John, Wickham Market, S., gent.	373 Youngs
1835	Howard, Jonathan, Smallburgh, N.	230 Harrowing
1827	Howard, Martha, Hockering, N., widow	162 Wood
1828	Howard, Robert, Ludham, N., shopkeeper	249 Farrow
1829	Howard, Robert, Beighton, N., farmer	513 Green
1852	Howard, Robert, Wells, N., hairdresser	333 Latten
1853	Howard, Robert, Hockham, N., schoolmaster	445 Veale
1820	Howard, Sarah, Sparham, N., widow	656 Mack
1838	Howard, Tabitha, Bury St Edmunds, S.	469 Skepper
1832	Howard, Thomas, Hoveton St Peter, N., husbandman	489 Cooke
1853	Howard, Thomas, Beccles, S., yeoman	180 Veale
1854	Howard, Thomas, Norwich, N., millwright	548 Day
1827	Howard, William, Blofield, N., husbandman	516 Wood
1833	Howard, William, St Cuthberts, Thetford, N., blacksmith and farrier	220 Cubitt
1836	Howard, William, East Dereham, N., farmer	332 Smith
1838	Howard, William Edward, Honingham, N., farmer	860 Skepper
1838	Howard, alias Button, William, Monk Soham, S., farmer	745 Skepper
1843	Howard, William, Colkirk, N., carpenter	320 Miles
1855	Howarth, Samuel, East Dereham, N., innkeeper	579 Whitty

1837	Howe, John, Hevingham, N., carpenter	30 Warren
1835	Howe, Margaret, Helhoughton, N., spinster	119 Harrowing
1823	Howe, Matthew, Gately, N., labourer	278 Tann
1834	Howe, Matthew, Great Ryburgh, N., farrier	585 Lane
1842	Howe, Rhoda Augusta, Great Ryburgh, N., widow	508 Canler
1851	Howe, William, Wacton, N., farmer	172 Friar
1851	Howell, Dinah, North Elmham, N., widow	357 Friar
1853	Howell, Elizabeth Thornhill, Hybla Castleknock, Co. Dublin, widow	275 Veale
1832	Howell, George, Corton, S., yeoman	575 Cooke
1855	Howell, Hannah, St Martin at Palace, Norwich, N., widow	729 Whitty
1845	Howell, John, North Elmham, N., farmer	896 Pedgrift
1847	Howell, John, North Elmham, N., farmer	347 Broom
1853	Howell, Robert, Gateley, N., farmer	143 Veale
1839	Howell, Stephen, Southwold, S., yeoman	470 Calton
1842	Howell, Susanna, Norwich, N., widow	O.W. 286
1857	Howes, Ambrose, Methwold, N., farmer	277 Youngs
1856	Howes, Benjamin, Great Yarmouth, N., brewer	272 Code
1850	Howes, Charles, Upper Hellesdon, N.	296 Cuthbert
1853	Howes, Edward, Catfield, N.	531 Veale
1857	Howes, Elizabeth, Crostwick, N., widow	136 Youngs
1831	Howes, Esther, Great Yarmouth, N., widow	164 Hart
1851	Howes, James, Heigham, Norwich, N., gent.	499 Friar
1822	Howes, John, Stratton St Mary, N., farmer	164 Sadler
1830	Howes, John, Rickinghall Superior, S., wheelwright	260 Pettingill
1834	Howes, John, Anmer, N., gardener	587 Lane
1844	Howes, John, Mundesley, N., farmer	308 Ebbage
1848	Howes, John, Long Stratton, N., gent.	815 Denny
1849	Howes, John, Tasburgh, N., formerly of Aslacton, farmer	513 Womack
1855	Howes, Mary, Strumpshaw, N., wife of Thomas Howes, bricklayer	522 Whitty
1824	Howes, Richard, Thorpe, Norwich, carter	357 Borrett
1822	Howes, Susan, Palgrave, S., widow of Thomas Howes, cook	185 Sadler
1846	Howes, Thomas, Filby, N., yeoman	549 Baret
1846	Howes, Thomas, Norwich, N., hotpresser	294 Baret
1857	Howes, Thomas, Lingwood, N., bricklayer	648 Youngs
1819	Howes, William, Topcroft, N., yeoman	148 Le Neve
1826	Howes, William, Horning, N., marshman	57 Davy
1832	Howlett, Ann Mary, Fakenham, N., spinster	479 Cooke
1841	Howlett, Ann, Redenhall with Harleston, N., widow	27 Traxton
1852	Howlett, Benjamin, Mettingham, S., farmer	305 Latten
1851	Howlett, Charlotte, Heacham, N., spinster	167 Friar
1837	Howlett, Frances, Kings Lynn, N., widow	220 Warren
1841	Howlett, George, St Margarets South Elmham, S., farmer	590 Traxton
1849	Howlett, George, Carlton Colville, S., farmer	575 Womack
1827	Howlett, Hannah, Diss, N., widow	617 Wood
1831	Howlett, Henry, Hempnall, N., farmer	233 Hart
1819	Howlett, John, Fakenham, N., innkeeper	94 Le Neve
1825	Howlett, John, Methwold, N., farmer	305 Hayward
1827	Howlett, John, Bowthorpe, N., gent.	2 Wood
1839	Howlett, John, Layham, S., farmer	89 Calton
1848	Howlett, John, Brockford, S., farmer	559 Denny
1855	Howlett, Joseph, Barnham Broom, N., carpenter	348 Whitty
1855	Howlett, Mary, Redgrave, S., widow	197 Whitty
1842	Howlett, Robert, Norwich, N., yeoman	182 Canler
1854	Howlett, Robert, Norwich, N., ironmonger	394 Day
1844	Howlett, Samuel, Yoxford, S., gent.	281 Ebbage
1847	Howlett, Sarah, Great Yarmouth, N., widow	317 Broom
1831	Howlett, Thomas, Weston, N., farmer	592 Hart
1820	Howlett, William, Wissett, S., husbandman	449 Mack
1831	Howlett, William, Debenham, S., wooldealer	437 Hart

1832	Howman, Roger Freston, Beccles, S., formerly of Hockering, N., clerk	454 Cooke
1845	Howse, Edward, Wangford, S., yeoman	329 Pedgrift
1857	Howse, Edward, Wangford, S., shopkeeper	5 Youngs
1855	Howse, John, Smallburgh, N., wheelwright	704 Whitty
1839	Howsen, Edward, St Augustines, Norwich, N., worstead weaver	287 Calton
1840	Howsham, John, Norwich, N., gent.	591 Turner
1841	Howsham, Sarah, Heigham, Norwich, N., widow	233 Traxton
1841	Hubbard, Dale, Wymondham, N., police officer	463 Traxton
1839	Hubbard, Ebenezer, Dickleburgh, N., farmer	463 Calton
1828	Hubbard, Hannah, Melton, S., widow	278 Farrow
1827	Hubbard, Mary, Kings Lynn, N., spinster	483 Wood
1833	Hubbard, Robert senior, Wacton, N., blacksmith	503 Cubitt
1854	Hubbard, Robert, Lyng, N., farmer	77 Day
1828	Hubbard, Samuel Henry, Trimingham, N., yeoman	312 Farrow
1841	Hubbard, Stephen, Brockford, S., farmer	218 Traxton
1835	Hubbard, Susan, Norwich, N., widow	409 Harrowing
1847	Hubbard, Susanna, Great Yarmouth, N., widow	10 Broom
1825	Hubbard, Thomas, Wendling, N.	25 Hayward
1843	Hubbard, Thomas, Great Yarmouth, N., shipmaster	530 Miles
1826	Hubbard, William, Thetford, N., carpenter	275 Davy
1840	Hubbard, William, Mickfield, S., labourer	327 Turner
1848	Hubbard, William, North Tuddenham, N.	205 Denny
1837	Huby, Dorothy, St Saviour, Norwich, N., widow	221 Warren
1835	Huby, John, St Saviour, Norwich, whitesmith	267 Harrowing
1828	Hudson, Edward, Swaffham, N., carter	338 Farrow
1847	Hudson, Elizabeth, Heigham, Norwich, N., widow	60 Broom
1852	Hudson, Jane, Swaffham, N., widow	474 Latten
1833	Hudson, John, Attleborough, N., schoolmaster	409 Cubitt
1835	Hudson, John, Garveston, N., smith	481 Harrowing
1839	Hudson, John, East Walton, N., farmer	4 Calton
1846	Hudson, Robert, Holme Hale, N., farmer	269 Baret
1829	Hudson, Tillitt, Sporle, N., thatcher	15 Green
1832	Hudson, William, Hoveton St John, N., marshman	435 Cooke
1845	Hudson, William, Wereham, N., gardener	602 Pedgrift
1831	Huggins, Henry, Kings Lynn, N., butcher	178 Hart
1845	Huggins, James, Shottesham All Saints, N., farmer	505 Pedgrift
1844	Huggins, John, South Lopham, N., butcher and farmer	94 Ebbage
1844	Huggins, John, Wreningham, N., farmer	622 Ebbage
1827	Huggins, Phillis, Norwich, N., widow	394 Wood
1841	Hughes, John, Bunwell, N., farmer	93 Traxton
1841	Hughes, Robert, Holbrook, S., bricklayer	315 Traxton
1845	Hughes, Thomas, Bramford, S., yeoman	163 Pedgrift
1850	Huke, James, North Cove, S., gent.	414 Cuthbert
1852	Huke, Maria, North Cove, S., widow	836 Latten
1824	Huke, William, Aldeby, N., farmer	123 Borrett
1835	Hull, Thomas, Brancaster, N., gent.	451 Harrowing
1856	Humfreys, Ann, Gorleston, S., widow	204 Code
1826	Humfreys, Elizabeth, Rockland St Mary, N., widow	323 Davy
1853	Hummersley, Joseph, Lowestoft, S., fish merchant	202 Veale
1843	Humphrey, Charles, Harleston, N., tailor	228 Miles
1844	Humphrey, Dorothy, Burnham Westgate, N., formerly of Burnham Thorpe	549 Ebbage
1839	Humphrey, John Benjamin, Bintree, N., gent.	706 Calton
1842	Humphrey, John, Banham, N., gardener	263 Canler
1851	Humphrey, Jonathan, Thetford, N., yeoman	294 Friar
1822	Humphrey, Robert, Hainford, N., farmer	368 Sadler
1852	Humphrey, Robert, Great Yarmouth, N., house carpenter	756 Latten
1819	Humphreys, Ann, Banham, N., single woman	218 Le Neve
1856	Humphreys, Edmund, East Dereham, N., formerly Shipdham, farmer	63 Code
1852	Humphreys, Obadiah, Stratton St Mary, N., yeoman	667 Latten
1838	Humphreys, Susanna, Kenninghall, N.	331 Skepper
1822	Hunn, Jemima, Great Yarmouth, N., widow	304 Sadler

1845	Hunn, Mary, Briningham, N., widow	867 Pedgrift
1822	Hunt, Ann, Battisford, S., widow	98 Sadler
1825	Hunt, Ann, Great Yarmouth, N., spinster	512 Hayward
1830	Hunt, Benjamin, Occold, S., yeoman	125 Pettingill
1837	Hunt, Deborah Ann, Oulton, S., spinster	717 Warren
1819	Hunt, Elizabeth, Norwich, N., widow	176 Le Neve
1834	Hunt, Gillford, Botesdale, S., plumber and glazier	80 Lane
1836	Hunt, Henry, Oulton, S., farmer	171 Smith
1850	Hunt, James Edward, Norwich, N., gent.	335 Cuthbert
1854	Hunt, James Thomas, Norwich, N., tea dealer	171 Day
1823	Hunt, Jemima, Fressingfield, S., widow	116 Tann
1819	Hunt, John, Northwold, S.	O.W. 29
1828	Hunt, John, Thurlton, N., farmer	172 Farrow
1836	Hunt, John, Parham, S., farmer	189 Smith
1843	Hunt, John, Great Yarmouth, N., blacksmith	375 Miles
1845	Hunt, John, Stratford St Andrews, S., farmer	543 Pedgrift
1848	Hunt, John, Mendlesham, S., formerly of Blakenham, S.	490 Denny
1848	Hunt, Mary, Fressingfield, S., widow	195 Denny
1855	Hunt, Matthew, Hemsby, N., husbandman	351 Whitty
1836	Hunt, Robert, Downham Market, N., victualler	278 Smith
1841	Hunt, Samuel, Middleton, S., cordwainer	591 Traxton
1852	Hunt, Samuel John, Norwich, N., gent.	220 Latten
1851	Hunt, Sellsby, Woolpit, S., gent.	393 Friar
1829	Hunt, Susan, Bacton, S., widow	207 Green
1820	Hunt, Thomas, Great Yarmouth, N., beer brewer	465 Mack
1821	Hunt, Thomas, Orford, S., gent.	2 Dewell
1834	Hunt, Thomas, Bacton, S., miller	263 Lane
1854	Hunt, William, Old Buckenham, N., farmer	586 Day
1854	Hunten, Daniel, Redenhall with Harleston, N., bachelor	289 Day
1857	Hunter, Christopher Thomas Agrippa, Downham, N., surgeon	144 Youngs
1820	Hunter, John, Great Yarmouth, N., mariner	271 Mack
1847	Hunter, John, Ovington, N., farmer	722 Broom
1857	Hunter, John, Sparham, N., shepherd	613 Youngs
1850	Hunter, William, Kings Lynn, N., gent.	27 Cuthbert
1847	Hunting, Harley, Bungay, S., butcher	721 Broom
1821	Huntington, James, Hemsby, N.	339 Dewell
1847	Huntley, Edmund Boyee, Lowestoft, S., shipwright	O.W. 308
1850	Hupton, Job, Ashby, N., minister of the Gospel	138 Cuthbert
1825	Hurn, Elizabeth, Gresham, N., spinster	63 Hayward
1856	Hurn, Elizabeth, Heigham, Norwich, N., widow	642 Code
1853	Hurn, Robert, Moulton, N., farmer	463 Veale
1829	Hurn, William, Woodbridge, S., minister of the Gospel	489 Green
1821	Hurnard, William, Hingham, N., gent.	307 Dewell
1845	Hurren, John, Kelsale, S., shoemaker	132 Pedgrift
1834	Hurren, William, Kelsale, S., farmer and corn merchant	735 Lane
1828	Hurry, John, Thelveton, N., farmer	499 Farrow
1840	Hurry, Joshua, Pulham St Mary Magdalen, N., farmer	339 Turner
1845	Hurry, Sarah, Pulham St Mary Magdalen, N., widow	470 Pedgrift
1841	Hurst, Sarah, Yarmouth, N., widow	346 Traxton
1853	Huson, Robert, Ubbeston, S., farmer	305 Veale
1839	Hustler, Charles Edward, Thorpe Morieux, S.	51 Calton
1834	Hutchcraft, Margaret, East Rudham, N., spinster	629 Lane
1837	Hutchcraft, Robert, East Rudham, N., victualler	643 Warren
1834	Hutson, Frances, Denver, N., wife of John Hutson, cooper	297 Lane
1839	Hutson, John, Denver, N., gent.	94 Calton
1835	Hutson, Martha, Kelling, N., widow	488 Harrowing
1849	Hutson, Robert, Heigham, Norwich, N., accountant of excise	650 Womack
1831	Hutson, William, Great Yarmouth, N., mariner	65 Hart
1833	Hyde, William, Wood Ditton, C., gamekeeper	68 Cubitt
1849	Hyem, Richard, Walton, S., mariner and innkeeper	469 Womack
1825	Hylden, Robert, Great Massingham, N., farmer	466 Hayward
1852	Hylton, Edward, Hempnall, N., farmer	140 Latten
1849	Hylton, John Hayward, Saxthorpe, N., formerly of Edgefield, farmer	519 Womack

1835	Hylton, Susanna, Strumpshaw, N., widow	535 Harrowing
1821	Hylton, William, Strumpshaw, N., blacksmith	254 Dewell
1852	Ingate, Charles, Chediston, S., gent.	811 Latten
1839	Ingram, Joseph, Swaffham, N.	242 Calton
1837	Ireland, Jemima, Hethersett, N., widow	249 Warren
1837	Ireland, John, Salle, N., farmer	27 Warren
1840	Ireland, Samuel, Cawston, N., shopkeeper	373 Turner
1835	Ireland, William, Heydon, N., farmer	502 Harrowing
1840	Ireland, William, Cawston, N., farmer	661 Turner
1845	Irwin, David, Norwich, N., stationer	60 Pedgrift
1835	Irwin, Elizabeth, Carbrooke, N.	621 Harrowing
1848	Irwin, Elizabeth Richardson, Norwich, N., widow	523 Denny
1857	Irwin, Robert, Kings Lynn, N., boot and shoe maker	76 Youngs
1843	Isaac, Peter, Great Yarmouth, N., carpenter	374 Miles
1831	Isaacson, John, Landwade, C., farmer	490 Hart
1850	Isaacson, Mary, Soham, C., widow	515 Cuthbert
1848	Isaacson, Thomas, Soham, C., yeoman	372 Denny
1819	Ives, Ann, Wood Dalling, N., widow	92 Le Neve
1845	Ives, Barzilia, Halvergate, N., farrier	596 Pedgrift
1832	Ives, John, Erpingham, N., labourer	193 Cooke
1846	Ives, John, Great Yarmouth, N., yeoman	O.W. 260
1825	Ives, Samuel, Oulton, S., cordwainer	325 Hayward
1836	Iveson, Thomas, Kings Lynn, N., clerk	283 Smith
1834	Jackaman, Sarah, Ipswich, S., single woman	708 Lane
1832	Jackman, William, Kings Lynn, N., baker and confectioner	167 Cooke
1828	Jackson, Elizabeth, Dersingham, N., spinster	357 Farrow
1854	Jackson, Elizabeth, South Lynn All Saints, Kings Lynn, N., widow	320 Day
1856	Jackson, Elizabeth, Rattlesden, S., widow	316 Code
1846	Jackson, George, Norwich, N., baker	175 Baret
1833	Jackson, James, Gorleston, S., bricklayer	51 Cubitt
1827	Jackson, John, Ditchingham, N., formerly of Wymondham, N. and Great Yarmouth, N., esquire	362 Wood
1828	Jackson, John, Thetford, N., glover	256 Farrow
1835	Jackson, John the elder, Dennington, S., farmer	315 Harrowing
1857	Jackson, John, Fulmodeston with Croxton, N., farmer	643 Youngs
1821	Jackson, Richard, Great Snoring, N., shopkeeper	O.W. 145
1852	Jackson, Stephen, Newbourn, S., innkeeper	231 Latten
1846	Jackson, Thomas, Wiggenhall St Peter, N., farmer	406 Baret
1845	Jackson, William, Lakenham, Norwich, N., yeoman	83 Pedgrift
1831	Jacob, Elizabeth, Little Walsingham, N., widow	118 Hart
1839	Jacob, George, Hockwold cum Wilton, N., farmer	89 Calton
1852	Jacob, Robert, Ipswich, S., gent.	576 Latten
1823	Jacob, Susanna, Cromer, N., widow	172 Tann
1821	Jacobs, Samuel, Chattisham, S., wheelwright	23 Dewell
1853	Jacobs, Thomas, Alderton, S., labourer	547 Veale
1839	Jacobs, William, Elmsett, S., farmer	409 Calton
1834	Jagger, Mary, St Stephens, Norwich, N., widow	666 Lane
1824	Jagger, Robert Scott, Outwell, C., yeoman	159 Borrett
1844	Jakes, William, Downham Market, N., mustard miller	88 Ebbage
1826	James, Henry, Winfarthing, N., farmer	321 Davy
1820	James, Sarah, Norwich, N., widow	236 Mack
1848	James, Susanna, Ringshall, S., widow, shopkeeper	240 Denny
1831	James, William, Upwell, N., yeoman	83 Hart
1837	Jarmy, Charles, Burgh Castle, S., yeoman	567 Warren
1826	Jarmy, William the elder, Halesworth, S., patten maker	317 Davy
1829	Jarmy, William, Vinegar Yard, Drury Lane, Middlesex, painter and glazier	89 Green
1849	Jarmyn, Ann, West Dereham, N., wife of John Jarmyn, farmer	295 Womack
1855	Jarred, William, Whissonsett, N., farmer	82 Whitty
1841	Jarrett, William, Hempton, N., widow	266 Traxton
1857	Jarrett, James, Diss, N., yeoman	230 Youngs
1834	Jarrett, John, Burston, N., miller	118 Lane
1835	Jarrett, John, Hempton Abbey, N., farmer	175 Harrowing

1849	Jarrett, Sarah, Gressenhall, N., widow	394 Womack
1845	Jarrett, Thomas, Little Walsingham, N., collar maker	311 Pedgrift
1849	Jarvis, Anne, Wighton, N., widow	26 Womack
1843	Jarvis, Christopher, Wendling, N., miller	625 Miles
1822	Jarvis, Henry the elder, Washbrook, S., bricklayer	89 Sadler
1829	Jarvis, Henry, Sproughton, S., bricklayer	444 Green
1830	Jarvis, James, Cheveley, C.	157 Pettingill
1846	Jarvis, James, Cromer, N., plumber and glazier and house painter	654 Baret
1855	Jarvis, Mary, Cromer, N., widow	561 Whitty
1844	Jarvis, Robert, Grundisburgh, S., yeoman	27 Ebbage
1852	Jarvis, Thomas, Norwich, N., upholsterer	511 Latten
1823	Jary, Ann, Cley, N.	61 Tann
1833	Jary, Edmund, Shouldham Thorpe, N., farmer	222 Cubitt
1857	Jary, Elizabeth, St Peter Permountergate, Norwich, N., spinster	O.W. 334
1821	Jary, John, Cley next the Sea, N., late customs officer	162 Dewell
1857	Jary, Mary, Norwich, N., spinster	695 Youngs
1832	Jary, Sarah, Acle, N., spinster	229 Cooke
1835	Jary, William Thomas, Reedham, N., farmer	223 Harrowing
1855	Jay, Amy, Norwich, N., widow	706 Whitty
1842	Jay, Elizabeth, Great Yarmouth, N., widow	203 Canler
1849	Jay, George, Great Yarmouth, N., shipowner	664 Womack
1851	Jay, James, Catfield, N., farmer	496 Friar
1842	Jay, Robert, Great Thornham, S., farmer	325 Canler
1842	Jay, Samuel, South Town, S., merchant	461 Canler
1823	Jay, Thomas, Great Yarmouth, N., merchant	194 Tann
1830	Jaye, James, Ipswich, S., gunsmith	165 Pettingill
1820	Jealous, Thomas, West Somerton, N., farmer	535 Mack
1831	Jeary, John, Beeston, N., collar maker	531 Hart
1838	Jecks, Henry Bidewell, Oulton, S., gent.	529 Skepper
1843	Jecks, Henry Bidewell, Oxwick, N., gent.	662 Miles
1841	Jecks, Isaac, Norwich, N., gent.	323 Traxton
1848	Jecks, Mary Ann, Leicester Square, Middsx., widow	463 Denny
1851	Jecks, Mary, Framingham Pigot, N., formerly of Wisbech, C., widow	134 Friar
1819	Jee, Robert the elder, Weeting, N., yeoman	215 Le Neve
1819	Jefferies, Daniel the elder, Wetheringsett, S., farmer	52 Le Neve
1848	Jeffery, John Gifford, Great Yarmouth, N., surgeon	749 Denny
1842	Jeffries, Daniel, Wetheringsett, S., farmer	447 Canler
1855	Jeffries, Phoebe, Lowestoft, S.	562 Whitty
1830	Jeffreys, John, Pulham St Mary Magdalen, N. yeoman and farmer	334 Pettingill
1854	Jenner, James, Great Yarmouth, N., gent.	370 Day
1850	Jenner, Mary Ann, Great Yarmouth, N., single woman	21 Cuthbert
1847	Jennings, Charles, Bacton, S., gent.	79 Broom
1838	Jennings, George, Catton, N., farmer	180 Skepper
1828	Jennings, James, Crowfield, S., farmer	245 Farrow
1833	Jennings, John, Brandon, S., linen draper	462 Cubitt
1834	Jennings, John, Eyke, S., yeoman	307 Lane
1853	Jennings, William, Horham, S., farmer	93 Veale
1832	Jermy, Ann, Norwich, N., spinster	384 Cooke
1845	Jermy, Robert, Thurlton, N., labourer	584 Pedgrift
1840	Jermyn, Editha, Reydon, S., formerly of Lowestoft, S., spinster	15 Turner
1819	Jermyn, James, Limpenhoe, N., farmer	63 Le Neve
1828	Jermyn, Richard, Hempnall, N., tailor	22 Farrow
1851	Jermyn, William, Limpenhoe, N., carpenter	240 Friar
1825	Jessop, John, Worlingworth, S., farmer	360 Hayward
1855	Jessup, Abraham, Woodbridge, S., farmer	183 Whitty
1855	Jessup, Alexander, Woodbridge, S., merchant	303 Whitty
1857	Jessup, Robert, North Lopham, N., linen manufacturer	748 Youngs
1850	Jessup, Thomas the younger, Norwich, N., gent.	607 Cuthbert
1822	Jessup, William, Hockering, N., carpenter	219 Sadler

1828	Jesup, Sarah, Woodbridge, S., formerly of Theberton, spinster	125 Farrow
1844	Jex, Henry, Wiggenhall St Germains, N., farmer	402 Ebbage
1831	Jex, John, Thursford, N., farmer	379 Hart
1851	Jex, John, Shipmeadow, S., yeoman	289 Friar
1854	Jex, Jonathan, Great Massingham, N., blacksmith	68 Day
1850	Jex, Robert, Rackheath, N., butler	533 Cuthbert
1840	Jex, Thomas, Fulmodeston with Croxton, N., gent.	337 Turner
1852	Jickling, George, Hingham, N., gent.	526 Latten
1836	Jickling, Sarah, Thornham, N., widow	145 Smith
1835	Jillings, Dennis, Westhall, S., farmer	40 Harrowing
1855	Jillings, William, Cratfield, S., farmer	120 Whitty
1847	Jimpson, James, Salhouse, N., yeoman	795 Broom
1856	Johnson, Ann, Carlton Colville, S., spinster	640 Code
1828	Johnson, Benjamin the younger, St Giles in the Fields, Middlesex, and St Lawrence, Norwich, grocer	34 Farrow
1848	Johnson, Benjamin, Thetford, N., wheelwright	818 Denny
1836	Johnson, Christopher, Kenninghall, N., farmer	224 Smith
1850	Johnson, Edmund, South Lynn All Saints, N., yeoman	230 Cuthbert
1824	Johnson, Elizabeth, Thornham, N., widow	216 Borrett
1834	Johnson, Elizabeth, Downham Market, N., widow	292 Lane
1837	Johnson, Elizabeth, Norwich, N., spinster	O.W. 345
1847	Johnson, Elizabeth, Great Yarmouth, N., widow	658 Broom
1851	Johnson, Elizabeth, Southtown, Yarmouth, S., widow	438 Friar
1820	Johnson, Frederick, Kings Lynn, N., surgeon	113 Mack
1820	Johnson, Goddard, Little Dunham, N., farmer	14 Mack
1833	Johnson, Hannah, Little Dunham, N., widow	246 Cubitt
1850	Johnson, Isaac, Great Yarmouth, N., carter	265 Cuthbert
1821	Johnson, James, Stalham, N., gent.	312 Dewell
1842	Johnson, James, Wortwell, N., farmer	583 Canler
1845	Johnson, James, Brookmans Park, Hatfield, Herts, servant to Robert William Gaupen, esquire	651 Pedgrift
1847	Johnson, James, Southtown, Yarmouth, S., gent.	90 Broom
1854	Johnson, James, Halesworth, S., farmer	335 Day
1834	Johnson, Jeremiah James, Walton, N., merchant	453 Lane
1827	Johnson, John, Overstrand, N., farmer	612 Wood
1829	Johnson, John, Cockley Cley, N.	444 Green
1836	Johnson, John, Downham Market, N., baker	499 Smith
1836	Johnson, John, Norwich, N., gent.	451 Smith
1844	Johnson, John, Great Yarmouth, N., cowkeeper	34 Ebbage
1852	Johnson, John, Norwich, N., gent.	720 Latten
1856	Johnson, John, Bedingfield, S., farmer	69 Code
1827	Johnson, Jonathan, Hempnall, N., plumber and glazier	209 Wood
1854	Johnson, Jonathan, Soham, C., labourer	208 Day
1838	Johnson, Martha Ann, Bradwell, S., widow	633 Skepper
1842	Johnson, Martha, Norwich, N., widow	246 Canler
1819	Johnson, Mary, St Clement, Ipswich, S., widow	253 Le Neve
1827	Johnson, Mary, Bishopgate Hospital, Norwich, N., widow	268 Wood
1834	Johnson, Mary, Kings Lynn, N., widow	691 Lane
1837	Johnson, Mary, Upwell, N., spinster	47 Warren
1848	Johnson, Mary, Norwich, N., widow	34 Denny
1853	Johnson, Mary Ann, Norwich, N., wife of Jacob Johnson, haberdasher	199 Veale
1835	Johnson, Paul, Runton, N., clerk	438 Harrowing
1833	Johnson, Peter, North Elmham, N., baker	143 Cubitt
1819	Johnson, Rebecca, Badingham, S., widow	154 Le Neve
1834	Johnson, Richard, Redlingfield, S., farmer	233 Lane
1849	Johnson, Richard, Holt, N., innkeeper	518 Womack
1849	Johnson, Richard, Horsey, N., labourer	251 Womack
1826	Johnson, Robert, Norwich, N., worstead weaver	14 Davy
1832	Johnson, Robert, Bildestone, S., draper and grocer	250 Cooke
1842	Johnson, Robert, Little Dunham, N., gent.	549 Canler
1851	Johnson, Robert, Boyton, S., farmer	40 Friar
1821	Johnson, Samuel, New Buckenham, N., plumber and glazier	81 Dewell

1826	Johnson, Samuel, Thurning, N., gent.	371 Davy
1849	Johnson, Samuel, Mendham, N., farmer	465 Womack
1827	Johnson, Sarah, Great Yarmouth, N., widow	304 Wood
1841	Johnson, Sarah Maria, Norwich, N., widow	124 Traxton
1845	Johnson, Sarah, Stalham, N., widow	469 Pedgrift
1825	Johnson, Stephen, Levington, S., farmer	437 Hayward
1819	Johnson, Thomas, Fakenham, N., dissenting minister	141 Le Neve
1824	Johnson, Thomas, Norwich, silk weaver	214 Borrett
1841	Johnson, Thomas, Soham, C., cordwainer	464 Traxton
1844	Johnson, Thomas, East Lexham, N., yeoman	9 Ebbage
1845	Johnson, Thomas, Great Fransham, N., yeoman	619 Pedgrift
1856	Johnson, Thomas, Wymondham, N., governer of Wymondham bridewell	41 Code
1821	Johnson, William, Ludham, N., gent.	29 Dewell
1829	Johnson, William, Beighton, N., farmer	488 Green
1844	Johnson, William, Bawdeswell, N., farmer, gardener and cordwainer	64 Ebbage
1852	Johnson, William, North Elmham, N., earthenware dealer	227 Latten
1842	Jolley, Henry, North Lopham, N., linen weaver	556 Canler
1852	Jolley, William the elder, North Lopham, N., farmer	590 Latten
1822	Jolly, Ann, Palgrave, S., widow	166 Sadler
1848	Jolly, Elizabeth, New Buckenham, N.	591 Denny
1855	Jolly, James, Earlham, N.	521 Whitty
1857	Jolly, John, Wortham, S., farmer	131 Youngs
1821	Jolly, Thomas, Rickinghall Superior, S., shopkeeper	266 Dewell
1845	Jolly, William, Deopham, N., farmer	555 Pedgrift
1847	Jones, Edward, Brooke, N., innkeeper	479 Broom
1837	Jones, Elizabeth, Kings Lynn, N., wife of William Hancliffe Jones, gent.	464 Warren
1854	Jones, Elizabeth Mary, Eye, S., spinster	570 Day
1835	Jones, Hannah, Snettisham, N., widow	319 Harrowing
1853	Jones, James, Bungay, S., Wesleyan minister	150 Veale
1838	Jones, John, Beccles, S., baker	85 Skepper
1838	Jones, John, Kings Lynn, N., carter and milkman	495 Skepper
1855	Jones, Sarah, Great Yarmouth, N., widow	21 Whitty
1822	Jones, Susanna, Lowestoft, S., widow	273 Sadler
1830	Jones, Susanna, Newmarket, S., spinster	114 Pettingill
1837	Jones, Susanna, Glasgow, formerly of Lowestoft, S., spinster	293 Warren
1849	Jones, Walter, Lowestoft, S., music master	399 Womack
1823	Jones, William, Norwich, carpenter	303 Tann
1830	Jones, William, Beccles, S., watchmaker	360 Pettingill
1838	Jordan, Emmerson, Kelsale, S., labourer	171 Skepper
1857	Josh, Isaac, Swaffham, N., blacksmith	774 Youngs
1850	Josh, Judith, Swaffham, N., spinster	482 Cuthbert
1828	Joullain, Frances, Norwich, N., spinster	226 Farrow
1825	Joy, Daniel, St Augustines, Norwich, N., gent.	68 Hayward
1836	Joy, Edmund, Roughton, N., miller	93 Smith
1840	Joy, John, Irstead, N., gent.	583 Turner
1844	Joy, John, Massingham, N., surgeon	378 Ebbage
1851	Joy, John, Briston, N., farmer	381 Friar
1848	Joy, Mary, Roughton, N.	5 Denny
1819	Joy, Robert, Neatishead, N., wheelwright	105 Le Neve
1836	Joyce, Ann, Norwich, N., spinster	113 Smith
1857	Juby, Joseph, Scarning, N., farmer	551 Youngs
1846	Juby, Mary, Weston, N., widow	581 Baret
1829	Juby, Robert, Syleham, S., farmer	340 Green
1840	Juby, Thomas, Norwich, N., coal merchant	330 Turner
1851	Juby, William, Hemsby, N., farmer	441 Friar
1837	Judd, Charles, Wells next the Sea, N., farmer	438 Warren
1836	Jude, Thomas, Hingham, N., labourer	310 Smith
1820	Jugate, William, Huntingfield, S., farmer	97 Mack
1856	Jugg, William, Soham, C., farmer	439 Code
1825	Juler, John, North Walsham, N., clock and watch maker	371 Hayward

1833	Juler, John, Thetford, N., draper	165 Cubitt
1838	Julian, Naunton, Walton, S., gent.	663 Skepper
1823	Julians, John the elder, Shadingfield, S., yeoman	332 Tann
1847	Jungins, Joseph, Norwich, N., printer	632 Broom
1824	Juniper, Henry, Horning, N., husbandman	230 Borrett
1826	Just, John, Norwich, N., innkeeper	37 Davy
1825	Keddington, James, Norwich, N., yeoman	377 Hayward
1830	Kedington, Robert, Great Waldingfield, S., clerk	209 Pettingill
1839	Keeble, Francis, Bentley, S., gent.	236 Calton
1834	Keeble, John, Aldeburgh, S., carpenter	373 Lane
1845	Keeble, Martin, Norwich, N., woolcomber	655 Pedgrift
1825	Keeble, Thomas, Bildeston, S., yeoman	252 Hayward
1829	Keen, John, Clopton, S., farmer	493 Green
1852	Keer, Emma, Framlingham, S., spinster	581 Latten
1832	Keer, William, Worlingham, S., gent.	98 Cooke
1854	Kelf, Robert, Norwich, N., weaver	419 Day
1854	Kelf, Susan, Norwich, N.	446 Day
1838	Kemball, Richard, Stoke by Nayland, S., farmer	O.W. 368
1846	Kemble, Thomas, Kersey, S.	78 Baret
1827	Kemp, Charles, West Watton, N., farmer	193 Wood
1835	Kemp, David, Shouldham Thorpe, N., yeoman	603 Harrowing
1827	Kemp, Deborah, Yoxford, S., widow	390 Wood
1853	Kemp, Elizabeth, Docking, N., widow	214 Veale
1827	Kemp, Hannah, Beccles, S., wife of David Kemp, labourer	480 Wood
1847	Kemp, James, Poringland, N., miller and farmer	628 Broom
1847	Kemp, James the elder, Ubbeston, S., farmer	709 Broom
1820	Kemp, John, Saxmundham, S., saddler	87 Mack
1854	Kemp John Turner, Swardeston, N., esquire	365 Day
1854	Kemp, Mary, Mulbarton, N., spinster	402 Day
1842	Kemp, Richard, Wymondham, N., blacksmith	41 Canler
1838	Kemp, Robert the elder, Tannington, S., innkeeper	600 Skepper
1848	Kemp, Sarah, Swardeston, N., wife of John, Turner Kemp, gent.	682 Denny
1856	Kemp, Simon, Darsham, S., farmer	85 Code
1835	Kemp, Susanna, Docking, N., widow	106 Harrowing
1822	Kemp, Thomas, Kings Lynn, N., master mariner	145 Sadler
1838	Kemp, Thomas Benjamin, Swafield, N., esquire	695 Skepper
1834	Kemp, William, Kerdiston, N., farmer	389 Lane
1843	Kemp, William, Norwich, N., cordwainer	353 Miles
1853	Kemp, William, Tasburgh, N., yeoman	675 Veale
1855	Kemp, William, Hollesley, S., farmer	667 Whitty
1834	Kendall, Frances, Framingham Pigot, N., spinster	636 Lane
1853	Kendall, John, Burnham Overy, N., blacksmith	603 Veale
1840	Kendall, Joseph, West Raynham, N., formerly of Sculthorpe, blacksmith	221 Turner
1823	Kendall, alias Rendall, Mary, Whissonsett, N., widow	32 Tann
1834	Kendall, Mary, Fincham, N., widow	24 Lane
1846	Kendall, Robert Oxley, Shernbourne, N., farmer	482 Baret
1857	Kendall, Wright, Sculthorpe, N., publican	416 Youngs
1851	Kendle, William, Kings Lynn, N., customs officer	3 Friar
1822	Kent, Bowles, Hoxne, S., wheelwright	284 Sadler
1839	Kent, Edmund the elder, East Winch, N., gent.	690 Calton
1844	Kent, Henry senior, St Peter Mancroft, Norwich, N., shoemaker	388 Ebbage
1833	Kent, James, Thorndon, S., farmer	491 Cubitt
1828	Kent, John, Morningthorpe, N., farmer	197 Farrow
1857	Kent, John, Dallinghoo, S., farmer	716 Youngs.
1837	Kent, Mary, North Walsham, N.	513 Warren
1851	Kent, Mary Ann, Pakefield, S., spinster	63 Friar
1857	Kent, Naomi, Thornham Magna, S., spinster	561 Youngs
1855	Kent, Robert, Rattlesden, S., farmer	234 Whitty
1849	Kent, Thomas, St Gregorys, Norwich, N., gent.	446 Womack
1853	Kent, Thomas, Metfield, S.	295 Veale
1842	Kent, William, Syleham, S., farmer	328 Canler

1850	Kent, William, Hoxne, S.	574 Cuthbert
1828	Kerridge, Hannah, Bramford, S., wife of Daniel Kerridge the elder, merchant	219 Farrow
1829	Kerridge, John, Palgrave, S., yeoman	412 Green
1846	Kerridge, John, Norwich, N., yeoman	233 Baret
1855	Kerridge, Samuel, Hinderclay, S., farmer	161 Whitty
1835	Kerrison, Adam, Great Snoring, N., millwright	190 Harrowing
1845	Kerrison, James, Norwich, N., hairdresser	877 Pedgrift
1852	Kerrison, John, Pulham St Mary Magdalen, N., farmer	30 Latten
1830	Kerrison, Richard, North Elmham, N., blacksmith and farmer	96 Pettingill
1829	Kerrison, Roger, Panxworth, N., farmer	39 Green
1834	Kerry, George, Black Swan Inn, Horsham St Faiths, N.	116 Lane
1833	Kerry, James, Denham, S., farmer	518 Cubitt
1856	Kerry, Jeremiah, Haughley, S., gent.	499 Code
1823	Kerry, Joseph, Diss, N., yeoman	278 Tann
1825	Kerry, Richard, Eye, S., draper and tailor	80 Hayward
1821	Kersey, Abraham, Mulbarton, N., farmer	235 Dewell
1851	Kersey, Aldis, Lowestoft, S., baker	328 Friar
1833	Kersey, Frances, Debenham, S., spinster	282 Cubitt
1856	Kersey, Henry Pells, Old Newton, S., farmer	491 Code
1838	Kersey, John, Intwood, N.	107 Skepper
1848	Kersey, Joseph, Eye, S., formerly of Norwich, N., gent.	783 Denny
1849	Kersey, Joseph, Eye, S., gent.	282 Womack
1834	Kersey, Thomas the elder, Charsfield, S., farmer	60 Lane
1839	Kersey, Thomas, Great Glenham, S., farmer	517 Calton
1855	Kersey, Thomas Clarke, Stowmarket, S., watchmaker	384 Whitty
1829	Kett, Edward, Norwich, N., butcher	219 Green
1845	Kett, Hannah, Seething, N., widow	597 Pedgrift
1846	Kett, John, Bedingham, N., yeoman	8 Baret
1837	Kett, Mary, Bungay, S., spinster	150 Warren
1833	Kett, Michael, Lock and Key Yard, Ber St, Norwich, yeoman	264 Cubitt
1841	Kett, Robert, Norwich, N., yeoman	207 Traxton
1836	Kett, Sarah, Huntingfield, S., widow	388 Smith
1833	Kett, William, Shottisham, S., clerk	105 Cubitt
1820	Ketteridge, Susanna, Lowestoft, S., wife of John Ketteridge, mariner and pilot	222 Mack
1834	Kettle, James, Norwich, N., mahogany merchant	5 Lane
1840	Kettle, James, Northwold, N., innkeeper	672 Turner
1852	Kettle, Joseph, Caister next Great Yarmouth, N., farmer	249 Latten
1856	Kettle, John, Caister next Great Yarmouth, N., farmer	626 Code
1841	Kew, Flora, Norwich, N., widow	360 Traxton
1833	Key, Robert, Norwich, N., cooper	236 Cubitt
1853	Key, Robert, Great Yarmouth, N.	56 Veale
1849	Kidall, Ellen, Swaffham, N., widow	O.W. 300
1855	Kidd, John Richard, Norwich, N., dyer	611 Whitty
1853	Kiddell, James, Heydon, N., farmer	133 Veale
1857	Kiddell, Henry, Corpusty, N., farmer	60 Youngs
1854	Kiddell, William, Heydon, N., farmer	364 Day
1855	Kiddle, James, Kenninghall, N., carpenter	441 Whitty
1843	Kidman, William, Great Yarmouth, N., corn factor	705 Miles
1826	Kilbourn, Simon, Stanstead, S., blacksmith	36 Davy
1844	Killett, Elizabeth, Norwich, N., widow	697 Ebbage
1831	Killett, John, Beccles, S., gent.	432 Hart
1820	Killett, William, Bradwell, S., gent.	184 Mack
1852	Killigrew, Frances, Heigham, Norwich, N.	621 Latten
1839	Killingworth, Anthony the elder, Feltwell, N., yeoman	335 Calton
1848	Kindred, Betsy, Theberton, S., widow	260 Denny
1847	Kindred, Elizabeth, Woodbridge, S., spinster	453 Broom
1838	Kindred, Laura, Marlesford, S.	769 Skepper
1827	King, Abraham, Chelmondiston, S., cordwainer	107 Wood
1821	King, Allen, North Tuddenham, N., gent.	299 Dewell
1833	King, Ann, Methwold, N.	509 Cubitt
1836	King, Bett, Ipswich, S., widow	420 Smith

1820	King, Charles, Cringleford, N., miller	169 Mack
1842	King, Charles, Coltishall, N., innkeeper	16 Canler
1822	King, Elizabeth, Methwold, N., wife of Thomas King, farmer	106 Sadler
1827	King, Elizabeth, Holt, N., widow	296 Wood
1827	King, Elizabeth, Melford, S., widow	569 Wood
1824	King, George, Ditchingham, N., yeoman	170 Borrett
1829	King, George the elder, Pulham St Mary Magdalen, N., farrier and farmer	504 Green
1850	King, George, Geldeston, N., innkeeper	376 Cuthbert
1824	King, James, Tottenhill, N., farmer	302 Borrett
1831	King, James, Great Yarmouth, N., victualler	224 Hart
1834	King, James, Roydon, N., cordwainer	541 Lane
1838	King, James, Wenhaston, S., farmer	275 Skepper
1840	King, James, Fordham, C., plumber and glazier	454 Turner
1842	King, James, Glemsford, S., draper	714 Canler
1848	King, James, Caister St Edmund, N., yeoman	120 Denny
1851	King, James Gobbett, Gorleston, S., mariner	400 Friar
1835	King, John, Baconsthorpe, N.	204 Harrowing
1837	King, John, Preston St Marys, S., farmer	126 Warren
1831	King, Lydia, Halesworth, S., spinster	499 Hart
1837	King, Martha, Sudbury, S., widow	366 Warren
1833	King, Mary, Southwold, S., spinster	500 Cubitt
1839	King, Mary, Great Yarmouth, N., widow	86 Calton
1839	King, Mary, Pulham St Mary Magdalen, N., widow	190 Calton
1843	King, Mary, Halesworth, S., widow	697 Miles
1851	King, Mary, Great Yarmouth, N., spinster	408 Friar
1833	King, Robert, Methwold, N., miller and farmer	49 Cubitt
1843	King, Robert junior, Horning, N.	686 Miles
1820	King, Samuel, Norwich, N., gent.	576 Mack
1852	King, Samuel the elder, St Michaels South Elmham, S., yeoman	651 Latten
1848	King, Susan, Hilborough, N., widow	317 Denny
1833	King, Thomas, Wretton, N., farmer	351 Cubitt
1843	King, Thomas, Weston, S., farmer	415 Miles
1850	King, Thomas, Norwich, N., gent.	609 Cuthbert
1820	King, William, Methwold, N., farmer	396 Mack
1822	King, William, Ingham, N., yeoman	386 Sadler
1834	King, William, Swanton Morley, N., husbandman	503 Lane
1848	King, William, St Giles, Norwich, N., builder	561 Denny
1851	King, William, Wangford, S., victualler	545 Friar
1843	Kingaby, Samuel, Norwich, N., bricklayer	90 Miles
1822	Kinghorn, David, Norwich, N., minister of the Gospel	121 Sadler
1830	Kingsbury, alias Hammond, Hester, Bungay, S., widow	387 Pettingill
1827	Kingsbury, Judith, Caister next Yarmouth, N.	95 Wood
1824	Kingsbury, Susan, Ipswich, S., widow	246 Borrett
1843	Kinnell, John, Framlingham, S., surgeon	212 Miles
1821	Kinney, Mary, Coddenham, S.	32 Dewell
1828	Kirby, Sarah, Barham, S., wife of William Kirby, clerk	153 Farrow
1828	Kirk, William, Catfield, N., labourer	490 Farrow
1819	Kitson, Joseph, Sudbury, late of Nayland, S., farmer	117 Le Neve
1838	Kitteringham, Michael, Hoe next East Dereham, farmer	399 Skepper
1844	Kitton, Edward, Ringstead, N., farmer	603 Ebbage
1838	Knapp, John, Gorleston, S., wheelwright	461 Skepper
1848	Knapp, Sargeant, Bildeston, S., farmer	307 Denny
1832	Knevett, Elizabeth, Eye, S., widow	344 Cooke
1823	Knevett, Henry, Stradbroke, S., clerk	91 Tann
1853	Knight, William, Brooke, N.	708 Veale
1851	Knights, Anne, Great Yarmouth, N., widow	334 Friar
1828	Knights, Daniel, Pulham St Mary the Virgin, N., farmer	176 Farrow
1852	Knights, Daniel Thomas, Ditchingham, N., shopkeeper	485 Latten
1845	Knights, David, Rushall, N., farmer	100 Pedgrift
1824	Knights, Elizabeth, Pulham St Mary the Virgin, N., wife of David Knights, farmer	338 Borrett
1844	Knights, Francis, Cransford, S., shopkeeper and miller	571 Ebbage

1853	Knights, Henry, Forncett St Peter, N., miller and farmer	315 Veale
1820	Knights, James, Great Thornham, S., yeoman	259 Mack
1848	Knights, James, St Lawrence Ilketshall, S., farmer	343 Denny
1829	Knights, John, Norwich, N., tailor	236 Green
1851	Knights, John, Kelsale, S., farmer	535 Friar
1845	Knights, Robert, Scottow, N., yeoman	368 Pedgrift
1853	Knights, Robert, Seething, N., farmer	211 Veale
1832	Knights, Susan, Pulham St Mary Magdalen, N.	5 Cooke
1828	Knights, Susannah, Pulham St Mary Magdalen, N., wife of Thomas Knights, farmer	136 Farrow
1843	Knopwood, Elizabeth, Saham Toney, N., wife of Robert Knopwood, yeoman	299 Miles
1843	Knowles, Hannah, Great Yarmouth, N., widow	481 Miles
1849	Knowles, Henry, Great Yarmouth, N., mast and block maker	452 Womack
1838	Knowles, John, Diss, N., yeoman	182 Skepper
1837	Knowles, Richard, Great Yarmouth, N., lawyer	559 Warren
1819	Kurby, Job, Great Yarmouth, N., yeoman	137 Le Neve
1856	Kybird, Robert, Old Buckenham, N., wheelwright	572 Code
1838	Laccohee, John, Norwich, N., weaver	9 Skepper
1845	Lacey, Elizabeth, Great Yarmouth, N., widow	673 Pedgrift
1829	Lacey, Esaw, Stalham, N., bricklayer	673 Calton
1841	Lacey, James, Westwick, N., farmer	195 Traxton
1820	Lacey, John, Trunch, N., schoolmaster	246 Mack
1828	Lacey, John, Ludham, N., harness maker	135 Farrow
1832	Lacey, John Smith, Great Yarmouth, N., fish curer	342 Cooke
1832	Lacey, John, Stalham, N.	257 Cooke
1842	Lacey, Mary, North Elmham, N., wife of Richard Lacey, bricklayer	541 Canler
1843	Lacey, Richard, North Elmham, N., builder	334 Miles
1840	Lack, Charles, Holkham, N., butcher	248 Turner
1828	Lack, George, South Creake, N., thatcher	110 Farrow
1824	Lack, John, Holkham, N., cordwainer	118 Borrett
1848	Lack, John, Gaywood, N.	158 Denny
1852	Lack, John, South Creake, N., labourer	303 Latten
1838	Lack, Susan Woodrow, St Julian, Norwich, N., widow	73 Skepper
1851	Lack, William Rust, Ingham, N., farmer	163 Friar
1825	Lackford, Sarah, Bawdsey, S., widow	380 Hayward
1830	Lacon, Sarah, Great Yarmouth, N., widow	15 Pettingill
1839	Lacy, John, Little Plumstead, N., brickmaker	604 Calton
1854	Lacey, Robert, Colby, N., farmer	564 Day
1839	Ladbrooke, John, Colney, N., farmer	410 Calton
1825	Ladell, Margaret, Mileham, N., widow	307 Hayward
1823	Ladell, Sarah, Norwich, widow	40 Tann
1832	Ladell, William, Oulton, N., farmer	612 Cooke
1838	Laflin, Joseph, Thorpe, Norwich, N., gent.	703 Skepper
1854	Laflin, Philip, Ringshall, S., farmer and carpenter	470 Day
1849	Lainchbury, Phoebe, Kings Lynn, N., widow	90 Womack
1847	Laird, Benjamin, Kings Lynn, N., baker	65 Broom
1838	Lait, Charles, Eaton, Norwich, N., turner and gardener	140 Skepper
1839	Lake, Ann, Letheringsett, N., widow	241 Calton
1836	Lake, James, Letheringsett, N., yeoman	294 Smith
1841	Lake, John, Mendlesham, S., farmer	16 Traxton
1856	Lake, John, Holt, N., cordwainer	35 Code
1855	Lake, Shadrach, Lingwood, N., labourer	341 Whitty
1851	Lake, Susan, Hindringham, N.	376 Friar
1822	Lake, Thomas, St Margarets, Westminster	O.W. 171
1829	Lake, William, Framingham Pigot, N., butcher	63 Green
1830	Lake, William, Watton, N., bricklayer	419 Pettingill
1853	Lamb, Charles, Norwich, N., butcher	104 Veale
1837	Lamb, Elizabeth, St Peter Permountergate, Norwich, N., widow	92 Warren
1839	Lamb, Frederic, Loddon, N., farmer and wool dealer	348 Calton
1845	Lamb, James, Great Yarmouth, N., watchmaker	582 Pedgrift
1855	Lamb, Tamason, Great Yarmouth, N., widow	642 Whitty

1848	Lambard, James, Rushmere, S., labourer	480 Denny
1835	Lambert, Amy, Feltwell, N., wife of William Lambert, farmer	331 Harrowing
1853	Lambert, Charles, Alderton, S., labourer	220 Veale
1831	Lambert, Daniel, Hockwold cum Wilton, N., carpenter	87 Hart
1842	Lambert, Francis, Gooderstone, N., yeoman	637 Canler
1847	Lambert, Joseph, Banningham, N., boot and shoe maker	319 Broom
1842	Lambert, Mary, Hanworth, N., wife of Richard Lambert, cordwainer	12 Canler
1852	Lambert, Matthew, Wenhaston, S., labourer	449 Latten
1826	Lambert, Robert, Norwich, N., gardener	144 Davy
1848	Lambert, Thomas the elder, Happisburgh, N.	478 Denny
1853	Lambert, William, Swilland, S., shoemaker	633 Veale
1847	Lambress, John, Mutford, S., yeoman	706 Broom
1823	Lancaster, John, Swaffham, N., blacksmith	146 Tann
1847	Lancaster, John, St Giles, Norwich, N., brush maker	396 Broom
1838	Lanchester, Anna Maria, Long Melford, S.	284 Skepper
1834	Lanchester, Thomas, Knettishall, S., gent.	392 Lane
1834	Land, John, Boughton, N., gent.	660 Lane
1837	Land, John, Beccles, S., yeoman	514 Warren
1845	Land, Joseph, Harleston, N., glover	370 Pedgrift
1825	Land, Mary, Orford, S., widow	289 Hayward
1841	Land, Mary, Long Stratton, N., widow	122 Traxton
1831	Land, Sarah, Pulham St Mary the Virgin, N., spinster	123 Hart
1853	Land, Seth the elder, Blo Norton, N., farmer	440 Veale
1820	Land, Susanna, wife of John Land of Boughton, N., gent	9 Mack
1830	Land, William, Blo Norton, N., farmer	246 Pettingill
1838	Land, William, Tivetshall St Margaret, N., formerly of Pulham St Mary, yeoman	378 Skepper
1840	Land, William Loveck, Blo Norton, N., farmer	401 Turner
1854	Lane, Elizabeth, Great Yarmouth, N., widow	540 Day
1820	Lane, Groom, North Walsham, N., butcher	56 Mack
1855	Lane, Groom, North Walsham, N., currier	698 Whitty
1823	Lane, James, Wreningham, N., farmer	350 Tann
1834	Lane, James, St Swithins, Norwich, N.	1 Lane
1835	Lane, James, Hempton, N., innkeeper	267 Harrowing
1819	Lane, John, Heigham next Norwich, worstead weaver	305 Le Neve
1822	Lane, Michael, North Creake, N., gardener	188 Sadler
1827	Lane, Nicholas, All Saints, Norwich, N., woolcomber	106 Wood
1855	Lane, Richard, Norwich, N., chairmaker	443 Whitty
1837	Lane, Robert the elder, Norwich, N., cabinet maker	38 Warren
1844	Lane, Rosamund, Wymondham, N., spinster	122 Ebbage
1845	Lane, William, Colton, N., yeoman	395 Pedgrift
1853	Langham, William, Neatishead, N., yeoman	498 Veale
1820	Langin, James, private in sixth regiment of dragoons, called Inniskilings	53 Mack
1843	Langley, Susanna, Snettisham, N., widow	92 Miles
1837	Langton, Anne, Wells next the Sea, N., wife of Rev. Augustus Wenman Langton	105 Warren
1841	Langton, George Thomas, St Helier, Jersey	646 Traxton
1834	Lanham, Susan, Bredfield, S., single woman	222 Lane
1848	Lanman, Francis, Mickfield, S., farmer	670 Denny
1832	Lanman, John, Little Stonham, S., farmer	500 Cooke
1856	Lansdell. Isaac, Winfarthing, N., blacksmith	515 Code
1834	Lansdell, Richard, Flordon, N., blacksmith	245 Lane
1852	Lantaff, Mary, Kings Lynn, N., spinster	308 Latten
1854	Lantaff, Sophia, Kings Lynn, N., spinster	549 Day
1828	Large, Frances, Beeston by Mileham, N., widow	162 Farrow
1837	Large, Isaac, Outwell, N., farmer	417 Warren
1857	Large, Thomas, Stanfield, N., farmer	162 Youngs
1823	Large, William, Heacham, N., cordwainer	55 Tann
1844	Lark, Henry, Beccles, S., painter and glazier	454 Ebbage
1833	Lark, James, Great Yarmouth, N., house carpenter	399 Cubitt
1846	Lark, William, Gisleham, S., farmer	48 Baret

1857	Larke, Elizabeth May, Brooke, N., widow	489 Youngs
1833	Larke, Henry the elder, Beccles, S., yeoman	88 Cubitt
1832	Larke, William, Happisburgh, N., labourer	401 Cooke
1831	Larkman,James, Herringfleet, S., farmer	182 Hart
1831	Larner, Frances, Stoke Ferry, N., spinster	26 Hart
1848	Larner, John, East Dereham, N., maltster and bricklayer	617 Denny
1832	Larner, Robert, Lakenham, N., maltster	109 Cooke
1833	Larstone, John, Ormesby St Michael, N., husbandman	119 Cubitt
1855	Larter, Bridget, Botesdale, S., widow	84 Whitty
1843	Larter, Jemima, Fressingfield, S., wife of John Larter, farmer	720 Miles
1835	Larter, John, Fressingfield, S., farmer	517 Harrowing
1854	Larter, John, Walsham Le Willows, S., innkeeper	555 Day
1840	Larter, Thomas the elder, Weybread, S., alehouse keeper	205 Turner
1842	Larter, William, Sutton, S., hawker	651 Canler
1851	Laskey, John, Carleton Forehoe, N., labourer	129 Friar
1857	Laskey, Joseph, Hethersett, N., gardener	635 Youngs
1819	Last, Ann, Rumburgh, S., widow	209 Le Neve
1855	Last, Ann, Old Buckenham, N., spinster	405 Whitty
1855	Last, Edward, Beccles, S., yeoman	309 Whitty
1842	Last, Isaac, Occold, S., farmer	25 Canler
1828	Last, John, Newmarket, C., miller and baker	380 Farrow
1851	Last, John, Newmarket, S.	Index only
1853	Last, John, Aldeby, N., farmer	194 Veale
1820	Last, Mary, Otley, S., widow	491 Mack
1847	Last, William Hayward, Great Yarmouth, N., gent	135 Broom
1857	Last, William, Burgh St Peter, N., yeoman	769 Youngs
1852	Latten, Robert James, Kings Lynn, N., watch maker	1 Latten
1842	Laurence, Fanny, Stowmarket, S., widow	221 Canler
1823	Law, John, Stowupland, S., miller	293 Tann
1829	Lawes, John, Briston, N., gent	107 Green
1831	Lawne, Samuel, Thurlton, N., husbandman	266 Hart
1838	Lawrance, James, Melford, S., innkeeper	77 Skepper
1854	Lawrence, Alfred, Combs, S., currier	221Day
1828	Lawrence, James, Loddon, N., innkeeper	525 Farrow
1843	Lawrence, Joseph, Kings Lynn, N., gent.	528 Miles
1839	Lawrence, William, Wiveton, N., yeoman	472 Calton
1825	Laws, John, Crimplesham, N., labourer	483 Hayward
1853	Laws, John, Southwold, S., master mariner	471 Veale
1848	Lawter, Robert, Norwich, N., gent.	838 Denny
1832	Lay, Elizabeth, Snettisham, N., widow	520 Cooke
1847	Lay, Henry, Wangford, N.	O.W. 317
1845	Lay, John, Peasenhall, N., farmer and merchant	Index only
1820	Layton, Charles, Surlingham, N., innkeeper	391 Mack
1828	Layton, Frances, Surlingham, N., widow	303 Farrow
1847	Layton, Henry, Southtown, Yarmouth, S., gent.	625 Broom
1829	Leach, John, Upend, Kirtling, C., yeoman	497 Green
1854	Leach, Robert, South Lynn, N., innkeeper	424 Day
1835	Leach, Sarah, Foulden, N., widow	499 Harrowing
1834	Leach, William, St Stephens, Norwich, N., gent.	212 Lane
1820	Leader, Lucy, Lammas, N., widow	65 Mack
1822	Leak, Benjamin the elder, Shipden, Cromer, N.	390 Sadler
1832	Leak, Thomas Emery, Cromer, N., bootmaker	249 Cooke
1830	Leaman, Philip, Foulsham, N., gent.	456 Pettingill
1846	Leatherdale, James, Kelsale, S., yeoman	534 Baret
1834	Leatherdale, Susan, Alburgh, N., spinster	369 Lane
1840	Leatherdale, William, Reydon, S., farmer	365 Turner
1853	Leathes, Harriett Elizabeth, Herringfleet Hall, S., spinster	163 Veale
1831	Leathes, Sarah, Shropham Hall, N., formerly of Roydon, wife of George Reading Leathes, clerk	325 Hart
1831	Leaurence, William the elder, Alby, N., labourer	471 Hart
1841	Lee, Caroline, Wangford, S.	215 Traxton
1832	Lee, George, Barnby, S., yeoman	38 Cooke

1845	Lee, James, Hindringham, N., farmer	15 Pedgrift
1827	Lee, John, Paston, N., husbandman	316 Wood
1849	Lee, John, Cley next the Sea, N., merchant	126 Womack
1838	Leech, Aaron, Redgrave, S., innkeeper	806 Skepper
1848	Leech, Sarah, Methwold, N., spinster	613 Denny
1838	Leech, William, Kings Lynn, N., bricklayer	244 Skepper
1844	Leeder, George, Redenhall with Harleston, N., labourer	584 Ebbage
1836	Leeder, John, Carbrooke, N.	535 Smith
1844	Leeder, Robert, Little Walsingham, N., whitesmith	277 Ebbage
1850	Leeder, Robert the elder, Rockland All Saints, N., horse dealer	134 Cuthbert
1845	Leeder, Simon, Sheringham, N., gamekeeper	535 Pedgrift
1854	Leeder, Thomas, Deopham, N., farmer	4 Day
1845	Leeds, Ann, Hackford next Reepham, N., innkeeper	472 Pedgrift
1830	Leeds, Charles, St Stephens, Norwich, N., yeoman	3 Pettingill
1838	Leeds, Clement, Hackford next Reepham, N., cordwainer	453 Skepper
1855	Leeds, Edward Fisher, North Barsham, N., gent.	636 Whitty
1833	Leeds, Gibbs, Norwich, N., wire worker	217 Cubitt
1821	Leeds, Henrietta, Great Walsingham, N., widow	115 Dewell
1842	Leeds, James, Gressenhall, N., labourer	85 Canler
1838	Leeds, Jeremiah, otherwise Boome Gardiner, Coltishall, N., grocer, draper and shopkeeper	433 Skepper
1840	Leeds, John, Burnham Thorpe, N., farmer	473 Turner
1853	Leeds, Mary, Foulsham, N., spinster	431 Veale
1837	Leeds, Sarah, Norwich, N., spinster	358 Warren
1834	Leeds, Stephen senior, Hackford next Reepham, N., cordwainer	484 Lane
1831	Leeds, William, Whitwell, N., gent.	278 Hart
1847	Leeds, William Eldridge, Norwich, N., yeoman	615 Broom
1830	Leek, Spencer, Woodbridge, S., basket maker	170 Pettingill
1844	Leftley, Sophia, Needham, N., widow	524 Ebbage
1836	Legg, William, Spixworth, N., gent.	186 Smith
1840	Leggatt, Benjamin, Ringland, N., gent.	479 Turner
1846	Leggatt, John, Woodbridge, S., carpenter	225 Baret
1836	Leggatt, William, Dunston, N., yeoman	183 Smith
1841	Leggatt, William, Ringland, N., farmer	371 Traxton
1841	Leggett, Charles, Gorleston, S., pilot	500 Traxton
1846	Leggett, Charles, Gorleston, S.	Index only
1834	Leggett, Faith, Wells, N., wife of Samuel Leggett, baker	677 Lane
1853	Leggett, James, Wenhaston, S., yeoman	358 Veale
1822	Leggett, John, Witton, N., yeoman	432 Sadler
1841	Leggett, Mary, Witton, N., widow	235 Traxton
1855	Leggett, Samuel, Heigham, Norwich, N., publican	497 Whitty
1855	Leggett, Thomas, Kirtley next Lowestoft, S., gent.	434 Whitty
1857	Leggett, Thomas, Little Glenham, S., wheelwright	484 Youngs
1827	Leggett, William, Little Glenham, S., wheelwright	376 Wood
1842	Leggett, William, Saxtead, S., farmer	450 Canler
1847	Legood, Elizabeth, Hedenham, N widow	180 Broom
1840	Legood, James, North Walsham, N., gent.	539 Turner
1844	Legood, Robert, Earsham, N., yeoman	2 Ebbage
1844	Legood, Samuel, Woodton, N., innkeeper	361 Ebbage
1838	Legood, William, Aylsham, N., formerly of Bethnal Green, Middsx., carpenter and joiner	335 Skepper
1855	Le Grice, see under Grice	719 Whitty
1835	Le Grys, Thomas, East Harling, N., yeoman	323 Harrowing
1835	Leist, Amy, South Walsham, N., spinster	601 Harrowing
1842	Leist, Edward, Ingham, N., farmer	59 Canler
1839	Leist, John, Rackheath, N., farmer	507 Calton
1835	Leman, Barnabas, Norwich, N., esquire, alderman of Norwich	386 Harrowing
1857	Leman, Barnabas, Carleton Colville, S., farmer	151 Youngs
1843	Leman, Elizabeth Mary Argill, Brampton, S., spinster	200 Miles
1843	Leman, Henrietta Jane Argill, Brampton, S., widow	221 Miles
1832	Leman, Henry, Terrington, N., butcher	25 Cooke

1821	Leman, John, Glandford, N., farmer	184 Dewell
1825	Leman, Maria, Hoxne, S.	214 Hayward
1840	Leman, Robert, Stoke Holy Cross, N., yeoman	483 Turner
1852	Lemmon, Elizabeth, Norwich, N., widow	469 Latten
1851	Lemmon, John, Hockham, N., wheelwright	354 Friar
1855	Lemmon, William, Calthorpe, N., yeoman	649 Whitty
1854	Lemon, Elisha, Fressingfield, S., dealer	273 Day
1838	Lemon, George William, Downham Market, N., grocer and draper	121 Skepper
1841	Lemon, William the elder, Loddon, N., general shopkeeper	44 Traxton
1819	Le Neve, Charles, North Walsham, N., farmer	1 Le Neve
1852	Le Neve, Charles, Suffield, farmer and beast and sheep salesman	O.W. 358
1836	Le Neve, William, North Walsham, N., baker	465 Smith
1840	Lenney, James, Brundish, S., gent.	580 Turner
1836	Lenney, William, Wilby, S., gent.	555 Smith
1820	Lenny, Deborah, Redenhall with Harleston, N., widow	375 Mack
1826	Lenny, Simon Grimsby, Worlingham, S., farmer	276 Davy
1821	Leo, Susanna, Gayton, N., widow	201 Dewell
1845	Le Pla, Samuel, Upwell, C., farmer	232 Pedgrift
1845	Lester, Anne Emma, Alpington, N., widow	559 Pedgrift
1850	Le Strange, Susannah, Southwold, S., widow	568 Cuthbert
1849	Lettis, Elizabeth, Great Yarmouth, N., widow	163 Womack
1825	Lettis, John, Great Yarmouth, N., rope maker	410 Hayward
1848	Levell, Sarah, Pulham St Mary Magdalen, N., wife of Thomas Levell, yeoman	401 Denny
1848	Leveredge, Thomas, East Dereham, N., farmer	345 Denny
1842	Leverett, Charles, Syderstone, N., blacksmith	383 Canler
1839	Leverington, Elizabeth, All Saints, Norwich, N.	303 Calton
1853	Levett, William, Woodbridge, S., master mariner	421 Veale
1820	Levick, Henry, Flordon, N., farmer	430 Mack
1832	Lewell, Thomas, Carlton Rode, N., farmer	267 Cooke
1839	Lewes, James, Ipswich, S., yeoman	649 Calton
1820	Lewis, Edward, Shadingfield, S., woodman	463 Mack
1847	Libbis, John, Southtown, Yarmouth, S., gent., o.w. missing	343 Broom
1838	Licence, Nathaniel the elder, Wickham Market, S., linen weaver	300 Skepper
1836	Licence, William, Garboldisham, N., innkeeper	314 Smith
1827	Liffen, Robert, Beccles, S., yeoman	470 Wood
1820	Lighton, Ann, Catton, N., wife of James Lighton, cordwainer	349 Mack
1837	Lighton, James, St Clement, Norwich, N., cordwainer	586 Warren
1835	Limberd, John, Norwich, N., worstead weaver	513 Harrowing
1852	Limberd, Mary, St Simon and St Jude, Norwich, N., widow	334 Latten
1848	Limmer, James Hovell, Roudham, N., gent.	753 Denny
1827	Limmer, John, Old Buckenham, N., yeoman	184 Wood
1819	Lincoln, Amos, Pakefield, S., bricklayer	86 Le Neve
1855	Lincoln, Hackard, Thetford, N., yeoman	94 Whitty
1827	Lincoln, James, Linstead Parva, S., gent.	585 Wood
1836	Lincoln, James, Runham, N., yeoman	164 Smith
1846	Lincoln, Jeremiah, Fundenhall, N., well sinker	346 Baret
1825	Lincoln, John, Norwich, N., gent.	64 Hayward
1834	Lincoln, John, Pulham St Mary the Virgin, N., labourer	48 Lane
1848	Lincoln, John Salter, Lowestoft, S., gent.	605 Denny
1855	Lincoln, John, Great Yarmouth, N., merchant	709 Whitty
1843	Lincoln, Mary, Rushmere, S, widow	279 Miles
1831	Lincoln, Robert, Rushmere, S., gent.	338 Hart
1856	Lincoln, Sabina, St Ethelred, Norwich, N.	149 Code
1838	Lincoln, Tabitha, Long Stratton, N., widow	49 Skepper
1829	Lincoln, William, Lowestoft, S., fish curer	208 Green
1843	Lincoln, William, Scoulton, N., farmer	499 Miles
1846	Lincoln, William, Lowestoft, S., merchant	676 Baret
1850	Lincoln, William Allen, Lowestoft, S., mariner	378 Cuthbert
1853	Lincoln, Zachariah, Cookley, S., farmer	545 Veale
1851	Linder, Samuel Homer, Great Yarmouth, N., gent.	465 Friar

1854	Lindsey, Thomas the elder, Lowestoft, S., superannuated Trinity pilot	482 Day
1825	Lindsey, William, Mattishall, N., farmer	114 Hayward
1831	Linehan, Rebecca, Great Yarmouth, N., widow	192 Hart
1834	Lines, John, Reedham, N., grocer and baker	168 Lane
1847	Lines, John, Wetheringsett, S., farmer	156 Broom
1853	Lines, John, Diss, N., ironmonger	165 Veale
1831	Lines, Joseph, Ellingham, N., yeoman	423 Hart
1835	Lines, William, Thorpe Parva, N., yeoman	61 Harrowing
1827	Linford, Hannah, Salhouse, N., widow	565 Wood
1844	Linford, Richard, Norwich, N., innkeeper	488 Ebbage
1852	Linford, William, Norwich, N., carpenter	376 Latten
1831	Ling, Charles, Norwich, N., coal merchant	158 Hart
1834	Ling, Elizabeth, Norwich, N., wife of Charles Ling, coal merchant	310 Lane
1837	Ling, Frances, Framlingham, S., widow	238 Warren
1853	Ling, Hannah, Gunton, S., spinster	350 Veale
1826	Ling, Henry, Bildeston, S., formerly of Hoveringham Nottingham, yeoman	167 Davy
1837	Ling, Jacob the elder, St Margarets Ilketshall, S., farmer	411 Cubitt
1826	Ling, John, St Andrews, Norwich, N.	147 Davy
1840	Ling, William, Weston, S., husbandman and sexton	394 Turner
1847	Ling, William Senior, Norwich, N., bricklayer	412 Broom
1834	Linge, John, Thetford, N., yeoman	276 Lane
1839	Linhen, Samuel Michael, Great Yarmouth, N., baker	464 Calton
1842	Linstead, Ann, St Pauls, Norwich, N., widow	505 Canler
1829	Linstead, Henry, Norwich, N., butcher	529 Green
1826	Linstead, Randle, Kirton, S., husbandman	141 Davy
1843	Linwood, Isaac, Newmarket, S., bricklayer	399 Miles
1835	List, George, Great Yarmouth, N., mariner	220 Harrowing
1857	Lister, William, Norwich, N., cutler	765 Youngs
1835	Litsenburg, Warner, Ufford, S., labourer	605 Harrowing
1828	Little, William, Marham, N., victualler	108 Farrow
1855	Littleboy, Mary, Norwich, N., formerly of Stalham, wife of William Littleboy, farmer	635 Whitty
1825	Littlewood, Enoch, Beighton, N., yeoman	290 Hayward
1832	Littlewood, Mary, Hoveton St John, N., spinster	591 Cooke
1849	Littlewood, Sampson Mitchell, Salhouse, N., gent.	630 Womack
1852	Livock, Edmund, Irstead, N., labourer	186 Latten
1848	Livock, John, Winfarthing, N., harness maker	696 Denny
1827	Livock, Jonathan, Bracon Ash, N., tailor	143 Wood
1833	Lloyd, Elizabeth, Bawdeswell, N., widow	76 Cubitt
1842	Lloyd, Katherine, Bawdeswell, N., spinster	663 Canler
1845	Loads, James, North Walsham, N.	362 Pedgrift
1821	Loads, Sarah, Ludham, N., single woman	151 Dewell
1853	Lock, Daniel, Terrington St Clements, N., farmer	566 Veale
1844	Lock, Elizabeth, Palgrave, S., widow	332 Ebbage
1847	Lock, Elizabeth Metcalf, Norwich, N., spinster	84 Broom
1848	Lock, Elizabeth, Newmarket St Mary, S., widow	124 Denny
1844	Lock, Ezekiel, Haveringland, N., farmer	631 Ebbage
1820	Lock, Henry, Great Yarmouth, N., gardener	140 Mack
1842	Lock, James, Shelfanger, N., farmer	745 Canler
1850	Lock, John, Stowmarket, S., farmer	502 Cuthbert
1825	Lock, Joseph, Thelnetham, S., bricklayer	282 Hayward
1847	Lock, Joseph, Hinderclay, S., miller	598 Broom
1850	Lock, Nathan, Thorndon All Saints, S., miller	451 Cuthbert
1819	Lock, Nathaniel, Norwich, millwright	259 Le Neve
1830	Lock, Susanna, Bressingham, N., widow	131 Pettingill
1847	Lock, Thomas, Fritton, N., yeoman, formerly of Westwell, S.	258 Broom
1848	Lock, William, Pulham St Mary Magdalen, N., farmer	160 Denny
1839	Lockett, Margaret, Hainford, N., widow	614 Calton
1820	Lockett, Thomas, Kings Lynn, N., wine and spirit merchant	6 Mack
1823	Lockwood, Benjamin, Swaffham, N., watchmaker	27 Tann

1828	Lockwood, Edmund Coulson, Holton, S., nurseryman and seedsman	72 Farrow
1837	Lockwood, James, Rishangles, S., farmer	537 Warren
1823	Lockwood, Mary, Swaffham, N., wife of Benjamin Lockwood, watchmaker	337 Tann
1848	Lockwood, Rachel, Holton, S., widow	688 Denny
1819	Lockwood, Robert, Creeting St Mary, S., carpenter	28 Le Neve
1833	Lockwood, William, Beccles, S, bricklayer	213 Cubitt
1852	Loder, Edward, Woodbridge, S., principal of Seckfords hospital	388 Latten
1835	Loder, Elizabeth, Woodbridge, S., spinster	406 Harrowing
1821	Loder, Sarah, Woodbridge, S., widow	76 Dewell
1854	Lodge, John, Sisland, N., farmer	309 Day
1850	Lodge, Joseph the younger, Creeting St Peter, S., farmer	275 Cuthbert
1853	Lofty, Charles, Coltishall, N., butcher	231 Veale
1844	Lofty, William, Hethersett, N., farmer and butcher	221 Ebbage
1835	Logdon, John, Great Yarmouth, N., stone mason	37 Harrowing
1832	London, John, Norwich, N., wheelwright	113 Cooke
1835	London, William, Great Yarmouth, N., cordwainer	36 Harrowing
1848	Lone, James the elder, Great Yarmouth, N., gent.	370 Denny
1853	Long, Ann, Downham Market, N., widow	298 Veale
1837	Long, David, Ingham, N.	681 Warren
1856	Long, David, Dillington, N., gent.	14 Code
1851	Long, Edward, Downham Market, N., formerly of Stanhoe, N., farmer	293 Friar
1856	Long, Frances, Marham, N., spinster	464 Code
1840	Long, George, Spexhall, S., farmer	504 Turner
1849	Long, George, Lowestoft, S., carpenter	457 Womack
1833	Long, Henry, Stratton St Mary, N.	501 Cubitt
1845	Long, James, Metfield, N.	O.W. 407
1853	Long, James, Upwell, N., farmer	702 Veale
1824	Long, John, Besthorpe, N., farmer	151 Borrett
1840	Long, John, Hales, N., yeoman	493 Turner
1850	Long, John, Ingham, N., bricklayer	111 Cuthbert
1843	Long, Samuel, Antingham, N.	564 Miles
1819	Long, Sarah, Trimingham, N., widow	103 Le Neve
1831	Long, Stephen, Newton Flotman, N., farmer	290 Hart
1819	Long, Susanna, Tharston, N., spinster	181 Le Neve
1819	Long, William, Hoxne, S., husbandman	141 Le Neve
1832	Long, William, Hasketon, S., farmer	124 Cooke
1839	Long, William Filby, Diss, N., yeoman	460 Calton
1841	Long, William, Hindringham, N., blacksmith	163 Traxton
1836	Looes, William, Aldeburgh, S., gent.	378 Pettingill
1847	Looes, William, Hindringham, N., publican and farmer	178 Broom
1830	Loom, Elizabeth, Burgh, S., widow	407 Pettingill
1825	Loom, James, Burgh, S., farmer	180 Hayward
1832	Loombe, John, Kings Lynn, N., gent.	357 Cooke
1829	Loose, Isaac, Hunstanton, N., farmer	541 Green
1831	Loose, John, Holkham, N., yeoman	26 Hart
1837	Loose, Robert, Calthorpe, N., yeoman	626 Warren
1825	Lorke, Samuel, Hevingham, N., farmer	503 Hayward
1830	Lott, James, Washbrook, S., farmer	89 Pettingill
1819	Lott, Robert, Grundisburgh, S., common carrier	341 Le Neve
1821	Lound, William the elder, Salthouse, N., yeoman	11 Dewell
1820	Lovack, Sarah, Shropham, N., spinster	618 Mack
1839	Love, Ann, Burnham Westgate, N., widow	280 Calton
1842	Love, Daniel, Great Bittering, N., labourer	711 Canler
1853	Love, Sarah, Gressenhall cum Bittering, N., widow	680 Veale
1824	Love, Susanna Jane, Great Yarmouth, N., widow	28 Borrett
1851	Love, Thomas, North Walsham, N., yeoman	522 Friar
1855	Love, William, Swanton Morley, N., yeoman	164 Whitty
1852	Loveday, Richard, Blofield, N., yeoman	726 Latten
1855	Loveless, William Fulcher, Bressingham, N., blacksmith	232 Whitty

1845	Loveridge, Mary Ann, Norwich, N., formerly of Great Yarmouth, N., spinster	806 Pedgrift
1844	Lovett, Daniel, Wendling, N., farmer	512 Ebbage
1850	Lovett, Henry, Costessey, N., builder	362 Cuthbert
1843	Lovewell, Elizabeth, Southtown, Yarmouth, S., widow	592 Miles
1820	Lovewell, Isaac, Norwich, N., innkeeper	559 Mack
1824	Lovewell, James, Southtown, Little Yarmouth, S., shipbuilder	174 Borrett
1820	Lovick, Samuel, Horsham St Faiths, N., gent.	662 Mack
1831	Lovick, Thomas, Norwich, N., thatcher	59 Hart
1848	Lowden, John, Norwich, N., butcher	650 Denny
1845	Lowden, Joseph, Tilney St Lawrence, N., labourer	506 Pedgrift
1835	Lowden, Sarah, Heigham, Norwich, N., widow	423 Harrowing
1832	Lowdon, John, Heigham next Norwich, gent.	Index only
1851	Lowe, Henry, Great Yarmouth, N., bricklayer	370 Friar
1836	Lowe, Joseph, Kings Lynn, N., baker	42 Smith
1829	Lowe, William, Smallburgh, N.	319 Green
1837	Lown, Ann, Aylsham, N., widow	479 Warren
1820	Lowne, Isaac, St Augustine, Norwich, N.	632 Mack
1854	Lowne, William Charles, Norwich, N., master of the workhouse	286 Day
1838	Loynes, Joseph, Holt, N., blacksmith	457 Skepper
1852	Lubbock, Ann, Norwich, N., spinster	733 Latten
1853	Lubbock, Katherine, Kings Lynn, N., spinster	508 Veale
1852	Lubbock, Ursula, Great Yarmouth, N., widow	259 Latten
1838	Lubbock, Woolterton John, Blofield, N., miller	477 Skepper
1838	Lucas, Elizabeth, Kings Lynn, N., spinster	423 Skepper
1854	Lucas, John, Thetford, S., master of Thetford Union workhouse	419 Day
1829	Luckett, Thomas, Norwich, N., gent.	244 Green
1826	Lucock, Elizabeth, Orford, S.	21 Davy
1833	Ludbrook, John, Wenhaston, S.	452 Cubitt
1828	Ludkin, Henry, Bunwell, N., carpenter	475 Farrow
1840	Ludkin, Henry, Shropham, N., shoemaker	659 Turner
1847	Ludkin, John, Bunwell, N., farmer, formerly of Norwich, carpenter	142 Broom
1838	Lulman, Mary, East Dereham, N., widow	402 Skepper
1855	Lumber, James, Gorleston, S., gent.	337 Whitty
1825	Lumpkin, Nicholas, West Walton, N., farmer	262 Hayward
1853	Lund, William, Kings Lynn, N., formerly of Gaywood, yeoman	447 Veale
1849	Lunn, Elizabeth, South Lynn All Saints, Kings Lynn, N., widow	305 Womack
1822	Lunn, Robert, Kings Lynn, N., cordwainer	31 Sadler
1831	Lusher, Richard, East Wretham, N., labourer	551 Hart
1836	Lusher, Robert, Ashill, N., yeoman	534 Smith
1827	Lydamore, James, Beccles, S., innkeeper	673 Wood
1851	Lynes, William, Surlingham, N., wheelwright	139 Friar
1848	Lynn, Alice, Kings Lynn, N.	60 Denny
1852	Mabson, Frances, Toftmonks, N., spinster	173 Latten
1857	McCabe, Margaret, Gooderstone, N.widow	202 Youngs
1826	McCredie, William, Melton, S., gardener	152 Davy
1838	McDonald, Jane, Great Yarmouth, N., widow	310 Skepper
1824	Mace, Jacob, Haddiscoe, N., farmer	254 Borrett
1835	Mace, James, alias Clark, Bradwell, S., formerly of Gorleston, farmer	415 Harrowing
1854	Mace, Barnabas, Lyng, N.	170 Day
1839	Mace, William, Norwich, N., yeoman	114 Calton
1835	Mack, Ann, Norwich, N., widow	483 Harrowing
1830	Mack, Edward, North Tuddenham, N., farmer	42 Pettingill
1839	Mack, John, Brandeston, S., farm bailiff	81 Calton
1841	Mack, John, Tunstead, N., gent.	388 Traxton
1841	Mack, Martha, Burnham Norton, N., widow	624 Traxton
1820	Mack, Mary, Hickling, N., widow	1 Mack
1821	Mack, Mary, Tunstead, N., widow	84 Dewell
1850	Mack, Mary, Salthouse, N., spinster	608 Cuthbert
1837	Mack, Robert, Aylsham, N., yeoman	583 Warren

1842	Mack, Robert, Buxton, N., bricklayer	747 Canler
1824	Mack, Thomas, Swanton Morley, N., farmer	248 Borrett
1830	Mack, Thomas, Norwich, N., gent.	146 Pettingill
1838	Mack, Thomas, Thwaite, N., gent.	616 Skepper
1856	Mack, Thomas Bond, Baconsthorpe, N., farmer	229 Code
1839	Mack, William, Burnham Norton, N., farmer	177 Calton
1851	Mack, William, Metfield, S., clerk	141 Friar
1850	Mackenzie, Elizabeth, Kings Lynn, N., widow	572 Cuthbert
1832	Mackley, John Utting, Norwich, N., tailor	246 Cooke
1857	McPherson, Donald, Kings Lynn, N., gent.	731 Youngs
1835	Macro, Isaac, Tibbenham, N., parish clerk	365 Harrowing
1843	Macro, Isaac, Diss, N., gent.	418 Miles
1843	Maddis, William, Pakefield, S., gardener	517 Miles
1835	Maddison, Robert, Southwood, N., esqùire	135 Harrowing
1828	Maddle, William, Upton, N., farmer	328 Farrow
1837	Magnus, Richard, Wells, N., carpenter	427 Warren
1853	Magub, John the elder, Southwold, S., master at sea and ship owner	140 Veale
1835	Makemead, Robert, Marham, N., farmer	105 Harrowing
1821	Makens, Jeremiah, Gressenhall, N., yeoman	116 Dewell
1821	Makin, Henry, Somersham, S., grocer and draper	103 Dewell
1823	Makin, Sarah, Somersham, S., shopkeeper	306 Tann
1828	Makins, Robert, Ringshall, S., farmer	144 Farrow
1845	Malby, Elizabeth, Setchey, N., widow	296 Pedgrift
1857	Malden, Elizabeth, Soham, C., widow	344 Youngs
1833	Mallett, Elizabeth, St Peter Mancroft, Norwich	383 Cubitt
1851	Mallett, Elizabeth, Woodbridge, S., widow	282 Friar
1851	Mallett, Joshua, Neatishead, N., farmer	373 Friar
1819	Mallett, Nicholas, Norwich, N., shawl manufacturer	135 Le Neve
1849	Mallett, Peter, Limpenhoe, N., yeoman	354 Womack
1824	Mallett, Robert, Burlingham St Peter, N., husbandman	93 Borrett
1836	Mallett, Robert, Ashmanhaugh, N., farmer	98 Smith
1845	Mallett, Robert, Beetley, N., yeoman	559 Pedgrift
1839	Mallett, Thomas the elder, Kessingland, S., labourer	307 Calton
1851	Mallett, Thomas, Reedham, N., labourer	442 Friar
1825	Mallitt, Elizabeth, Stalham, N.	105 Hayward
1847	Mallows, John, Norwich, N., yeoman	585 Broom
1819	Mallows, Mary, Ashill, N., widow	131 Le Neve
1837	Malster, Stephen, Norwich, N., worstead weaver	612 Warren
1836	Malt, Jeffry, Brandon, S., yeoman	152 Smith
1845	Maltby, Sarah, Norwich, N., widow	660 Pedgrift
1820	Malyn, Reverend Robert, Eye, S., clerk	654 Mack
1837	Manby, Letitia, Horham, S., widow	535 Warren
1845	Manby, Matthew, Walsingham, N., esquire	92 Pedgrift
1831	Manby, Thomas, Horham, S., farmer	474 Hart
1833	Maning, Ann McKee, Lowestoft, S.	252 Cubitt
1819	Manlove, Mary, Great Yarmouth, N., widow	O.W. 184
1840	Mann, Ann, Thorpe next Norwich, N., spinster	640 Turner
1843	Mann, Ann, Norwich, N., widow	207 Miles
1850	Mann, Charlotte, Watton, N., widow	491 Cuthbert
1830	Mann, Christopher, St Lawrence, Norwich, N., gent.	255 Pettingill
1841	Mann, Edmund, Barney, N., cordwainer	36 Traxton
1832	Mann, Eleanor, Kings Lynn, N., widow	287 Cooke
1852	Mann, Elizabeth, Norwich, N., widow	164 Latten
1857	Mann, Hannah, North Walsham, N., formerly of Norwich, N., spinster	701 Youngs
1845	Mann, Job, St James South Elmham, S., shopkeeper	484 Pedgrift
1845	Mann, John, Shropham, N, gent.	538 Pedgrift
1851	Mann, John, St Michaels South Elmham, S., cordwainer	578 Friar
1824	Mann, alias Snitterly, Mary, Blakeney, N., widow	347 Borrett
1826	Mann, Mary, Thorpe Hamlet, Norwich, N., widow	168 Davy
1837	Mann, Mary, Soham, C., widow	295 Warren
1850	Mann, Mary, Soham, C., wife of James Mann, farmer	198 Cuthbert
1857	Mann, Mary, Kings Lynn, N., spinster	17 Youngs

1830	Mann, Michael, Norwich, N., gent.	395 Pettingill
1831	Mann, Robert, Norwich, N., watchmaker	215 Hart
1833	Mann, Robert, Fordham, C., bricklayer	388 Cubitt
1856	Mann, Sarah, North Tuddenham, N., widow	138 Code
1836	Mann, Susanna, Watton, N., widow	276 Smith
1828	Mann, Thomas, Plumstead, N., farmer	86 Farrow
1825	Manners, William, Norwich, N., yeoman, late of Great Yarmouth, N., mariner	465 Hayward
1832	Manning, Dinah, Hemsby, N., spinster	194 Cooke
1839	Manning, John, Eye, S., esquire	274 Calton
1830	Manning, Robert, Ashbocking, S.	145 Pettingill
1833	Manning, Robert, Castle Acre, N., carpenter	483 Cubitt
1824	Manning, William, Strumpshaw, N., carpenter	68 Borrett
1825	Manning, William, Ormesby St Michael, N., esquire	386 Hayward
1824	Mansbridge, James, Salthouse, N., gent, pensioner of Royal Train of Artillery	286 Borrett
1829	Manship, James, Blundeston, S., farmer	16 Calton
1831	Manship, Maria, Great Yarmouth, N., widow	444 Hart
1852	Manship, Richard, Ludham, N., farmer	120 Latten
1824	Manship, Robert, Hemsby, N., farmer	343 Borrett
1838	Manship, Thomas, Palling, N., mariner	329 Skepper
1847	Manship, William, Palling, N., fisherman	274 Broom
1851	Manthorpe, Samuel, Shottisham, S., innkeeper and farmer	396 Friar
1830	Mapelston, Francis, Aldeburgh, S., innkeeper	370 Pettingill
1840	Maplestone, Mary, Beccles, S., spinster	446 Turner
1827	March, Thomas, Southtown, Little Yarmouth, S., gent.	355 Wood
1849	Marcon, George Reginald, Swaffham, N., gent.	616 Womack
1851	Marfrey, Richard, Worstead, N., farmer	90 Friar
1835	Marfrey, Sherwood, Kirby Cane, N., farmer	159 Harrowing
1833	Margerom, Ann, Norwich, N., widow	405 Cubitt
1825	Margerom, Robert William, Norwich, N., cabinet maker	261 Hayward
1834	Margerom, Sarah, Norwich, N., spinster	365 Lane
1856	Margetson, Abraham, Shipdham, N., farmer	473 Code
1831	Margetson, Mary, Ludham, N., single woman	442 Hart
1852	Maris, James, East Dereham, N., innholder and maltster	348 Latten
1819	Maris, Margaret, Bacton, N., spinster	98 Le Neve
1832	Maris, Robert, Bacton, N., collar and harness maker	96 Cooke
1836	Maris, Thomas, Bacton, N., gent.	140 Smith
1840	Maris, Thomas Everitt, Westwick, N., farmer	594 Turner
1828	Mark, Elizabeth, Foulsham, N., spinster	23 Farrow
1827	Mark, Henry, Weybread, S., husbandman	423 Wood
1839	Mark, June, Wortham, S., yeoman	14 Calton
1849	Markant, Elizabeth, Fakenham, N., spinster	424 Womack
1846	Markant, Hamon, Hoe next East Dereham, N., farmer	85 Baret
1846	Markham, Mary, Norwich, N., widow	113 Baret
1829	Markham, Thomas, St Stephens, Norwich, N., shopkeeper	46 Green
1840	Markum, Samuel, Framlingham, S., cordwainer	65 Turner
1842	Markwell, John, Stuston, S., carpenter	13 Canler
1823	Marler, Benjamin, Oakley, S., yeoman	59 Tann
1837	Marriott, John, Little Stonham, S., farmer	144 Warren
1838	Marriott, Mary, Eye, S., widow	100 Skepper
1857	Marrison, Elizabeth, Norwich, N., widow	134 Youngs
1855	Marrison, Samuel, Norwich, N., gunmaker	580 Whitty
1842	Marrison, Thomas, Norwich, N., gent.	442 Canler
1839	Marsden, John Marmaduke, Henham, S., carpenter	126 Calton
1840	Marsh, Christopher, Burwell, C., gardener	657 Turner
1841	Marsh, Edward, Diss, N.	5 Traxton
1826	Marsh, John, Old Buckenham, N., labourer	313 Davy
1840	Marsh, John, Brome, S., farmer	86 Turner
1820	Marsh, Mary, Norwich, N., widow	206 Mack
1827	Marshal, Benjamin, Lound, S., yeoman	369 Wood
1823	Marshall, Elizabeth, Bacton, N., widow	375 Tann
1832	Marshall, James the elder, Holverstone, N.	425 Cooke
1844	Marshall, Jeremiah, Great Yarmouth, N., gent.	209 Ebbage

1836	Marshall, John, Upwell, N., farmer	237 Smith
1846	Marshall, John, Wiggenhall St Germains, N., farmer	203 Baret
1850	Marshall, John, Worlingworth, S., labourer	430 Cuthbert
1842	Marshall, Julia, Norwich, N., spinster	216 Canler
1836	Marshall, Michael, St Clements, Norwich, N., ensign of late 2nd Royal Veteran Battalion	246 Smith
1838	Marshall, Nicholas, St Miles Coslany, Norwich, N., dyer	514 Skepper
1824	Marshall, Phillis, Great Yarmouth, N., widow	169 Borrett
1825	Marshall, Robert, Norwich, N., late of Horsford, N., linen draper	211 Hayward
1836	Marshall, Ruth, Norwich, N., widow	505 Smith
1857	Marshall, Sarah, Great Yarmouth, N., widow	415 Youngs
1853	Marshall, William, Eye, S., ironmonger	575 Veale
1831	Marshall, Zaccheus, St John Sepulchre, Norwich, N., gent.	482 Hart
1856	Marsters, Ann, Tivetshall St Mary, N., widow	118 Code
1844	Marsters, Thomas, Gaywood, N., gent.	161 Ebbage
1826	Marston, Elizabeth, Great Yarmouth, N., widow	150 Davy
1842	Marston, Hannah, St Stephen, Norwich, N., widow	416 Canler
1826	Marston, Sarah, Bramford, S., wife of William Meek Marston, gent.	46 Davy
1834	Mash, Sarah, Gillingham, N., widow	70 Lane
1846	Mason, Christopher, Bramfield, S., clerk	305 Baret
1855	Mason, Elizabeth, Great Yarmouth, N., widow	267 Whitty
1829	Mason, George Lingley, Cheveley, C., blacksmith	310 Green
1834	Mason, Henry, Charing Cross, Norwich, N., household broker	657 Lane
1846	Mason, Henry the elder, Burwell, C., farmer	641 Baret
1847	Mason, Henry, North Elmham, N., gent.	227 Broom
1853	Mason, John, Scarning, N., gent.	117 Veale
1857	Mason, John, Whissonsett, N., yeoman	261 Youngs
1838	Mason, Maria, Great Yarmouth, N., widow	857 Skepper
1820	Mason, Robert, Bury St Edmunds, S., carpenter	152 Mack
1827	Mason, Robert the elder, Scoulton, N., farmer	22 Wood
1842	Mason, Robert, Norwich, N., gent.	173 Canler
1851	Mason, Robert, St Swithins, Norwich, N., gent.	377 Friar
1821	Mason, Samuel, North Elmham, N., farmer and butcher	297 Dewell
1819	Mason, William, Sparham, N., farmer	242 Le Neve
1847	Mason, William, Stanfield, N., farmer	272 Broom
1853	Mason, William, Wereham, N., yeoman	208 Veale
1856	Massey, Thomas, Blofield, N., gent.	480 Code
1850	Massingham, James, Gunthorpe, N., farmer	369 Cuthbert
1827	Massingham, John, Kings Lynn, N., pilot	430 Wood
1834	Massingham, John, Swanton Abbott, N.	365 Lane
1822	Massingham, Margaret, Kings Lynn, N., widow	114 Sadler
1820	Massingham, Mary, Holt, N., spinster	172 Mack
1820	Massingham, Ann, Saxthorpe, N., widow	414 Mack
1855	Masterson, Thomas, Lowestoft, S., pilot	425 Whitty
1843	Masterson, William, Lowestoft, S., fish merchant	180 Miles
1831	Martin, Benjamin, Ilketshall St Margaret, S., farmer	589 Hart
1824	Martin, Charles, Downham Market, N.	308 Borrett
1853	Martin, James, Washbrook, S., formerly of Ellough, S., gent.	684 Veale
1831	Martin, John, Hollesley, S.	533 Hart
1852	Martin, John the elder, Lowestoft, S., collar maker	194 Latten
1830	Martin, Margaret, Beccles, S., widow	279 Pettingill
1844	Martin, Mary, St Margarets Ilketshall, S., widow	532 Ebbage
1847	Martin, Mary Annie, Bury St Edmunds, S., widow	25 Broom
1827	Martin, Nathaniel, Worlington, S., blacksmith	249 Wood
1856	Martin, Richard, Soham, C., turfman	435 Code
1854	Martin, Susan, Brundish, S., spinster	178 Day
1824	Martin, Susanna, Bressingham, N., widow	242 Borrett
1853	Martin, Susannah, Thornham Parva, S.	42 Veale
1838	Martin, Thomas, Finningham, S., farmer	31 Skepper
1845	Martin, Thomas, Norwich, N., cabinet maker	Index only
1825	Martin, William, Hinderclay, S., farmer	292 Hayward

1834	Martin, William, Norwich, N., fishmonger	618 Lane
1857	Martins, Mary, Ingham, N., widow	157 Youngs
1832	Martins, William, Runton, N., farmer	609 Cooke
1847	Martins, William, Palling, N., farmer	544 Broom
1846	Massingham, Joseph, Coltishall, N., schoolmaster	45 Baret
1825	Mathias, Sarah, widow	345 Hayward
1835	Matsell, Jane, Wells next the Sea, N., widow	368 Harrowing
1838	Matsell, Thomas, Burnham Norton, N., husbandman	272 Skepper
1853	Matsell, Thomas, Burnham Norton, N., yeoman	602 Veale
1853	Matthew, Edward, Wickham Skeith, S., farmer	144 Veale
1835	Matthew, John, Mendlesham, S., farmer	212 Harrowing
1837	Matthews, Charles, St Nicholas South Elmham, S., farmer	484 Warren
1828	Matthews, Elizabeth, Ingham, N., wife of John Matthews, miller	290 Farrow
1839	Matthews, James, Wells next the Sea, N., shoemaker	143 Calton
1852	Matthews, Jasper, Barningham, N., yeoman	649 Latten
1825	Matthews, Rebecca, Stalham, N., widow	363 Hayward
1836	Matthews, Thomas William, Norwich, N., plumber and glazier	570 Smith
1825	Matthews, William, Norwich, N., cordspinner	469 Hayward
1835	Matthews, William, Ringsfield, S., farmer	524 Harrowing
1841	May, Ann, Ipswich, S., widow	583 Traxton
1843	May, Gamaliel, Upwell, N., farmer	196 Miles
1848	May, John, Southtown, Little Yarmouth, N., gent.	496 Denny
1852	May, John, Outwell, N., farmer and grazier	319 Latten
1855	May, John, Kings Lynn, N., victualler and dealer in marine stores	380 Whitty
1853	May, Mary, Southtown, S.	Index only
1855	May, Robert, Brinton, N., yeoman	75 Whitty
1835	Mayers, Joseph, Great Yarmouth, N., shopkeeper	291 Harrowing
1840	Mayes, Charles, Pulham St Mary the Virgin, formerly of Rumburgh, S., yeoman	163 Turner
1838	Mayes, Edward, Norwich, N., vintner and printer	712 Skepper
1820	Mayes, George, South Creake, N., drover	299 Mack
1819	Mayes, John, Holme next the Sea, N., yeoman	246 Le Neve
1826	Mayes, John, Caister next Yarmouth, N., farmer	294 Davy
1828	Mayes, John, Falkenham, S., yeoman	489 Farrow
1851	Mayes, John, St Georges Colegate, Norwich, N., shopkeeper	372 Friar
1845	Mayes, Margaret, Alburgh, N., widow	156 Pedgrift
1838	Mayes, Richard, East Dereham, N., farmer	408 Skepper
1827	Mayes, Thomas, Felmingham, N., farmer	530 Wood
1847	Mayes, Thomas, St Saviours, Norwich, N., carpenter	395 Broom
1855	Mayes, Thomas, Baconsthorpe, N., gent.	385 Whitty
1843	Mayes, William, Crostwick, N., yeoman	576 Miles
1854	Mayhew, Amos, Bungay, S., tailor	157 Day
1844	Mayhew, James, Westacre, N., farmer	71 Ebbage
1847	Mayhew, James, Combs, S., grocer, baker and beer seller	69 Broom
1849	Mayhew, James, Pettaugh, S., farmer	107 Womack
1827	Mayhew, Jeremiah, Newmarket, S., blacksmith	104 Wood
1820	Mayhew, John, Cotton, S., labourer	432 Mack
1823	Mayhew, John, Redisham, S., farmer	247 Tann
1825	Mayhew, John, Upwell, N.	275 Hayward
1840	Mayhew, John Gardiner, Helmingham, S., farmer	461 Turner
1856	Mayhew, John, Beccles, S., wherryman	387 Code
1850	Mayhew, Joseph William, Halesworth, S. dissenting minister	86 Cuthbert
1847	Mayhew, Lot, Metfield, S., yeoman	595 Broom
1827	Mayhew, Mary, Norwich, N.	506 Wood
1843	Mayhew, Mary, Bath, formerly of Norwich, N., spinster	615 Miles
1846	Mayhew, Rebekah, Mutford, S., widow	231 Baret
1835	Mayhew, Robert the elder, Henham, S., farmer	514 Harrowing
1844	Mayhew, Robert, Mendlesham, S., farmer	658 Ebbage
1837	Mayhew, Samuel, Wickham Skeith, S.	261 Warren
1829	Mayhew, Sarah, Earl Stonham, S., spinster	519 Green

1841	Mayhew, Sarah Ann, Halesworth, S., wife of Joseph William Mayhew, dissenting minister	628 Traxton
1850	Mays, Edward, Stowmarket, S.	526 Cuthbert
1821	Mays, James, Stowupland, S., cordwainer	13 Dewell
1836	Mays, Richard, East Rudham, N., innkeeper	268 Smith
1830	Mays, William, Foulsham, N., gent.	226 Pettingill
1844	Mayston, Hannah, North Elmham, N., wife of Joshua Mayston, miller	644 Ebbage
1829	Mayston, Samuel, Norwich, N., gent.	414 Green
1847	Mayston, Sarah, Norwich, N., widow	228 Broom
1843	Meacham, Edward, Beccles, S.	609 Miles
1838	Meacham, Charles, Yaxham, N., farmer	407 Skepper
1819	Meachem, John, Burwell, C., yeoman	311 Le Neve
1820	Mead, Stephen, Hempnall, N., farmer and carrier	574 Mack
1849	Meadows, James, Norwich, N., cordwainer	327 Womack
1843	Meadows, Louisa, Great Yarmouth, N., wife of Henry William Meadows, chemist and druggist	313 Miles
1826	Meadows, Robert, Tivetshall St Mary, N., yeoman	88 Davy
1829	Meadows, William, Stradbroke, S., cooper	10 Green
1852	Mear, Daniel, Trowse Millgate, N., miller	555 Latten
1853	Meares, Hannah, Brooke, N., widow	707 Veale
1824	Mears, Jeremiah, Norwich, N., vintner	194 Borrett
1846	Medcalf, William, Tilney St Lawrence, N., farmer and grazier	651 Baret
1819	Medlar, Henry, Hevingham, N., labourer	12 Le Neve
1842	Medler, Edward, St Michael at Plea, Norwich, N., clothier	712 Canler
1838	Medler, William, Great Bircham, N., labourer	581 Skepper
1831	Medley, William, St Mary at the Tower, Ipswich, S., formerly of Thorpe. Essex, widower	55 Hart
1840	Meek, Isaac, Thetford, N., yeoman	477 Turner
1854	Meek, William, Norwich, N., cowkeeper	582 Day
1822	Meen, James the elder, Redenhall w. Harleston, collar maker	168 Sadler
1829	Meen, John, Gillingham, N.	70 Green
1823	Meen, Thomas, Fressingfield, S., miller	208 Tann
1842	Meggs, John the elder, Acton, S., blacksmith	490 Canler
1856	Melton, Mary, Tittleshall, N., widow	420 Code
1853	Melton, Richard, Tittleshall, N., hurdle maker	10 Veale
1841	Melvin, Sarah, Norwich, N., widow	3 Traxton
1827	Mendham, Frances, Norwich, N., widow	35 Wood
1825	Mendham, John, Hockering, N., tailor	447 Hayward
1848	Mendham, William, Mattishall, N tailor	38 Denny
1852	Merrison, James, Norwich, N., watch and clock maker	215 Latten
1848	Merrison, Judith, West Newton, N., wife of Robert Merrison, miller	59 Denny
1855	Merrison, Thomas, West Barsham, N., farmer	25 Whitty
1829	Messling, Thomas, Thetford, N., publican	191 Green
1850	Metcalf, Joseph, Great Yarmouth, N., master mariner	144 Cuthbert
1829	Mickleburgh, Samuel, Shelfanger, N., yeoman	211 Green
1832	Mickleburgh, Martha, Cromer, N., widow	536 Cooke
1853	Mickleburgh, Mary, Rushall N., widow	312 Veale
1852	Mickleburgh, Robert, Woodbridge, S., corn chandler	784 Latten
1853	Mickleburgh, Samuel, Horstead, N., farmer	304 Veale
1856	Mickleburgh, Sarah, Great Yarmouth, N., spinster	137 Code
1834	Mickleburgh, William, Broome, N., farmer	138 Lane
1850	Micklefield, Roger, Stoke Ferry, N., gent.	4 Cuthbert
1833	Micklefield, Timothy, Ipswich, S., shopkeeper	433 Cubitt
1850	Middleton, Charles, Norwich, N., gent.	332 Cuthbert
1845	Middleton, James, Norwich, N., weaver	812 Pedgrift
1855	Middleton, Mary, Mendham, N., farmer	608 Whitty
1835	Middleton, Matthew, Burnham Overy, N., mariner	222 Harrowing
1854	Middleton, Thomas Blunderfield, Fakenham, N., bankers clerk	232 Day
1856	Middleton, Thomas, Rickinghall Superior, S., yeoman	253 Code
1850	Middleton, William, East Tuddenham, N., farmer	322 Cuthbert
1827	Mileham, John, Dilham, N., husbandman	494 Wood

1840	Mileham, Robert, Trimingham, N., carpenter	521 Turner
1828	Miles, Ann, Norwich, N., widow	272 Farrow
1852	Miles, Benjamin, Mattishall, N., schoolmaster	880 Latten
1824	Miles, Elias, Great Yarmouth, N., master mariner	107 Borrett
1822	Miles, Francis, Rollesby, N., blacksmith	248 Sadler
1839	Miles, John, Alburgh, N., farmer	147 Calton
1842	Miles, John, Wroxham, N., gent.	Index only
1843	Miles, John Cannell, Needham, N., farmer	1 Miles
1843	Miles, Robert, Great Bircham, N., cordwainer	347 Miles
1824	Miles, Stephen, Alburgh, N., farmer and dealer	141 Borrett
1841	Miles, William, Mattishall, N., farmer	242 Traxton
1846	Millatt, Ann, Kettlestone, N., wife of Robert Millatt, timber merchant	520 Baret
1838	Millatt, Hamlet, Elsing, N., farmer and blacksmith	192 Skepper
1844	Millatt, Jonathan, Billingford, N., blacksmith	397 Ebbage
1856	Millatt, William, Elsing, N., blacksmith	92 Code
1845	Miller, Elizabeth, St Michaels, Coslany, Norwich, widow	499 Pedgrift
1856	Miller, James, Bramerton, N., gent.	391 Code
1833	Miller, Jasper, North Barningham, N., yeoman	279 Cubitt
1822	Miller, Jeffrey, Methwold, N., farmer	376 Sadler
1848	Miller, John, Great Yarmouth, N., fish merchant	334 Denny
1848	Miller, John, Stokesby, N., boatman	328 Denny
1851	Miller, John the elder, Walsham Le Willows, S., gent.	395 Friar
1852	Miller, John, Broome, N., farmer	676 Latten
1848	Miller, Margaret, North Runcton, N., single woman	643 Denny
1855	Miller, Mary Ann, Bungay, S., widow	759 Whitty
1835	Miller, Robert Reynolds, Liverpool, Lancs, victualler	565 Harrowing
1836	Miller, Robert, Holt, N., gent.	378 Smith
1850	Miller, Sarah, Walsham Le Willows, S., wife of John Miller, gent.	469 Cuthbert
1846	Miller, Stephen, Great Yarmouth, N., linen draper	489 Baret
1853	Miller, Stephen, Gorleston, S., gent.	623 Veale
1852	Miller, William, Norton, S., farmer	553 Latten
1857	Miller, William, Kings Lynn, N., meter	226 Youngs
1839	Miller, Winnifred, Downham Market, N., widow	620 Calton
1829	Millerd, Edward, St Peters, Thetford, N., yeoman	388 Green
1834	Millett, Ham, Framingham Pigot, N., farmer	390 Lane
1855	Millett, Hamlet, Woodton, N., wheelwright	135 Whitty
1845	Millett, Sarah, Framingham Pigot, N., widow	117 Pedgrift
1825	Millett, Van, Hedenham, N.	292 Hayward
1855	Mills, Ann, Norwich, N., widow	198 Whitty
1854	Mills, Ebenezer, Norwich, N., gent.	254 Day
1857	Mills, Francis, Lowestoft, S., blacksmith	768 Youngs
1827	Mills, George, Sproughton, S., gardener	230 Wood
1837	Mills, George, Bungay, S., gent.	753 Warren
1839	Mills, John, Reydon, S., farmer	382 Calton
1844	Mills, John, Great Yarmouth, N., shipwright	660 Ebbage
1837	Mills, Mary, Thetford, N., widow	592 Warren
1856	Mills, Sheppard, Saxmundham, S., beerhouse keeper	329 Code
1857	Mills, Simon, Mendlesham, S., o.w. missing	44 Youngs
1850	Mills, Thomas, Rushall, N., farmer	225 Cuthbert
1834	Mills, William Smith, Ditchingham, N., hemp cloth manufacturer and farmer	682 Lane
1856	Milnes, Elizabeth, Norwich, N., wife of Charles Milnes, stone mason	618 Code
1848	Mines, Edward, Diss, N., gent.	810 Denny
1849	Mines, Thomas, Scole, N., farmer	506 Womack
1848	Mingay, Edward, Panxworth, N., horse dealer	277 Denny
1827	Mingay, George, Orford, S., gent.	597 Wood
1854	Mingay, James, Holton, S., shoemaker	225 Day
1852	Mingay, William James, Thornham, N., farmer	309 Latten
1823	Minister, Edward, Wickhampton, N., yeoman	417 Tann
1856	Minns, Ann, Seething, N., spinster	585 Code
1853	Minns, Benjamin Atterton, Norwich, N.	246 Veale

1819	Minns, John, Edgefield, N., gent.	202 Le Neve
1841	Minns, John, Thwaite, N., yeoman	657 Traxton
1842	Minns, John, Eysefield, S.	Index only
1838	Minns, Martin, Ditchingham, N., farmer	717 Skepper
1827	Minns, Mary, St Georges, Colegate, Norwich, N., spinster	558 Wood
1833	Minns, Nathaniel Downing, Bungay, S., draper	238 Cubitt
1819	Minns, Robert, Neatishead, N., husbandman	258 Le Neve
1849	Minter, John, Great Yarmouth, N., fish merchant	10 Womack
1848	Minter, Robert, Wickham Market, S., wine merchant	245 Denny
1840	Mitcham, Elizabeth, Dilham, N.	35 Turner
1837	Mitchel, John, Ingham, N., farmer	382 Warren
1824	Mitchell, Charles, Necton, N., farmer	10 Borrett
1836	Mitchell, Henry, Norwich, N., baker	421 Smith
1850	Mitchell, Henry, Fakenham, N., farmer	73 Cuthbert
1850	Mitchell, Page, Great Yarmouth, N., house carpenter	312 Cuthbert
1837	Mitchell, Richard, Strumpshaw, N., farmer	761 Warren
1841	Mitchell, Robert, Little Ryburgh, N., farmer	237 Traxton
1837	Mitchley, Edward, Kings Lynn, N., carpenter and builder	738 Warren
1842	Mitchley, Robert, Kings Lynn, N., master mariner	37 Canler
1841	Mobbs, John, Ringsfield, S., carpenter	647 Traxton
1827	Mole, John, Nacton, S., schoolmaster	666 Wood
1828	Moll, Edward, Blofield, N., husbandman	487 Farrow
1828	Moll, John, Norwich, N., innkeeper	27 Farrow
1829	Money, Cammant, Somerleyton, S., esquire	5 Green
1835	Money, Elizabeth, St Benedicts, Norwich, N., widow	528 Harrowing
1834	Money, John, St Benedicts, Norwich, N., cow keeper	123 Lane
1839	Money, Thomas, Norwich, N., lieut. on half pay of Her Majesties Army	119 Calton
1837	Money, William, Barney, N., husbandman	170 Warren
1838	Moneyment, George, Norwich, N., veterinary surgeon	19 Skepper
1819	Moneyment, Henry, Norwich, N., gent.	221 Le Neve
1819	Moneyment, Robert, Horsham St Faiths, N., blacksmith	116 Le Neve
1830	Monsey, Issabella, Stalham, N., widow	113 Pettingill
1829	Monsey, Martha, Norwich, N., widow	406 Green
1820	Monsey, Robert, Kirby Bedon, N., farmer	196 Mack
1821	Monument, Joseph, Great Yarmouth, N., mariner	106 Dewell
1820	Mood, John, Thurlton, N., yeoman	447 Mack
1845	Moon, Elizabeth, Finningham, S., widow	65 Pedgrift
1845	Moon, Prudence, Great Yarmouth, N., widow	822 Pedgrift
1819	Moon, Thomas, Great Yarmouth, N., yeoman	213 Le Neve
1856	Moor, Charles, Woodbridge, S., gent.	152 Code
1855	Moore, Abraham, Reymerstone, N., blacksmith	137 Whitty
1850	Moore, Ann, Norwich, N., spinster	156 Cuthbert
1846	Moore, Anne, Norwich, N., widow	200 Baret
1855	Moore, Benjamin, Great Hautbois, N., farmer	516 Whitty
1848	Moore, Charlotte, Soham, C., widow	849 Denny
1839	Moore, Daking Ireland, Creeting St Mary, S., gent.	403 Calton
1836	Moore, Edmund, Kelsale, S., gent.	484 Smith
1820	Moore, Edward, Great Witchingham, N., gent.	4 Mack
1851	Moore, Ellen, Thorndon, S.	107 Friar
1844	Moore, Esther, Broome, N., widow	446 Ebbage
1832	Moore, Francis, Wendling, N., blacksmith	39 Cooke
1824	Moore, George, Norwich, N., worstead weaver	104 Borrett
1838	Moore, George, Aylsham, N., farmer	622 Skepper
1825	Moore, Henry, Ubbeston, S., late of Huntingfield, farmer	453 Hayward
1852	Moore, Henry, Badingham, S., farmer	596 Latten
1832	Moore, James, Diss, N., farmer	360 Cooke
1834	Moore, James, St Margarets South Elmham, S., yeoman	346 Lane
1837	Moore, James, Bedfield, S., blacksmith	581 Warren
1857	Moore, James, Norwich, N., yeoman	334 Youngs
1825	Moore, John, Burnham Westgate, N., labourer	90 Hayward
1830	Moore, John, Norwich, N., tailor	228 Pettingill
1836	Moore, John, Fressingfield, S., farmer	116 Smith
1840	Moore, John, Filby, N., bricklayer	167 Turner

1840	Moore, John Barker, Old Newton, S., farmer	548 Turner
1842	Moore, John, Thwaite, S., farmer	294 Canler
1843	Moore, John, Filby, N., yeoman, formerly of Burgh St Margaret	321 Miles
1844	Moore, John, Winston, S., yeoman	114 Ebbage
1846	Moore, John, Gissing, N.	77 Baret
1847	Moore, John, Denham, S., farmer	149 Broom
1848	Moore, John, Skeyton, N., gent.	820 Denny
1832	Moore, Mary, Lowestoft, S., widow	2 Cooke
1834	Moore, Mary Ann, Great Yarmouth, N., spinster	601 Lane
1839	Moore, Mary Elizabeth, Worlingham, S., widow	555 Calton
1842	Moore, Mary, Great Yarmouth, N., widow	688 Canler
1850	Moore, Mary, Great Yarmouth, N., spinster	612 Cuthbert
1840	Moore, Moses, Overstrand, N., farmer	610 Turner
1831	Moore, Richard, Ditchingham, N., labourer	263 Hart
1842	Moore, Robert, Hickling, N., farmer	115 Canler
1845	Moore, Sarah, Flixton, S., widow	830 Pedgrift
1837	Moore, Susana, St Nicholas, Ipswich, S., widow	21 Warren
1826	Moore, Thomas, Cromer, N., thatcher	153 Davy
1839	Moore, Thomas, Broome, N., innkeeper	493 Calton
1839	Moore, Thomas, Hilborough, N.	414 Calton
1844	Moore, Thomas, Acle, N., carpenter	526 Ebbage
1844	Moore, Thomas, Kirby Bedon, N., formerly of Norwich, N., farmer	371 Ebbage
1846	Moore, Thomas, Heigham, Norwich, N., yeoman	497 Baret
1837	Moore, William, Norwich, N., upholsterer	602 Warren
1844	Moore, William, Baconsthorpe, N., farmer	399 Ebbage
1847	Moore, William, Catfield, N., yeoman	701 Broom
1857	Moppett, Esther, St Peter Mancroft, Norwich, N., spinster	809 Youngs
1821	Mordey, Esau, Costessey, N.	65 Dewell
1823	Mordy, John, St Michael at Plea, Norwich, horse dealer	243 Tann
1829	More, Elizabeth, Spexhall, S., widow	88 Green
1845	More, James Vincen, Redenhall, N., farmer	136 Pedgrift
1850	More, Robert, Leiston, S., farmer	88 Cuthbert
1821	More, Walter, Halesworth, S., saddler and harness maker	91 Dewell
1856	More, William, Wortwell, N., farmer	161 Code
1856	Moretti, Guiseppe Casserra, Kings Lynn, N., jeweller	503 Code
1857	Morfoot, John Fountain, Methwold, N., farmer	650 Youngs
1853	Morgan, Edward the elder, Beccles, S., yeoman	501 Veale
1831	Morgan, James, Great Yarmouth, N., gent.	232 Hart
1844	Morgan, John the younger, Woodbridge, S., grocer	621 Ebbage
1851	Morgan, John, Kings Lynn, N., currier	561 Friar
1827	Morgan, Mary, Wickham Skeith, S., spinster	242 Wood
1849	Morgan, Mary Anne, Rendham, S., wife of Rev. Rowland Morgan	401 Womack
1850	Morley, Corben, Gislingham, S., farmer	360 Cuthbert
1838	Morley, James, Lakenheath, S., farmer	496 Skepper
1838	Morley, John, Stow Bardolph, N., turfman	10 Skepper
1835	Morley, Mary, Great Yarmouth, N., widow	417 Harrowing
1826	Morley, Thomas, Brandon, S., widower	247 Davy
1847	Morley, Thomas, Gorleston, S.	459 Broom
1820	Morphew, John, Thorpe, N.	611 Mack
1837	Morris, George the younger, Norwich, N., slater	26 Warren
1828	Morris, Jesse Tuck, Bungay, S., surgeon	507 Farrow
1856	Morris, Lucy, Burgh Castle, S., widow	310 Code
1823	Morris, Samuel, Acle, N., formerly of Cawston, labourer	373 Tann
1856	Morris, Samuel, Shipdham, N., wine and brandy merchant	343 Code
1837	Morrison, John, St Stephens, Ipswich, S., gardener	607 Warren
1834	Morrison, Thomas, Kings Lynn, N., master mariner	377 Lane
1827	Morse, James, Great Yarmouth, N., inn keeper	477 Wood
1830	Morse, John, Swaffham, N.	422 Pettingill
1831	Morse, John, Leiston, S., labourer	384 Hart
1835	Morse, Sarah, Lowestoft, S., spinster	576 Harrowing
1849	Morse, Thomas, Walpole, S., gent.	427 Womack
1834	Morsley, Francis, Bawdsey, S., labourer	195 Lane

1829	Morss, Sarah, Elmham St Cross, S., widow	351 Green
1819	Morter, Richard, Thursford, N., publican	201 Le Neve
1846	Mortimer, Margaret, Thetford, N., widow	363 Baret
1832	Mortimer, Sarah, Polstead, S.	424 Cooke
1852	Morton, John, Caister, N., clerk	488 Latten
1839	Moss, Ann, Burlingham St Andrew, N., widow	347 Calton
1843	Moss, Ann, Norwich, N., spinster	22 Miles
1825	Moss, Samuel, Norwich, N., late of New Buckenham, gent.	516 Hayward
1836	Mott, Mary, Brisley, N., widow	445 Smith
1852	Mott, William, West Newton, N., bricklayer	490 Latten
1844	Mottram, James Nasmith, Norwich, N., gent.	522 Ebbage
1825	Motts, William, Fressingfield, S., farmer	379 Hayward
1856	Motum, Thomas, Charsfield, S., blacksmith	421 Code
1834	Moule, Solomon, Eye, S., carpenter	834 Lane
1821	Moulton, Mary, Bawdeswell, N.	43 Dewell
1841	Moulton, Noah, West Winch, N., farmer	354 Traxton
1847	Moulton, Thomas, Worlingworth, S., farmer	352 Broom
1846	Mounser, Charles, Great Yarmouth, N., gardener	307 Baret
1855	Mount, John, Needham Market, S., innkeeper and lime burner	342 Whitty
1821	Mouse, Mary, Great Yarmouth, N., widow of Phillip Mouse, house carpenter	221 Dewell
1830	Mouser, Mary, Framsden, S., widow	412 Pettingill
1852	Moxon, William, Upwell, Isle of Ely, formerly of Welney, yeoman	84 Latten
1841	Moy, James, Colby, N., yeoman	330 Traxton
1838	Moy, William, Diss, N., publican	832 Skepper
1853	Moyce, John, Gaywood, N., shoemaker	442 Veale
1832	Moyce, Martha, Kings Lynn, N., widow	107 Cooke
1833	Moye, Mary, Syderstone, N., widow	281 Cubitt
1828	Moyes, Hannah Maria, Norwich, N., widow	188 Farrow
1826	Moyse, John, Carlton Colville, S., farmer	67 Davy
1851	Moyse, Sarah, Ipswich, S., widow	253 Friar
1843	Mudd, Ann, Darmsden, S., widow	309 Miles
1827	Mudd, James, Lowestoft, S., husbandman	510 Wood
1837	Mudd, John the elder, Beccles, S., yeoman	48 Warren
1848	Mudd, John, Upwell, N., farmer	196 Denny
1850	Mudd, Thomas, Great Yarmouth, N., yeoman	524 Cuthbert
1820	Mullender, Daniel, Great Yarmouth, N., mariner	183 Mack
1835	Mullender, John, Kirkley, S., fisherman	197 Harrowing
1839	Mullener, William, Palgrave, S., butcher	545 Calton
1856	Mullenger, Henry Debenham, Rickinghall, S., yeoman	315 Code
1850	Mullenger, Marcia, St Stephens, Norwich, N., widow	521 Cuthbert
1855	Mullenger, Thomas, Little Thornham, S., labourer	68 Whitty
1841	Mulley, Richard, Shipdham, N., innkeeper	114 Traxton
1825	Munday, Amy	437 Hayward
1857	Munday, John, Norwich, N., gent.	794 Youngs
1835	Mundford, John, Newmarket St Mary, S., yeoman	496 Harrowing
1854	Munford, Peter, East Dereham, N., carpenter, builder and pump maker	158 Day
1826	Munnings, Elizabeth, Bredfield, S., widow	366 Davy
1846	Munson, Robert, Wells next the Sea, N., master mariner	424 Baret
1857	Murfet, Sarah, Soham, C., widow	346 Youngs
1855	Murfet, William, Soham, C., carrier	687 Whitty
1827	Murphy, Keziah, Bracondale, Norwich, N widow	O.W. 307
1832	Murray, alias Thurtell, James, Loddon, N.	243 Cooke
1833	Murray, Joseph, Bawdeswell, N., farmer	348 Cubitt
1829	Murrell, Ann, Norwich, N., single woman	357 Green
1842	Murrell, Charles, Woodbridge, S., plumber and glazier	5 Canler
1847	Murrell, Gibbs, Surlingham, N., gent.	562 Broom
1832	Murrell, James, Little Cressingham, N., auctioneer and farmer	334 Cooke
1824	Murrell, John, Carbrooke, N., miller	270 Borrett
1820	Murrell, Jonathan, Wymondham, N., gent.	31 Mack
1843	Murton, Edmund, Burston, N., linen weaver	132 Miles
1844	Murton, Ellis, Bildeston, S., innkeeper	32 Ebbage

1827	Murton, Richard, Hepworth, S.	91 Wood
1828	Murton, William, Kenninghall, N., farmer	242 Farrow
1835	Musk, Edmund, Halesworth, S., harness maker	68 Harrowing
1846	Musk, Samuel, Carlton Rode, N., farmer	659 Baret
1835	Muskett, Andrew Hart, Thelveton, N., farmer	613 Harrowing
1824	Muskett, Charles, Yelverton, N., farmer	176 Borrett
1852	Muskett, Henry, Clippesby, N., esquire	177 Latten
1834	Muskett, John, Spixworth, N.	495 Lane
1824	Muskett, Jonathan, Yelverton, N., bachelor	89 Borrett
1829	Muskett, Jonathan, Carleton Rode, N., yeoman	43 Green
1833	Muskett, Martha, St Clements, Norwich, N., spinster	497 Cubitt
1857	Muskett, Mary, Heigham next Norwich, N., widow	559 Youngs
1856	Muskett, Robert, Heigham, Norwich, N., gent.	311 Code
1820	Muskett, Thomas, Wacton, N., farmer	644 Mack
1846	Muskett, Thomas, Norwich, N.	446 Baret
1848	Muskett, William, Attleborough, N., gent.	405 Denny
1849	Mussett, James, Swanton Novers, N., husbandman	615 Womack
1855	Mussett, William, Swanton Novers, N., hurdle maker	647 Whitty
1841	Must, Elizabeth, Sudbury, S., widow	386 Traxton
1852	Mutimer, John, Hoxne, S., farmer	90 Latten
1828	Myall, Ann, Thornham, N., widow	249 Farrow
1821	Myhiles, Francis, Bruisyard, S., labourer	134 Dewell
1851	Myhill, Augustus, Norwich, N., carpenter and builder	146 Friar
1829	Myhill, James, West Somerton, N., farmer	104 Green
1851	Myhill, John, Southtown, Yarmouth, S., victualler	185 Friar
1848	Myhill, Lewis, Catfield, N., shoemaker	36 Denny
1854	Myhill, Mary, North Walsham, N., widow	138 Day
1833	Myhill, Samuel, Honing, N., yeoman	294 Cubitt
1845	Myhill, Samuel, Great Yarmouth, N., gent.	302 Pedgrift
1847	Myhill, William, Horsey, N., carpenter	693 Broom
1855	Myhill, William, Hemsby, N., yeoman	91 Whitty
1843	Narburgh, Richard the elder, Earsham, N., yeoman	112 Miles
1827	Nash, Thomas, Great Yarmouth, N., leather cutter	102 Wood
1852	Nash, Henry, Norwich, N., chemist and druggist	39 Latten
1820	Nash, James, Hainford, N.	587 Mack
1857	Nash, John Allen, Wymondham, N., gent.	508 Youngs
1843	Nash, Samuel, Barford, N., farmer	581 Miles
1853	Nash, Spooner, Norwich, N., rag and paper merchant	84 Veale
1840	Nash, William, Hethersett, N., tailor	7 Turner
1845	Naunton, Charles the elder, Southwold, S., yeoman	430 Pedgrift
1844	Nave, James, Great Yarmouth, N., gent.	514 Ebbage
1832	Neal, Barnard, Felthorpe, N., farmer	123 Cooke
1840	Neal, Elizabeth, Neatishead, N., widow	522 Turner
1849	Neal, John, Docking, N., shoemaker	70 Womack
1847	Neal, Nathaniel, Whissonsett, N.	669 Broom
1820	Neal, Sarah, Saham Toney, N., spinster	400 Mack
1844	Neal, Thomas, St Margarets Ilketshall, S., farmer	508 Ebbage
1832	Neale, Anne, Wells next the Sea, N., widow	356 Cooke
1847	Neale, Fountain, Hainford, N., farmer	348 Broom
1827	Neale, Henry, Newmarket, C., formerly of Wood Ditton, gent.	541 Wood
1822	Neale, John, Great Witchingham, N., husbandman	33 Sadler
1829	Neale, John Lawrence, Heigham, Norwich, N., gardener	347 Green
1830	Neale, John, Norwich, N., yeoman	319 Pettingill
1826	Neave, Ann, Wymondham, N., widow	71 Davy
1851	Neave, Charles, Moulton, N., farmer	402 Friar
1851	Neave, Elizabeth, Flixton, S., widow	191 Friar
1850	Neave, Isaac, Smallburgh, N., labourer	150 Cuthbert
1857	Neave, Jacob, Hickling, N., blacksmith	626 Youngs
1832	Neave, John, Scarning, N., farmer	235 Cooke
1839	Neave, John, Marlingford, N., yeoman	400 Calton
1844	Neave, John, Tharston, N., farmer	367 Ebbage
1836	Neave, Mary Ann, Great Yarmouth, N., widow	298 Smith
1837	Neave, Philip, Mattishall, N., husbandman	419 Warren
1849	Neave, Samuel, St Stephens, Norwich, N., musician	682 Womack

1857	Neave, Thomas, East Dereham, N., gent.	771 Youngs
1841	Neave, William, Smallburgh, N., yeoman	375 Traxton
1832	Neech, John, Framingham Pigott, N., farmer	163 Cooke
1851	Neech, Thomas William, Beccles, S., cattle dealer	165 Friar
1819	Neeld, Clement, Upwell, N., bricklayer	42 Le Neve
1847	Neep, Francis, Tilney All Saints, N., farmer	419 Broom
1851	Neep, Francis, Walpole St Peter, N., farmer	210 Friar
1852	Neeve, Elizabeth, Aldeburgh, S., widow	507 Latten
1837	Neeve, Mary, Aldeburgh, S., widow	226 Warren
1852	Neeve, Mary, Lowestoft, S., widow	787 Latten
1837	Neeve, Philip, Lowestoft, S., gent.	49 Warren
1828	Nelson, Elizabeth, Worstead, N., widow	187 Farrow
1838	Nelson, James, Sparham, N., gent.	66 Skepper
1841	Nelson, James, Melford, S., carpenter	136 Traxton
1844	Nelson, Mary, East Dereham, N., widow	187 Ebbage
1837	Neslen, Catherine, Great Yarmouth, N., widow	22 Warren
1833	Neslen, William, Flixton, S., farmer	439 Cubitt
1824	Neve, Susannah, Dersingham, N., widow	30 Borrett
1849	Neve, Thomas, Norwich, N., gent.	526 Womack
1827	Newark, alias Newrick, Henry, Great Yarmouth, N., yeoman	93 Wood
1845	Newbery, John, Westhall, S., farmer	510 Pedgrift
1855	Newby, Elizabeth, Great Yarmouth, N., widow	622 Whitty
1841	Newby, Phebe, Great Yarmouth, N., spinster	257 Traxton
1855	Newham, William Howard, Ilketshall St Lawrence, S., farmer	312 Whitty
1850	Newhouse, James, Coltishall, N., gent.	353 Cuthbert
1825	Newhouse, Thomas, Horstead, N., carpenter	96 Hayward
1828	Newland, Joseph, Trunch, N., carpenter	410 Farrow
1843	Newman, Alfred, St Peter Mancroft, Norwich, N., tea dealer	555 Miles
1839	Newman, Charles, St Peter Mancroft, Norwich, N., tea dealer	415 Calton
1824	Newman, Elizabeth, Norwich, N., widow	241 Borrett
1857	Newman, Hannah, Brumstead, N., wife of John Newman, farmer	612 Youngs
1844	Newman, James, Tacolnestone, N., farmer	677 Ebbage
1824	Newman, John, Felmingham, N., public house keeper	320 Borrett
1832	Newman, John, Surlingham, N., farmer	371 Cooke
1835	Newman, John, Little Plumstead, N., farmer	564 Harrowing
1841	Newman, John, Hickling, N., farmer	486 Traxton
1843	Newman, John, East Tuddenham, N., farmer	678 Miles
1845	Newman, John, Norwich, N., bricklayer	474 Pedgrift
1847	Newman, John, Newmarket, S., baker	257 Broom
1852	Newman, John, Little Ormesby, N., husbandman	22 Latten
1841	Newman, Joseph, Cawston, N., gardener	212 Traxton
1841	Newman, Mary, Hickling, N., widow	100 Traxton
1857	Newman, Mary, Great Yarmouth, N., widow	527 Youngs
1853	Newman, Richard, Trimingham, N., gent.	495 Veale
1822	Newman, Robert, Heigham, Norwich, N., carpenter and shopkeeper	63 Sadler
1848	Newman, Robert, Beccles, S., farmer	718 Denny
1840	Newman, Susan, Middleton, N., wife of William Newman, farmer	55 Turner
1826	Newman, Thomas, Overstrand, N., publican	286 Davy
1837	Newman, Thomas, Reepham, N., carpenter	657 Warren
1847	Newman, Thomas, Norwich, N., baker	193 Broom
1833	Newman, Thomas Fitzherbert, Bassingham, N.	O.W. 231
1827	Newrick, alias Newark, Henry, Great Yarmouth, N., yeoman	93 Wood
1835	Newrick, Susan, Great Yarmouth, N., widow	91 Harrowing
1853	Newsham, Susan, Framingham Pigot, N., widow	682 Veale
1828	Newson, Benjamin, Great Yarmouth, N., house carpenter	267 Farrow
1853	Newson, Cornelius, Stradbroke, S., gentlemans servant	480 Veale
1827	Newson, Elizabeth, Sotherton, S., widow	300 Wood
1825	Newson, Hannah, Beccles, S., widow	433 Hayward
1823	Newson. Mary, Norwich, widow	277 Tann
1852	Newson, Mary, Ilketshall St Andrew, S., widow	126 Latten
1823	Newson, Richard, Diss, N., schoolmaster	306 Tann
1856	Newson, Thomas, Gorleston, S., pilot	486 Code
1855	Newson, William, Blundeston, S., yeoman	724 Whitty

1829	Newstead, Benjamin Powell, Wounded Hart Inn, St Peter Mancroft, Norwich	532 Green
1833	Newstead, John, Colby, N., farmer	19 Cubitt
1852	Newstead, John, Rickinghall Superior, S., farmer	378 Latten
1821	Newstead, Nathaniel, Overstrand, N., carpenter	61 Dewell
1854	Newstead, Philip Shickle, Norwich, N., gardener	275 Day
1832	Newstead, Robert, Eye, S., yeoman	597 Cooke
1840	Newton, George, Great Yarmouth, N., shipwright	348 Turner
1845	Newton, George, Southtown, S., shipwright	46 Pedgrift
1834	Newton, James, Horsford, N.	815 Lane
1831	Newton, John, Methwold, N., farmer	247 Hart
1841	Newton, Robert, Downham Market, N., common carrier	256 Traxton
1842	Newton, William, Methwold, N., farmer	361 Canler
1847	Newton, William, North Walsham, N., gardener	763 Broom
1840	Nice, John, Nedging, S., farmer	545 Turner
1855	Nicholds, Dinah, Foulden, N.	81 Whitty
1823	Nicholes, Henry, Forncett St Peter, N., farmer	17 Tann
1828	Nicholls, James, Heacham, N., labourer	110 Farrow
1850	Nichols, Edward, Norwich, N., confectioner	374 Cuthbert
1850	Nichols, Fitt, Little Plumstead, N., farmer and carpenter	231 Cuthbert
1842	Nichols, James, St Stephens, Norwich, N., worstead weaver	138 Canler
1819	Nichols, Jeremiah, Reedham, N., farmer	40 Le Neve
1837	Nichols, John, Tivetshall St Mary, N., farmer	693 Warren
1857	Nichols, John, Ormesby St Margaret, N., house carpenter	239 Youngs
1846	Nichols, Mary, Mautby, N., spinster	342 Baret
1847	Nichols, Mary, Ormesby St Margaret, N., widow	53 Broom
1821	Nichols, Stephen, Sloley, N.	9 Dewell
1828	Nichols, Thomas, St John Timberhill, Norwich, N., cordwainer	241 Farrow
1856	Nicholson, Elizabeth, North Elmham, N., widow	517 Code
1846	Nicholson, Francis, East Dereham, N., gunsmith	488 Baret
1849	Nicholson, Maria, East Dereham, N., wife of Daniel Nicholson, farmer	121 Womack
1819	Nickalls, Carolina Maria, Shipden, Cromer, N., widow	293 Le Neve
1831	Nickalls, John, Norwich, N., gent.	419 Hart
1848	Nickalls, Susan, Norwich, N., widow	552 Denny
1850	Nickels, Benjamin, Orford, S., innkeeper	248 Cuthbert
1844	Nickels, William, Wickham Market, S., innkeeper	602 Ebbage
1851	Nickhols, Rachel, Polstead, S., spinster	254 Friar
1842	Nickless, Mary, New Buckenham, N., widow	409 Canler
1845	Nickless, Noah, Forncett St Peter, N., farmer	587 Pedgrift
1833	Nickols, Thomas, Walcot, N., gent.	154 Cubitt
1855	Nightingale, Charles, Great Yarmouth, N., yeoman	86 Whitty
1820	Nightingale, Francis, Great Yarmouth, N., coalmeter	256 Mack
1849	Nightingale, Maria, Great Yarmouth, N., spinster	498 Womack
1827	Nightingale, Robert the younger, Great Yarmouth, N., confectioner	572 Wood
1840	Nightingale, Samuel, Great Yarmouth, N., book keeper	50 Turner
1841	Ninham, John, St Georges Tombland, Norwich, plumber, glazier and painter	288 Traxton
1857	Ninham, Mary, Great Yarmouth, N., spinster	388 Youngs
1849	Nobbs, Charles, Heigham, Norwich, N., dealer	74 Womack
1824	Nobbs, Francis, Brandon, S., labourer	358 Borrett
1837	Nobbs, James, Brockdish, N., formerly of Dissand, gent.	228 Warren
1830	Nobbs, Robert, Little Snoring, N., alehouse keeper	236 Pettingill
1849	Nobbs, Thomas, Stratton Strawless, N., farmer	644 Womack
1854	Nobbs, Thomas, Norwich, N.	175 Day
1830	Nobel, Elizabeth, Ipswich, S., widow	17 Pettingill
1819	Noble, Ann, Little Walsingham, N., spinster	252 Le Neve
1853	Nockall, James, St Marys, Norwich, N., manufacturer	670 Veale
1855	Nockall, Joseph, Norwich, N., carpenter and builder	138 Whitty
1839	Nockall, Robert, St Augustines, Norwich, N., gauze weaver	536 Calton
1845	Nockolds, Henry, Mundesley, N., farmer	412 Pedgrift
1831	Nockolds, William, Neatishead, N., yeoman	228 Hart

1852	Nockolds, William, Great Yarmouth, N., carter and fish curer	541 Latten
1852	Nokes, Mary Elizabeth, Norwich, N., widow	313 Latten
1843	Nolbrow, John, Great Yarmouth, N., cordwainer	205 Miles
1842	Nolbrow, Susanna, Acle, N., widow	710 Canler
1844	Nolloth, Abraham, Wingfield, S., yeoman	520 Ebbage
1839	Norburn, Richard, Downham Market, N., farmer	455 Calton
1835	Norburn, Thomas, Downham Market, N., gent.	351 Harrowing
1831	Norfor, Robert, Great Yarmouth, N., labourer	561 Hart
1827	Norfor, William, Great Yarmouth, N., ropemaker	601 Wood
1852	Norfor, William, Great Yarmouth, N., town surveyor	324 Latten
1833	Norgate, Elias, Hethersett, N., gent.	O.W. 232
1823	Norman, Ann, St Clements, Norwich, N., wife of Thomas Norman, gent.	15 Tann
1853	Norman, Charles, Norwich, N., blacksmith	181 Veale
1835	Norman, Elizabeth, Felthorpe, N., widow	266 Harrowing
1848	Norman, Elizabeth, Stuston, S., spinster	368 Denny
1847	Norman, James, Burwell, C., saddler and collar maker	636 Broom
1825	Norman, John, Somersham, S., carpenter	240 Hayward
1833	Norman, John, Thetford, S., yeoman	225 Cubitt
1857	Norman, Joseph, Beccles, S., carpenter	639 Youngs
1839	Norman, Robert, Thetford, N., waterman	668 Calton
1823	Norman, Thomas, St Georges Colegate, Norwich, gent.	205 Tann
1844	Norman, Thomas, Whitwell, N., yeoman	253 Ebbage
1834	Norman, William, Gazeley, S., farmer	395 Lane
1834	Norman, Willam, Thetford, N., baker	175 Lane
1837	Norman, William, Thetford, N., waterman	301 Warren
1844	Norman, William, Harpley, N., miller and baker	297 Ebbage
1840	Norris, John, Norwich, N., cabinet maker	243 Turner
1845	Norton, Alice, St Peter Mancroft, Norwich, N., spinster	862 Pedgrift
1825	Norton, Amy Crisp, Norwich, N., spinster	42 Hayward
1842	Norton, Elizabeth, Great Yarmouth, N., widow	577 Canler
1832	Norton, Frances, Ipswich, S., spinster	388 Cooke
1837	Norton,Hannah, Colton, N., wife of William Norton, bricklayer	305 Warren
1829	Norton, James, Stokesby, N., farmer	293 Green
1855	Norton, James, Ringstead, N., farmer	509 Whitty
1830	Norton, John, East Dereham, N., miller	291 Pettingill
1855	Norton, Maria, Norwich, N., widow	45 Whitty
1821	Norton, Mary, Ormesby St Margaret, N., widow	262 Dewell
1823	Norton, Robert, East Dereham, N., miller	213 Tann
1851	Norton, Robert, Norwich, N., grocer and tea dealer	512 Friar
1851	Norton, Sarah Cobb, Great Yarmouth, N., spinster	340 Friar
1855	Norton, Sophia Louisa, Lowestoft, S., wife of Edmund Norton, gent.	289 Whitty
1849	Norton, Thomas, Heigham, Norwich, N., carpenter	462 Womack
1851	Norton, Thomas, Holt, N., farmer and common brewer	117 Friar
1822	Norton, William, Snettisham, N., gent.	298 Sadler
1829	Norton, William, Cawston, N., farmer	211 Green
1845	Norton, William, Colton, N., yeoman	901 Pedgrift
1840	Notcutt, Ann, Ipswich, S., spinster	116 Turner
1826	Notley, Robert, Shottesham All Saints, N., farmer	178 Davy
1831	Notley, William, Hoxne, S., farmer	154 Hart
1822	Nott, William, Carleton Rode, N., farmer	211 Sadler
1838	Noy, William, Ufford, S., yeoman	262 Skepper
1834	Nudds, Robert, St Stephens, Norwich, N., carpenter	795 Lane
1826	Nunn, Edmund, Botesdale, S., yeoman	170 Davy
1847	Nunn, Isaac, Burgate, S., labourer	21 Broom
1821	Nunn, John King, Hitcham, S., yeoman	62 Dewell
1846	Nunn, John, Hitcham, S., butcher	408 Baret
1837	Nunn, Margaret, Spexhall, S., widow	495 Warren
1838	Nunn, Robert, Hepworth, S., gent.	107 Skepper
1830	Nunn, Thomas the elder, Hitcham, S., butcher	182 Pettingill
1847	Nunn, Thomas, Thelnetham, S., farmer	469 Broom
1828	Nunn, William, Brome, S., yeoman	389 Farrow

1826	Nurse, George, Titchwell, N., yeoman	314 Davy
1851	Nurse, James, Diss, N., maltster	360 Friar
1841	Nurse, Mary Ann, Stoke Ferry	208 Traxton
1822	Nurse, William the elder, Feltwell, N., farmer	245 Sadler
1846	Nurse, William, Wormegay, N.	614 Baret
1852	Nurse, William the elder, Colchester, Essex, gent.	579 Latten
1830	Nuthall, Elizabeth, East Winch, N., wife of Nevil Nuthall, farmer	348 Pettingill
1842	Nuthall, Nevil, East Winch, N., farmer	295 Canler
1839	Nutman, Elizabeth, Fakenham, N., widow	165 Calton
1823	Nutman, Samuel, Fakenham, N., currier	201 Tann
1849	Oakes, John, Yaxley, S.	645 Womack
1842	Oakes, Rachel, Norwich, N., widow	509 Canler
1842	Oakes, Robert, Thrandeston, S., yeoman	199 Canler
1849	Oakes, Sarah, Great Yarmouth, N., widow	488 Womack
1826	Oakes, Thomas, Norwich, N., gent.	351 Davy
1855	Oakes, William, Downham Market, N., grocer	688 Whitty
1820	Oatley, Bathsheba, Snettisham, N., widow	67 Mack
1848	Offley, Henry the elder, Terrington St Clements, N., farmer	258 Denny
1821	Offord, James, New Buckenham, N.	107 Dewell
1819	Offord, Thomas, Rickinghall Inferior, S., yeoman	187 Le Neve
1837	Ogden, Ann, Hilgay, N., widow	221 Warren
1835	Olby, Robert, Brandon, S., gunflint maker and furrier	187 Harrowing
1833	Oldfield, Edmund, Walton, N., postmaster	362 Cubitt
1819	Oldfield, John, Grimston, N., farmer	299 Le Neve
1833	Oldfield, John, Upwell, N., farmer	221 Cubitt
1841	Oldfield, Henry, Ashill, N., farmer	263 Traxton
1827	Oldman, John, Wereham, N., miller	652 Wood
1838	Oldman, John, Wells next the Sea, N., fisherman	71 Skepper
1841	Oldman, John, Wheatacre All Saints, N., yeoman	9 Traxton
1820	Oldman, Mary, Thetford, N., widow	228 Mack
1847	Oldman, Robert, Wells next the Sea, N., fisherman	126 Broom
1846	Oldman, William Senior, Thetford, N., miller	503 Baret
1833	Oldmeadow, Thomas, North Runcton, N.	453 Cubitt
1836	Oldmeadow, William, Kings Lynn, N.	147 Smith
1848	Oldrin, Edward, Willingham, S., farmer	2 Denny
1852	Oldrin, Samuel, Kirby Cane, N.	483 Latten
1848	Oldring, James the elder, Southwold, S., butcher	230 Denny
1849	Oldring, Henry, Southwold, S., twinespinner	571 Womack
1826	Olifer, Juniper, Hevingham, N., yeoman	140 Davy
1841	Oliver, John, Brandeston, N., yeoman	580 Traxton
1842	Oliver, John, South Creake, N., farmer, maltster and brewer	239 Canler
1846	Oliver, Margaret, South Creake, N., widow	478 Baret
1837	Oliver, Shore, St Clements, Norwich, N., yeoman	216 Warren
1852	Oliver, William, Great Yarmouth, N., twinespinner	10 Latten
1853	Ollett, Tweed, Denver, N., farmer	289 Veale
1821	Olley, Frances, Norwich, N., spinster	296 Dewell
1834	Olley, Henry, Great Yarmouth, N., mariner	314 Lane
1843	Olley, John, West Somerton, N., yeoman	16 Miles
1820	Olley, Mary, Lowestoft, S., spinster	503 Mack
1822	Olley, Stephen, Norwich, N., dyer	371 Sadler
1828	Olley, Thomas, West Somerton, N.	114 Farrow
1838	Olley, Thomas, Barney, N., farmer	17 Skepper
1843	Olphin, John, Upwell, C.	15 Miles
1843	Orbell, James, Chellesworth, S., horse dealer	712 Miles
1850	Orfeur, John, Great Yarmouth, N., master mariner	384 Cuthbert
1842	Orford, George, Sporle, N., shoemaker	107 Canler
1822	Orford, John, Brooks Hall, Ipswich, S., gent.	268 Sadler
1843	Orford, Samuel, Sotherton, S., farmer	355 Miles
1824	Orford, William, West Dereham, N., farmer	21 Borrett
1857	Orfour, Elizabeth, Great Yarmouth, N., widow	362 Youngs
1847	Orman, Charles Joseph, Shouldham, N.	O.W. 313
1838	Orris, John, Hindringham, N., gent.	234 Skepper
1852	Orris, alias Smith, William, Kings Lynn, N., butcher	861 Latten

1837	Orsbon, William, Ipswich, S., yeoman	642 Warren
1841	Orsborn, George, Horsham St Faith, N.	527 Traxton
1841	Orsborn, Mark, Norwich, N., shoemaker	491 Traxton
1820	Orttewell, Frank, Mellis, S., linen weaver	252 Mack
1851	Osborn, Elizabeth, Blofield, N., spinster	291 Friar
1854	Osborn, John, Surlingham, N., labourer	543 Day
1857	Osborn, John, Rockland St Peter, N., farmer	472 Youngs
1851	Osborn, Mary, Blofield, N., spinster	291 Friar
1823	Osborn, William, Newmarket, S., carrier	281 Tann
1839	Osborn, William, Griston, N., gent.	245 Calton
1823	Osborne, Isaac, Norwich, alehouse keeper	280 Tann
1827	Osborne, Joseph, Newmarket, S., carrier	306 Wood
1829	Osborne, Robert, Kings Lynn, N., widower	158 Green
1825	Osborne, William, Woodbridge, S., cabinet maker	150 Hayward
1834	Osler, Thomas, Kings Lynn, N., master mariner	30 Lane
1833	Osler, William, Kings Lynn, N., bone merchant	273 Cubitt
1833	Ostler, James, -alias Hostler	344 Cubitt
1830	Ostwick, alias Astwick, Robert, Repps with Bastwick, N., yeoman	257 Pettingill
1832	Ostwick, alias Astwick, Thomas, Repps with Bastwick, farmer and coachmaker	192 Cooke
1831	Oswick, William, North Elmham, N., farmer	530 Hart
1845	Otty, Tabitha, Edgefield, N., spinster	371 Pedgrift
1829	Overed, James, Blofield, N., farmer	228 Green
1834	Overed, William, Blofield, N., veterinary surgeon	506 Lane
1854	Overton, John, Fakenham, N., attorney at law	90 Day
1845	Overton, Richard, Bodham, N., farmer	554 Pedgrift
1847	Overton, Samuel, Southrepps, N., yeoman	768 Broom
1857	Overton, William, Little Barningham, N., miller	525 Youngs
1845	Owen, Elizabeth, Halesworth, S., widow	851 Pedgrift
1848	Owen, Thomas, Sculthorpe, N., farmer	441 Denny
1828	Owers, Dorothy Ann, Mendlesham, S., widow	458 Farrow
1837	Owles, James, Yarmouth, N., grocer	707 Warren
1831	Owles, John, Huntingfield, S., cordwainer	12 Hart
1833	Owles, Mary, Huntingfield, S., spinster	242 Cubitt
1841	Owles, Thomas, St Michaels South Elmham, farmer	635 Traxton
1848	Oxborrow, James, Tannington, S., farmer	63 Denny
1857	Oxborrow, Mary Ann, Woodbridge, S., schoolmistress	640 Youngs
1851	Oxborrow, Stephen, Bredfield, S., yeoman	64 Friar
1831	Oxley, James, Norwich, N., gent.	483 Hart
1850	Oxley, John Prescott, Wroxham, N., gent.	540 Cuthbert
1855	Oxley, Mary, Norwich, N., spinster	185 Whitty
1827	Pack, Frances, East Dereham, N., widow	225 Wood
1831	Packard, George, Denton, N., formerly of Plumstead, Kent, blacksmith	85 Hart
1830	Packard, John Harrison, Hasketon, S., gent.	118 Pettingill
1824	Packard, William, Denton, N., farmer	349 Borrett
1849	Padgett, William, Congham, N., farmer	632 Womack
1830	Page, Ann, Ipswich, S., widow	O.W. 250
1854	Page, Ann, Itteringham, N., widow	410 Day
1856	Page, Anna, South Town, Yarmouth, S., widow	545 Code
1850	Page, - alias Cubitt, Cubitt, Burgh next Aylsham	375 Cuthbert
1836	Page, Elizabeth, St Andrews, Norwich, N., widow	185 Smith
1854	Page, Fanny, Cawston, N., wife of Samuel Page, farmer	277 Day
1848	Page, Frances, Heigham, Norwich, N., wife of Joseph Page, gent.	513 Denny
1850	Page, Hannah Elizabeth, Attlebridge, N., widow	269 Cuthbert
1821	Page, James, Charsfield, S., farmer	219 Dewell
1850	Page, James, Besthorpe, N., farmer	544 Cuthbert
1851	Page, James, Stow Bardolph, N., farmer	556 Friar
1852	Page, James, Carleton Rode, N.	472 Latten
1857	Page, James, Great Yarmouth, N., tailor	557 Youngs
1853	Page, Jeremiah, Bressingham, N., farmer	443 Veale
1826	Page, John, Stratton St Mary, N., gent.	331 Davy

1827	Page, John, East Dereham, N., farmer and tanner	465 Wood
1829	Page, John, Beccles, S., bricklayer	341 Green
1833	Page, John the elder, Walton, S., yeoman	192 Cubitt
1838	Page, John, Ellingham, N., farmer	59 Skepper
1853	Page, John, Kelsale, S., builder	318 Veale
1851	Page, Joseph, Norwich, N., gent.	79 Friar
1845	Page, Joshua, Wortwell, N., farmer	774 Pedgrift
1841	Page, Martha, Great Yarmouth, N., spinster	236 Traxton
1839	Page, Mary, Ipswich, S., widow	138 Calton
1854	Page, Philip, Field Dalling, N., farmer	O.W. 267
1855	Page, Robert, Dilham, N., butcher	46 Whitty
1845	Page, Samuel the elder, Wymondham, N., farmer	616 Pedgrift
1851	Page, Samuel, Catfield, N., carpenter	480 Friar
1820	Page, Thomas, Ormesby St Michael, N., bricklayer	174 Mack
1836	Page, Thomas, Ormesby St Margaret, N., farmer	202 Smith
1838	Page, Thomas, East Ruston, N., yeoman	719 Skepper
1847	Page, Thomas, Downham Market, N., pipe maker	578 Broom
1849	Page, Thomas, Great Yarmouth, N., labourer	574 Womack
1856	Page, Thomas, Walpole, S., gent.	33 Code
1857	Page, Thomas, Norwich, N., porter	212 Youngs
1820	Page, William, Norwich, N., innkeeper	608 Mack
1856	Page, William, Great Yarmouth, N., mariner	221 Code
1827	Pagnell, Joseph, Redgrave, S., yeoman	151 Wood
1854	Paine, Jane, Bury St Edmunds, S., spinster	382 Day
1844	Painter, Edmund, Holt, N., plumber and glazier	432 Ebbage
1838	Palgrave, James, Ludham, N., yeoman	613 Skepper
1827	Palgrave, Philip, North Runcton, N.	182 Wood
1833	Pallant, John, Aldburgh, S.	451 Cubitt
1826	Pallant, Robert, Thetford, N., blacksmith	350 Davy
1849	Palmer, Ambrose, Great Yarmouth, N., shipbuilder	308 Womack
1846	Palmer, Ann, Diss, N., wife of George Palmer, farmer	444 Baret
1854	Palmer, Betty, Norwich, N., spinster	368 Day
1848	Palmer, Charles, Pulham St Mary Magdalen, N., postman	441 Denny
1837	Palmer, Edward the elder, Thetford, S., farmer	661 Warren
1844	Palmer, Edward, Halvergate, N., yeoman	65 Ebbage
1820	Palmer, Elizabeth, St Andrews Hill, Norwich, N., widow	587 Mack
1851	Palmer, Francis, Soham, C., farmer	274 Friar
1850	Palmer, Frederick Nathaniel, Great Yarmouth, N., surgeon	106 Cuthbert
1838	Palmer, George, Lenwade, Great Witchingham, N., blacksmith	489 Skepper
1838	Palmer, George, Thetford, S., coachmaker	316 Skepper
1839	Palmer, George, St Johns Maddermarket, Norwich, N., broker	99 Calton
1856	Palmer, Hannah Pottle, Old Buckenham, N., shopkeeper	173 Code
1856	Palmer, Henry Norton, New Buckenham, N., esquire	114 Code
1847	Palmer, Isaac, Soham, C., yeoman	664 Broom
1819	Palmer, Isabella, Old Buckenham, N., wife of Robert Palmer, farmer	59 Le Neve
1820	Palmer, John, Wicken, C., yeoman	328 Mack
1842	Palmer, John, East Dereham, N., carpenter	725 Canler
1847	Palmer, John, Welborne, N., farmer	308 Broom
1849	Palmer, Jonathan, Broome, N., yeoman	617 Womack
1834	Palmer, Mary, Soham, C., spinster	18 Lane
1840	Palmer, Mary, Pulham St Mary Magdalen, N., widow	669 Turner
1855	Palmer, Mary, Great Yarmouth, N., widow	5 Whitty
1840	Palmer, Phillis, Wilby, N., spinster	466 Turner
1844	Palmer, Richard, Thompson, N., farmer	155 Ebbage
1827	Palmer, Robert, Rockland All Saints, N., farmer	460 Wood
1832	Palmer, Robert Bailey, Upwell, N., wheelwright	85 Cooke
1835	Palmer, Samuel, Bramford, S., carpenter	466 Harrowing
1822	Palmer, Sarah, South Lynn All Saints, Kings Lynn, N., widow	311 Sadler
1853	Palmer, Sarah, Great Yarmouth, N., widow	314 Veale
1851	Palmer, Thomas, Shipdham, N., gent.	226 Friar
1857	Palmer, Thomas, Beeston, N., gent.	350 Youngs
1834	Palmer, William Danby, Great Yarmouth, N., esquire	762 Lane
1838	Palmer, William, Thetford, N.	16 Skepper

1840	Palmer, William, Broome, N., yeoman	646 Turner
1835	Pamment, Jane, Bury St Edmunds, S., widow	366 Harrowing
1841	Pane, Mayham, Cley, N., blacksmith	139 Traxton
1845	Pank, Elizabeth, St Michaels Coslany, Norwich, N., widow	17 Pedgrift
1822	Pank, Matthew, Shipden, Cromer, N., bricklayer	133 Sadler
1836	Pank, Sherringham, White Hart Inn, Norwich, N., innkeeper and stone mason	313 Smith
1845	Panks, Robert, Grimston, N., yeoman	360 Pedgrift
1837	Parfrey, Thomas, Wilton, N., labourer	594 Warren
1828	Parish, Edward, Norwich, N., worstead weaver	106 Farrow
1852	Parish, James Broughton, Marham, N., grocer and draper	772 Latten
1854	Park, John, Wiggenhall St Mary, N., gardener	434 Day
1840	Parke, Elizabeth, Norwich, N., single woman	O.W. 265
1833	Parke, James, Hoxne, S., farmer	353 Cubitt
1851	Parke, John, Bawdeswell, N., farmer	135 Friar
1830	Parke, Ruth, Norwich, N., widow	367 Pettingill
1839	Parke, Thomas, Brome, S., farmer	57 Calton
1837	Parke, William Baldy, Norwich, N., gent.	786 Warren
1845	Parker, Dorothy, Whissonsett, N., widow	88 Pedgrift
1833	Parker, Elizabeth, Bildeston, S., widow	327 Cubitt
1822	Parker, George, Weybread, S., gent.	34 Sadler
1835	Parker, James, Great Yarmouth, N., accomptant	413 Harrowing
1824	Parker, John, Bildeston, S., butcher	168 Borrett
1827	Parker, John, Thurne with Oby, N., yeoman	490 Wood
1833	Parker, John, Bildeston, S., esquire	476 Cubitt
1834	Parker, John, North Walsham, N., fishmonger	551 Lane
1838	Parker, John, Diss, N., gardener	134 Skepper
1847	Parker, Mary, Blofield, N., widow	620 Broom
1854	Parker, Mary, Eye, S., widow	154 Day
1829	Parker, Robert the elder, Whissonsett, N., blacksmith	238 Green
1833	Parker, Robert, Whissonsett, N., blacksmith	435 Cubitt
1836	Parker, Robert, Winfarthing, N., tailor	2 Smith
1842	Parker, Robert, Hopton, S., labourer	17 Canler
1851	Parker, Samuel, Bungay, S., currier	102 Friar
1820	Parker, Thomas, Tattersett, N., gent.	189 Mack
1838	Parker, William, Grundisburgh, S., bricklayer and plasterer	118 Skepper
1853	Parker, William, Lowestoft, S., master mariner	435 Veale
1854	Parkerson, Carter John, Loddon, N., farmer	330 Day
1856	Parkerson, Charlotte, Pulham St Mary Magdalen, N., spinster	233 Code
1834	Parkerson, James, Pulham St Mary Magdalen, N., gent.	88 Lane
1845	Parkerson, John Carter, Loddon, N., farmer	238 Pedgrift
1823	Parkerson, Lydia, Pulham St Mary Magdalen, N., wife of James Parkerson, gent.	77 Tann
1823	Parkhurst, Benjamin, Ipswich, S.	308 Tann
1827	Parkhurst, John the elder, Ipswich, S., coal meter	684 Wood
1827	Parkinson, Jane, South Lynn All Saints, Kings Lynn, N., widow	205 Wood
1834	Parment, James, Great Dunham, N., butcher	403 Lane
1849	Parmeter, Ann, South Town, S., wife of John Parmeter, gent.	275 Womack
1827	Parnell, Elizabeth, Cley next the Sea, N., wife of Thomas Parnell, labourer	297 Wood
1855	Parnell, Henry, Bircham Magna, N., shopkeeper	648 Whitty
1841	Parnell, Robert, Norwich, N., stone mason	490 Traxton
1823	Parr, Ann, Norwich, N., widow of Rev. Robert Parr	O.W. 180
1831	Parr, Mark the elder, Burwell, C., yeoman	54 Hart
1853	Parr, Mary, Stalham, N., widow, o.w. missing	703 Veale
1857	Parr, Mary, Stalham, N., widow	378 Youngs
1832	Parr, Robert, Neatishead, N., farmer	290 Cooke
1827	Parr, William, Burwell, C., miller	298 Wood
1855	Parr, William Mark, Burnham Overy, N., mariner	458 Whitty
1825	Parrish, Sarah, Norwich, widow	18 Hayward
1854	Parry, Harvy, Thetford, N., miller	204 Day
1820	Parry, John Gascoigne, Ipswich, S.	241 Mack
1834	Parry, Susanna, Southwold, S., widow	607 Lane

1855	Parry, Thomas, Thetford, N., veterinary surgeon	392 Whitty
1822	Pars, Albertus, Newmarket, S., gent.	372 Sadler
1833	Pars, Charles, Newmarket, S., shopkeeper	235 Cubitt
1840	Parsey, William, Thorpe, Norwich, N., weaver	392 Turner
1836	Parsley, James, Metfield, S., farmer	410 Smith
1844	Parsley, William, Henstead with Hulverstreet, S., farmer	249 Ebbage
1829	Parson, Henry, Boxford, S., gent.	79 Green
1835	Parson, Shadrack, Wacton, N., farmer	171 Harrowing
1839	Parson, Thomas, Norwich, N., plumber and glazier	234 Calton
1820	Parson, William, Upper Downham, Wymondham, N., farmer	620 Mack
1839	Parsons, James, Lessingham, N., yeoman	578 Calton
1857	Parsons, Mary, Wilby, S.	85 Youngs
1855	Parsons, Robert, Snettisham, N., farmer	652 Whitty
1838	Parsons, Samuel Wild, Great Yarmouth, N., licensed victualler	91 Skepper
1835	Parsonson, William, Sudbury, S., cordwainer	343 Harrowing
1845	Partrick, William, Thursford, N., shopkeeper	356 Pedgrift
1840	Partridge, Elizabeth, Bury St Edmunds, S., spinster	420 Turner
1824	Partridge, Joseph, St Edmunds, Norwich, weaver	122 Borrett
1839	Partridge, Joseph, St Julian, Norwich, N., publican	247 Calton
1833	Partridge, Mary, Norwich, N., spinster	149 Cubitt
1852	Partridge, Mary, Norwich, N., widow	518 Latten
1826	Partridge, Rebecca, Wolterton, N., widow	223 Davy
1837	Partridge, Richard, Great Yarmouth, N., ship master	193 Warren
1820	Partridge, Robert, Stoke by Nayland, S., yeoman	54 Mack
1851	Partridge, Robert, Horstead, N., esquire	76 Friar
1856	Partridge, Robert Ansell, Layham, S., gent.	98 Code
1841	Partridge, Sarah, Kersey, S., widow	380 Traxton
1819	Partridge, William, Wiston, S., farmer	83 Le Neve
1856	Pashley, Rebecca, Great Yarmouth, N., widow	107 Code
1847	Pashley, Samuel, Great Yarmouth, N., mariner	134 Broom
1854	Pashly, Charles, Norwich, N., music teacher	272 Day
1833	Paske, George, Needham Market, S., esquire	311 Cubitt
1846	Passon, Frances, Great Yarmouth, N., widow	194 Baret
1827	Patfield, Luke, Hackford next Reepham, N., blacksmith	619 Wood
1828	Patrick, James, Alburgh, N., farmer	524 Farrow
1839	Patrick, Mary, Foulsham, N., widow	458 Calton
1845	Patrick, Parlet, Barnby, S., farmer	939 Pedgrift
1821	Pattern, John, Walpole St Peter, N., farmer	67 Dewell
1845	Patterson, John, Halesworth, S., innholder	813 Pedgrift
1830	Pattle, John, Knodishall, S., farmer	276 Pettingill
1851	Pattle, Robert the younger, Tannington, S., farmer	105 Friar
1842	Paul, Ann, Gresham, N., widow	678 Canler
1829	Paul, John, Gresham, N., gent.	373 Green
1846	Paul, Lydia, Pentney, N., spinster	517 Baret
1820	Paul, William, Norwich	569 Mack
1841	Paul, William, Pentney, N., farmer	O.W. 308
1831	Pavis, Ann, Bunwell, C., widow	385 Hart
1838	Pavis, John, Cheveley, C., yeoman	776 Skepper
1823	Pavis, Joseph, Kirtling, C., miller	219 Tann
1856	Paxman, Ann Smith, Stowmarket, S., draper	640 Code
1847	Paxman, Christopher, Yoxford, S., yeoman	358 Broom
1856	Paxman, James, Stowmarket, S., grocer and draper	111 Code
1841	Paxman, John, Great Bradley, S., thatcher	140 Traxton
1828	Payn, Mary, Debach, S., widow	369 Farrow
1840	Payne, George, Sibton, S., farmer	588 Turner
1845	Payne, James, Saham Toney, N., farmer	703 Pedgrift
1835	Payne, John, Gorleston, S., pilot	491 Harrowing
1841	Payne, John, St Peter Mancroft, Norwich, N., gent.	593 Traxton
1844	Payne, John, Coston, N.	46 Ebbage
1855	Payne, John the younger, Diss, N., innkeeper	413 Whitty
1856	Payne, John, Thetford, S., yeoman	612 Code
1837	Payne, Richard, Westgate St., Long Melford, S.	251 Warren
1842	Payne, Simon, Ipswich, S., gent.	759 Canler

1849	Payne, Simon, Ipswich, S.	Index only
1842	Payne, William, South Burgh, N., farmer	601 Canler
1837	Peachy, Edward Fox, Brancaster, N., wheelwright	629 Warren
1838	Peachey, James, Fordham, C., thatcher	778 Skepper
1838	Peachey, John, Mildenhall, S., farmer	296 Skepper
1848	Peachey, Mary, Wicken, C., spinster	233 Denny
1827	Peachey, Reuben, Beck Row, Mildenhall, S., thatcher	415 Wood
1823	Peachey, Samuel, Burwell, C., farmer	350 Tann
1834	Peacock, Agnes, Great Yarmouth, N., widow	321 Lane
1844	Peacock, John, Ipswich, S., formerly of Blakenham Magna, S., gent.	606 Ebbage
1851	Peacock, Mary, Ipswich, S., widow	352 Friar
1851	Peacock, Thomas, North Tuddenham, N., rector	511 Friar
1853	Peacock, Thomas, Upwell, N.	524 Veale
1826	Peairce, John, Newton St Faiths, N., weaver	143 Davy
1846	Peake, Mary, Rushall, N., single woman	114 Baret
1833	Peake, Robert, Brockdish, N., husbandman	102 Cubitt
1820	Peake, Thomas, East Harling, N., blacksmith	223 Mack
1844	Peake, Thomas, Pulham St Mary the Virgin, N., farmer	694 Ebbage
1842	Pearce, James, St Clements, Norwich, N.	143 Canler
1842	Pearce, Margaret, Heigham, Norwich, N.	144 Canler
1831	Pearce, Mary, Newton St Faiths, N., widow	28 Hart
1839	Pearce, Richard, Norwich, N., carpenter and joiner	468 Calton
1822	Pearce, Samuel, Pulham St Mary, N., farmer	151 Sadler
1842	Pearl, George, Hoxne, S., gent.	624 Canler
1832	Pearl, Samuel, Hitcham, S., farmer	155 Cooke
1840	Pearse, Elizabeth, Bungay, S., spinster	519 Turner
1855	Pearse, Fredric, Toftmonks, N., farmer	17 Whitty
1845	Pearse, Henry Neale, Hainford, N., tailor and draper	853 Pedgrift
1841	Pearse, John, Bungay, S., innholder	239 Traxton
1827	Pearse, Richard, Longham, N., carpenter	119 Wood
1832	Pearson, Catherine, Cromer, N.	276 Cooke
1825	Pearson, Elizabeth, Kings Lynn, N., wife of George Pearson, victualler	442 Hayward
1837	Pearson, James, Northrepps, N., farmer	735 Warren
1857	Pearson, James, Norwich, N., gent.	255 Youngs
1851	Pearson, John, Colby, N., bricklayer	159 Friar
1831	Pearson, Joseph, Tibbenham, N., farmer	445 Hart
1828	Pearson, Samuel, Kings Lynn, N., teacher of mathematics	66 Farrow
1839	Pearson, Susannah, Great Yarmouth, N., widow	84 Calton
1845	Pearson, William, St Benedicts, Norwich, N., plasterer	777 Pedgrift
1849	Pearson, William, Northrepps, N., farmer	243 Womack
1837	Peck, John, Litcham, N., jobber	683 Warren
1839	Peck, John, Rishangles, S., farmer and miller	541 Calton
1843	Peck, John, Brockford, S., gent.	457 Miles
1847	Peck, John, Wenhaston, S., husbandman	580 Broom
1844	Peck, Judith, Great Yarmouth, N., widow	214 Ebbage
1846	Peck, Priscilla, Brockford, S., widow	276 Baret
1842	Peck, Robert, Wilby, N., farmer	554 Canler
1838	Peck, Thomas, Mendlesham, S., gent.	129 Skepper
1841	Peck, Thomas, Cheveley, C., carpenter	36 Traxton
1831	Peck, William, Shipdham, N., farmer	81 Hart
1843	Peck, William, Cheveley, C., carpenter	693 Miles
1852	Peck, William, Norwich, N., gent.	93 Latten
1840	Peckett, William, Southery, N., grocer and draper	150 Turner
1831	Peckover, Sarah, Lowestoft, S., widow	215 Hart
1847	Peddar, Charles, Shelland, S., shopkeeper, formerly of Stowmarket	483 Broom
1831	Pedder, Frances, Aylsham, N., widow	155 Hart
1827	Pedder, John, Aylsham, N., gent.	444 Wood
1855	Pedgrift, James, Harleston, N., stone mason	677 Whitty
1845	Pedgrift, John, Alburgh, N., bricklayer	1 Pedgrift
1857	Pedgrift, Robert Augustus, Halesworth, S., surgeon	776 Youngs

1839	Peebles, Juliet, Neatishead, N., wife of Thomas Peebles, carpenter	358 Calton
1855	Peek, Susan, Soham, C., widow	O.W. 343
1839	Peeke, Charlotte, Norwich, N., widow	586 Calton
1839	Peele, Edmund, Cromer, N., yeoman	672 Calton
1830	Peeny, William, South Lynn All Saints, N., master mariner	214 Pettingill
1820	Pegg, Ann, Aslacton, N., widow	274 Mack
1846	Pegg, Elizabeth, Great Waldingfield, S., spinster	35 Baret
1842	Pegg, Hannah, Aylsham, N., wife of Robert Pegg	269 Canler
1827	Pegg, Henry, Sheringham, N., farmer	169 Wood
1848	Pegg, John, Lower Sheringham, N., farmer	336 Denny
1849	Pegg, John, Sheringham, N., farmer	94 Womack
1850	Pegg, Joseph, Guestwick, N., farmer	181 Cuthbert
1839	Pegg, Margaret, Sheringham, N., widow	631 Calton
1852	Pegg, Matthew, Colby, N., farmer	407 Latten
1854	Pegg, Thomas, Sheringham, N., farmer	147 Day
1835	Pegg, William, Ringshall, S., farmer	606 Harrowing
1832	Peglar, Daniel, Nayland, S., gent.	4 Cooke
1843	Peirson, Alfred, Shadingfield, S., gent.	255 Miles
1831	Peirson, Elizabeth, Shadingfield, S., widow	513 Hart
1825	Peirson, John the elder, Stoven, S., farmer	27 Hayward
1835	Peirson, Mary, Acle, N., wife of John Peirson, surgeon	231 Harrowing
1854	Peirson, Robert, Somerleyton, S., yeoman	537 Day
1840	Pell, Susanna, Kings Lynn, N., widow	279 Turner
1844	Pells, John, Aylmerton, N., farmer	642 Ebbage
1855	Pells, John the elder, Ipswich, S., bricklayer	47 Whitty
1854	Pells, Samuel, Beccles, S., yeoman	67 Day
1831	Pells, William, Frostenden, S., carpenter	128 Hart
1846	Pendal, William, Tannington, S., wheelwright	455 Baret
1838	Pennington, Ann, Lowestoft, S., spinster	595 Skepper
1836	Penny, Sarah, Great Yarmouth, N., widow	273 Smith
1826	Pennyman, Isaac, St Gregory, Norwich, N., publican	369 Davy
1854	Penrice, Charles, Little Plumstead, N., clerk	91 Day
1850	Pentin, John, Norwich, N., broker	163 Cuthbert
1845	Pentin, Paul, Norwich, N., gent.	10 Pedgrift
1841	Pentney, Richard, Norwich, N., carpenter	234 Traxton
1857	Pepper, Hannah, Laxfield, S., wife of James Pepper, carpenter	296 Youngs
1825	Pepper, Samuel the elder, Ipswich, S., merchant	457 Hayward
1855	Percival, Richard, Lowestoft, S., yeoman	685 Whitty
1845	Perk, William, Cheveley, C.	Index only
1854	Perkins, Frances, Carleton St Peter, N., farmer	233 Day
1850	Perkins, Jeremiah, East Dereham, N., tinman and plate worker	316 Cuthbert
1825	Perkins, Henry Sparbanke, Coltishall, N., gent.	60 Hayward
1837	Perkins, Percy, Coltishall, N., spinster	152 Warren
1837	Perkins, Richard, Thornham, N., brickmaker	573 Warren
1826	Perowne, John, Stalham, N., gent.	O.W. 176
1842	Perowne, William, Barney, N., gent.	498 Canler
1847	Perren, John, Wood Ditton, C.	411 Broom
1831	Perriment, Ann, Great Whelnetham, S., widow	418 Hart
1853	Perring, Dame Ann, Southwold, S., widow	245 Veale
1848	Perry, John, Watlington, N., builder	527 Denny
1851	Perry, William, Swaffham, N., veterinary surgeon	585 Friar
1845	Pert, William, Aylsham, N., plumber, glazier and painter	504 Pedgrift
1843	Pestell, Joseph, Great Yarmouth, N., yeoman	133 Miles
1857	Pestell, Robert, Horning, N., horse dealer	534 Youngs
1838	Petchey, Benjamin the younger, Dersingham, N., wheelwright	829 Skepper
1854	Petchey, Lydia, Dersingham, N., widow	156 Day
1832	Petchy, Benjamin, Dersingham, N., wheelwright	108 Cooke
1833	Peters, Mary, Norwich, N., spinster	110 Cubitt
1828	Peters, Robert, Worstead, N., farmer	302 Farrow
1822	Peterson, Ann, Norwich, N., alias Whitehand	309 Sadler
1857	Petre, the Hon. Catherine, Westwick House, N., widow	653 Youngs

1847	Pett, Robert, Ashill, N., farmer	433 Broom
1848	Pettet, John, Oakley, S., basket maker	491 Denny
1831	Pettett, Martha, Kirtling, C., widow	414 Hart
1846	Pettett, Mary, Gorleston, S., widow	57 Baret
1852	Pettett, Samuel, Eye, S., shoemaker	47 Latten
1856	Pettingall, Elizabeth, Great Yarmouth, N., spinster	458 Code
1838	Pettingall, Robert, Tharston, N., farmer	41 Skepper
1855	Pettingill, Ann, Southtown, Little Yarmouth, S., spinster	418 Whitty
1845	Pettingill, Edmund, Hemsby, N., farmer	586 Pedgrift
1848	Pettingill, Elizabeth, Mautby, N., widow	325 Denny
1853	Pettingill, John, Fritton, S., farmer	26 Veale
1830	Pettingill, Robert, Filby, N., yeoman	1 Pettingill
1853	Pettingill, William, Burgh St Margaret, N., farmer	148 Veale
1823	Pettingle, Elizabeth, Blofield, N., widow	O.W. 178
1853	Pettingle, Elizabeth, Ludham, N., spinster	181 Veale
1844	Pettingle, John, Fritton, S., yeoman	626 Ebbage
1821	Pettingle, Thomas, Blofield, N., farmer	O.W. 146
1842	Pettit, Elizabeth, Oakley, S., widow	631 Canler
1838	Pettit, John, Ellingham, N., yeoman	216 Skepper
1844	Pettit, William, Soham, C., yeoman	706 Ebbage
1826	Pettitt, Jonathan, Osmondiston (Scole), N., basket maker	356 Davy
1820	Pettrie, Susanna, Great Yarmouth, N., widow	66 Mack
1857	Petty, Charles, Belton, S., labourer	610 Youngs
1834	Phetham, William, South Lynn All Saints, Kings Lynn, N., labourer	376 Lane
1846	Phillips, Abraham senior, Old Buckenham, N., carpenter	399 Baret
1828	Phillips, Jacob, Old Buckenham, N.	424 Farrow
1826	Phillips, John, East Bergholt, S.	63 Davy
1828	Phillips, Pullyn, Old Buckenham, N., farmer	215 Farrow
1857	Phillipo, Edward, Horningtoft, N., farmer	270 Youngs
1842	Phillipo, George, Barney, N., yeoman	187 Canler
1851	Phillipo, James, Norton, N., farmer	351 Friar
1830	Philo, James, East Dereham, N.	61 Pettingill
1837	Philo, John Bocking, Swaffham, N., leather cutter	280 Warren
1842	Philpot, David, Brundish, S., miller	288 Canler
1854	Philpott, John, Walpole, S., farmer	163 Day
1825	Pickering, Hobman, Buxton, N., shopkeeper	201 Hayward
1834	Pickering, Mary, Buxton, N., widow	287 Lane
1837	Pickers, Thomas, Great Yarmouth, N., gent.	223 Warren
1826	Pickrell, John, Hillington, N., farmer	42 Davy
1846	Pidgeon, Elizabeth, Hulver, S., widow	387 Baret
1842	Pidgeon, Thomas, Middleton, N., farmer	207 Canler
1851	Pigg, Alice, Wells, N., widow	189 Friar
1850	Pigg, Elizabeth, Great Yarmouth, N., widow	314 Cuthbert
1838	Pigg, John, St Augustines, Norwich, N., carpenter	61 Skepper
1825	Pigg, Joseph, Great Yarmouth, N.	233 Hayward
1825	Pigg, Thomas, Norwich, N., gent.	295 Hayward
1850	Pigg, William, Norwich, N., broker	299 Cuthbert
1845	Pigge, Andrew, Heacham, N., gent.	379 Pedgrift
1829	Pigge, Thomas, Wiveton, N., gent.	O.W. 241
1842	Pigge, Valentine, Wells next the Sea, N., farmer	676 Canler
1831	Piggin, Benjamin, Thorpe next Norwich, N., toll bar keeper	430 Hart
1853	Piggin, John, Norwich, N., gent.	168 Veale
1856	Piggin, John, Norwich, N., watchmaker	665 Code
1849	Piggins, Stephen the elder, Great Yarmouth, N., gent.	545 Womack
1844	Pightling, Anna Maria, Coltishall, N., widow	189 Ebbage
1833	Pightling, William, Coltishall, N., gent.	15 Cubitt
1826	Pigney, Edward, Great Yarmouth, N., yeoman	325 Davy
1846	Pigott, William, Weybourne, N., yeoman	68 Baret
1852	Pike, John, Great Yarmouth, N., gent.	358 Latten
1819	Pilch, Thomas, North Walsham, N., farmer	20 Le Neve
1827	Pile, William, Yarmouth, N., mariner	154 Wood
1825	Pilgrem (Pilgrim), Mary, Hoe, N., widow	322 Hayward
1846	Pilgrim, James, Hempstead, N., farmer	162 Baret

1826	Pilgrim, Jeremiah, North Walsham, N., yeoman	257 Davy
1834	Pilgrim, John, Wattisham, S., farmer	837 Lane
1840	Pilgrim, Lydia, Winfarthing, N., single woman	408 Turner
1840	Pilgrim, Maurice, Winfarthing, N., farmer	9 Turner
1836	Pinchen, James, West Bradenham, N., blacksmith	236 Smith
1827	Pinchin, Charles, Cley next the Sea, N., coal porter	232 Wood
1829	Pinkney, Thomas, Hasketon, S., gent.	286 Green
1852	Pinnock, Margaret, Wells next the Sea, N., widow	82 Latten
1829	Pipe, James, Bedfield, S., farmer	437 Green
1831	Pipe, James, Ipswich, S., innkeeper	519 Hart
1835	Pipe, Mary, Framlingham, S., spinster	498 Harrowing
1846	Pipe, Philip, Stradbroke, S., yeoman	298 Baret
1855	Pipe, Philip, Kings Lynn, N., brewer	668 Whitty
1834	Pipe, Samuel, Friston, S., tailor	186 Lane
1857	Pipe, Susanna, Shadbrooke, S., widow	22 Youngs
1850	Piper, Edmund, Mileham, N., yeoman	306 Cuthbert
1832	Piper, Isaac, Beccles, S., shoemaker	189 Cooke
1820	Piper, William, Weeting, N., carpenter	30 Mack
1831	Pitcher, James, Beccles, S., yeoman	457 Hart
1832	Pitcher, John, Docking, N., wheelwright	476 Cooke
1849	Pitcher, Kirk, Easton, N., farmer	381 Womack
1829	Pitcher, Robert, South Lynn All Saints, Kings Lynn, N., tide surveyor	3 Green
1825	Pitchers, Jane, Geldeston, N.	272 Hayward
1849	Pitchers, Mary, Barsham, S., widow	194 Womack
1839	Pitches, John, Exning, S., innkeeper	73 Calton
1837	Pitt, James, Great Yarmouth, N., gent.	773 Warren
1844	Pitts, John, Shernborne, N., publican	182 Ebbage
1824	Pitts, Thomas, late of Burgate, S., now London, gent.	88 Borrett
1839	Pitts, William, Denver, N., yeoman	53 Calton
1841	Pitts, William, Holme next Sea, N., yeoman	588 Traxton
1856	Pittuck, John, Eye, S., yeoman	359 Code
1825	d'Piza, Anne Maria, - see Depiza	
1852	Pizzy, William, Norton, S., veterinary surgeon	69 Latten
1851	Plaford, Elizabeth, Holt, N., widow	272 Friar
1848	Plaford, Thomas Page, Mannington, N., gent.	635 Denny
1824	Plane, Edward, Foulsham, N., cord winder	243 Borrett
1829	Plane, Edward, Aylsham, N., gent.	114 Green
1851	Plane, William, Great Witchingham, N., farmer	197 Friar
1820	Plant, Edmund the elder, North and Great Glemham, S., farmer	341 Mack
1837	Plant, Elizabeth, Saxmundham, S., widow	596 Warren
1852	Plant, John, Trowse Newton, N., farmer	347 Latten
1844	Plant, Robert, Horham, S., gent.	406 Ebbage
1846	Platfoot, Lydia, Wighton, N., widow	628 Baret
1839	Platfoot, Wighton, N., tailor	675 Calton
1857	Platford, Elizabeth, Necton, N., widow	566 Youngs
1829	Platford, William, Horning, N., yeoman	44 Green
1836	Platt, Samuel, Heydon, N., gent.	181 Smith
1857	Platten, Peter, Norwich, N., livery stable keeper	656 Youngs
1852	Platten, William, Thornham, N., farmer	468 Latten
1845	Playford, George, Norwich, N., butcher	850 Pedgrift
1849	Playford, George, Great Yarmouth, N., pawnbroker	480 Womack
1843	Playford, John, Gillingham, N., farmer	670 Miles
1848	Playford, Robert, Bungay, S., yeoman	761 Denny
1841	Playford, Thomas, Thornage, N., farmer	83 Traxton
1849	Playford, William the elder, Norton Subcourse, N., gent.	135 Womack
1852	Playford, William, Limpenhoe, N., yeoman	413 Latten
1852	Playford, William, Soham, C., bookseller, stationer and printer,	373 Latten
1853	Pleasance, Charles, Sutton Woodbridge, S., publican	205 Veale
1856	Pleasance, William, Woodbridge, S., innkeeper	34 Code
1857	Pleasants, Ann, Great Yarmouth, N., widow	268 Youngs
1853	Pleasants, Thomas, Horsham St Faiths, N., gent.	167 Veale
1838	Pleasants, William, Toft Monks, N., blacksmith	587 Skepper

1835	Plow, William, Hardley, N., yeoman	587 Harrowing
1852	Plowman, Ann, Wells next the Sea, N., widow	543 Latten
1841	Plowman, Jane, Great Yarmouth, N., widow	511 Traxton
1850	Plowman, Sophia, Bungay, S., widow	432 Cuthbert
1822	Plowman, Thomas, Broome, N., farmer	345 Sadler
1841	Plowman, William, Wells next the Sea, N., sieve maker	200 Traxton
1833	Plowright, Ann, South Lynn All Saints, Kings Lynn, N., widow	45 Cubitt
1824	Plowright, George, Swaffham, N., late brazier	62 Borrett
1819	Plowright, John, Swaffham, N., plumber and glazier	93 Le Neve
1845	Plowright, Thomas, Kings Lynn, N., linen draper	708 Pedgrift
1846	Plowright, Thomas, Kings Lynn, N., brazier	63 Baret
1847	Plowright, William Tomling, Swaffham, N., ironmonger	424 Broom
1829	Plumb, Ann, Sculthorpe, N., spinster	59 Green
1841	Plumb, Curtis, Ipswich, S., gent.	110 Traxton
1856	Plumb, James, Brancaster Town, N., shepherd	675 Code
1857	Plumbley, Charles, East Dereham, N., publican	16 Youngs
1857	Plumbtree, John, Upwell, N., farmer	274 Youngs
1819	Plummer, Charles, East Ruston, N., yeoman	291 Le Neve
1819	Plummer, Elizabeth, Norwich, N., widow	226 Le Neve
1853	Plummer, John, Great Yarmouth, N., gent.	499 Veale
1852	Plummer, Mary, St John de Sepulchre, Norwich, N., widow	59 Latten
1831	Plumton, Robert, Attleborough, N., ironmonger and blacksmith	295 Hart
1843	Plunkett, James, Norwich, N., weaver	225 Miles
1833	Podd, Mary, Farnham, S., widow	301 Cubitt
1826	Pointer, William, Thornham, N., carrier	54 Davy
1832	Pointer, William, Norwich, N., yeoman	309 Cooke
1851	Pole, Noah, Belton, S., house carpenter	247 Friar
1838	Poll, James, Downham Market, N., miller and baker	79 Skepper
1845	Poll, James, Wymondham, N., weaver	523 Pedgrift
1838	Poll, John, Downham Market, N., miller	274 Skepper
1846	Poll, Philip, Bungay, S., clock and watchmaker	620 Baret
1841	Pollard, Charles, Martham, N., gent.	475 Traxton
1850	Pollard, Robert, Catfield, N., husbandman	182 Cuthbert
1856	Pollard, Thomas, Bungay, S., yeoman	637 Code
1822	Pollyn, John, Tilney St Lawrence, N., yeoman	295 Sadler
1852	Pollyn, William, Tilney St Lawrence, N., farmer	16 Latten
1837	Pond, Henry, Beccles, S., dyer	289 Warren
1826	Pond, John, Great Dunham, N., farmer	180 Davy
1827	Pond, John, Diss, N., dyer	639 Wood
1835	Pond, Mary, East Dereham, N., widow	295 Harrowing
1832	Pond, Robert, Shropham, N., farmer	594 Cooke
1829	Pond, Susanna, Diss, N., widow	96 Green
1838	Ponder, Lydia, Newmarket All Saints, C., spinster	297 Skepper
1821	Pool, Zepheniah, Bildeston, S., plumber and glazier	328 Dewell
1845	Poole, Joseph, Southtown, S.	38 Pedgrift
1848	Poole, Mary, Burwell, C., wife of James Poole, yeoman	45 Denny
1831	Poole, Thomas Zephaniah, Bildeston, S., plumber and glazier	505 Hart
1838	Poole, Thomas, Mendham, N., draper	540 Skepper
1837	Poole, William, Debenham, S., gent.	789 Warren
1848	Pooley, Henry, Woodbridge, S., baker	700 Denny
1845	Pooley, Jane, Wilton near Hockwold, N., housekeeper	306 Pedgrift
1848	Pooley, John, Debenham, S., farrier	651 Denny
1832	Pooley, Mary Ann, Winston, S.	367 Cooke
1839	Pooley, Rachel, Ipswich, S., spinster	436 Calton
1852	Popay, Charles, Winterton, N., tailor	728 Latten
1825	Popay, James, Winterton, N., tailor	502 Hayward
1843	Pope, Anne, Blaxhall, S., widow	579 Miles
1856	Pope, Hannah, Orford, S., servant	537 Code
1835	Pope, Henry, Thurlton, N., thatcher	362 Harrowing
1855	Pope, Susannah, Great Yarmouth, N., formerly of Lowestoft, S., widow	56 Whitty
1853	Pope, Thomas, Southtown, Yarmouth, S., ferryman	412 Veale
1855	Pope, William, Lound, S., labourer	55 Whitty
1854	Popjoy, Joseph, Heigham, Norwich, N., gent.	239 Day

1845	Poppey, Sarah, Ipswich, S., widow	471 Pedgrift
1853	Popplewell, Mary Ann Neech, Great Yarmouth, N., widow	20 Veale
1820	Poppy, Edward, Hoxne, S., farmer	329 Mack
1834	Poppy, Frances, Weybread, S.	496 Lane
1843	Poppy, Jonathan, Great Yarmouth, N., hat manufacturer	604 Miles
1857	Poppy, Robert, Topcroft, N., tailor and draper	480 Youngs
1847	Porrett, James, Welborne, N., butcher	738 Broom
1842	Porter, Christopher, Southery, N., yeoman	154 Canler
1853	Porter, Darius, Methwold, N., yeoman	661 Veale
1853	Porter, Elizabeth, Moulton, N., widow	198 Veale
1849	Porter, Gamaliel, Southery, N., shoemaker	48 Womack
1839	Porter, George the elder, Rickinghall Superior, formerly of Weybread, S., farmer	294 Calton
1849	Porter, George Brooks, Newmarket St Mary, S., grocer	222 Womack
1836	Porter, Jacob, - alias Read	
1822	Porter, James, Kings Lynn, N., gent.	4 Sadler
1828	Porter, James, Freethorpe, N., farmer	483 Farrow
1828	Porter, John, Holbrook, S., house carpenter	13 Farrow
1845	Porter, John, Thorpe, Norwich, N., gent.	384 Pedgrift
1857	Porter, John, Blakeney, N., mariner	510 Youngs
1847	Porter, Kibble, Southery, N., farmer	338 Broom
1831	Porter, Osler, Southery, N., yeoman	460 Hart
1855	Porter, Robert, Kings Lynn, N., meat salesman	616 Whitty
1827	Porter, Thomas, Southery, N., farmer	310 Wood
1828	Porter, William, Southery, N., labourer	106 Farrow
1845	Porter, William, Newmarket, S., gent.	97 Pedgrift
1827	Postle, Ann, Burgh next Aylsham, N., widow	698 Wood
1852	Postle, Hannah, Thelnetham, S., wife of Samuel Postle, gent.	42 Latten
1851	Postle, Henry, Burgh next Aylsham, N., carpenter	335 Friar
1847	Postle, John, Ingham, N., gent.	509 Broom
1855	Postle, John, Smallburgh, N., esquire	314 Whitty
1830	Postle, Samuel, East Ruston, N., gent.	250 Pettingill
1855	Potter, Catherine, Fakenham, N., spinster	101 Whitty
1856	Potter, Daniel, Old Buckenham, N., farmer	225 Code
1854	Potter, Francis, Little Dunham, N., yeoman	39 Day
1838	Potter, George Simpson Densley, Attleborough, N., surgeon	13 Skepper
1841	Potter, Robert, Old Buckenham, N., yeoman	317 Traxton
1845	Potter, Robert the younger, Moulton, N., publican	675 Pedgrift
1857	Potter, Robert Roper, Bressingham, N., farmer	778 Youngs
1827	Potter, Samuel, Wighton, N., farmer	79 Wood
1839	Potter, Thomas, Nayland, S., corn dealer	682 Calton
1851	Potter, Thomas, Forncett St Peter, N., husbandman	563 Friar
1822	Potter, William, Sudbury, S., innkeeper	72 Sadler
1827	Potter, William, Aslacton, N.	23 Wood
1833	Potter, William, Leziate, N., farmer	162 Cubitt
1841	Potts, John, Kessingland, S., farmer	240 Traxton
1851	Powditch, Thomas, Wells, N., mariner	255 Friar
1844	Powell, Charles, Wighton, N., farmer	403 Ebbage
1828	Powell, John, Norwich, N., gardener	189 Farrow
1841	Powell, John, Norwich, N., linen draper	534 Traxton
1852	Powell, John, North Walsham, N., yeoman	328 Latten
1855	Powell, John, Antingham, N., blacksmith and farrier	571 Whitty
1823	Powell, Mary, Aylsham, N., widow	159 Tann
1833	Powell, Stephen, Norwich, N., linen draper	298 Cubitt
1841	Powell, William, Wormegay, N., esquire	304 Traxton
1849	Powell, William, North Walsham, N., draper	524 Womack
1837	Powley, Ann, Little Fransham, N., widow	4 Warren
1845	Powley, Bartholomew, Little Dunham, N., farmer	720 Pedgrift
1828	Powley, Mary, Swaffham, N., widow	21 Farrow
1845	Powley, Mary, Newton, N., widow	676 Pedgrift
1847	Powley, Richard, Great Yarmouth, N., baker	172 Broom
1833	Powley, William, Newton by Castleacre, N., miller	373 Cubitt
1851	Powley, William, Norwich, N., livery stable keeper	73 Friar
1850	Pratt, Ann, Felthorpe, N., widow	116 Cuthbert

1856	Pratt, Ann, Norwich, N., spinster	232 Code
1828	Pratt, Benjamin, Norwich, N., maltster	104 Farrow
1846	Pratt, Daniel, Mendham, S., gent.	242 Baret
1824	Pratt, George the elder, Ringstead, N., farmer	32 Borrett
1846	Pratt, Hannah, Norwich, N., spinster	619 Baret
1851	Pratt, Henry, Snettisham, N., farmer	267 Friar
1832	Pratt, James, Needham, N., gent.	347 Cooke
1838	Pratt, Jeremiah, Ipswich, S., formerly of Kings Lynn, N., cork cutter	327 Skepper
1838	Pratt, John, Horsford, N., farmer	710 Skepper
1845	Pratt, Mary, Thetford, N., widow	614 Pedgrift
1857	Pratt, Maud, Norwich, N., widow	773 Youngs
1846	Pratt, Richard, Felthorpe, N., farmer	326 Baret
1850	Pratt, Samuel, Weston, N., farmer	487 Cuthbert
1831	Pratt, Sarah, Saham Toney, N., widow	132 Hart
1856	Pratt, Sarah, Norwich, N., widow	89 Code
1835	Pratt, Thomas, Norwich, N., currier	205 Harrowing
1836	Pratt, Thomas, Norwich, N., currier	307 Smith
1836	Pratt, William, Felthorpe, N., farmer	21 Smith
1850	Pratt, William, Burwell, C., yeoman	161 Cuthbert
1856	Pratt, William, Antingham, N., yeoman	263 Code
1839	Pratt, Zachariah, Gissing, N., single man	644 Calton
1854	Precious, Elizabeth, Lowestoft, S., wife of Robert Precious, whitesmith	526 Day
1836	Prentice, Manning, Stowmarket, S.	506 Smith
1828	Prentice, Rachel, Bungay, S.	9 Farrow
1832	Prentice, Sarah, Bungay, S., widow	282 Cooke
1836	Presant, William, Gorleston, S.	272 Smith
1840	Presant, William, Gorleston, S.	Index only
1855	Press, Edward, Southtown, Yarmouth, S., miller	620 Whitty
1850	Press, Elizabeth, Norwich, N., widow	93 Cuthbert
1848	Press, Jane, St Peter Hungate, Norwich, N., widow	137 Denny
1836	Press, John Latham, Hoxne, S., gent.	121 Smith
1846	Press, John, North Walsham, N., draper	29 Baret
1852	Press, John, Beccles, S., innkeeper	747 Latten
1837	Press, Lydia, North Walsham, N., widow	546 Warren
1839	Press, Mary, Trunch, N., spinster	82 Calton
1832	Press, Thomas, Coltishall, N., cordwainer	487 Cooke
1844	Press, Thomas, Hethersett, N., gent.	4 Ebbage
1836	Prestney, Thomas, Nayland, S., soap boiler	576 Smith
1847	Preston, Francis, Burwell, C., turf digger	451 Broom
1846	Preston, Jane, Beeston Park, N., widow	580 Baret
1821	Preston, Thomas, Naughton, S., farmer	69 Dewell
1845	Prestwidge, George the elder, Southwold, S., yeoman	963 Pedgrift
1824	Pretty, James, Snettisham, N., gent.	75 Borrett
1855	Pretty, John, Thetford, N., plumber and glazier	485 Whitty
1849	Pretty, Mary, Tibbenham, N., spinster	176 Womack
1830	Pretty, Robert, Tibbenham, N., farmer	85 Pettingill
1838	Pretty, Robert, Rickinghall Inferior, higgler	597 Skepper
1845	Pretty, Robert, Tibbenham, N., farmer	943 Pedgrift
1846	Pretty, Robert the younger, Eye, S., draper and tailor	348 Baret
1852	Pretty, Susan, Yaxley, S., spinster	778 Latten
1848	Price, Charles, Cheveley, C., farmer and miller	716 Denny
1831	Price, George, Wood Ditton, C., farmer	93 Hart
1840	Price, Sarah, Sculthorpe, N., widow	627 Turner
1830	Pridgeon, Samuel, North Runcton, N., farmer	116 Pettingill
1838	Pridgeon, Thomas, Kings Lynn, N.	121 Skepper
1843	Priest, Elizabeth Neale Frances, St Giles, Norwich, N., spinster	65 Miles
1844	Priest, Hannah Arnall, Norwich, N., spinster	113 Ebbage
1825	Priest, John, Burnham Norton, N.	385 Hayward
1826	Priest, Joseph, - alias Whitby	
1846	Priest, Richard, Redenhall with Harleston, N., gent.	532 Baret
1852	Priest, Robert Raven, Norwich, N., druggist	77 Latten

1852	Priest, William, Great Walsingham, N., bricklayer	213 Latten
1829	Priestley, Mary, Heacham, N., widow	51 Green
1844	Prigg, Mary, Alpheton, S., spinster shopkeeper	150 Ebbage
1820	Prime, Harriet, Rushall, N., wife of William Prime, farmer	534 Mack
1849	Prime, James, Rumburgh, S., farmer	309 Womack
1844	Prime, John, Flordon, N., bailiff	280 Ebbage
1838	Prime, William, Toft Monks, N., carpenter	333 Skepper
1847	Prime, William, Palgrave, S., shoemaker	9 Womack
1851	Prime, William, Huntingfield, S., labourer	581 Friar
1830	Primett, Thomas the elder, Beccles, S., butcher	452 Pettingill
1834	Primrose, Ann, Trunch, N., widow	686 Lane
1832	Primrose, William, Trunch, N., gent.	546 Cooke
1837	Primrose, William, Norwich, N.	689 Warren
1839	Prince, Ann, Newmarket, S., widow	595 Calton
1857	Prince, Charlotte, St Augustines, Norwich, N., widow	583 Youngs
1837	Prior, Charles, Hackford next Reepham, N., saddler	361 Warren
1824	Prior, Joseph, Wiggenhall St Germains, N., toll bar keeper	344 Borrett
1851	Pritchard, John, Great Yarmouth, N., surgeon	14 Friar
1830	Pritty, Thomas, Haughley, S., shopkeeper	370 Pettingill
1831	Proctor, Robert, Coddenham, S., butcher	30 Hart
1855	Proudfoot, Henry, Stanhoe, N., gent.	124 Whitty
1854	Proudfoot, Thomas, Scottow, N., husbandman	O.W. 268
1837	Pryke, Margaret, Stoke next Nayland, S., widow	617 Warren
1846	Pryor, Mary, Combs, S., widow	310 Baret
1848	Pulham, Charles, Weybread, S., husbandman	624 Denny
1819	Pulham, John, Great Yarmouth, N., furniture broker	255 Le Neve
1835	Pummell, John, Norwich, N., throwsterer	618 Harrowing
1843	Punchard, Robert, Downham Market, N., yeoman	243 Miles
1856	Punt, James, Bressingham, N., labourer	412 Code
1843	Punt, Joseph, Bressingham, N., yeoman	602 Miles
1844	Purcell, Joseph, Lyng, N.	206 Ebbage
1852	Purdey, Robert, Stoke next Norwich, N., farmer	764 Latten
1840	Purdy, Henry, Heigham, Norwich, N., carpenter	475 Turner
1836	Purdy, Thomas, Foulsham, N., maltster	180 Smith
1854	Purdy, Thomas, Kings Lynn, N., carpenter	544 Day
1848	Purling, Ann, Little Ryburgh, N., widow	210 Day
1847	Purling, William, Yarmouth, N., farmer, formerly of Little Ryburgh, N.	366 Broom
1834	Purple, Henry, Longham, N., labourer	190 Lane
1852	Purr, Robert, Stowmarket, S., cabinet maker and upholsterer	653 Latten
1846	Purr, William, Great Finborough, S., blacksmith	634 Baret
1835	Purse, William, Rickinghall Superior, S., labourer	550 Harrowing
1838	Puxley, James, St Peter Mancroft, Norwich, N., innkeeper	463 Skepper
1837	Puxley, John, Norwich, N., cordwainer	307 Warren
1827	Puxley, Mary, Caister next Yarmouth, N., widow, o.w. missing	492 Wood
1830	Puxley, Mary, Caister next Yarmouth, N., widow	220 Pettingill
1831	Pye, Elizabeth, Cawston, N., widow	465 Hart
1853	Pye, John, Bungay, S., cordwainer	80 Veale
1840	Pye, Sarah, Swannington, N., widow	13 Turner
1855	Pye, Susannah, St Benedicts, Norwich, N., widow	575 Whitty
1825	Pye, Thomas, Salle, late of Bawdeswell, N., farmer	17 Hayward
1854	Pyle, William, Thornage, N., baker	401 Day
1821	Pyman, John the elder, Besthorpe, N., farmer	199 Dewell
1855	Pyman, John, Stowupland, S., gent.	491 Whitty
1854	Pymar, Thomas, Beccles, S., gent.	59 Day
1833	Quadling, John, Bedingham, N., farmer	390 Cubitt
1829	Quadling, Mary, Norwich, N., widow	99 Green
1839	Quantrell, Christopher, Norwich, N., cordwainer	129 Calton
1848	Quantrell, Richard, Heigham, Norwich, N., bricklayer	623 Denny
1826	Quantrill, Joseph, Old Buckenham, N., farmer	280 Davy
1844	Quantrill, Sarah, Diss, N., widow	650 Ebbage
1838	Quarles, Francis Thomas, Foulsham, N., gent.	367 Skepper
1827	Quinton, James, Earl Stonham, S., farmer	701 Wood
1841	Quinton, John, Great Yarmouth, N., mariner	29 Traxton

1856	Quinton, John, Mickfield, S.	187 Code
1856	Quinton, John, Needham Market, S., chemist and druggist	554 Code
1835	Raby, Edmund, Gaywood, N.	256 Harrowing
1841	Raby, George the elder, Downham Market, N., farmer	330 Traxton
1836	Racey, Thomas, Lakenham, Norwich, N., gent.	578 Smith
1835	Rackham, Ann, Wrentham, S., widow	367 Harrowing
1824	Rackham, Catherine, Norwich, N., widow	141 Borrett
1856	Rackham, alias Rant, Edward, Mendham, S., farmer	287 Code
1830	Rackham, Elizabeth, Norwich, N., spinster	458 Pettingill
1837	Rackham, Elizabeth, Norwich, N., spinster	648 Warren
1833	Rackham, George, Bedingham, N., gent.	303 Cubitt
1830	Rackham, Henry, Earsham, N., farmer	90 Pettingill
1837	Rackham, Henry, Bungay, S., yeoman	785 Warren
1834	Rackham, John, Snape, S.	613 Lane
1837	Rackham, John, Earl Soham, S., yeoman	387 Warren
1851	Rackham, John, Alburgh, N., farmer	321 Friar
1854	Rackham, Martha, Aylsham, N., widow	430 Day
1822	Rackham, Mary, Norwich, N., widow	387 Sadler
1855	Rackham, Roger, Westhall, S., farmer	187 Whitty
1829	Rackham, Simon, Foulsham, N., gent.	234 Green
1834	Rackham, Simon, St Margarets South Elmham, S., yeoman	115 Lane
1848	Rackham, Thomas, Aylsham, N., gent.	580 Denny
1853	Rackham, Thomas Charles, Kenninghall, N., Master of Guiltcross Union Workhouse	257 Veale
1850	Raffe, James, Stowmarket, S., cordwainer	149 Cuthbert
1830	Rainbird, Priscilla, Norwich, N., widow	218 Pettingill
1827	Rainer, Francis, Great Yarmouth, N., master to sea	153 Wood
1820	Raker, Ann, Rattlesden, S., widow	195 Mack
1850	Rallison, Mary Ann, Haughley, S., widow	15 Cuthbert
1822	Ralph, Robert, Woolverstone, S., farmer	142 Sadler
1836	Ralph, Robert, Leiston, S., labourer	393 Smith
1829	Ram, Ann, Swaffham, N., widow	426 Green
1855	Ram, Thomas, Hethersett, N., yeoman	590 Whitty
1823	Ramm, Eleanor, Wiveton, N., widow	29 Tann
1820	Ramm, Jipporah, Norwich, N., widow	194 Mack
1845	Ramm, Richard, Shouldham, N., farmer	638 Pedgrift
1833	Ramm, Wilson, Norwich, N., dyer	87 Cubitt
1832	Rampley, William, Blofield, N., innkeeper	362 Cooke
1857	Rampling, Edward the elder, Eye, S., carpenter	382 Youngs
1856	Ramsdale, Matthew, East Dereham, N., leather cutter	516 Code
1831	Ramsey, Robert, St Stephens, Norwich, N., gent.	200 Hart
1844	Ramsey, William, St John Maddermarket, Norwich, N., plumber, glazier and painter	413 Ebbage
1837	Ramus, James, Bungay, S., bricklayer	780 Warren
1824	Rand, Hewett the younger, Norwich, N., gent.	O.W. 179
1857	Randall, George, Moulton, N., farmer	661 Youngs
1848	Randall, John, Little Glemham, S.	170 Denny
1828	Randall, Martha, Charsfield, S., farmer	282 Farrow
1827	Randall, Samuel, Aldeburgh, S., coach maker	227 Wood
1826	Randall, Thomas, Snape, S., veterinary surgeon	256 Davy
1833	Randell, John, Ipswich, S., master mariner	101 Cubitt
1839	Rands, Israel, Debenham, S., schoolmaster	387 Calton
1857	Ranier, alias Campling, Susanna, Great Yarmouth, N., widow	386 Youngs
1843	Ranner, Ralph, Newmarket, S., yeoman	699 Miles
1838	Rannow, Henry, Hartest, S., farmer	239 Skepper
1848	Ransbey, Samuel, Bawdsey, S., shoemaker	619 Denny
1843	Ransom, Doiby Scott, Cromer, N., mariner	715 Miles
1848	Ransom, Frances, Cromer, N., spinster	289 Denny
1832	Ransom, Henry, Cromer, N., victualler	421 Cooke
1827	Ransom, James, Holkham, N., beer brewer	160 Wood
1834	Ransom, Judith Susanna, Cromer, N., widow	79 Lane
1855	Ransom, Robert, Wells next the Sea, N., carpenter	668 Whitty
1845	Ransome, Ann, Great Yarmouth, N., widow	599 Pedgrift
1852	Ransome, Henry, Norwich, N., watchmaker	191 Latten

1842	Ransome, James, Norwich, N., haberdasher	163 Canler
1837	Ransome, John, Ludham, N., farmer	748 Warren
1853	Ransome, Robert, Rollesby, N., farmer	235 Veale
1831	Ransome, William, Burgh St Margaret, N., miller	239 Hart
1828	Ranson, Frances, Hintlesham, S., widow	204 Farrow
1844	Ranson, Sarah, Chediston, S., widow	243 Ebbage
1852	Rant, George, Mendham, S., esquire	316 Latten
1844	Rant, James, Bungay, S., innkeeper	570 Ebbage
1856	Rant, alias Rackham, Edward, Mendham, S., farmer	287 Code
1841	Rattee, Anne, Fundenhall, N., widow	173 Traxton
1833	Rattee, James, Ashwellthorpe, N., blacksmith	157 Cubitt
1820	Raven, Benjamin, Horningtoft, N., farmer	163 Mack
1831	Raven, Elizabeth, Burnham Westgate, N.	25 Hart
1824	Raven, Frances, Swaffham, N., widow	295 Borrett
1846	Raven, James, Swaffham, N., farmer	154 Baret
1855	Raven, Jane, Gorleston, S., spinster	602 Whitty
1827	Raven, John, Stoven Green, S., woodman	55 Wood
1830	Raven, John, Wiggenhall St Germains, N., gent.	254 Pettingill
1838	Raven, John, Sotterley, S., carpenter	702 Skepper
1850	Raven, John, Norwich, N., gent.	387 Cuthbert
1826	Raven, Margaret, Swaffham, N., widow	97 Davy
1839	Raven, Mary Ann, Docking, N., wife of John Raven, esquire	437 Calton
1856	Raven, Richard, Kings Lynn, N., gent.	647 Code
1837	Raven, Sarah, Bawdeswell, N., spinster	783 Warren
1851	Raven, Stephen, Watton, N., formerly of Norwich, innkeeper	126 Friar
1820	Rawling, James, Cockley Cley, N., yeoman	580 Mack
1855	Rawling, Sarah, Gressenhall, N., spinster	200 Whitty
1819	Rawling, William, Brandon, S., yeoman	26 Le Neve
1821	Rawson, John, Norwich, N., gunmaker	311 Dewell
1843	Ray, Charles, Needham, N.	286 Miles
1837	Ray, Elizabeth, Norwich, N., spinster	488 Warren
1838	Ray, Francis, Norwich, N., glover	176 Skepper
1821	Ray, Thomas, Hardwick, N., yeoman	46 Dewell
1842	Ray, Thomas, Kings Lynn, N., gent.	18 Canler
1853	Ray, Walter, Tostock, S., esquire	229 Veale
1838	Raymes, Joseph, Hevingham, N., shopman	276 Skepper
1830	Raymond, Benjamin, Ipswich, S., shipbuilder	396 Pettingill
1825	Rayner, Ann, Kessingland, S., late of Wrentham, S., carpenter	330 Hayward
1819	Rayner, Benjamin, Holt, N., husbandman	82 Le Neve
1857	Rayner, Frances, Langmere, N., widow	393 Youngs
1847	Rayner, James, Middleton, N., baker	653 Broom
1834	Rayner, John, Stratton St Mary, N., yeoman, formerly of Earsham, N.	819 Lane
1839	Rayner, John Rix, Thornham, N., farmer	417 Calton
1844	Rayner, John, Thorpe next Norwich, N., farmer and gardener	38 Ebbage
1839	Rayner, Jonathan, Diss, N., formerly of Roydon, N., farmer	392 Calton
1850	Rayner, Mark, Newmarket, S., fish merchant	77 Cuthbert
1843	Rayner, Mary, Fulmodeston with Croxton, N., widow	80 Miles
1849	Rayner, Philip, Diss, N., publican and coal dealer	212 Womack
1844	Rayner, Robert, Hilgay, N., yeoman	5 Ebbage
1848	Rayner, Thomas, Thornham, N., farmer	131 Denny
1838	Rayner, William, Rougham, N., victualler	782 Skepper
1837	Raynham, Thomas, Bildeston, S., carpenter	262 Warren
1829	Raynor, John, Kirtling, C., farmer	326 Green
1840	Rayson, Thomas, Hardingham, N., farmer	255 Turner
1824	Read, Ann, Great Yarmouth, N., widow	243 Borrett
1857	Read, Anne, Great Yarmouth, N., spinster	810 Youngs
1850	Read, Elizabeth, Bungay, S., spinster	278 Cuthbert
1826	Read, George, Hollesley, S., shopkeeper	70 Davy
1845	Read, George, Orford, S., carpenter and boat builder	59 Pedgrift
1832	Read, Henry, Wighton, N., farmer	416 Cooke
1855	Read, Henry, Beccles, S., gent.	111 Whitty
1856	Read, Henry, Gissing, N., yeoman	677 Code

1836	Read, Jacob, alias Porter, Halesworth, S., basket maker	536 Smith
1854	Read, James, Great Yarmouth, N., builder	42 Day
1823	Read, John, Aldeby, N., farmer	56 Tann
1827	Read, John, Great Yarmouth, N., gent.	353 Wood
1830	Read, John, Loddon, N., farmer	300 Pettingill
1836	Read, John, East Dereham, N., farmer	530 Smith
1839	Read, John, Eye, S., publican	101 Calton
1841	Read, John, St Nicholas South Elmham, S., farmer	132 Traxton
1845	Read, John Thomas, Stowmarket, S.	299 Pedgrift
1846	Read, John, Yarmouth, N.	498 Baret
1827	Read, Joseph, Woodbridge, S., shoemaker	211 Wood
1822	Read, Margaret, Great Yarmouth, N., widow	254 Sadler
1832	Read, Martha, Freethorpe, N., widow	47 Cooke
1829	Read, Robert, Westleton, S., blacksmith	269 Green
1833	Read, Robert, Ormesby St Michael, N., farmer	385 Cubitt
1846	Read, Robert, Needham Market, S., beer seller	594 Baret
1839	Read, Samuel, Alburgh, N., bricklayer	338 Calton
1851	Read, Sarah, Mautby, N., spinster	143 Friar
1830	Read, Stephen, Fakenham, N., brewer	363 Pettingill
1837	Read, Susan, Norwich, N., single woman	11 Warren
1846	Read, Susanna, Wickham Skeith, S., spinster	369 Baret
1842	Read, Thomas, Frettenham, N., farmer	88 Canler
1823	Read, William, Great Yarmouth, N., innkeeper	218 Tann
1824	Read, William, Great Yarmouth, N., gent.	280 Borrett
1843	Read, William, Heigham, Norwich, N., bricklayer	605 Miles
1843	Read, William, Norwich, N., cordwainer	331 Miles
1849	Read, William, Hopton, S., cordwainer	123 Womack
1852	Read, William, Wortham, S., farmer	431 Latten
1851	Read, Zachariah, Pulham St Mary Magdalen, N., yeoman	523 Friar
1841	Readwin, Mary, Fakenham, N., widow	593 Traxton
1840	Readwin, William Leist, Fakenham, N., builder and carpenter	570 Turner
1831	Reason, Mary, Bungay, S., widow	127 Hart
1845	Reddish, Hannah, Rattlesden, S., widow	279 Pedgrift
1834	Reddish, William, Stowmarket, S., poulterer	512 Lane
1835	Redgment, Thomas, West Bradenham, N., yeoman	511 Harrowing
1824	Redgrave, Daniel, New Buckenham, N., yeoman	36 Borrett
1855	Redgrave, Hannah, Norwich, N., widow	518 Whitty
1846	Redgrave, Joseph, St Etheldred, Norwich, N., drayman	268 Baret
1852	Redgrave, Samuel, Bungay, S., yeoman	289 Latten
1832	Redit, Nathaniel, Grundisburgh, S., schoolmaster	273 Cooke
1851	Reeder, Michael, Norwich, N., gent.	184 Friar
1824	Reeder, alias Wright, William, Swaffham, N.	
1827	Reeder, William, Great Bradenham, N., bricklayer	578 Wood
1855	Reeder, William the elder, Kirstead, N., farmer	597 Whitty
1828	Reeve, Ann, Kenninghall, N., single woman	194 Farrow
1846	Reeve, Ann, Little Walsingham, N., widow	284 Baret
1853	Reeve, Dinah, Wyverstone, S., widow	641 Veale
1821	Reeve, Daniel, Brisley, N., gent.	279 Dewell
1848	Reeve, Edward, Heigham, Norwich N., schoolmaster	239 Denny
1826	Reeve, Elizabeth, Norwich, N., widow	246 Davy
1841	Reeve, Elizabeth, Thuxton, N., widow	33 Traxton
1832	Reeve, George, Kenninghall, N., farmer	247 Cooke
1829	Reeve, James, Kings Lynn, N., cabinet maker	389 Green
1840	Reeve, John, Oxwick, N., farmer	492 Turner
1842	Reeve, John, Wighton, N., gent.	61 Canler
1843	Reeve, John Sayer, Norwich, N., baker	575 Miles
1844	Reeve, John, Briston, N., miller	393 Ebbage
1829	Reeve, Owen, Wymondham, N., weaver	393 Green
1830	Reeve, Rebecca, Great Yarmouth, N., spinster	159 Pettingill
1837	Reeve, Richard, Barney, N., gent.	171 Warren
1841	Reeve, Richard, Halesworth, S., gent.	674 Traxton
1830	Reeve, Robert, Kenninghall, N., late of Mulbarton, N., carpenter	343 Pettingill
1848	Reeve, Robert, Yaxley, S., innkeeper	220 Denny

1846	Reeve, Samuel, Kenninghall, N., farmer	247 Baret
1853	Reeve, Susanna, Honingham, N., widow	324 Veale
1820	Reeve, Thomas, Neatishead, N., butcher	438 Mack
1832	Reeve, Thomas Gosling, Gislingham, S., esquire	O.W. 258
1841	Reeve, Thomas, Honingham, N., farmer	390 Traxton
1823	Reeve, William, Wainford Mills, near Bungay, S., carpenter	416 Tann
1836	Reeve, William, Great Yarmouth, N., whitesmith	406 Smith
1841	Reeve, William, Thuxton, N., farmer	38 Traxton
1843	Reeve, William, Downham Market, N., carpenter	129 Miles
1853	Register, Edward, Southery, N., yeoman	663 Veale
1847	Reid, Walter, Great Yarmouth, N., gent.	131 Broom
1853	Remblance, Robert, Belton, S., yeoman	666 Veale
1823	Remmonds, John, Ludham, N., yeoman	412 Tann
1823	Rendall, alias Kendall, Mary, Whissonsett, N., widow	32 Tann
1857	Revans, Edward, Yoxford, S., gent.	406 Youngs
1825	Revans, John, Woodbridge, S., master mariner	497 Hayward
1823	Revans, William, Yoxford, S., esquire	45 Tann
1849	Revett, Alfred, Stowmarket, S., builder	228 Womack
1823	Revill, Marmaduke, North Walsham, N., shopkeeper	316 Tann
1852	Reyner, Rawling, Litcham, N.	162 Latten
1845	Reynolds, Abraham, East Bergholt, S., thatcher	312 Pedgrift
1853	Reynolds, Ann, Bramfield, S., widow	469 Veale
1844	Reynolds, Charles, St Martin at Oak, Norwich, N., gent.	152 Ebbage
1833	Reynolds, Francis, Forncett St Peters, N., farmer	415 Cubitt
1856	Reynolds, Isaac, East Bergholt, S., yeoman	228 Code
1819	Reynolds, James, Brandon, S., labourer	137 Le Neve
1852	Reynolds, James the elder, Burgh St Peter, N., labourer	524 Latten
1846	Reynolds, Jeremiah, East Bradenham, N., farmer	173 Baret
1826	Reynolds, John, Hoxne, S., gent.	368 Davy
1834	Reynolds, John, Wymondham, N., farmer	861 Lane
1839	Reynolds John, Mendlesham, S., ironmonger	48 Calton
1852	Reynolds, John, Norwich, N., Wesleyan minister, o.w. missing	188 Latten
1822	Reynolds, Joseph, North Walsham, N., farmer	116 Sadler
1841	Reynolds, Mary, Norton Subcourse, N., widow	101 Traxton
1837	Reynolds, Richard, Burgh, N., yeoman	640 Warren
1853	Reynolds, Robert, Norwich, N.	19 Veale
1839	Reynolds, Sarah, Gayton, N., widow	101 Calton
1838	Reynolds, Stephen, Bramfield, S., yeoman	372 Skepper
1832	Reynolds, Thomas, Loddon, N., gent.	261 Cooke
1844	Reynolds, Thomas, Upwell, N., yeoman	90 Ebbage
1822	Reynolds, William, Benhall, S., yeoman	157 Sadler
1844	Reynolds, William, Exning, S., maltster	196 Ebbage
1852	Reynolds, William, Thurning, N., miller	478 Latten
1856	Reynolds, William, Newton St Faiths, N., farmer	303 Code
1828	Rhodes, Samuel, Outwell, N., waterman	49 Farrow
1842	Ribbands, Stephen, Coltishall, N., labourer	193 Canler
1829	Rice, Catharine, Norwich, N., wife of James Luke Rice, tailor and draper	304 Green
1837	Rice, Edmund, Mulbarton, N., yeoman	309 Warren
1828	Rice, James Luke, Norwich, N., river surveyor	515 Farrow
1832	Rice, Margaret, Emneth, N.	88 Cooke
1835	Rice, Thomas, Lammas, N., farmer	432 Harrowing
1845	Rice, Thomas, Langham, N., labourer	55 Pedgrift
1854	Rice, Thomas, Lammas, N., farmer	383 Day
1848	Richards, William, Hempnall, N., butcher	321 Denny
1824	Richardson, Charles, Norwich, N., worstead weaver	100 Borrett
1823	Richardson, Clement, Docking, N., farmer and blacksmith	113 Tann
1832	Richardson, Jacob, Hackford, N., farmer	12 Cooke
1843	Richardson, Abraham, Bredfield, S., yeoman	192 Miles
1834	Richardson, Edward, St Giles, Norwich, N., publican	249 Lane
1844	Richardson, Edward, Hempton, N., yeoman	586 Ebbage
1854	Richardson, Elizabeth, Alby, N., widow of Samuel Richardson, late of Suffield, farmer	380 Day
1839	Richardson, James, Wretton, N., bricklayer	397 Calton

1840	Richardson, James, Shipdham, N., farmer	99 Turner
1841	Richardson, John the elder, Feltwell, N., millwright	30 Traxton
1846	Richardson, Robert, Great Snoring, N., shepherd	300 Baret
1843	Richardson, Sally, Woodbridge, S., wife of Abraham Richardson, butcher	187 Miles
1838	Richer, Ann, Rattlesden, S., spinster	591 Skepper
1826	Richer, Nicholas, St Gregory, Norwich, N., bookbinder	200 Davy
1854	Riches, Ann, Althorpe, N., widow	437 Day
1843	Riches, Anne, Freethorpe, N., spinster	587 Miles
1837	Riches, Elizabeth, East Ruston, N., formerly of Brumstead, N., wife of Isaac Riches, blacksmith	323 Warren
1841	Riches, Elizabeth, Great Yarmouth, N., widow	302 Traxton
1854	Riches, Francis, Shipdham, N., farmer	292 Day
1847	Riches, Henry, Poringland, N., yeoman,	421 Broom
1822	Riches, Isaack, Reedham, N., husbandman	273 Sadler
1848	Riches, Jeremiah, Pentney, N., miller	251 Denny
1829	Riches, John, St Marys Coslany, Norwich, N., carpenter	346 Green
1836	Riches, John, Attleborough, N., husbandman	327 Smith
1836	Riches, John, Mileham, N., carpenter	304 Smith
1845	Riches, John, East Rudham, N., tailor	486 Pedgrift
1845	Riches, John, Wrenningham, N., gent.	856 Pedgrift
1849	Riches, John, West Rudham, N., grocer, draper and tailor	182 Womack
1853	Riches, John, Hardley, N., yeoman	502 Veale
1855	Riches, John, North Walsham, N., hairdresser	620 Whitty
1857	Riches, John, Sutton, N., boatman	506 Youngs
1842	Riches, Mary, East Dereham, N., spinster	528 Canler
1851	Riches, Richard, Salhouse, N., cordwainer	606 Friar
1820	Riches, Robert, Neatishead, N., farmer	134 Mack
1840	Riches, Robert Kendall, Fakenham, N., cordwainer	665 Turner
1847	Riches, Robert, Mulbarton, N., yeoman, formerly of East Dereham, N.	790 Broom
1828	Riches, Samuel, Neatishead, N., beer brewer and boatman	112 Farrow
1849	Riches, Susannah, Laxfield, S., widow	106 Womack
1828	Riches, Thomas Reeve, Neatishead, N., farmer	30 Farrow
1846	Riches, Thomas, Worlingworth, S., carpenter	139 Baret
1847	Riches, Thomas, Walcot, N., farmer and coal merchant	460 Broom
1820	Riches, William, Worlingworth, S.	437 Mack
1828	Riches, William, Laxfield, S., boot and shoemaker	335 Farrow
1829	Riches, William, St Benedicts, Norwich, N., wheelwright	231 Green
1834	Riches, William, Great Yarmouth, N., gent.	725 Lane
1849	Riches, William, Stoke Holy Cross, N., carpenter	587 Womack
1854	Riches, William, Norwich, N., gent.	109 Day
1857	Riches, William Barber, Neatishead, N.	381 Youngs
1857	Richmond, Edward, Southtown, Little Yarmouth, S., merchant	64 Youngs
1848	Richmond, Elizabeth, Ditchingham, N.	420 Denny
1821	Richmond, Samuel, Ditchingham, N., whitesmith	195 Dewell
1821	Richmond, Thomas, Ditchingham, N., yeoman	44 Dewell
1825	Richold, Peter, Melford, S., coachmaker	338 Hayward
1845	Rickbell, Philip, Middleton, S, yeoman, o.w. missing	336 Pedgrift
1827	Riddlesworth, Isaac, Reymerstone, N., farmer	511 Wood
1854	Rider, Robert, Cawston, N., shoemaker	38 Day
1823	Ridley, Grace, Kings Lynn, N., widow	13 Tann
1840	Ridley Henry, Ipswich, S., wine merchant	403 Turner
1823	Rigby, Joseph, Ipswich, S., shopkeeper	296 Tann
1824	Rigby, Sarah, Norwich, N., wife of Edward Rigby, surgeon	337 Borrett
1824	Ringe, Samuel, Old Newton, S., gent.	362 Borrett
1837	Ringer, Benjamin, Tharston, N., farmer and miller	730 Warren
1837	Ringer, James, Norwich, N., cabinet and chair maker	445 Warren
1838	Ringer, John, Tuttington Hall, N., esquire	500 Skepper
1843	Ringer, John Manship, Norwich, N., grocer	508 Miles
1851	Ringer, John, Blofield, N., yeoman	91 Friar
1838	Ringer, Richard, Lingwood, N., husbandman	586 Skepper
1849	Ringer, Robert, Wymondham, N., yeoman	533 Womack
1842	Ringer, Samuel Saunders, Norwich, N., hosier	134 Canler

1845	Ringwood, Hammond Farrer, Halesworth, S., gent.	110 Pedgrift
1831	Rippin, Ann, Norwich, N., widow	108 Hart
1830	Rippin, James, Norwich, N., tailor	435 Pettingill
1846	Rirabell, Philip, Huddleston, S.	Index only
1843	Rising, Benjamin, Thorndon, S., farmer and maltster	168 Miles
1832	Rising, John, Paston, N., gent.	61 Cooke
1841	Rising, Robert, Horsey, N., esquire	599 Traxton
1834	Rising, Stephen, Horning, N.	46 Lane
1854	Rising, William, Great Yarmouth, N.	3 Day
1854	Rising, William, Great Yarmouth, N., shipwright	227 Day
1833	Rivers, John, Shotley, S., farmer	429 Cubitt
1833	Rivers, John, Stoke Ferry, N., yeoman	335 Cubitt
1848	Rivett, Francis, Great Ellingham, N., fowl merchant	481 Denny
1825	Rivett, John, Wacton, N., yeoman	461 Hayward
1852	Rivett, John, Fritton, S., yeoman	879 Latten
1835	Rivett, Michael Albrow, - alias Albrow	260 Harrowing
1829	Rivett, Thomas, Ringland, N., miller	478 Green
1838	Rix, Benjamin, Heacham, N., farmer	251 Skepper
1856	Rix, Bridget, Brundall, N., widow	23 Code
1841	Rix, Esther, Norwich, N., widow	585 Traxton
1845	Rix, Hannah, Kings Lynn, N., spinster	106 Pedgrift
1837	Rix, Henry, Swaffham, N., innkeeper	273 Warren
1849	Rix, Henry, Panxworth, N., shopkeeper	133 Womack
1838	Rix, Hephzibah, Oulton, S., wife of Nathaniel Rix, gent.	767 Skepper
1835	Rix, John, Drayton, N., butcher	421 Harrowing
1840	Rix, John, Stoke Holy Cross, N., tailor	125 Turner
1844	Rix, John the younger, Dersingham, N.	248 Ebbage
1843	Rix, Mary, Great Yarmouth, N., spinster	358 Miles
1825	Rix, Peter, Aylsham, N., innkeeper	435 Hayward
1821	Rix, Robert, Yaxham, N., farmer	207 Dewell
1856	Rix, Thomas, Tittleshall, N., farmer	277 Code
1824	Rix, William, Barnby, S., yeoman	298 Borrett
1839	Rix, William, Swaffham, N., corn merchant	242 Calton
1855	Rix, William Loades, Little Walsingham, N., gent.	639 Whitty
1838	Roach, Anna Lucy, Thorndon, S., spinster	70 Skepper
1830	Roach, Mary, St Giles, Norwich, N., widow	295 Pettingill
1849	Roan, Thomas, Oxborough, N., victualler	661 Womack
1849	Robberds, William Tooley, Tombland, Norwich, N., gent.	317 Womack
1834	Roberson, Robert, St George South Elmham, S., farmer	426 Lane
1855	Roberson, Robert, Stradsett, N., formerly of Gayton, N., bricklayer	77 Whitty
1826	Roberson, Thomas, Hockwold cum Wilton, N., farmer	64 Davy
1845	Roberts, Edward, Fakenham, N., yeoman	30 Pedgrift
1841	Roberts, Elizabeth, Snettisham, N.	Index only
1821	Roberts, George, Downham Market, N., yeoman	229 Dewell
1857	Roberts, George, Bungay, S., yeoman	300 Youngs
1838	Roberts, Hannah, Tivetshall St Mary, N., spinster	204 Skepper
1857	Roberts, Henry Mann, Seething, N., gent.	204 Youngs
1857	Roberts, James the elder, Hempnall, N., wheelwright	32 Youngs
1840	Roberts, John, Kelsale, S., gardener	453 Turner
1855	Roberts, Nichael, Mundham, N., gent.	734 Whitty
1835	Roberts, Nelson, Kings Lynn, N., cooper	60 Harrowing
1854	Roberts, Richard, Oulton, N., independent minister	305 Day
1856	Roberts, Roger, Hempnall, N., farmer	648 Code
1841	Roberts, Thomas, Belton, S., gent.	528 Traxton
1832	Roberts, William, Downham Market, N., farmer	393 Cooke
1844	Roberts, William, Runcton Holme, N., farmer	354 Ebbage
1830	Robertson, John, Somerleyton, S.	357 Pettingill
1829	Robins, Alice, Denver, N., widow	449 Green
1833	Robins, Aquila, Bayfield Lodge, N., farmer	406 Cubitt
1840	Robins, Sarah, Cawston, N.	Index only
1844	Robinson, Caroline, Halesworth, S., spinster	541 Ebbage
1830	Robinson, Elizabeth, Hardwick, N., widow	297 Pettingill
1843	Robinson, Helen, Norwich, N., widow	388 Miles

1828	Robinson, Jacob, Combs, S., farmer	180 Farrow
1822	Robinson, James, Carleton Rode, N., farmer	358 Sadler
1839	Robinson, James, Kings Lynn, N., brewers clerk	67 Calton
1835	Robinson, John, Cringleford, N., miller	360 Harrowing
1838	Robinson, John Syer, Palgrave, S., yeoman	439 Skepper
1842	Robinson, John, Barking, S., farmer	586 Canler
1845	Robinson, John Clarke, St Pauls, Norwich, N., plumber, painter and glazier	491 Pedgrift
1852	Robinson, John, Peasenhall, S., yeoman	216 Latten
1820	Robinson, Margaret, Norwich, N., widow	513 Mack
1848	Robinson, Margaret, Halesworth, S., widow	249 Denny
1837	Robinson, Martin, Combs, S., farmer	189 Warren
1830	Robinson, Mary, Norwich, N., widow	O.W. 251
1852	Robinson, Mary, Bressingham, N., farmer	37 Latten
1822	Robinson, Nathan, Holt, N., grocer, draper and cordwainer	298 Sadler
1848	Robinson, Robert, Huntingfield, S., farmer	148 Denny
1823	Robinson, Samuel, Blakeney, N., servant	411 Tann
1844	Robinson, Samuel, Great Yarmouth, N., gent.	185 Ebbage
1830	Robinson, Sarah, Kings Lynn, N., widow	41 Pettingill
1833	Robinson, Sarah, Mileham, N., widow	14 Cubitt
1846	Robinson, Susanna, South Lynn All Saints, Kings Lynn, N., widow	261 Baret
1822	Robinson, Thomas, Norwich, N., schoolmaster	O.W. 173
1844	Robinson, Thomas, Norwich, N., gent.	333 Ebbage
1835	Robinson, William, Norwich, N., cork cutter	9 Warren
1847	Robinson, William, Tunstall, S., blacksmith	640 Broom
1857	Robinson, William, Great Yarmouth, N., carpenter	411(a) Youngs
1831	Robison, Archibald, Norwich, N., salesman	279 Hart
1827	Robson, Benjamin, Barnby, S., thatcher	314 Wood
1830	Robson, Sarah, Lowestoft, S., widow	330 Pettingill
1827	Robson, Thomas, Carleton Forehoe, N., gamekeeper	74 Wood
1856	Robson, Thomas, Thornham, N., formerly of West Newton, farmer	154 Code
1852	Rockhill, Robert Henry, Eye, S., bankers clerk	750 Latten
1847	Roddwell, Charles Miller, Pulham St Mary the Virgin, N., yeoman	372 Broom
1835	Rodham, James, Whitwell, N., farmer	433 Harrowing
1832	Rodwell, Alice, Great Yarmouth, N., widow	60 Cooke
1851	Rodwell, Edward, Wetheringsett cum Brockford, S., bricklayer	463 Friar
1849	Rodwell, George, Burnham Deepdale, N., gent.	198 Womack
1836	Rodwell, James, Wangford, S., labourer	354 Smith
1855	Rodwell, Mary, Hethersett, N., spinster	265 Whitty
1834	Rodwell, Thomas, Great Yarmouth, N., carpenter	277 Lane
1845	Rodwell, Thomas, Thorndon, S., bricklayer	147 Pedgrift
1845	Rodwell, William, Pulham St Mary Magdalen, N., farmer	375 Pedgrift
1845	Roe, Edmund, St Martins at Palace, Norwich, N., worstead weaver	405 Pedgrift
1847	Roe, Edward, Oulton, S., farmer	Index only
1831	Roe, John, Beccles, S., cooper	165 Hart
1852	Roe, Michael, Lowestoft, S., farmer	34 Latten
1854	Roe, Rebecca Walker, Lowestoft, S., widow	85 Day
1831	Roe, Richard, Beccles, S., cooper	166 Hart
1847	Roe, Robert, Woodton, N., gent.	499 Broom
1828	Roe, Thomas, Great Yarmouth, N., innkeeper	310 Farrow
1845	Roe, William Haylett, Norwich, N., tavern keeper	768 Pedgrift
1843	Rofe, Ann, Great Yarmouth, N., widow	531 Miles
1827	Rofe, Charles, Great Yarmouth, N., shopkeeper	374 Wood
1836	Rogers, Hugh, Hempnall, N., formerly of Norwich, brushmaker	490 Smith
1850	Rogers, James Master, Great Yarmouth, N., iron and brass founder	537 Cuthbert
1828	Rogers, John the younger, Woodbridge, S., auctioneer	16 Farrow
1847	Rogers, John, Lowestoft, S., shoemaker	594 Broom
1847	Rogers, Jonas, Fakenham, N., cordwainer and farmer	302 Broom
1856	Rogers, Phoebe, Felthorpe, N., widow	552 Code
1841	Rogers, Robert, Newmarket St Mary, S., bookseller	650 Traxton

1830	Rogers, Samuel, Lowestoft, S., twine spinner	198 Pettingill
1831	Rogers, Thomas, Norwich, N., cordwainer	O.W. 251
1829	Rogers, William, Rockland, N., yeoman	328 Green
1833	Rogers, William, Thetford, N., carpenter	140 Cubitt
1838	Rogers, William the elder, Redgrave, S., farmer	566 Skepper
1853	Rogers, William, Costessey, N., carpenter	484 Veale
1843	Rogerson, Charles Josiah, Beccles, S., gent.	505 Miles
1824	Rolfe, John, Norwich, N., carpenter	253 Borrett
1829	Rolfe, John, Stonham Aspal, S., farmer	186 Green
1819	Rolfe, Joseph, Methwold Hithe, N., farmer	123 Le Neve
1829	Rolfe, Thomas, Stow Bardolph, N., yeoman	272 Green
1824	Rolfe, William, Ipswich, S., cork cutter	370 Borrett
1825	Roll, William, Sutton, N., yeoman	182 Hayward
1828	Rolle, Susannah, Colchester, Essex, widow	456 Farrow
1841	Rolling, John, East Rudham, N., innkeeper	55 Traxton
1835	Roof, William, Crostwick, N.	450 Harrowing
1844	Roofe, Robert, Felmingham, N., thatcher	529 Ebbage
1846	Roofe, Samuel, Horsham St Faiths, N., baker	560 Baret
1834	Root, James, Norwich, N., whitesmith	559 Lane
1850	Rope, Aaron, Little Plumstead, N., farmer	367 Cuthbert
1847	Rope, Ann, Hemblington, N.	818 Broom
1833	Rope, Elizabeth, Beighton, N., widow	475 Cubitt
1837	Rope, John, Gorleston, S., gent.	73 Warren
1831	Rope, Richard, Ubbeston, S., farmer	562 Hart
1843	Rope, Robert, Gorleston, S., yeoman	72 Miles
1843	Roper, Amy, Wortham, S., widow	39 Miles
1851	Roper, Charlotte, Halesworth, S., book seller and glass and china dealer	66 Friar
1854	Roper, Eliza, Fordham, N.	208 Day
1853	Roper, Emma, Kings Lynn, N., formerly of East Dereham, widow	574 Veale
1820	Roper, John, Saint Etheldred, Norwich, N., maltster	84 Mack
1848	Roper, John, Bunwell, N.	426 Denny
1843	Roper, Lionel, Bedfield, S., labourer	298 Miles
1846	Roper, Osborn, Badingham, S., farmer	142 Baret
1841	Roper, Priscilla, West Dereham, N., wife of William Roper, farmer	96 Traxton
1839	Roper, Robert, Wetheringsett, S., farmer	259 Calton
1855	Roper, Robert Land, Boughton, N., farmer	710 Whitty
1827	Roper, Sarah, Sutton, S., widow	46 Wood
1842	Roper, Samuel, Halesworth, S., bookseller and dealer in china, glass and Staffordshire ware	250 Canler
1824	Roper, Snelling, Colby, N., gent.	223 Borrett
1848	Roper, Snelling Drozier, Colby, N., gent.	499 Denny
1844	Roper, Thomas, Fordham, N., farmer	13 Ebbage
1849	Roper, Thomas, Wortham, S., labourer	476 Womack
1821	Roper, William, Thurgarton, N., gent.	247 Dewell
1823	Roper, William, Lakenheath, S., farmer	371 Tann
1828	Roper, William, Exning, S., gardener	358 Farrow
1844	Roper, William, West Dereham, N., farmer	436 Ebbage
1842	Ropkins, James, St Georges Colegate, Norwich, N., weaver	93 Canler
1825	Rortherham, John Beccles, S., pawnbroker	360 Hayward
1845	Rose, Edmund, Halesworth, S., carpenter	207 Pedgrift
1823	Rose, Elizabeth, Downham Market, N., widow	344 Tann
1842	Rose, John, North Barsham, N., farmer	686 Canler
1844	Rose, Philippa, Great Ellingham, N., widow	36 Ebbage
1844	Rose, Reuben, Hardingham, N., farmer	510 Ebbage
1843	Rose, Samuel, Barford, N., farmer	537 Miles
1847	Rose, Sarah, Corpusty, N.	409 Broom
1850	Rose, Susan, Wissett, S., widow	389 Cuthbert
1838	Rose, William, Wickham Skeith, S., farmer	664 Skepper
1841	Rose, William, Great Ellingham, N., shopkeeper	300 Traxton
1847	Rose, William, Mundesley, N., farmer	773 Broom
1831	Roseberry, Sarah, Walsoken, N., wife of John Roseberry, yeoman	204 Hart
1821	Roseberry, John, New Buckenham, N., bricklayer	146 Dewell

1822	Roughton, William, Roydon, N., linen weaver	107 Sadler
1833	Rounce, Henry, Carlton Colville, S., wheelwright	374 Cubitt
1837	Rounce, Samuel, Topcroft, N., farmer	354 Warren
1856	Rounce, Samuel, Carlton Colville, S., wheelwright	95 Code
1829	Rounce, William, Rushmere, S., farmer	204 Green
1838	Rounce, William, Gunton, N., gamekeeper	827 Skepper
1844	Rounce, William, Colby, N., farmer	11 Ebbage
1856	Rounce, William, Rushmere, S.	Index only
1832	Rous, Samuel, Wrentham, S., husbandman	579 Cooke
1832	Rouse, Richard, Mattishall Burgh, N., farmer	167 Cooke
1854	Rouse, William, Snape, S., husbandman	47 Day
1847	Rout, James, Stowmarket, S., plumber and glazier	595 Broom
1837	Rout, Samuel, Felthorpe, N., farmer	393 Warren
1845	Row, James the younger, Badingham, S., formerly of Bruisyard	551 Pedgrift
1820	Row, Robert, Bruisyard, S., farmer	612 Mack
1838	Row, William, Yoxford, S., collar and harness maker	375 Skepper
1836	Rowe, William, Kings Lynn, N., victualler	564 Smith
1840	Rowell, John, Northwold, N., gent.	38 Turner
1849	Rowley, Thomas, Hacheston, S., yeoman	486 Womack
1853	Rowling, Henry, Eye, S., innkeeper	166 Veale
1844	Rowling, William, St Stephens, Norwich, N., carpenter	99 Ebbage
1827	Royal, Robert, Hindolveston, N.	425 Wood
1847	Royall, James, Colton, N., farmer	138 Broom
1820	Royall, Rachel, Wrentham, S., widow	157 Mack
1846	Rubland, Roberta, Halesworth, S.	Index only
1852	Rudd, Ann, Swanton Morley, N., widow	285 Latten
1855	Rudd, Francis Gray, Surlingham, N., gent.	127 Whitty
1857	Rudd, Henry, Whitwell, N.	211 Youngs
1836	Rudd, John, East Ruston, N., gent.	427 Smith
1829	Rudd, Leah, Ashwicken, N., spinster	408 Green
1847	Rudd, Martha, Sutton, N., wife of John Rudd, gent.	394 Broom
1820	Rudd, Mary, Brandon, S., spinster	29 Mack
1850	Rudd, Mary, North Walsham, N., widow	459 Cuthbert
1847	Rudd, Robert Cock, Surlingham, N., gent.	75 Broom
1841	Rudd, Sarah, Great Yarmouth, N., widow	366 Traxton
1847	Rudd, William, Wymondham, N., yeoman	481 Broom
1830	Ruddiman, John, Kings Lynn, N., gent.	6 Pettingill
1836	Ruddock, John, Bridgham, N., miller	416 Smith
1839	Rudge, Edward Batch, Aylsham, N., gent.	95 Calton
1835	Rudkin, Mary, Nayland, S., spinster	176 Harrowing
1827	Rudland, John, Ipswich, S., hairdresser	203 Wood
1837	Rudland, Nehemiah, Fakenham, N., butcher	348 Warren
1828	Rudland, William, Kings Lynn, N., corn chandler	155 Farrow
1841	Rudledge, William, Crownthorpe, N., wheelwright	643 Traxton
1855	Rudlen, William, Flordon, N., gardener	207 Whitty
1834	Rudrum, Frederick William, Norwich, N., surgeon	474 Lane
1831	Rudrum, Harriet, Norwich, N., widow	16 Hart
1838	Rudrum, Samuel the elder, Norton Subcourse, N., farmer	297 Skepper
1849	Rumbell, Matthew, Upwell, N., labourer	7 Womack
1832	Rumble, John, Scarning, N., farmer	17 Cooke
1847	Rummer, Richard, Norwich, N., gent.	438 Broom
1850	Rump, Christopher, North Elmham, N., farmer	108 Cuthbert
1844	Rump, Hugh Robert, Wells next the Sea, N., surgeon	48 Ebbage
1852	Rump, Jeremiah Robert, Wells next the Sea, N., surgeon	384 Latten
1838	Rump, John, Booton, N., gent.	81 Skepper
1840	Rump, John, Castle Acre, N., victualler	44 Turner
1825	Rump, Maria Ann, Catton, N., spinster	44 Hayward
1834	Rump, Maria Ann, Swaffham, N., widow	505 Lane
1848	Rump, Rebecca, Field Dalling, N., spinster	780 Denny
1855	Rump, Thomas, Swanton Morley, N., gent.	10 Whitty
1843	Rump, William Elden, Banningham, N., yeoman	543 Miles
1856	Rump, William, Dilham, N., farmer	535 Code
1848	Rumsby, James, Kirkley, S., gardener	146 Denny

1845	Rumsey, James, Stutton, S., cordwainer	513 Pedgrift
1830	Runnacles, Mark, Hollesley, S.	84 Pettingill
1834	Runnicus, Robert the elder, Blo Norton, N., farmer	142 Lane
1847	Rush, Edmund, Carleton Rode, N., farmer	601 Broom
1825	Rush, Edward, Creeting St Peter, S., gent.	530 Hayward
1857	Rush, Elizabeth, Wingfield, S., widow	2 Youngs
1835	Rush, Francis, Cley, N.	431 Harrowing
1839	Rush, James, Eye, S., formerly of Wetheringsett, farmer	122 Calton
1853	Rush, James, Thwaite, S., farmer	503 Veale
1857	Rush, James the younger, Thwaite, S., farmer	524 Youngs
1827	Rush, John, Carleton Rode, N., farmer	37 Wood
1823	Rush, Marlborough, Old Buckenham, N., farmer	392 Tann
1830	Rush, Robert, Offton, S., farmer	12 Pettingill
1839	Rushbrook, Ann, Repps with Bastwick, N., widow	315 Calton
1819	Rushbrook, Elizabeth, Salhouse, N., widow	132 Le Neve
1825	Rushbrook, Maria, Salhouse, N., widow	202 Hayward
1850	Rushbrook, William, Thetford, S., yeoman	186 Cuthbert
1829	Rushbrooke, Elizabeth, Salhouse, N., spinster	362 Green
1833	Rushbrooke, Jane, Coddenham, S., widow	88 Cubitt
1853	Rushbrooke, Thomas Allen, Scoulton, N., farmer	473 Veale
1847	Rushbroke, Ann, Hingham, N., wife of Reuben Rushbroke, gent.	465 Broom
1836	Rushmer, Charles, Bergh Apton, N., yeoman	66 Smith
1853	Rushmer, James, Halvergate, N., yeoman	196 Veale
1852	Rushmer, Joshua, Billockby, N., farmer	357 Latten
1846	Rushmer, Thomas, Limpenhoe, N., cordwainer	343 Baret
1829	Rushmor, William, Thurlton, N., marshman	119 Green
1857	Rushmore, Anthony, Blofield, N., yeoman	87 Youngs
1836	Russell, Benjamin, Norwich, N., watchmaker	O.W. 233
1855	Russell, Benjamin, Croxton, Fulmodeston, N., farmer	568 Whitty
1831	Russell, George, Combs, S., farmer	120 Hart
1824	Russell, James, Guist, N., farmer	124 Borrett
1847	Russell, James, Norwich, N., grocer and tallow chandler	O.W. 315
1825	Russell, Jenny, Whittington, Northwold, N., widow	311 Hayward
1845	Russell, John, Norwich, N.	268 Pedgrift
1847	Russell, Mary, Thursford, N., wife of William Russell, farmer	388 Broom
1857	Russell, Thomas, Whittington, Northwold N., farmer	801 Youngs
1841	Rust, Elizabeth, South Lynn All Saints, N., widow	500 Traxton
1857	Rust, Elizabeth, East Dereham, N., wife of John Rust, blacksmith	692 Youngs
1832	Rust, Hannah, Cromer, N., widow	149 Cooke
1819	Rust, John, Trunch, N., yeoman	284 Le Neve
1829	Rust, John, Kings Lynn, N., innkeeper	82 Green
1840	Rust, John Edgar, Stowmarket, S., esquire	351 Turner
1844	Rust, Michael, Swaffham, N., farmer	240 Ebbage
1836	Rust, Richard Johnson, Swaffham, N., carpenter and builder	401 Smith
1842	Rust, Thomas, Stowmarket, S., draper and tailor	376 Canler
1846	Rust, Thomas, Thrandeston, S., gent.	374 Baret
1838	Rust, William, Briningham, N., cooper	783 Skepper
1842	Ryder, Samuel, Hingham, N., labourer	167 Canler
1822	Rye, Richard, Hemingstone, S., yeoman	O.W. 172
1820	Saar, John the elder, Wangford, S., farmer	402 Mack
1845	Sabberton, Thomas, Norwich, N., yeoman	826 Pedgrift
1848	Sadd, Hannah, Ipswich, S., widow	287 Denny
1855	Sadd, James, Bungay, S., gent.	128 Whitty
1831	Sadd, John, Homersfield, S., farmer	173 Hart
1831	Sadd, John, St Michael Coslany, Norwich, N., gent.	374 Hart
1839	Saddington, John, South Lynn, N., butcher and labourer	390 Calton
1834	Sadler, John, Cley next the Sea, N., master mariner	19 Lane
1834	Sadler, John, Costessey, N., yeoman	642 Lane
1844	Sadler, Martha, Norwich, N., widow	84 Ebbage
1822	Sadler, Mary, Ipswich, S., widow	1 Sadler
1837	Sadler, Rachel, Great Yarmouth, N., spinster	247 Warren
1824	Sadler, Robert, St Martin at Oak, Norwich, worstead weaver	137 Borrett

1823	Sadler, Susanna, North Walsham, N., widow	314Tann
1844	Sadler, William, Great Yarmouth, N., bricklayer	350 Ebbage
1852	Sadler, William, Sea Palling, N., yeoman	142 Latten
1840	Saffery, Mary, Upwell, N., widow	270 Turner
1823	Sage, Deborah, Trimley St Mary, S., spinster	359 Tann
1838	Sage, Joseph, Ipswich, S., formerly of City of London, bookbinder and stationer	492 Skepper
1838	Sage, Ralph, Ipswich, S., gent.	626 Skepper
1856	Saint, Robert, Halvergate, N., yeoman	224 Code
1848	St John, Mary, Hackford next Reepham, N., widow	204 Denny
1829	St John, Thomas, Hackford, N., shopkeeper	365 Green
1839	Sales, Arthur, Hemsby, N., labourer	416 Calton
1839	Sales, John, St Georges Colegate, Norwich, N., linen draper	340 Calton
1838	Salmon, George, Merton, N., shoemaker	117 Skepper
1834	Salmon, Mary, Babingley, N., widow	615 Lane
1835	Salmon, Mary, Lower Sheringham, N.	145 Harrowing
1831	Salmon, Richard, Sutton, N., boatman	63 Hart
1845	Salmon, Richard, Worstead, N., carpenter	436 Pedgrift
1849	Salmon, Richard, Fakenham, N., miller	173 Womack
1837	Salmon, Thomas, Norwich, N.	O.W. 346
1831	Salmon, William, Raveningham, N., farmer	460 Hart
1835	Salter, John, Westerfield, S., wheelwright	326 Harrowing
1837	Salter, Jonathon, Winterton, N., mariner	492 Warren
1827	Salton, John, Aldeburgh, S., carpenter	17 Wood
1833	Sampson, Aaron, Norwich, N., confectioner	178 Cubitt
1854	Sampson, Elizabeth, Kings Lynn, N., widow	347 Day
1842	Sampson, John, St Lawrence Ilketshall, S., farmer	299 Canler
1845	Sampson, Moses, Great Yarmouth, N., yeoman	914 Pedgrift
1820	Sampson, Sarah, Wickham Skeith, S., widow	18 Mack
1838	Sampson, William the elder, St Margarets Ilketshall, S., bricklayer	174 Skepper
1835	Sanctuary, John, East Dereham, N., hosier	328 Harrowing
1849	Sandal, Sarah, Kirby Bedon, N., widow	482 Womack
1837	Sanders, John Hopkin, Upwell, C., miller	744 Warren
1830	Sandford, Henry, Shipden, Cromer, N., merchant	51 Pettingill
1834	Sandling, William, Wells next the Sea, formerly of Fakenham, N., whitesmith	420 Lane
1841	Sandling, William, Wells next the Sea, N.	Index only
1852	Sands, Hercules, Hindringham, N., tailor	754 Latten
1854	Sands, Richard Copeman, Blakeney, N., innkeeper and tailor	401 Day
1853	Sands, Robert, Little Walsingham, N., cooper	456 Veale
1820	Sands, Thomas, Croxton, N., yeoman	106 Mack
1826	Sands, Thomas, Twyford, N., tailor	172 Davy
1851	Sands, William, Swaffham, N., carpenter	361 Friar
1823	Sannevill, Isaac, St Michael at Thorn, Norwich, dyer	31 Tann
1843	Sanneville, Thomas, Norwich, N., gent.	393 Miles
1834	Sansum, Robert, Melford, S., wheelwright	338 Lane
1855	Santy, William, Rougham, N., butcher	679 Whitty
1839	Sare, John, South Lopham, N., miller	290 Calton
1830	Sarjeant, Joseph, Great Yarmouth, N., late officer of excise	274 Pettingill
1841	Sarter, John, Halesworth, S., gent.	21 Traxton
1857	Saul, Edward, Panxworth, N., miller	357 Youngs
1833	Saul, Mary, Little Plumstead, N., widow	3 Cubitt
1840	Saul, Thomas, Cawston, N., husbandman	277 Turner
1826	Saul, William, Norwich, N., builder	31 Davy
1834	Saunders, Benjamin, Diss, N., farmer	281 Lane
1839	Saunders, Charles, Barton Mills, S., farmer	526 Calton
1857	Saunders, Edmond, South Cove, S., farmer	129 Youngs
1841	Saunders, John, Cranworth, N., labourer	433 Traxton
1827	Saunders, Jonathan, Sudbourn, S., marshman	629 Wood
1843	Saunders, Jonathan, Ranworth, N., husbandman	328 Miles
1838	Saunders, Richard, Wiggenhall St Mary Magdalen, N., farmer	582 Skepper
1852	Saunders, Samuel, Strumpshaw, N., gent.	457 Latten

1855	Saunders, Samuel, Ranworth, N., labourer	426 Whitty
1835	Saunders, Sarah, Cantley, N., spinster	400 Harrowing
1833	Saunders, Thomas, Burston, N., linen weaver	292 Cubitt
1820	Saunders, William, Blo Norton, N., gardener	227 Mack
1834	Saunders, William, Wissett, S., bachelor	370 Lane
1848	Saunders, William, Great Yarmouth, N., merchant	174 Denny
1853	Saunders, William, Great Yarmouth, N.	See 1848
1828	Savage, Ann, Horsford, N., wife of Robert Savage, yeoman	467 Farrow
1845	Savage, Francis, Norwich, N., gent.	631 Pedgrift
1827	Savage, John, Shipdham, N., farmer	71 Wood
1857	Savage, John, Rickinghall Superior, S., yeoman	44 Youngs
1833	Savage, Robert, Horsford, N., yeoman	404 Cubitt
1838	Savory, Coulsey, Bixley, N.	606 Skepper
1831	Savory, Elizabeth, Burnham Westgate, N., widow	126 Hart
1829	Savory, Samuel Henry, Twyford Hall, N., clerk	525 Green
1846	Savory, William, Sutton, N., gent.	468 Baret
1856	Savory, William, Great Yarmouth, N., yeoman	212 Code
1835	Sawer, Everard, Leiston, S., breeches maker	185 Harrowing
1845	Sawford, Thomas, Walsoken, N., farmer	347 Pedgrift
1840	Sawyer, Charles, Southwold, S., cabinet maker and upholsterer	541 Turner
1830	Sawyer, Sarah, Ipswich, S., spinster	359 Pettingill
1845	Sawyer, Thomas, Boyton, S., wheelwright and carpenter	197 Pedgrift
1834	Sawyer, William, Woodbridge, S., farmer and chaise proprietor	763 Lane
1846	Sawyer, William, Saxmundham, S., cabinet maker	210 Baret
1847	Say, Henry, Wangford, S., surgeon	O.W. 317
1850	Say, Jeremiah, Wortwell, N., yeoman	237 Cuthbert
1826	Say, Thomas, Norwich, N., plumber and glazier	126 Davy
1846	Say, Thomas Robert Skipper, Norwich, N., plumber and glazier	499 Baret
1852	Sayer, Benjamin, Bungay, S., farmer	689 Latten
1855	Sayer, Daniel, Shottesham St Mary, N., farmer	625 Whitty
1837	Sayer, James, Bodham, N., farmer	461 Warren
1841	Sayer, John, St Andrew Ilketshall, S., woodman	97 Traxton
1854	Sayer, John, Sculthorpe, N., farmer	502 Day
1849	Sayer, Samuel, Great Yarmouth, N., baker	374 Womack
1836	Sayer, William, Catton, N., yeoman	254 Smith
1838	Sayer, William, Sotterley, S.	642 Skepper
1856	Sayer, William, Beccles, S., gent.	257 Code
1844	Sayers, James Gambling, West Basham, N., farmer	207 Ebbage
1836	Sayers, John Gambling, Bodham, N., farmer	12 Smith
1838	Sayers, Mary Saunderson, Ormesby, N.	94 Skepper
1853	Sayers, Robert, South Creake, N., miller and butcher	209 Veale
1839	Sayle, Robert, Southery, N., farmer	461 Calton
1847	Sayles, Jane, Kings Lynn, N., wife of John Sayles, yeoman	8 Broom
1847	Sayles, John, Kings Lynn, N., yeoman	2 Broom
1849	Scace, Joseph, Framsden, S., farmer	82 Womack
1847	Scales, Charlotte, Norwich, N., single woman	774 Broom
1820	Scales, John, Northwold, N., farmer	358 Mack
1855	Scales, Maria, Coltishall, N., widow	639 Whitty
1828	Scales, Robert, Beachamwell, N., farmer	518 Farrow
1823	Scales, Sarah, Pulham St Mary Magdalen, N., widow	105 Tann
1851	Scales, Stephen, Old Buckenham, N., farmer	521 Friar
1855	Scales, Susannah, Hackford next Reepham, N., widow	178 Whitty
1830	Scales, Thomas, Limpenhoe, N., brick maker	139 Pettingill
1854	Scales, William, Belaugh, N., farmer	279 Day
1848	Scarf, James, Great Yarmouth, N., fishing merchant	848 Denny
1835	Scarfe, Jonas, otherwise Jonah, Blo Norton, N., farmer	146 Harrowing
1828	Scarfe, William, Haughley, S., carpenter	269 Farrow
1856	Scarle, Richard, Lowestoft, S., confectioner and baker	189 Code
1851	Scarlett, Dameron, Trimley St Mary, S., butcher and innkeeper	145 Friar
1849	Scarlett, Daniel, Heigham next Norwich, gent.	457 Womack
1850	Scarlett, Elizabeth, Redenhall with Harleston, N., widow	10 Cuthbert
1838	Scarlett, James, Lowestoft, S., wheelwright	37 Skepper
1839	Scarlett, James, Norton Subcourse, N., farmer	208 Calton
1819	Scarlett, John, Repps with Bastwick, N., miller	325 Le Neve

1844	Scarlett, Robert, Saxmundham, S., yeoman	302 Ebbage
1854	Scarll, William, Lowestoft, S., gent.	27 Day
1820	Scarnel, John, Tilney All Saints, N., blacksmith	659 Mack
1843	Scarnell, Hannah, Earlham, Norwich, N., widow	103 Miles
1852	Scase, Robert the elder, Laxfield, S., gent.	820 Latten
1827	Scholding, Hannah, Whitton, S., spinster	419 Wood
1837	Schulen, George, Ipswich, S., potter	571 Warren
1837	Scogging, James the elder, Coddenham, S., gamekeeper	335 Warren
1848	Scopes, George Seur, Creeting St Mary, S., bricklayer	83 Denny
1819	Scotchmer, Catherine, Monk Soham, S., spinster	44 Le Neve
1850	Scotchmer, Thomas, Bacton, S., wheelwright	24 Cuthbert
1821	Scott, Charles, Great Yarmouth, N., mariner	193 Dewell
1852	Scott, Elizabeth, Norwich, N.	650 Latten
1819	Scott, Francis, Burwell, C., farmer	124 Le Neve
1850	Scott, Hannah, Ipswich, S., widow	98 Cuthbert
1843	Scott, James, Great Yarmouth, N., baker	503 Miles
1847	Scott, Janette Louisa, Gresham, N., widow	295 Broom
1846	Scott, John, Thetford, N., draper	526 Baret
1845	Scott, Jonathan Leman, Gresham, N., farmer	116 Pedgrift
1826	Scott, Mary, Ipswich, S.	23 Davy
1832	Scott, Mary, Needham Market, S., spinster	172 Cooke
1846	Scott, Nathaniel James, Hoxne, S., esquire	18 Baret
1833	Scott, Robert, North Walsham, N., confectioner	152 Cubitt
1842	Scott, Robert, Norwich, N., cabinet maker and upholsterer	671 Canler
1845	Scott, Robert, Tharston, N., blacksmith	26 Pedgrift
1848	Scott, Robert, Saddlebow, N., victualler	165 Denny
1852	Scott, Samuel, Norwich, N., brazier and ironmonger	537 Latten
1839	Scott, Sarah, Kenninghall, N.	516 Calton
1842	Scott, Spencer, Lowestoft, S., master mariner	348 Canler
1844	Scott, Thomas, Needham Market, S., formerly of Badley, gent.	30 Ebbage
1855	Scott, Thomas Charles, Shadingfield Hall, S., gent.	550 Whitty
1828	Scott, William, Aldham, S., farmer	206 Farrow
1829	Scott, William, St Andrews, Norwich, N., confectioner	124 Green
1830	Scott, William, Norwich, N.	63 Pettingill
1833	Scott, William, St Andrews, Norwich, N., confectioner	61 Cubitt
1844	Scott, William, Sudbury, S.	494 Ebbage
1848	Scott, William, North Walsham, N., yeoman	207 Denny
1850	Scott, William, Hilgay, N., yeoman	466 Cuthbert
1845	Scotter, Peter, Norwich, N., carpenter	269 Pedgrift
1840	Scotter, Samuel senior, Northrepps, N., farmer	341 Turner
1845	Scotto, Ann, Aylsham, N., widow	84 Pedgrift
1848	Scowen, Christopher, Boxford, S., maltster	418 Denny
1845	Scowen, Thomas, Bures St Mary, S., beerseller	106 Pedgrift
1849	Scraggs, James, South Lynn All Saints, N., artist	61 Womack
1826	Scrutton, Samuel the elder, Chelmondiston, S., farmer	174 Davy
1836	Sculfor, Anne, Dersingham, N., spinster	326 Smith
1843	Scurll, Brettingham, Bergh Apton, N., yeoman	20 Miles
1832	Scurll, Lydia, Hackford next Reepham, N., spinster	438 Cooke
1852	Seaber, Robert Fyson, Fordham, C., farmer	129 Latten
1842	Seaber, William, Fordham, C., farmer	270 Canler
1820	Seadon, Agnes, Newmarket, S., widow	528 Mack
1819	Seadon, Samuel, Elmswell, S., innholder	296 Le Neve
1829	Seago, Mary, Barnby, S., widow	74 Green
1835	Seago, William the elder, Southrepps, N., farmer	1 Harrowing
1834	Sealy, Isaac, Ringstead, N., yeoman	291 Lane
1850	Seaman, Ann, Oulton, N., widow	17 Cuthbert
1836	Seaman, James, Worlingworth, S., wheelwright	199 Smith
1837	Seaman, James, Heigham, Norwich, N.	46 Warren
1848	Seaman, Jane Sare, Coney Weston, S.	714 Denny
1826	Seaman, John the elder, Fressingfield, S., farmer	302 Davy
1833	Seaman, John, Stratton St Mary, N., yeoman	422 Cubitt
1834	Seaman, John, Felmingham, N., gent.	714 Lane
1835	Seaman, John, Bixley, N., farmer	97 Harrowing
1852	Seaman, John, Fressingfield, S., farmer	239 Latten

1854	Seaman, John, Walsham Le Willows, S., wheelwright	560 Day
1855	Seaman, John the younger, Brockford, S., gent.	705 Whitty
1851	Seaman, Luke, Finningham, S., shopkeeper	299 Friar
1839	Seaman, Martha, Norwich, N., spinster	481 Calton
1835	Seaman, Robert, Norwich, N., cordwainer	596 Harrowing
1849	Seaman, Robert, Guestwick, N., farmer	558 Womack
1857	Seaman, Robert, Rickinghall Superior, S., yeoman	709 Youngs
1848	Seaman, Samuel, Sporle, N., shepherd	814 Denny
1822	Seaman, William senior, Foulsham, N., farmer	253 Sadler
1842	Seaman, William the elder, Stratton St Mary, N., yeoman	764 Canler
1854	Seaman, William, Foulsham, N., farmer	562 Day
1850	Seamans, James, Chediston, S., farmer	435 Cuthbert
1853	Seamans, Mary, Chediston, S., widow	206 Veale
1846	Searle, Richard, Terrington St Clements, N., farmer	319 Baret
1821	Seayears, Robert, Upwell, N., farmer	206 Dewell
1850	Seayears, Sarah, Upwell, N., widow	472 Cuthbert
1820	Secker, Robert, Syderstone, N., yeoman	506 Mack
1840	Secker, Robert, Fakenham, N., basket maker	80 Turner
1844	Secker, Tabitha, Norwich, N., widow	72 Ebbage
1833	Secret, Margaret, St Michael at Plea, Norwich, formerly of Ormesby, N., spinster	463 Cubitt
1846	Seel, Edward, Thursford, N., farmer	675 Baret
1842	Seely, Isaiah, Norwich, N., pork butcher	321 Canler
1849	Seely, John, Salle, N., farmer	500 Womack
1850	Seely, Sarah, Great Yarmouth, N., widow	297 Cuthbert
1842	Seely, William, Fordham, C., gent.	695 Canler
1855	Self, Edward, West Bradenham, N., farmer	226 Whitty
1834	Self, John, Pulham St Mary Magdalen, N., gent.	406 Lane
1837	Self, John, Roydon, N., yeoman	493 Warren
1851	Self, John, Dickleburgh, N., gent.	608 Friar
1821	Self, Joseph, Aldeburgh, S., limeburner	224 Dewell
1842	Self, Samuel John, Woodbridge, S., innholder	224 Canler
1848	Self, Stephen, Mendham, S., husbandman	626 Denny
1853	Selfe, Thomas James, East Dereham, N., cabinet maker	460 Veale
1847	Semmence, William, Wymondham, N., farmer	406 Broom
1835	Sendall, Martin, Norwich, N., spirit dealer	8 Harrowing
1821	Sendall, Richard, East Tuddenham, N., farmer	109 Dewell
1828	Sendall, Robert, Great Yarmouth, N., farrier	304 Farrow
1856	Sendall, Samuel, Norwich, N., commercial traveller	6 Code
1829	Senkler, Charles, Docking, N., gent.	460 Green
1840	Seppings, Anne, Kings Lynn, N.	450 Turner
1823	Seppings, Elizabeth, Fakenham, N., spinster	119 Tann
1826	Seppings, John, Gressenhall, N., farmer	367 Davy
1851	Seppings, Mary, Syderstone, N., wife of Thomas Seppings, esquire	176 Friar
1835	Seppings, Thomas the elder, South Creake, N., gent.	623 Harrowing
1851	Seppings, William, Fakenham, N., innkeeper	187 Friar
1848	Sessions, Thomas, West Lynn St Peters, N., yeoman	35 Denny
1850	Sewell, Ann, Eye, S., widow	444 Cuthbert
1855	Sewell, Ann, Redenhall with Harleston, N., widow	208 Whitty
1824	Sewell, Daniel, St Giles, Norwich, gent.	125 Borrett
1854	Sewell, Drake, North Walsham, N., grocer	423 Day
1837	Sewell, Edward, Swaffham, N., gent.	274 Warren
1845	Sewell, George, Eye, S., farmer	788 Pedgrift
1824	Sewell, Hannah, Norwich, wife of David Sewell	O.W. 180
1850	Sewell, Henry, Yaxley, S., clerk	586 Cuthbert
1823	Sewell, John, Bracon Ash, N., farmer	326 Tann
1841	Sewell, John, Eye, S., farmer	455 Traxton
1841	Sewell, John, Hitcham, S., thatcher	379 Traxton
1842	Sewell, Mary, Felmingham, N., widow	578 Canler
1838	Sewell, Robert, Eye, S., formerly of Wortham, yeoman	809 Skepper
1839	Sewell, Robert, Attleborough, N., innkeeper	614 Calton
1843	Sewell, Robert, Castle Meadow, Norwich, N., music teacher	126 Miles
1847	Sewell, Rosamund, Felmingham, N.spinster	346 Broom

1838	Sewell, Samuel the elder, Thurlton, N., gent.	152 Skepper
1843	Sewell, Samuel, Hackford next Reepham, N., builder	631 Miles
1852	Sewell, Samuel the elder, North Walsham, N., bootmaker and shopkeeper	470 Latten
1827	Sewell, Thomas, Buxton, N., tailor	527 Wood
1829	Sewell, Thomas, Felmingham, N., miller	26 Green
1831	Sewell, Thomas E., Blofield, N., tailor	18 Hart
1834	Sewell, Thomas, Wherstead, S., innkeeper	13 Lane
1836	Sewell, William, Hitcham, S., thatcher	398 Smith
1843	Sewell, William, Thorpe next Norwich, N., gent.	569 Miles
1828	Sexton, John, Hainford, N., yeoman	500 Farrow
1850	Sexton, John, Brinton, N., formerly of Mileham, N., baker	529 Cuthbert
1851	Sexton, Sarah, Catton, Norwich, N.	550 Friar
1851	Sexton, Thomas, Norwich, N., gent.	188 Friar
1820	Sexton, William, Great Wenham, S., farmer	11 Mack
1827	Seymour, William, Great Yarmouth, N., gent.	681 Wood
1822	Shafto, George, Norwich, N., millwright	65 Sadler
1819	Shalders, Richard, Norwich, N., currier	227 Le Neve
1827	Shall, James, Gorleston, S., pilot	461 Wood
1820	Shanly, Francis Henry, Fincham, N., surgeon	560 Mack
1856	Shardalow, Benjamin, Beccles, S., gent.	482 Code
1846	Shardalow, George the elder, Raveningham, N., farmer	472 Baret
1835	Shardelow, Margaret Maria, Kenninghall, N.	158 Harrowing
1830	Sharlock, Henry, Great Yarmouth, N., mariner	83 Pettingill
1854	Sharman, Henry Francis, Great Yarmouth, N., formerly of Halvergate, farmer	416 Day
1844	Sharman, John, Scarning, N., farmer	691 Ebbage
1854	Sharman, John, Dennington, S., tailor	577 Day
1845	Sharman, Robert, Beccles, S., brickmaker	403 Pedgrift
1823	Sharman, Samuel, Pettaugh, S., miller	114 Tann
1837	Sharman, Susanna, Diss, N., wife of John Sharman, Norwich, surgeon	403 Warren
1843	Sharman, William, Mendham, N., gent.	539 Miles
1844	Sharp, William, Walpole St Peters, N., collector of marshland smeeth and fen taxes	630 Ebbage
1829	Sharpe, Ann, Isleham, C., widow	321 Green
1843	Sharpe, Anne, Aldborough, N., wife of Charles Sharpe, clerk	229 Miles
1828	Sharpe, Edward, Kings Lynn, N., collector of excise	331 Farrow
1825	Sharpe, George, Melton, S., late of Petworth, Sussex, esquire	33 Hayward
1840	Sharpe, George, Westwick, N.	102 Turner
1848	Sharpe, John, Norwich, N., gent.	6 Denny
1850	Sharpe, John, North Walsham, N., yeoman	578 Cuthbert
1821	Sharpe, Mary, Witnesham, S., widow	257 Dewell
1846	Sharpe, Mary Atkins, Westwick, N., widow	82 Baret
1847	Sharpe, Samuel, Wisbech St Peters, Isle of Ely, C., yeoman	575 Broom
1849	Sharpen, Robert, Aylmerton, N., farmer	649 Womack
1857	Sharpin, Elizabeth, Wickmere, N., spinster	445 Youngs
1834	Sharpin, Robert, Hindringham, N., yeoman	242 Lane
1855	Sharpin, Robert, Banningham, N., farmer	588 Whitty
1837	Sharping, John, Wormegay, N., butcher	334 Warren
1834	Shave, Martha, Woolpit, S., formerly of Wyvestone, S., widow	32 Lane
1848	Shaw, Elizabeth, Burwell, C., widow	319 Denny
1851	Shaw, Esther, Gillingham, N., spinster	51 Friar
1846	Shaw, John, Wells next the Sea, N., woollen draper and tailor	360 Baret
1853	Shaw, John, Diss, N., innkeeper	325 Veale
1851	Shaw, Mary Ann, Norwich, N., spinster	614 Friar
1831	Shaw, Richard, Gillingham, N.	176 Hart
1855	Shaw, Sarah, Aylsham, N., spinster	377 Whitty
1823	Shaw, William, Old Buckenham, N., yeoman	259 Tann
1848	Shawl, David, Middleton, N., labourer	228 Denny
1846	Shearing, Ann, Saint Cross South Elmham, S., widow	544 Baret
1825	Shearing, Robert, Norwich, N., smith and iron dealer	283 Hayward
1829	Shearing, Thomas, Rumburgh, S., farmer	442 Green

1840	Shelcott, John, Woodbridge, S., master mariner	523 Turner
1838	Sheldrake, Charles, Mendlesham, S., gent.	565 Skepper
1841	Sheldrake, Deborah, Stowmarket, S., spinster	549 Traxton
1845	Sheldrake, Frances, Ipswich, S., wife of Jeremiah Sheldrake, gent.	393 Pedgrift
1828	Sheldrake, Isaac Everitt, Aldham, S., farmer	332 Farrow
1854	Sheldrake, John, Wingfield, S., farmer	384 Day
1834	Sheldrake, Thomas, Wetheringsett, S., farmer	153 Lane
1850	Sheldrake, William Joseph, Tibbenham, N., harness maker	552 Cuthbert
1840	Sheldrick, Thomas, Horham, S., farmer	449 Turner
1857	Shelley, Benjamin the elder, Peasenhall, S., farmer	703 Youngs
1834	Shepard, Ambrose the elder, Glemsford, S., farmer	205 Lane
1848	Shephard, Christopher, Norwich, N., gent.	469 Denny
1846	Shephard, Thomas, Melton Constable, N., farmer	253 Baret
1829	Shepheard, John, Fakenham, N.	522 Green
1839	Shepheard, Samuel, Erpingham, N., formerly of Colby, N., gent.	637 Calton
1843	Shepheard, Susanna, Erpingham, N., widow	294 Miles
1856	Shepherd, Charles, Sloley, N., gent.	O.W. 280
1847	Shepherd, James, Brome, S., carter	597 Broom
1828	Shepherd, John, Weybread, S., carpenter	68 Farrow
1844	Shepherd, John, Diss, N., shoemaker	112 Ebbage
1820	Shepherd, Mary, Great Yarmouth, N., widow	333 Mack
1855	Shepherd, Sarah, Great Yarmouth, N., widow	625 Whitty
1838	Sheppard, Daniel, Ipswich, S., merchant	877 Skepper
1841	Sheppard, James, Bungay St Mary, S., gent.	552 Traxton
1823	Sheppard, William, Eye, S.	212 Tann
1843	Sheppeard, Edmund, Belstead, S., farmer	351 Miles
1845	Sheppeard, Elizabeth, Winston, S., spinster	485 Pedgrift
1819	Shepperd, Mary, Acle, N., widow	193 Le Neve
1849	Sheriffe, Sarah, Southwold, S., widow	262 Womack
1846	Sherman, George, Occold, S., farmer	256 Baret
1850	Sherman, Mary, Occold, S., widow	600 Cuthbert
1853	Sherman, Thomas Roper, Rishangles, S., grocer and draper	336 Veale
1826	Sherrell, Mary, St Andrews, Norwich, N., single woman	O.W. 177
1824	Sherringham, James, Foulsham, N., bricklayer	19 Borrett
1825	Sherrington, Robert, Great Yarmouth, N., coal meter	288 Hayward
1845	Sherrington, Samuel, Great Yarmouth, N., gent.	74 Pedgrift
1857	Sherwood, John, South Cove, S., brickmaker	679 Youngs
1842	Shibley, Henry, Rushall, N., labourer	506 Canler
1823	Shickell, John, Great Yarmouth, N., tallow chandler	42 Tann
1823	Shickle, Ann, Great Yarmouth, N., widow	43 Tann
1834	Shickle, James, Norwich, N., plasterer	416 Lane
1857	Shickle, John, Attleborough, N., examiner of weights and measures	753 Youngs
1822	Shickle, Philip, North Walsham, N., late of Gimingham, farmer	385 Sadler
1835	Shilling, Shadrack Meshack, (Shadrack Shillings), Gorleston, S., mariner	474 Harrowing
1837	Shingles, Daniel, Acle, N., waterman	72 Warren
1837	Shingles, John, East Ruston, N., farmer	602 Warren
1832	Shingles, Mary, Happisburgh, N., widow	402 Cooke
1852	Shingles, Mary, Wicklewood, N., widow	450 Latten
1822	Ship, Robert, Thetford, N.	272 Sadler
1838	Shiplee, Edward, Haddiscoe, N., gardener	13 Skepper
1830	Shipp, William, Appleton cum Flitcham, N., farmer	408 Pettingill
1829	Shirley, Francis, Stanhoe, N.	520 Green
1831	Shore, James, Gresham, N., farmer	32 Hart
1855	Short, John, Norwich, N., silk manufacturer	296 Whitty
1849	Short, Thomas Lettis, Great Yarmouth, N., agent	499 Womack
1843	Shreeve, Elizabeth, Heigham, Norwich, N., spinster	160 Miles
1831	Shreeve, Henry, St Augustines, Norwich, N., maltster	13 Hart
1831	Shreeve, Jane, St Augustines, Norwich, N., widow	72 Hart
1839	Shreeve, Susan, Beccles, S., widow	25 Calton

1842	Shreeve, Susanna, Thurne, N., widow	282 Canler
1820	Shreeve, William, Norwich, N., gent.	307 Mack
1855	Shribley, Jonas, Rendham, S., yeoman	33 Whitty
1850	Shrimplin, Sarah, Norwich, N., widow	240 Cuthbert
1847	Shrimpton, Joseph, Clerkenwell, Middsx., gent.	477 Broom
1854	Shuckford, Benjamin, Great Yarmouth, N., merchant	181 Day
1850	Shuckford, Isaac, Lowestoft, S., basket maker	249 Cuthbert
1830	Shufflebottom, Robert, Bungay, S., clerk	45 Pettingill
1845	Shulver, James, Aspall, S., gent.	832 Pedgrift
1841	Shulver, John, Bedingfield, S., farmer	63 Traxton
1849	Siddle, Rose, Brancaster, N., spinster	637 Womack
1838	Sidel, Ann, Norwich, N., widow	104 Skepper
1819	Sidel, John, St Augustines, Norwich, shoemaker	182 Le Neve
1853	Sidney, Thomas, St Augustines, Norwich, N., yeoman	394 Veale
1825	Siely, Alexander, Happisburgh, N., gent.	308 Hayward
1830	Siely, Hannah, Norwich, N., spinster	207 Pettingill
1842	Siely, John, Stalham, N., surgeon and apothecary	230 Canler
1839	Siggers, Richard, Woodbridge, S., glover	22 Calton
1838	Siggers, Sarah, Metton, N., widow	250 Skepper
1834	Silcock, Obadiah, Stalham, N., grocer	627 Lane
1834	Silcock, Rebecca, Stalham, N., widow	532 Lane
1840	Sillett, James, Norwich, N., artist	309 Turner
1839	Sillett, John, Kelsale, S., farmer	547 Calton
1823	Sillett, Lionel, Kelsale, S., innkeeper	399 Tann
1847	Sillett, Robert, Fakenham, N., gent.	796 Broom
1845	Sillett, Thomas, Saxlingham Nethergate, N., husbandman	668 Pedgrift
1835	Sillis, James, Feltwell, N.	9 Harrowing
1844	Silverwood, Mary Ann, Kings Lynn, N., spinster	407 Ebbage
1839	Silvey, Robert, Norwich, N., confectioner	401 Calton
1852	Silvey, Thomas, South Lopham, N., farmer	594 Latten
1837	Simkin, Samuel the younger, Sudbury, S., hairdresser	36 Warren
1849	Simmons, Ann, Great Yarmouth, N., widow	421 Womack
1835	Simmons, James, Belton, S., carpenter	264 Harrowing
1849	Simmons, Lydia, Weasenham, N., widow	364 Womack
1828	Simmons, Martha, Hemblington, N., widow	47 Farrow
1856	Simmons, Mary, Heigham, Norwich, N., spinster	533 Code
1844	Simmons, Peter, Hindringham, N.	568 Ebbage
1841	Simmons, Philip, Great Yarmouth, N., carpenter	109 Traxton
1845	Simmons, Thomas, Weasenham All Saints, N., labourer	40 Pedgrift
1854	Simms, Law, Brancaster, N., farmer	265 Day
1845	Simonds, Charles, Redenhall with Harleston, N., veterinary surgeon	868 Pedgrift
1838	Simonds, Edmund, Norwich, N., hoop maker	220 Skepper
1846	Simonds, John the elder, Halesworth, S., yeoman	545 Baret
1845	Simonds, Mary, St Stephens, Norwich, N., widow	20 Pedgrift
1827	Simonds, Nathaniel, Burgh, S.	217 Wood
1823	Simonds, Samuel, Bungay, S., farmer	154 Tann
1833	Simonds, Samuel, Bungay, S., blacksmith and farrier	248 Cubitt
1836	Simons, Abraham, Methwold, N., farmer	187 Smith
1838	Simons, Elizabeth, Methwold, N., wife of John Simons, farmer	760 Skepper
1844	Simons, Mary, Methwold, S., widow	180 Ebbage
1831	Simons, Samuel, Cromer, N., carpenter	19 Hart
1846	Simpkin, Jonas, Wicken, C., labourer	37 Baret
1834	Simpson, Benjamin, North Walsham, N., collar maker	680 Lane
1827	Simpson, George, Stonham Aspall, S., farmer and butcher	120 Wood
1851	Simpson, Harriet, North Walsham, N., widow	580 Friar
1827	Simpson, James, Woodbridge, S., stationer and writing master	345 Wood
1829	Simpson, James, Ipswich, S., cordwainer	385 Green
1820	Simpson, John, Winston, S., farmer	406 Mack
1822	Simpson, John the elder, Bramford, S., formerly of Badley, gent.	138 Sadler
1837	Simpson, John, Bildeston, S., innkeeper	252 Warren

1845	Simpson, Joseph, Brockford, S., yeoman, formerly of Thwaite, S.	262 Pedgrift
1831	Simpson, Sarah, Ipswich, S., spinster	133 Hart
1827	Simpson, Thomas, North Runcton, N., yeoman	128 Wood
1835	Simpson, Thomas, Mellis, S., innholder	478 Harrowing
1840	Simpson, Thomas, Sutton, S., farmer	382 Turner
1846	Sims, Ann, Hackford next Reepham, N., spinster	568 Baret
1839	Sims, Edward, Sheringham, N., general shopkeeper	602 Calton
1840	Sims, James, Bungay, S., plumber, glazier, and house painter	135 Turner
1835	Sims, John the younger, Norwich, N., chemist and druggist	336 Harrowing
1848	Sims, John, Foxley, N., farmer	172 Denny
1852	Sims, John, Lessingham, N., thatcher	515 Latten
1834	Sims, Robert, East Ruston, N., shopkeeper	41 Lane
1832	Sims, Sarah, Kings Lynn, N., widow	315 Cooke
1838	Sims, Sarah, South Lynn All Saints, Kings Lynn, N., spinster	800 Skepper
1833	Sims, William, East Ruston, N., carpenter	138 Cubitt
1852	Sissen, William, Norwich, N., hairdresser	724 Latten
1819	Sizeland, Thomas, Norwich, N., baker	146 Le Neve
1852	Sizer, Ann, Woodbridge, S., widow	405 Latten
1823	Skeet, John, Wells next the Sea, N., yeoman	71 Tann
1838	Skeet, Nicholas, Marlesford, S., farmer	835 Skepper
1830	Skelton, Edward, St John Maddermarket, Norwich, N.	320 Pettingill
1853	Skelton, John the elder, Necton, N., farmer	464 Veale
1825	Skelton, Sarah, Eye, S., widow	192 Hayward
1838	Skepper, Breame, Oulton, S., farmer	1 Skepper
1836	Skepper, Edmund, Oulton Hall, S., gent.	469 Smith
1841	Skidmore, Meremoth, Calthorpe, N., gent.	517 Traxton
1839	Skillington, William, Kings Lynn, N., publican	306 Calton
1836	Skinner, Elizabeth, Great Yarmouth, N., widow	203 Smith
1838	Skinner, John the elder, Bungay, S., labourer	213 Skepper
1845	Skinner, Mary the younger, Walsoken, N., spinster	344 Pedgrift
1820	Skinner, Richard, West Walton, N., farmer	627 Mack
1827	Skipp, John, Neatishead, N., carpenter	559 Wood
1835	Skipp, William, Hoveton St John, N., gent.	304 Harrowing
1843	Skipper, Elizabeth, Heigham, Norwich, N., single woman	134 Miles
1855	Skipper, John, Hardingham, N., carpenter	445 Whitty
1819	Skippon, Ann, Mintlyn and South Lynn, N., spinster	226 Le Neve
1844	Skippon, John, Swanton Novers, N., carpenter	96 Ebbage
1855	Skippon, John, South Lynn All Saints, Kings Lynn, N.	668 Whitty
1844	Skippon, Luke, Crimplesham, N., carpenter and joiner	23 Ebbage
1834	Skitter, Levi, Capel St Mary, S., collar maker	180 Lane
1840	Skoyles, Elizabeth, Great Yarmouth, N., widow	269 Turner
1845	Skoyles, Samuel, Holkham, N., farmer and innkeeper	203 Pedgrift
1857	Skrimshire, George, Kettlestone, N., farmer	308 Youngs
1839	Skulthorpe, Mary, Kettleburgh, S., widow	438 Calton
1852	Slann, Richard, Southtown, S., historical engraver to the Queen	619 Latten
1821	Slapp, Matthew, Hanworth, N., yeoman	152 Dewell
1853	Slapp, Thomas, Great Yarmouth, N., gent.	540 Veale
1828	Slater, John, Rollesby, N., husbandman	495 Farrow
1841	Slegg, John, Docking, N., innkeeper	241 Traxton
1826	Slipper, Thomas, Hemsby, N., yeoman	345 Davy
1856	Slipper, Thomas the elder, Ludham, N., gent.	643 Code
1835	Slipper, William, Acle, N., shoemaker	125 Harrowing
1851	Sloman, William Waters, Scratby, N., gent.	53 Friar
1842	Sly, Ann, Norwich, N., wife of Samuel Sly, watchmaker	122 Canler
1842	Sly, Samuel, St Peter Mancroft, Norwich, N., clock and watchmaker	618 Canler
1846	Smallman, Francis, Newmarket, C., gent.	621 Baret
1829	Smart, William, Ipswich, S., merchant	471 Green
1825	Smeaton, John, Wells next the Sea, N., patten maker	195 Hayward
1837	Smetham, Elizabeth Jane, Kings Lynn, N., widow	324 Warren
1841	Smith, Aaron, Needham Market, S.	619 Traxton
1836	Smith, Ann, Neatishead, N., widow	138 Smith

1839	Smith, Ann, Norwich, N., widow	554 Calton
1856	Smith, Ann, Bungay, S., widow	402 Code
1840	Smith, Benjamin, St Giles, Norwich, N., cabinet maker	281 Turner
1849	Smith, Benjamin, Hickling, N., bricklayer	267 Womack
1852	Smith, Benjamin, Heigham, Norwich, N., gent.	677 Latten
1830	Smith, Christopher, Stradbrooke, S., farmer,	167 Pettingill
1827	Smith, Daniel, Coltishall, N., shopkeeper	148 Wood
1838	Smith, Daniel, Lessingham, N., labourer	483 Skepper
1842	Smith, Daniel, Greenwich Hospital pensioner	249 Canler
1843	Smith, Daniel, Beccles, S., currier	113 Miles
1856	Smith, Daniel Stannard, Bergh Apton, N.	672 Code
1851	Smith, David Wanly, North Delph, Upwell, N., farmer	283 Friar
1840	Smith, Edgar, East Dereham, N., miller	416 Turner
1857	Smith, Edward, Stokesby, N., bricklayer	807 Youngs
1835	Smith, Eleanor, Canterbury, Kent, spinster	O.W. 280
1836	Smith, Elizabeth, Norwich, N.	51 Smith
1839	Smith, Elizabeth, Norwich, N., widow	169 Calton
1841	Smith, Elizabeth, Norwich, N., spinster	631 Traxton
1842	Smith, Elizabeth, Newmarket, S., spinster	235 Canler
1850	Smith, Elizabeth, Norwich, N., widow	465 Cuthbert
1851	Smith, Elizabeth, Soham, C., widow	486 Friar
1853	Smith, Elizabeth, Ipswich, S., widow	81 Veale
1854	Smith, Elizabeth, Bungay, S., spinster	183 Day
1856	Smith, Elizabeth, Bungay, S., widow	509 Code
1846	Smith, Esther Ellen, Beccles, S., widow	51 Baret
1839	Smith, Fanny, Lakenham, Norwich, N., spinster	337 Calton
1820	Smith, Frances, Norwich, N., widow	149 Mack
1830	Smith, Francis, Fakenham, N., bricklayer	156 Pettingill
1832	Smith, Francis, Norwich, N., wine cooper	191 Cooke
1854	Smith, Francis, Wells next the Sea, N., gent.	128 Day
1821	Smith, George, Cratfield, S., farmer	279 Dewell
1823	Smith, George, St Stephens, Norwich, N., household broker	90 Tann
1841	Smith, George William, Norwich, N., clerk	166 Traxton
1847	Smith, George, Postwick, N., farmer	250 Broom
1852	Smith, George, Colkirk, N., farming bailiff	392 Latten
1857	Smith, George, Frenze, N.	264 Youngs
1834	Smith, Hannah, Kersey, S., widow	794 Lane
1821	Smith, Harriet, Bungay, S., spinster	166 Dewell
1840	Smith, Henry, Brancaster, N., bricklayer	36 Turner
1846	Smith, Henry, Brooke, N., yeoman, formerly of Swardeston	339 Baret
1849	Smith, Henry, Weasenham All Saints, N., husbandman	661 Womack
1823	Smith, Isaac, Ipswich, S., cordwainer	102 Tann
1825	Smith, Isaac, Weston, S., farmer	186 Hayward
1819	Smith, James, Weybread, S., yeoman	247 Le Neve
1826	Smith, James, St Clement, Norwich, N., gent.	21 Davy
1828	Smith, James Edward, St Stephens, Norwich, N., knight	150 Farrow
1829	Smith, James, Frenze Hall, N., gent.	539 Green
1830	Smith, James, Yaxham, N., farmer	26 Pettingill
1833	Smith, James, Bunwell, N., yeoman	421 Cubitt
1834	Smith, James, East Rudham, N., baker	112 Lane
1834	Smith, James, Kenninghall, N., gardener	705 Lane
1836	Smith, James, Burgh, S., farmer	488 Smith
1837	Smith, James, Eye, S., brazier	483 Warren
1843	Smith, James, Pulham St Mary Magdalen, N., farmer	477 Miles
1849	Smith, James, Little Glenham, S., blacksmith	65 Womack
1850	Smith, James, Stokesby, N., husbandman	132 Cuthbert
1851	Smith, James, Thetford, N., carpenter	473 Friar
1854	Smith, James, Norwich, N., brushmaker	196 Day
1855	Smith, James, Ipswich, S., gent.	225 Whitty
1857	Smith, James, Bungay, S., tailor	175 Youngs
1857	Smith, Jemima, Lowestoft, S., wife of William Smith, innkeeper	727 Youngs
1852	Smith, Jeremiah, Kings Lynn, N., dyer	242 Latten
1819	Smith, John, Pakefield, S., gardener	47 Le Neve

1820	Smith, John the elder, Kings Lynn, N., butcher	277 Mack
1821	Smith, John, Lyng, N., farmer	35 Dewell
1826	Smith, John, Great Yarmouth, N., coach maker	271 Davy
1826	Smith, John the younger, Norwich, N., tailor	221 Davy
1826	Smith, John, St Peter Mancroft, Norwich, N., hay and corn porter	115 Davy
1826	Smith, John, Salthouse, N., mariner	291 Davy
1827	Smith, John, Dersingham, N., yeoman	190 Wood
1830	Smith, John, Feltwell, N., yeoman	317 Pettingill
1831	Smith, John, Fressingfield, S cordwainer	517 Hart
1831	Smith, John, Hackford next Reepham, N., cordwainer	378 Hart
1831	Smith, John, St Mary Tower, Ipswich, S., tailor	191 Hart
1832	Smith, John, Melton, N., farmer	101 Cooke
1833	Smith, John, Norwich, N., draper	347 Cubitt
1836	Smith, John Chinery, Fritton, N., farmer	514 Smith
1837	Smith, John, Mettingham, S., farmer	467 Warren
1838	Smith, John, Bracon Ash, N., farmer	11 Skepper
1841	Smith, John, Eye, S., currier	570 Traxton
1841	Smith, John, St Stephens, Norwich, N., grocer	620 Traxton
1841	Smith, John Dodman, West Winch, N., farmer	O.W. 306
1842	Smith, John, Hevingham, N., farmer	248 Canler
1842	Smith, John, Tasburgh, N., yeoman	566 Canler
1847	Smith, John, Gorleston, S., surgeon	417 Broom
1848	Smith, John, Kings Lynn, N., butcher	487 Denny
1852	Smith, John, Great Yarmouth, N., Primitive Methodist minister	102 Latten
1853	Smith, John, Wells, N., formerly of Dersingham, N.	681 Veale
1857	Smith, John, Cromer, N., warrener	315 Youngs
1857	Smith, John, Hilgay, N., tailor	541 Youngs
1827	Smith, Jonathan, Gorleston, S., labourer	7 Wood
1822	Smith, Joseph, Norwich, N.	32 Sadler
1835	Smith, Joseph, Palgrave, S., yeoman	141 Harrowing
1845	Smith, Joseph, Ditchingham, N., yeoman	911 Pedgrift
1846	Smith; Joseph, Barking, S., farmer	546 Baret
1847	Smith, Joseph, Bungay, S., carpenter	755 Broom
1842	Smith, Joshua, Boxford, S., farmer	241 Canler
1851	Smith, Leonard Claxton, Grimston, N., veterinary surgeon	48 Friar
1829	Smith, Lewis, Loddon, N., collar maker	116 Green
1845	Smith, Martha, Great Yarmouth, N., widow	13 Pedgrift
1826	Smith, Mary, Earl Soham, S., widow	65 Davy
1832	Smith, Mary, Orford, S., spinster	339 Cooke
1837	Smith, Mary, Heigham, Norwich, N., widow	697 Warren
1854	Smith, Mary, Wiveton, N.	O.W. 266
1831	Smith, Peter, Winston, S., brickmaker	554 Hart
1838	Smith, Philip, Chedgrave, N., innkeeper	801 Skepper
1843	Smith, Philip, Syleham, S., blacksmith	687 Miles
1848	Smith, Rebecca, Benacre, S.	549 Denny
1830	Smith, Richard, St Mary's Coslany, Norwich, N.	238 Pettingill
1820	Smith, Robert, Norwich, N., cabinet maker	13 Mack
1820	Smith, Robert, Smallburgh, N., yeoman	102 Mack
1821	Smith, Robert, Great Yarmouth, N., blacksmith	260 Dewell
1828	Smith, Robert Cooper, Great Yarmouth, N., builder	439 Farrow
1829	Smith, Robert, Bungay, S., baker	409 Green
1830	Smith, Robert, Ipswich, S., master mariner	339 Pettingill
1832	Smith, Robert, Broome, N., yeoman	312 Cooke
1834	Smith, Robert, Stockton, N., farmer	268 Lane
1837	Smith, Robert, Cromer, N., carpenter	540 Warren
1845	Smith, Robert, East Winch, N., cattle jobber	684 Pedgrift
1846	Smith, Robert, Henstead, S., labourer	563 Baret
1849	Smith, Robert, Foulsham, N., publican	218 Womack
1851	Smith, Robert, Marlesford, S., carpenter	94 Friar
1852	Smith, Robert, Bradwell, S., boot and shoe maker	638 Latten
1852	Smith, Robert, Burnham Westgate, N., baker	522 Latten
1852	Smith, Rueben, Yelverton, N., farmer	48 Latten
1845	Smith, Samuel, Halvergate, N., blacksmith	284 Pedgrift

1846	Smith, Samuel, Bungay, S., yeoman, formerly of The Plough Inn	170 Baret
1854	Smith, Samuel, Fakenham, N., yeoman	290 Day
1854	Smith, Samuel, Norwich, N., gent.	323 Day
1822	Smith, Sarah, Chattisham, S., widow	186 Sadler
1837	Smith, Sarah, Ipswich, S., widow	704 Warren
1837	Smith, Sarah, Woodbridge, S., widow	403 Warren
1843	Smith, Sarah, Norwich, N., widow	O.W. 263
1856	Smith, Sarah, Beccles, S., widow	207 Code
1830	Smith, Simon, Raveningham, N., yeoman	303 Pettingill
1857	Smith, Sophia Martham, Kirkley, S., widow	14 Youngs
1857	Smith, Stephen, Lingwood, N., farmer	367 Youngs
1851	Smith, Susannah, Redenhall with Harleston, N., widow	388 Friar
1854	Smith, Susannah, Woodbridge, S., widow	46 Day
1820	Smith, Thomas, Carbrooke, N., yeoman	468 Mack
1820	Smith, Thomas, Ludham, N., cordwainer	42 Mack
1824	Smith, Thomas, Little Glemham, S., innholder	388 Borrett
1832	Smith, Thomas, Norwich, N., plumber and glazier	112 Cooke
1836	Smith, Thomas, Fressingfield, S., carpenter	443 Smith
1841	Smith, Thomas, Norwich, N., tailor	633 Traxton
1847	Smith, Thomas, Ditchingham, N., gardener	507 Broom
1852	Smith, Thomas, Rushall, N., farmer	106 Latten
1847	Smith, Una, Cley next the Sea, N., widow	63 Broom
1825	Smith, William, Docking, N., plumber and glazier	522 Hayward
1828	Smith, William, Denver, N.	101 Farrow
1830	Smith, William, Bressingham, N.	233 Pettingill
1832	Smith, William, Seething, N., gent.	460 Cooke
1834	Smith, William, Great Yarmouth, N., mariner	556 Lane
1836	Smith, William, East Carlton, N., farmer	392 Smith
1836	Smith, William, Swaffham, N., surgeon	35 Smith
1836	Smith, William, Wells next the Sea, N., labourer	1 Smith
1841	Smith, William, Middleton, N., farmer	622 Traxton
1844	Smith, William, Great Cornard, S., carpenter	543 Ebbage
1844	Smith, William, Stowmarket, S., innkeeper	63 Ebbage
1845	Smith, William, Redenhall with Harleston, N., plumber and glazier	5 Pedgrift
1846	Smith, William, Rendenhall, N.	Index only
1848	Smith, William, Swefling, S., farmer	725 Denny
1849	Smith, William, Bungay, S., gardener	640 Womack
1849	Smith, William, Norton, S., innkeeper	52 Womack
1849	Smith, William, Halesworth, S., former clothes salesman	277 Womack
1850	Smith, William, Thetford, N.	257 Cuthbert
1851	Smith, William, Billingford, N., yeoman	504 Friar
1852	Smith, alias Orris, William, Kings Lynn, N.	861 Latten
1852	Smith, William, New Catton, Norwich, N., manufacturer	124 Latten
1856	Smith, William, Kings Lynn, N.	48 Code
1857	Smith, William, Stowmarket, N., blacksmith	125 Youngs
1825	Smithbone, James, East Rudham, N., carpenter	321 Hayward
1821	Smithson, Robert, Barford, N., blacksmith	60 Dewell
1834	Smyth, Eliza, Cringleford Hall, N., widow	52 Lane
1839	Smyth, George, St Mary at the Elms, Ipswich, S., corn drill maker	505 Calton
1856	Smyth, George, Bredfield, S., farmer	237 Code
1831	Smyth, James, Swefling, S., cooper	371 Hart
1843	Smyth, Mary, Great Glemham, S., spinster	628 Miles
1844	Smyth, Rebecca, Chellesworth, S., widow	1 Ebbage
1819	Smyth, Richard, Ipswich, S., cooper	10 Le Neve
1834	Snape, Samuel, Great Whelnetham, S., farmer	264 Lane
1838	Snare, Henry, Brandon, S., stone mason	482 Skepper
1845	Snare, Robert the elder, Thetford, N., stone mason and brickmaker	184 Pedgrift
1827	Snare, Thomas, Thetford, N., wheelwright	632 Wood
1854	Snasdell, Oliver, Tilney All Saints, N., farmer	512 Day
1831	Snell, Harriet, Snettisham, N., spinster	261 Hart

1850	Snell, John, Swefling, S., timber merchant and farmer	532 Cuthbert
1837	Snell, Robert, Easton, S., woodreeve	702 Warren
1854	Snelling, John, Wetheringsett, S., labourer	162 Day
1826	Snelling, Joseph the elder, Tivetshall St Margaret, N., farmer	40 Davy
1834	Snelling, Joseph, Tivetshall St Mary, N., yeoman	105 Lane
1832	Snelling, Thomas, Old Buckenham, N., yeoman	48 Cooke
1824	Snitterly, alias Mann, Mary, Blakeney, N., widow	347 Borrett
1839	Snow, William, Norwich, N., tavern keeper	671 Calton
1836	Snowden, John, Capel St Andrews, S., shepherd	5 Smith
1832	Snowley, John, Blofield, N., bricklayer	289 Cooke
1843	Soames, Thomas, Harleston, N., hosier	371 Miles
1857	Soanes, John, Corton, S., mariner	419 Youngs
1825	Soanes, Richard, Roydon, N.	267 Hayward
1845	Softly, Mary, Norwich, N., spinster	168 Pedgrift
1846	Sooley, Frances, Little Fransham, N., widow	249 Baret
1855	Sooley, Samuel, Appleton, N., farmer	59 Whitty
1820	South, Charles, Burwell, C., yeoman	651 Mack
1837	Southgate, Ann, Heacham, N., widow	227 Warren
1848	Southgate, Christopher, Norwich, N., millwright	558 Denny
1851	Southgate, George, Ludham, N., husbandman	510 Friar
1826	Southgate, Hannah, Gorleston, S., wife of Isaac Southgate	352 Davy
1829	Southgate, Isaac, Gorleston, S., bricklayer	265 Green
1824	Southgate, James, Rushmere, S., innholder	183 Borrett
1836	Southgate, John, Banham, N., gent.	277 Smith
1851	Southgate, Mary, Thetford, S., spinster	12 Friar
1820	Southgate, Robert, Great Snoring, N., farmer	657 Mack
1841	Southgate, Robert, Norwich, N., mail coach guard	188 Traxton
1842	Southgate, Robert, Norwich, N., gent.	129 Canler
1838	Southgate, Susanna, Melford, S., widow	345 Skepper
1837	Southgate, Theophilus, Hackford, N.	35 Warren
1845	Southgate, Thomas John, Thetford, N., yeoman	305 Pedgrift
1846	Southgate, Thomas Green, Ludham, N., brickmaker	414 Baret
1837	Southgate, William the elder, Stowupland, S., labourer	683 Warren
1853	Southgate, William, Kirstead, N., yeoman	560 Veale
1856	Southgate, William, Botesdale, S., licensed victualler	329 Code
1829	Southwell, James, Emneth, N., blacksmith	123 Green
1821	Southwell, Parker, Gayton, N., gent.	145 Dewell
1836	Sowels, William, Norwich, N., yeoman	214 Smith
1840	Sowter, James, Sotherton, S., farmer	272 Turner
1840	Sowter, Robert, Uggeshall, S., farmer	364 Turner
1826	Spalding, Frances, Diss, N., wife of John Spalding, husbandman	3 Davy
1854	Spalding, Francis, Keswick, N., farmer and land agent	23 Day
1845	Spalding, Mary, Cratfield, S., widow	913 Pedgrift
1845	Spalding, Richard, Laxfield, S., gent.	93 Pedgrift
1854	Spalding, Thomas, Mettingham, S., gent.	474 Day
1852	Spall, Edward, Bungay, S., yeoman	873 Latten
1838	Spall, Robert, Yoxford, S., farmer	790 Skepper
1857	Spall, Susan, Holton, S., wife of James Smith Spall	468 Youngs
1857	Spanton, Christopher, Attleborough, N., gent.	665 Youngs
1847	Spanton, Hannah, Heigham, Norwich, N., widow	6 Broom
1841	Spanton, Robert, Blofield, N., drover	540 Traxton
1856	Sparham, John, Lowestoft, S., mariner	597 Code
1824	Spark, John, Eriswell, S., farmer	228 Borrett
1840	Spark, John, Swannington, N., wheelwright	273 Turner
1843	Sparke, Elizabeth, Norwich, N., widow, formerly of Billingford, N.	17 Miles
1820	Sparke, Frances, Mildenhall, S., widow	291 Mack
1851	Sparke, Job, Stoke Ash, S., miller	562 Friar
1825	Sparke, Mary, Mellis, S., spinster	525 Hayward
1822	Sparke, Matthew, Bildeston, S., jobbing smith and patten maker	314 Sadler
1829	Sparke, Robert, Cratfield, S., inn keeper	82 Green
1820	Sparkes, Sarah, Beccles, S., widow	460 Mack
1826	Sparkes, Thomas, Aldeburgh, S., gent.	190 Davy

1844	Sparkhall, Bower, Norwich, N., yeoman	32 Ebbage
1842	Sparks, Ann, Eye, S., spinster	280 Canler
1833	Sparks, John, Burgh St Peters, N., labourer	61 Cubitt
1828	Sparks, Martha, Buxton, N.	472 Farrow
1836	Sparrow, Ann, Acle, N., wife of John Sparrow, farmer	350 Smith
1843	Sparrow, Ann, St Swithins, Norwich, N., publican	606 Miles
1841	Sparrow, William, St John Maddermarket, Norwich, N., publican	378 Traxton
1841	Sparrow, William, Tibbenham, N., farmer	142 Traxton
1820	Sparshall, Judith, North Walsham, N., wife of John Sparshall, merchant	135 Mack
1841	Spaul, Augustine, Letheringsett, N., husbandman	189 Traxton
1847	Spaul, Henry, Buxton, N.	56 Broom
1819	Spaul, John, Hevingham, N., farmer	99 Le Neve
1857	Spaul, John, Costessey, N., blacksmith	62 Youngs
1849	Spence, Frances, Southtown, Yarmouth, S., widow	460 Womack
1834	Spence, John the elder, Loddon, N., cooper and farmer	382 Lane
1855	Spence, John, Ditchingham, N., formerly of Bedingham, N., farmer	587 Whitty
1823	Spence, Samuel, Bedingham, N., yeoman	356 Tann
1823	Spence, William, Ditchingham, N., farmer	99 Tann
1849	Spencer, Ann Temperance, St Julian, Norwich, N., widow	633 Womack
1834	Spencer, Clark, Feltwell, N., yeoman	137 Lane
1847	Spencer, Daniel, Norwich, N., shopkeeper	213 Broom
1819	Spencer, Francis, Feltwell, N., yeoman	313 Le Neve
1836	Spencer, John, Norwich, N., manufacturer	414 Smith
1843	Spencer, John, St John Timberhill, Norwich, N., gent.	102 Miles
1849	Spencer, John, Feltwell, N., thatcher	211 Womack
1852	Spencer, Matthew, Kings Lynn, N., gun maker	748 Latten
1846	Spencer, Robert, Downham Market, N., plumber, painter and glazier	672 Baret
1834	Spencer, Samuel, Feltwell, N., yeoman	555 Lane
1822	Spencer, William, Ipswich, S., innholder	43 Sadler
1853	Spendlove, John Simpson, Thetford, N., clock and watchmaker	337 Veale
1846	Spice, Thomas, Norwich, N., carpenter	616 Baret
1820	Spilling, James, Holy Trinity, Bungay, S., yeoman	159 Mack
1849	Spink, Charles, Thetford, S., warrener	473 Womack
1848	Spink, James, Aylsham, N., hay trusser	111 Denny
1857	Spink, Robert, Swanton Abbott, N., farmer	649 Youngs
1835	Spinks, Abraham, Feltwell, N., farmer	332 Harrowing
1830	Spinks, George, Thetford, N., innkeeper	294 Pettingill
1855	Spinks, Mary, Mileham, N., spinster	722 Whitty
1824	Spinks, William, Norwich, N., yeoman	232 Borrett
1839	Spinks, William, Mileham, N., farmer	557 Calton
1834	Spooner, Edward, Norwich, N., draper	630 Lane
1819	Spooner, John, Ipswich, S., banker	Index only
1844	Spooner, John, St Lawrence, Norwich, N.	228 Ebbage
1852	Spooner, Rhoda, Ipswich, S., widow	463 Latten
1839	Spooner, William, Stanhoe, N., wheelwright	150 Calton
1855	Spratt, George Denny, Fressingfield, S., dissenting minister	581 Whitty
1823	Spratt, Henry, Heigham next Norwich, N., silk weaver	176 Tann
1833	Spratt, Sarah Elizabeth, Norwich, N., spinster	412 Cubitt
1819	Spratt, Stephen, Great Yarmouth, N., cordwainer	78 Le Neve
1845	Spratt, William, Norwich, N., coachmaker	731 Pedgrift
1835	Spring, Peter, Ballingdon cum Brunden, Essex, wheelwright	278 Harrowing
1831	Springall, Conred, Lyng, N., bricklayer	392 Hart
1822	Springall, Elizabeth, Horsham St Faiths, N., formerly Felthorpe, widow	369 Sadler
1848	Springall, Elizabeth, Great Yarmouth, N., widow	665 Denny
1848	Springall, John, St Clements, Norwich, N., wheelwright	315 Denny
1848	Springall, Joseph, Alby, N., farmer	631 Denny
1821	Springall, Samuel, Reepham, N., bricklayer	646 Wood

1841	Springall, William, North Tuddenham, N., farmer	262 Traxton
1840	Springfield, Harmer	578 Turner
1827	Springfield, John Sparrow, Stoke Ferry, N., plumber and glazier	171 Wood
1840	Springfield, Thomas, Thorpe, Norwich, N., gent.	387 Turner
1849	Spruce, Susan, Marham, N., spinster	169 Womack
1829	Sprunt, James, Wrentham, S., farmer	54 Green
1853	Sprunt, Simon, Redisham, S., yeoman	259 Veale
1839	Spurgen, George, Docking, N., farmer	264 Calton
1837	Spurgeon, Benjamin, Great Witchingham, N., collar maker	490 Warren
1846	Spurgeon, Elizabeth, Alderford, N., widow	39 Baret
1855	Spurgeon, William the elder, Hales, N., farmer	211 Whitty
1834	Spurgin, Stephen the elder, Sudbury, S., innkeeper	266 Lane
1852	Spurling, Jonathon, Bolton-Le-Moors, Lancaster, railway clerk	787 Latten
1820	Spurling, Thomas senior, Aldeburgh, S., mariner	148 Mack
1845	Spurling, William, Burston, N., farmer	841 Pedgrift
1852	Spurling, William, Weybread, S., farmer	86 Latten
1868	Spurr, David, Kings Lynn, N., iron founder	377 Skepper
1837	Spurrell, John, Bressingham, N., gent.	446 Warren
1827	Spurrell, William, Thurgarton, N., gent.	163 Wood
1851	Squire, David, Harleston, N., tailor and draper	390 Friar
1819	Squire, Edward, Norwich, N., gent.	315 Le Neve
1820	Squire, John, Metfield, S., farmer	316 Mack
1853	Squire, Nathaniel, Pakefield, S., master in Royal Navy	210 Veale
1829	Squire, William, Homersfield, S., farmer	474 Green
1845	Squirrell, Samuel, Shottisham, S., Baptist minister	520 Pedgrift
1853	Squirrell, Sarah, Shottisham, S., widow	260 Veale
1852	Staff, Stephen, Happisburgh, N., cordwainer	546 Latten
1847	Staff, William Winson, Norwich, N., soap manufacturer	690 Broom
1842	Stafford, William, Fordham, N., victualler	346 Canler
1837	Stagg, Ann, Great Yarmouth, N., wife of Edward Stagg, book keeper	326 Warren
1824	Stagg, James, Shipdham, N., cordwainer	356 Borrett
1848	Staines, William, Reymerstone, N., farmer	801 Denny
1822	Standley, Miles, Wymondham, N., alehouse keeper	297 Sadler
1837	Stanford, Charlotte, Snettisham, N., spinster	491 Warren
1840	Stanford, Henry, Sporle, N., labourer	284 Turner
1827	Stanford, William, Great Yarmouth, N., watchmaker	475 Wood
1838	Stanford, William, Hardingham, N., labourer	301 Skepper
1844	Stanforth, Silvester, Whissonsett, N., shopkeeper	652 Ebbage
1826	Stalham, Benjamin, Ellingham Magna, N., labourer	321 Davy
1851	Stanley, John, Pulham St Mary Magdalen, N., farmer	609 Friar
1836	Stannard, Edward Simpson, Downham Market, N., yeoman	221 Smith
1841	Stannard, Elizabeth, Blofield, N., widow	369 Traxton
1856	Stannard, Harriet, Corton, S., spinster	133 Code
1857	Stannard, Henry, Syleham, S., gent.	100 Youngs
1824	Stannard, Isaac Shreeve, Thurlton, N., cordwainer	317 Borrett
1827	Stannard, John, North Burlingham St Andrew, N., wheelwright	34 Wood
1830	Stannard, John Smith, Norwich, N., plumber and glazier	184 Pettingill
1833	Stannard, John, Thorpe next Norwich, N., limeburner	2 Cubitt
1825	Stannard, Joseph, Norwich, N., worstead weaver	304 Hayward
1830	Stannard, Samuel, Stalham, N.	268 Pettingill
1826	Stannard, William, Lowestoft, S., cooper	292 Davy
1834	Stannard, William, Strumpshaw, N., yeoman	846 Lane
1837	Stannard, William, Corton, S., farmer	164 Warren
1840	Stannard, William, Norwich, N., worstead weaver	293 Turner
1829	Stanton, James, Pulham St Mary the Virgin, N., miller and baker	448 Green
1832	Stanton, Mary, Thornham, N., widow	151 Cooke
1841	Stanton, Mary, South Lynn All Saints, Kings Lynn, N., widow	120 Traxton
1846	Staples, Edward, Soham, C., farmer	159 Baret
1854	Staples, Jeoffery, Soham, C., farmer	306 Day
1850	Staples, Luke, Wicken, C., farmer	358 Cuthbert

1852	Staples, William, Burwell, C., relieving officer	215 Latten
1832	Star, Benjamin, Wiggenhall St Mary Magdalen, N., lime burner	403 Cooke
1832	Stark, James, Hockwold with Wilton, N., yeoman	343 Cooke
1820	Starke, Robert, Southburgh, N., farmer	596 Mack
1821	Starkey, Robert, Norwich, N., gent.	169 Dewell
1839	Starkey, William Roper, Oby, N., farmer	383 Calton
1838	Starlee, Elizabeth, Great Yarmouth, N., widow	383 Skepper
1857	Starling, Edmund, Norwich, N., yeoman	43 Youngs
1850	Starling, Eleanor, South Repps, N., widow	527 Cuthbert
1832	Starling, Henry, Blakeney, N., mariner	391 Cooke
1847	Starling, Joseph, Great Yarmouth, N., gent.	696 Broom
1855	Starling, John, Great Yarmouth, N., hatter	630 Whitty
1841	Starling, William the elder, Wiveton, N., farmer	345 Traxton
1852	Starling, William, Barton Turf, N., thatcher	552 Latten
1824	Starne, Thomas, Thetford, N., carpenter	50 Borrett
1843	Staygle, William, Great Yarmouth, N., master mariner	584 Miles
1848	Stearman, James, Aylsham, N., gardener	42 Denny
1840	Stearman, Richard, North Walsham, N., yeoman	526 Turner
1842	Stearman, Thomas, Buxton, N., husbandman	177 Canler
1840	Stearn, Molly, Woodbridge, S., widow	190 Turner
1835	Stearn, Sarah, Elmsett, S., widow	475 Harrowing
1843	Stearn, Thomas, Elmsett, S., miller	535 Miles
1822	Stebbens, Ann, Mellis, S.	185 Sadler
1836	Stebbing, George, St Lawrence, Norwich, N., publican	383 Smith
1820	Stebbing, Isaac, Battisford, S., farmer	600 Mack
1850	Stebbing, Zachariah, Downham Market, N., nurseryman	172 Cuthbert
1855	Stebbings, John, Old Buckenham, N., blacksmith	180 Whitty
1820	Stedman, Jane, Naughton, S., wife of John Stedman, farmer	475 Mack
1844	Stedman, John, Stowupland, S., farmer	158 Ebbage
1853	Steed, Simon, Feltwell, N., innkeeper	618 Veale
1827	Steel, Elizabeth, Bucklesham, S., spinster	379 Wood
1831	Steel, Maria, Great Yarmouth, N., single woman	4 Hart
1842	Steel, Mary, Great Ellingham, N., spinster	247 Canler
1851	Steggall, Jonathan, Rickinghall Superior, S., farmer	35 Friar
1824	Steggals, John, Thetford, N., wheelwright	180 Borrett
1850	Steggles, John, Rickinghall Inferior, S., bricklayer	337 Cuthbert
1857	Stephenson, George, Stoke Holy Cross, N., starch maker	655 Youngs
1824	Stephenson, Richard, Feltwell, N., clerk	85 Borrett
1819	Stephenson, Margaret, Norwich, N., spinster	196 Le Neve
1850	Sterry, William, Great Yarmouth, N., ship master	418 Cuthbert
1832	Stevens, Charlotte Wilhelmina, Norwich, N., spinster	583 Cooke
1826	Stevens, Joseph, Beccles, S., cattle drover	173 Davy
1838	Stevens, Martha, Aldeburgh, S., widow	391 Skepper
1835	Stevens, Sarah, Charsfield, S., widow	33 Harrowing
1828	Stevenson, Elizabeth, Norwich, N., widow	452 Farrow
1831	Stevenson, John, Bunwell, N., horsedealer	96 Hart
1856	Stevenson, Joseph, Wingfield, S., yeoman	9 Code
1819	Stevenson, Samuel, Great Yarmouth, N., twinespinner	6 Le Neve
1837	Stevenson, Sarah, Bungay, S., spinster	742 Warren
1857	Steverson, Robert, Topcroft, N., general shopkeeper	118 Youngs
1834	Steward, Catharine, Woodbastwick, N., wife of George Steward, clerk	765 Lane
1850	Steward, Elizabeth, Great Yarmouth, N., widow	126 Cuthbert
1833	Steward, George, Norwich, N., ironmonger	296 Cubitt
1839	Steward, Henry, Stokesby, N., labourer	606 Calton
1846	Steward, Henry, Great Yarmouth, N., esquire, formerly of Cambridge, C.	625 Baret
1820	Steward, John, Brandon, S., carpenter	604 Mack
1839	Steward, John, Bixley, N., labourer	135 Calton
1841	Steward, Margaret, Terrington St Clements, N., widow	229 Traxton
1820	Steward, Martha, Bury St Edmunds, S., widow	87 Mack
1822	Steward, Richard, Honing, N., farmer	167 Sadler
1841	Steward, Richard, Thorpe next Norwich, N., gent.	367 Traxton
1850	Steward, Richard, Southtown, Yarmouth, S., gent.	295 Cuthbert

1834	Steward, Robert, Norwich, N., market gardener	9 Day
1834	Steward, Samuel, Nayland, S., gent.	332 Lane
1839	Steward, Samuel, Norwich, N., gent.	67 Calton
1848	Steward, Samuel, Boughton, N., farmer	444 Denny
1849	Steward, Samuel, Tivetshall St Margaret, N., formerly of Belaugh, farmer	369 Womack
1850	Steward, Samuel, Wereham, N., farmer	497 Cuthbert
1830	Steward, Sarah, St Edmunds, Norwich, N., widow	75 Pettingill
1845	Steward, Sarah, Norwich, N., widow	727 Pedgrift
1852	Steward, Susanna, Great Yarmouth, N., widow	267 Latten
1837	Steward, Timothy, Great Yarmouth, N., merchant	98 Warren
1845	Steward, William, Norwich, N., carpenter	350 Pedgrift
1849	Steward, William, Edingthorpe, N., wheelwright	219 Womack
1854	Stidson, William West, Great Yarmouth, N., master mariner	439 Day
1831	Stimpson, Benjamin, Alderford, N., farmer	573 Hart
1840	Stimpson, Elizabeth, Bury St Edmunds, S., single woman	586 Turner
1825	Stimpson, Francis, Corpusty, N., carpenter	23 Hayward
1847	Stimpson, John, Corpusty, N., carpenter	85 Broom
1841	Stimpson, Sarah, Hilgay, N., spinster	249 Traxton
1820	Stimpson, Thomas, Moulton, N.	279 Mack
1852	Stirling, William Fordon, Saham Toney, N., formerly of Trinity College, Oxford, esquire	241 Latten
1849	Stoakley, John, South Lynn All Saints, Kings Lynn, master mariner	19 Womack
1820	Stockdale, John, Kings Lynn, N., merchant	80 Mack
1822	Stockens, Ann, Harleston, N., single woman	24 Sadler
1836	Stocking, Allen, Scottow, N., farmer	196 Smith
1853	Stockings, Robert, Scottow, N., farmer	433 Veale
1856	Stofer, Samuel, Wissett, S., farmer	415 Code
1836	Stoker, Robert the younger, Great Yarmouth, N., master mariner	256 Smith
1838	Stoker, Robert, Holt, N., gent.	564 Skepper
1846	Stokes, James, Moulton, N., farmer	553 Baret
1829	Stoman, Elizabeth, Great Yarmouth, N., widow	17 Green
1848	Stone, Deborah, Stalham, N., widow	100 Denny
1853	Stone, Esther, St Peter Permountergate, Norwich, N.	422 Veale
1836	Stone, Francis, Norwich, N., architect and surveyor	239 Smith
1839	Stone, John, St Peters, Thetford, N.	269 Calton
1838	Stone, Susannah, Great Yarmouth, N., spinster	401 Skepper
1852	Stone, William, Thetford, N., carrier	255 Latten
1855	Stone, William, Great Yarmouth, N., merchant	568 Whitty
1825	Stonex, Benjamin, Bawdeswell, N., wheelwright	51 Hayward
1855	Stonex, Elizabeth, Bawdeswell, N., widow	501 Whitty
1836	Stops, William, Swaffham, N., farmer	407 Smith
1828	Storey, Elizabeth, Briston, N., wife of Stephen Storey, miller	410 Farrow
1842	Storey, John Ringwood, Norwich, N., hairdresser	359 Canler
1831	Storey, Robert, Baconsthorpe, N., gent.	104 Hart
1850	Storey, William, Great Yarmouth, N., gent.	183 Cuthbert
1838	Stort, Ann, Kings Lynn, N.	68 Skepper
1834	Story, Edward, Northrepps, N., gardener	547 Lane
1831	Stout, Joseph, Cantley, N., blacksmith	293 Hart
1823	Stout, Simon, Upton, N., blacksmith	57 Tann
1819	Stow, Nehemiah, Semer, S.	340 Le Neve
1820	Stowton, Susannah, Norwich, N., spinster	276 Mack
1827	Strain, Elizabeth, Aylsham, N., widow	134 Wood
1845	Strange, Henry, Thorndon, S., farmer	969 Pedgrift
1834	Strange, John the younger, Denton, N., yeoman	581 Lane
1836	Strange, Susan, Denton, N., spinster	418 Smith
1843	Stratford, William, Beighton, N., farmer	296 Miles
1854	Stratton, Margaret, Swaffham, N., spinster	412 Day
1833	Street, Samuel, East Dereham, N., salesman	164 Cubitt
1839	Stringer, Mary, East Dereham, N., widow	182 Calton
1830	Strowger, Samuel, Redenhall with Harleston, N., surgeon	161 Pettingill

1827	Strutt, Benjamin, Ipswich, S., gent.	689 Wood
1834	Strutt, Elizabeth, Nayland, S., widow	331 Lane
1855	Strutt, Mary, Norwich, N., widow	96 Whitty
1843	Stuart, Wardell, alias Wenn, Downham Market, N., merchant	342 Miles
1837	Stuckey, Charlotte, Swaffham, N.	183 Warren
1845	Studd, Jonathon Abbott, Great Cornard, S., formerly of Melton, S., esquire	779 Pedgrift
1857	Studwell, Paul Green, Heigham next Norwich, N., gent.	689 Youngs
1855	Sturley, Thomas, Docking, N.	612 Whitty
1838	Sturman, Juby, Stibbard, N., farmer	848 Skepper
1845	Sturman, Robert, Bunwell, N., farmer	423 Pedgrift
1852	Sturtevant, Mary Ann, Hampstead, Middlesex, wife of Richard Lawrence Sturtevant, Sergeant Major 2nd Regiment Dragoons	829 Latten
1845	Stygall, Robert, North Walsham, N., cordwainer	230 Pedgrift
1834	Subbury, Samuel, Swaffham, N., stationer and printer	439 Lane
1842	Suckling, Rebecca, North Lopham, N., widow	320 Canler
1836	Sudbury, Daniel, Swaffham, N., gent.	51 Smith
1824	Sudbury, Mary, Norwich, N., widow	140 Borrett
1825	Sudbury, William, Swaffham, N., upholsterer	21 Hayward
1838	Suffield, Henry, Thorpe next Norwich, N., gent.	882 Skepper
1831	Suffling, Samuel, Sutton, N.	590 Hart
1826	Suffolk, Rachel, Great Yarmouth, N., widow	344 Davy
1830	Suggate, Robert, Sotherton, S., yeoman	155 Pettingill
1854	Suggett, Samuel, Stibbard, N., wheelwright	393 Day
1848	Summers, John, Burwell, C., yeoman	497 Denny
1832	Summers, Robert, Happisburgh, N., gent.	129 Cooke
1827	Summons, Beilby, Belton, S., husbandman	645 Wood
1848	Summons, William, Norwich, N., gent.	662 Denny
1855	Sunman, Elijah Francis, Sheringham, N., innkeeper	666 Whitty
1820	Sunstead, Daniel, Great Yarmouth, N., gent.	7 Mack
1831	Sunstead, Daniel, Norwich, N., grocer	289 Hart
1832	Sussams, Charles, Great Yarmouth, N., victualler	565 Cooke
1853	Sutherland, John, Southwold, S., surgeon	187 Veale
1856	Sutton, Abigail, Swaffham N., widow	11 Code
1828	Sutton, Ann, Great Yarmouth, N., widow	239 Farrow
1830	Sutton, Ann, Norwich, N., widow	111 Pettingill
1836	Sutton, Bettina, Heigham, Norwich, N., spinster	340 Smith
1828	Sutton, Edmund, Norwich, N., carpenter	43 Farrow
1844	Sutton, Elizabeth, Roughton, N., wife of Stephen Sutton, farmer	689 Ebbage
1852	Sutton, George Crispin, Worlingham, S., farmer	301 Latten
1850	Sutton, James, Swaffham, N., gun maker	69 Cuthbert
1828	Sutton, Joseph Amis, Winterton, N., fisherman	88 Farrow
1837	Sutton, Mary Ann, Bungay, S.	576 Warren
1838	Sutton, Samuel, Smallburgh, N., farmer	777 Skepper
1847	Sutton, Samuel, Bungay, S., tailor and draper	657 Broom
1835	Sutton, Susannah, Lowestoft, S., spinster	617 Harrowing
1851	Sutton, Thomas, East Tuddenham, N., farmer	478 Friar
1852	Sutton, Thomas, Stanfield, N., seed merchant	691 Latten
1849	Sutton, William, Holt, N., cordwainer	594 Womack
1836	Swallow, John, Hunworth, N., farmer	270 Smith
1850	Swallow, Rachel, Wroxham, N., spinster	Original will only
1849	Swallow, Sarah, Wroxham, N.	Index only
1848	Swallow, Thomas, Redenhall with Harleston, N., tailor	480 Denny
1850	Swan, Lionel, Beccles, S., plumber and glazier	70 Cuthbert
1855	Swann, Elizabeth, Stalham, N., spinster	300 Whitty
1848	Swann, John, Castle Acre, N., gent.	676 Denny
1839	Swann, Robert, Castle Acre, N., tanner	155 Calton
1848	Swann, Robert, Stalham, N., gent.	189 Denny
1842	Swann, Thomas, Norwich, N., glover	460 Canler
1840	Swatman, Edward, Little Fransham, N., clerk	152 Turner
1841	Swatman, Mary, St Stephens, Norwich, N., widow	499 Traxton
1845	Swatman, Mary, Rickinghall Superior, S., widow	259 Pedgrift

1844	Sweeting, Richard, Lessingham, N., carpenter	188 Ebbage
1833	Swift, John, Norwich, N., gent.	210 Cubitt
1824	Swift, Mary, Great Yarmouth, N., widow	235 Borrett
1837	Swift, Mary, Norwich, N., widow	379 Warren
1819	Swinburn, Mercy, Hadleigh, S., widow	O.W. 180
1854	Swirles, David, Great Yarmouth, N., builder	373 Day
1854	Swirles, Elizabeth, Great Yarmouth, N., widow of David Swirles, carpenter	400 Day
1848	Sword, Benjamin, Catton, N., husbandman	168 Denny
1837	Sword, Elizabeth, Norwich, N., single woman	147 Warren
1843	Sword, Henry, Norwich, N., coach porter	O.W. 264
1837	Sword, John, Norwich, N., mail coachman	574 Warren
1845	Sword, Robert, Botesdale, S., builder	444 Pedgrift
1844	Sydell, Dinah, Norwich, N., wife of George Sydell, butcher	290 Ebbage
1819	Sydell, Sarah, Norwich, N., widow	257 Le Neve
1857	Syer, Hastings, Longham, N., farmer	772 Youngs
1823	Syer, John, Melton, S., doctor of medicine	22 Tann
1834	Syer, Thomas, Melton, S., gent.	57 Lane
1841	Sykes, Frances, Norwich, N., widow	508 Traxton
1822	Symmons, William, Hemblington, N., brickmaker	302 Sadler
1838	Symonds, Edward, Dallinghoo, S., yeoman	429 Skepper
1824	Symonds, Elizabeth, Thornham, N.	O.W. 178
1820	Symonds, John, Norwich, N., alehouse keeper	511 Mack
1827	Symonds, John, Great Yarmouth, N., gent.	19 Wood
1853	Symonds, John, Great Yarmouth, N., merchant	407 Veale
1825	Symonds, Mary, Norwich, N., widow	70 Hayward
1820	Symonds, Robert, Scottow, N., yeoman	439 Mack
1852	Symonds, William, Great Yarmouth, N., hairdresser	58 Latten
1857	Taber, John, Copdock, N., husbandman	213 Youngs
1825	Tabrum, Swan, Merton, N., yeoman	205 Hayward
1851	Tacon, Abraham, Bressingham, N., farmer	443 Friar
1843	Tacon, John, Stratford, S., farmer	337 Miles
1823	Tacon, Mary, Kingsfield, S., widow	186 Tann
1832	Talbot, Thomas Sugden, Tivetshall, N., clerk	440 Cooke
1855	Tallent, Ann, Wrentham, S., widow	505 Whitty
1854	Tallent, Ethelind Elizabeth Hero, Wrentham, S., spinster	392 Day
1853	Tallent, Horace Leander, Reydon, S., gent.	578 Veale
1827	Tallent, John, Redenhall with Harleston N.	609 Wood
1829	Tallent, William, Chediston, S.	466 Green
1831	Tallent, William, Rushmere, S., farmer	5 Hart
1833	Tallent, William John, Reydon, S., farmer	457 Cubitt
1853	Tallent, William, Rushmere, S., farmer	107 Veale
1843	Talman, John, Southolt, S, farmer	157 Miles
1823	Tann, Thomas, Bawdeswell, N., farmer	1 Tann
1822	Tann, William, Ludham, N., meal seller	215 Sadler
1836	Targett, Henry, Thompson, N., farmer	33 Smith
1838	Tate, James, Barton Turf, N., gardener	101 Skepper
1850	Tate, James, Ludham, N.	123 Cuthbert
1838	Taylor, Adeline, Redenhall with Harleston, N., spinster	148 Skepper
1819	Taylor, Ann, North Walsham, N., widow	O.W. 179
1827	Taylor, Anna Maria, Redenhall with Harleston, N., spinster	125 Wood
1834	Taylor, Benjamin, Briston, N., carpenter	678 Lane
1857	Taylor, Bridget, Wickham Market, S.	825 Youngs
1849	Taylor, Charles, Norwich, N., innkeeper	292 Womack
1856	Taylor, David, Upton, N., farmer	394 Code
1839	Taylor, Dorothy, Spexhall, S., widow	7 Calton
1827	Taylor, Elizabeth, Great Yarmouth, N., widow	519 Wood
1828	Taylor, Elizabeth, St Clements, Ipswich, S., single woman	276 Farrow
1837	Taylor, Ezekiel, Ringshall, S., farmer	157 Warren
1825	Taylor, George, Diss, N., collar maker	348 Hayward
1834	Taylor, George, Wretton, N., gent.	130 Lane
1843	Taylor, George, Burwell, C., yeoman	694 Miles
1848	Taylor, George, Horsford, N., clerk	120 Denny
1845	Taylor, Hannah, Levington, S., wife of William Taylor	225 Pedgrift

1852	Taylor, Henry, Burnham Norton, N.	335 Latten
1852	Taylor, Henry, Heigham, Norwich, N., carpenter	679 Latten
1856	Taylor, Isaac, Earl Stonham, S., farmer	323 Code
1830	Taylor, James Shepherd, Fishley, N., gent.	429 Pettingill
1852	Taylor, James, Great Yarmouth, N., builder	282 Latten
1823	Taylor, John, Barham, S.	301 Tann
1838	Taylor, John, Banham, N., bricklayer	677 Skepper
1838	Taylor, John, Oakley, S., farmer	609 Skepper
1838	Taylor, John, Spexhall, S., farmer	113 Skepper
1841	Taylor, John, St Clements, Norwich, N., weaver	465 Traxton
1847	Taylor, John Edward, St Peter Mancroft, Norwich, N., goldbeater and publican	398 Broom
1830	Taylor, Michael, Norwich, N., gardener	173 Pettingill
1832	Taylor, Penelope, Breckles, N., spinster	478 Cooke
1839	Taylor, Pleasance, Ringshall, S., widow	271 Calton
1851	Taylor, Rebecca, Burnham Westgate, N., widow	124 Friar
1833	Taylor, Richard, Heigham, Norwich, gent.	152 Cubitt
1829	Taylor, Robert, Attleborough, N., cordwainer	420 Green
1834	Taylor, Robert, Hoxne, S., farmer	99 Lane
1844	Taylor, Roger, Ipswich, S., gent.	310 Ebbage
1839	Taylor, Samuel, Framlingham, S., watchmaker	103 Calton
1841	Taylor, Samuel, New Buckenham, N., gent.	155 Traxton
1852	Taylor, Samuel, Ipswich, S., coachman, o.w. missing	500 Latten
1840	Taylor, Sarah, Diss, N., spinster	422 Turner
1841	Taylor, Sarah, New Buckenham, N., spinster	422 Traxton
1852	Taylor, Sarah, Mendlesham, S., farmer	364 Latten
1839	Taylor, Stephen, Hopton, S., farmer	265 Calton
1819	Taylor, Susanna, Lowestoft, S., spinster	O.W. 183
1821	Taylor, Thomas, North Walsham, N., glazier	225 Dewell
1842	Taylor, Thomas, Kings Lynn, N., draper	226 Canler
1839	Taylor, Walford, Coltishall, N., surgeon and apothecary	337 Calton
1820	Taylor, William, Norwich	216 Mack
1821	Taylor, William, North Creake, N., formerly of Cromer, yeoman	16 Dewell
1840	Taylor, William, Lowestoft, S., fish merchant	24 Turner
1843	Taylor, William Robert, Holt, N., clerk	O.W. 265
1845	Taylor, William, Levington, N., yeoman	227 Pedgrift
1852	Taylor, William the younger, Holme next the Sea, N., labourer	866 Latten
1854	Taylor, William, Gayton, N., blacksmith	75 Day
1854	Taylor, William, Winston, S., yeoman	342 Day
1855	Taylor, William, Woolpit, S., farmer	433 Whitty
1832	Tayor, Susanna, Brook St, Ipswich, S., spinster	51 Cooke
1854	Tebbitt, Mary, Soham, C., spinster	204 Day
1821	Tebble, Henry, South Creake, N., tailor and shopkeeper	66 Dewell
1855	Tedder, Elizabeth, Methwold, N., widow	693 Whitty
1840	Tedder, John, Methwold, N., farmer	11 Turner
1840	Tedder, John, Stoke Ferry, N., yeoman	268 Turner
1840	Temple, James, North Barsham, N., farmer	628 Turner
1836	Temple, Mary, North Barsham, N., widow	391 Smith
1845	Temple, Robert, Wells next the Sea, N., mariner	685 Pedgrift
1848	Temple, William, Southrepps, N., yeoman	66 Denny
1857	Temple, William, Stoke Ferry, N., farmer	423 Youngs
1821	Tench, James, Norwich, N., yeoman	131 Dewell
1827	Tennant, Francis, Filby, N., thatcher	15 Wood
1851	Tennant, Mark, Brancaster, N., yeoman	292 Friar
1838	Tennant, Martha, Ormesby St Margaret, N., innkeeper	2 Skepper
1843	Terrey, Mary, Walsingham, N., widow	209 Miles
1833	Terry, Robert, Norwich, N.	O.W. 233
1838	Terry, Robert, Wangford, S., baker	O.W. 369
1832	Thacker, Mary, Great Yarmouth, N., wife of John Thacker, gent,	251 Cooke
1834	Thacker, Nicholas, Middleton, N., shopkeeper	856 Lane
1834	Thain, John, Hickling, N., blacksmith	641 Lane
1832	Thain, Robert, Metfield, S., blacksmith	174 Cooke

1843	Thain, Robert, Hickling, N., blacksmith and farmer	520 Miles
1841	Thain, William, Topcroft, N., farmer	138 Traxton
1847	Thaxter, Ann, Potter Heigham, N., widow	69 Broom
1849	Thaxter, Eliza, Melton Constable, N., widow	478 Womack
1842	Thaxter, Maria, Beccles, S., widow	507 Canler
1847	Thaxter, Robert, Colkirk, N., cordwainer	119 Broom
1827	Thaxter, Samuel Davy, Potter Heigham, N., gent.	24 Wood
1855	Thaxter, William Flaxman, Ludham, N., gent.	656 Whitty
1849	Theobald, Elizabeth Day, Great Yarmouth, N., single woman	444 Womack
1831	Theobald, John, Norwich, N., leather seller	368 Hart
1841	Theobald, John, Starston, N., farmer	536 Traxton
1830	Theobald, Robert Benting, Great Yarmouth, N., master at sea	240 Pettingill
1834	Theobald, Robert Benting, Great Yarmouth, N., master mariner	315 Lane
1853	Theobald, Sarah, Norwich, N., spinster	360 Veale
1842	Theobald, Thomas, Norwich, N., gent.	322 Canler
1824	Theobald, William, Syleham, S., farmer	115 Borrett
1835	Theodorick, John, Holt, N., stone cutter	282 Harrowing
1835	Thetford, John, Woolverston, S., yeoman	405 Harrowing
1849	Thetford, Robert, Poringland, N., publican	11 Womack
1840	Thilthorpe, John, Castle Acre, N., labourer	283 Turner
1828	Thirkettle, Henry, Pulham St Mary Magdalen, N., farmer	387 Farrow
1837	Thirkettle, Henry the elder, Redenhall with Harleston, N., carpenter and builder	508 Warren
1845	Thirkettle, Henry, Loddon, N., farmer	270 Pedgrift
1851	Thirkettle, John, New Orleans, Louisiana, U.S.A.	412 Friar
1850	Thirkettle, Mary, Great Yarmouth, N., wife of James Thirkettle, coal meter	318 Cuthbert
1830	Thirkettle, Richard, Beighton, N., husbandman	181 Pettingill
1830	Thirtle, James, Lowestoft, S., yeoman	20 Pettingill
1842	Thirtle, Thomas, Norwich, N., livery stable keeper and hackney-master	513 Canler
1848	Thomas, Elizabeth, South Lynn All Saints, Kings Lynn, N., widow	235 Davy
1832	Thomas, Mary, Holt, N., wife of William Thomas, clerk	571 Cooke
1825	Thompson, Ann, Great Yarmouth, N., widow	197 Hayward
1827	Thompson, Ann, Norwich, N., widow	439 Wood
1828	Thompson, Elizabeth, North Walsham, N.	105 Farrow
1819	Thompson, George, Great Yarmouth, N., esquire	337 Le Neve
1838	Thompson, George the elder, Fakenham, N., cordwainer	752 Skepper
1857	Thompson, George, Burnham Market, N., yeoman	144 Youngs
1832	Thompson, Hannah, Norwich, N., widow	558 Cooke
1832	Thompson, James, Ingham, N., husbandman	173 Cooke
1832	Thompson, James, Norwich, N., bricklayer	106 Cooke
1833	Thompson, James, Swaffham, N., drillman	243 Cubitt
1857	Thompson, James, Paston, N., cordwainer	3 Youngs
1827	Thompson, John, Culpho, S., farmer	92 Wood
1835	Thompson, John, Ovington, N., farmer	149 Harrowing
1836	Thompson, John the elder, Happisburgh, N., blacksmith	150 Smith
1839	Thompson, John, Norwich, N., bricklayer	123 Calton
1847	Thompson, John, Beccles, S., plumber and glazier	210 Broom
1832	Thompson, Mary Love, Norwich, N., spinster	112 Cooke
1848	Thompson, Mary, Martham, N., widow	585 Denny
1847	Thompson, Richard Bunn, Great Yarmouth, N., painter	5 Broom
1838	Thompson, Sarah, Holt, N., widow	315 Skepper
1850	Thompson, Simon, Great Yarmouth, N., gent.	373 Cuthbert
1857	Thompson, Sophia, Beccles, S., spinster	560 Youngs
1827	Thompson, Thomas, Thornham, N., farmer	83 Wood
1831	Thompson, William the elder, Tottenhill, N., farmer	42 Hart
1835	Thompson, William the elder, Sculthorpe, N., cordwainer	63 Harrowing
1856	Thompson, William, Norwich, N., victualler	670 Code
1856	Thorndick, Thirza, Great Yarmouth, N., widow	274 Code
1845	Thorndick, William, Great Yarmouth, N., gent.	443 Pedgrift
1825	Thorne, Hannah, Norwich, N., widow	348 Hayward

1836	Thorne, Robert, Weston, N., farmer	346 Smith
1826	Thorne, Susanna, Norwich, N., spinster	O.W. 178
1836	Thorne, William, Heigham, Norwich, N., gent.	71 Smith
1854	Thornton, John, Eye, S., yeoman	64 Day
1830	Thornton, Sarah, Great Yarmouth, N., widow	195 Pettingill
1853	Thornton, Thomas, Great Yarmouth, N., gent.	665 Veale
1835	Thorp, John, Wattisham, S., huckster	485 Harrowing
1848	Thorp, Sophia, Norwich, N., spinster	229 Denny
1852	Thorpe, Frederick, Salthouse, N., labourer	363 Latten
1853	Thorpe, John, Carlton Colville, S., farmer	622 Veale
1839	Thorpe, Joseph, Marham, N., baker	539 Calton
1845	Thorpe, Thomas, St Margarets, Norwich, N., publican	658 Pedgrift
1854	Thorpe, William, Fakenham, N., butcher	542 Day
1820	Thorrold, Richard, Shipdham, N., gent.	229 Mack
1837	Thorrold, Robert, West Dereham, N., farmer	428 Warren
1844	Thorrold, Robert, Pentney, N., farmer	402 Ebbage
1848	Threadgill, William, Outwell, N., farmer	565 Denny
1853	Thrower, Aaron, Southtown, Yarmouth, S., gent.	13 Veale
1853	Thrower, Hannah, Eye, S., spinster	517 Veale
1853	Thrower, Louisa, Hempnall, N., wife of Alexander Thrower, farmer	328 Veale
1850	Thrower, Mary, Starston, N., widow	221 Cuthbert
1829	Thrower, Noah, Tivetshall St Mary, N., miller	464 Green
1856	Thrower, Sarah, Eye, S., spinster	579 Code
1855	Thurling, Elizabeth, East Tuddenham, N., widow	569 Whitty
1844	Thurlow, Abram, Palgrave, S.	435 Ebbage
1836	Thurlow, Ann, Norwich, N., spinster	34 Smith
1839	Thurlow, Elizabeth, Beccles, S., wife of James Thurlow, gent.	252 Calton
1832	Thurlow, Frances, Wortham, S., widow	437 Cooke
1838	Thurlow, George, Dallinghoo, S., farmer	431 Skepper
1847	Thurlow, Honor, North Lopham, N., widow	233 Broom
1832	Thurlow, Jane, Downham Market, N., widow	570 Cooke
1830	Thurlow, John, Downham Market, N., wool comber	136 Pettingill
1850	Thurlow, John, Saxmundham, S., stone mason	391 Cuthbert
1856	Thurlow, Lydia, Palgrave, S., wife of Henry Thurlow, carpenter	315 Code
1834	Thurlow, Margaret, Wortham, S., wife of Thomas Thurlow, linen weaver	36 Lane
1827	Thurlow, Thomas, Old Buckenham, N., yeoman	157 Wood
1839	Thurlow, Thomas, Norwich, N., gent.	341 Calton
1845	Thurlow, William, Eye, S., blacksmith	398 Pedgrift
1857	Thurlow, William, Norwich, N., innkeeper and horse master	725 Youngs
1827	Thurmot, William, Stonham Aspall, S., farmer	202 Wood
1842	Thursby, Elizabeth, Norwich, N.	724 Canler
1833	Thurst, John, Bawdeswell, N., labourer	174 Cubitt
1830	Thurston, John, Norwich, N., surgeon	282 Pettingill
1849	Thurston, Mary, Old Newton, S., spinster	598 Womack
1827	Thurston, Robert the elder, Cley next the Sea, N., farmer	674 Wood
1847	Thurston, Robert, Tharston, N., farmer	314 Broom
1837	Thurston, Samuel, St John Maddermarket, Norwich, N.	371 Warren
1847	Thurston, Sarah, Norwich, N., spinster	125 Broom
1855	Thurston, Thomas, Hindringham, N., dealer	580 Whitty
1838	Thurston, William, Lowestoft, S., carpenter	821 Skepper
1841	Thurtell, Frederick, Brookes, Morpeth, Australia	569 Traxton
1854	Thurtell, George, Flixton and Lound, S., farmer	484 Day
1832	Thurtell, alias Murray, James, Loddon, N.	243 Cooke
1843	Thurton, George, Alderton, - S., farmer	19 Miles
1819	Tiars, Elizabeth, Downham Market, N., widow	193 Le Neve
1834	Tibbenham, John, Kirstead, N., yeoman	107 Lane
1847	Tibbett, Edward, Methwold, N., shepherd	321 Broom
1852	Tibbett, Robert Greenacre, Downham Market, N., carpenter	825 Latten
1824	Tibbett, Thomas, Methwold, N., shepherd	83 Borrett
1825	Tice, Edward the elder, Aylsham, N.	92 Hayward
1825	Tice, John, Filby, N., husbandman	271 Hayward

1835	Tice, John Bennett, Cromer, N., boot and shoe maker	95 Harrowing
1819	Ticken, Elizabeth, Norwich, N.	O.W. 74
1851	Tidnam, William, North Tuddenham, N.	65 Friar
1852	Tiffen, Amos, Acton, S., farmer	235 Latten
1855	Tiffin, Thomas, Boxford, S., miller	155 Whitty
1856	Tiler, Matthew, Wiggenhall St Germains, N., wheelwright and carpenter	383 Code
1829	Tillbrook, Jonathan, St Marys, Newmarket, S., innkeeper	222 Green
1830	Tillett, Frances, Worstead, N., spinster	333 Pettingill
1822	Tillett, James, St John Maddermarket, Norwich, N., whitesmith	252 Sadler
1848	Tillett, John, Bracon Ash, N., farmer	841 Denny
1853	Tillett, John, Norwich, N., silk weaver	429 Veale
1827	Tillett, Martha, Burgh next Aylsham, N., spinster	699 Wood
1853	Tillett, Mary Ann, Norwich, N., grocer	480 Veale
1854	Tillett, Rachel, Norwich, N., widow	212 Day
1844	Tillott, James, Eye, S.	395 Ebbage
1834	Tillott, John, Wissett, S., farmer	693 Lane
1829	Tillott, Thomas, Gipping, S., farmer	285 Green
1855	Tillyard, Abraham Crispin, St Saviours, Norwich, N., shoe maker	596 Whitty
1847	Tillyard, Robert the elder, Norwich, N., leather cutter	332 Broom
1835	Tilney, Henry, Hockwold cum Wilton, N., clerk	133 Harrowing
1821	Tilney, Nathaniel, Hoxne, S., innkeeper	270 Dewell
1845	Tilney, William, Little Walsingham, N., carpenter	187 Pedgrift
1823	Tilson, Margaret, Holt, N., widow of Reverend Edward Tilson	294 Tann
1828	Tingey, Mary, West Dereham, N., widow	313 Farrow
1826	Tingey, Stephen, West Dereham, N.	22 Davy
1823	Tinker, Richard, Worstead, N., yeoman	62 Tann
1830	Tinker, William, Letheringsett, N., carpenter	305 Pettingill
1835	Tinkler, John the younger, Heigham, Norwich, N.	9 Harrowing
1849	Tiplod, William, Beccles, S., gent.	436 Womack
1848	Tippell, Jonathan, St Stephens, Norwich, N., bookseller	368 Denny
1856	Tippell, Thomas, Halesworth, S., bookseller and stationer	214 Code
1850	Tipple, John, Oulton, N., widower	494 Cuthbert
1823	Tipple, Robert, Botesdale, S., innkeeper	117 Tann
1824	Tipple, William, East Rudham, N., yeoman	67 Borrett
1827	Tite, John, Bunwell, N., yeoman	317 Wood
1837	Titter, Benjamin Palmer, Lakenham, Norwich, N.	303 Warren
1841	Todd, Anthony, Oakley, S., farmer	359 Traxton
1842	Todd, Charles, Carlton Colville, S., yeoman	80 Canler
1854	Todd, James, Runham, N., farmer	107 Day
1845	Todd, John, Little Walsingham, N., whitesmith	783 Pedgrift
1829	Todd, Noah William, Norwich, N.	O.W. 242
1826	Todd, Richard, Rickinghall Superior, S., stone mason	332 Davy
1854	Todd, Robert, Brampton, S., bricklayer	413 Day
1846	Tokelove, Hannah, Upwell, N., widow	27 Baret
1834	Tokelove, John, Upwell, N., shopkeeper	38 Lane
1821	Tokelove, Robert, Feltwell, N., wheelwright	148 Dewell
1844	Toll, Ann, St Peter Mancroft, Norwich, N., spinster	353 Ebbage
1829	Toll, Robert, Norwich, N., warehouseman	30 Green
1850	Toller, Mary, Benhall, S., widow	353 Cuthbert
1826	Tolme, David, Great Yarmouth, N., merchant	100 Davy
1849	Tolson, Richard, St Georges Colegate, Norwich, N., yarn factor	118 Womack
1830	Tolver, Elizabeth, Great Yarmouth, N., widow	143 Pettingill
1842	Tolworthy, William, Chippenham, C., carpenter	375 Canler
1831	Tomlinson, Robert, Norwich, N., tailor and draper	501 Hart
1834	Tomlinson, Susanna, Acle, N., spinster	367 Lane
1832	Tomlinson, Virtue, Norwich, N., wife of William Tomlinson, hatter	302 Cooke
1842	Tomlinson, William, Pulham, N., gent, formerly Norwich, ironmonger	700 Canler
1857	Tomlinson, William, Norwich, N., upholsterer	101 Youngs

1829	Tompson, Elizabeth, Great Yarmouth, N., widow	36 Green
1851	Tompson, Elizabeth, Foulsham, N., widow	597 Friar
1847	Tompson, Francis, see No. 49 - 1859	642 Broom
1845	Tompson, Henry, Saxlingham Nethergate, N., formerly of Hapton, thatcher	508 Pedgrift
1855	Tompson, Richard Mills, Wickmere, N., farmer	627 Whitty
1839	Tompson, William, St Giles, Norwich, N., cordwainer	633 Calton
1843	Tomson, Ann, Mildenhall, S.	339 Miles
1827	Tomson, Thomas, Mildenhall, S., yeoman	344 Wood
1856	Tongate, John, Kelsale, S., grocer and draper	4 Code
1850	Took, William, Castle Acre, N., tanner	447 Cuthbert
1847	Tooke, James, Norwich, N., gent.	O.W. 316
1845	Tooke, John, Sprowston, N., formerly of Watton, N., shoemaker	359 Pedgrift
1827	Tooke, Samuel, Kings Lynn, N., brewer	237 Wood
1848	Tooke, Samuel, Kings Lynn, N.	Index only
1837	Tooke, William Carpenter, Kings Lynn, N., watch maker	778 Warren
1829	Tooley, Anna, Norwich, N., widow	186 Green
1839	Tooley, Philip, Mattishall Burgh, N., farmer	223 Calton
1829	Tooley, Susan, St Peter Permountergate, Norwich, N.	402 Green
1837	Tooley, William, Great Yarmouth, N., gent.	258 Warren
1823	Toosey, Joseph the elder, Ipswich, S., wine merchant	179 Tann
1844	Topple, John the elder, Alderton, S.	135 Ebbage
1856	Towell, Elizabeth, Lynn, N., wife of Edward Towell, corn merchant	291 Code
1835	Towell, - alias Fowell, Henry, Ipswich, S., wine merchant	99 Harrowing
1854	Towell, Martin, Cawston, N., yeoman	165 Day
1838	Towell, Mary, Cawston, N., spinster	868 Skepper
1852	Towell, Richard, South Lynn All Saints, N., mariner	383 Latten
1836	Towler, Hannah, Norwich, N., widow	163 Smith
1843	Towler, Robert, Great Yarmouth, N., gent, formerly of Foulsham, N.	378 Miles
1825	Towler, Thomas, North Runcton, N., farmer	151 Hayward
1835	Townly, Mary, Wretton, N., widow	275 Harrowing
1820	Townsend, Thomas, Campsey Ash, S., yeoman	282 Mack
1853	Townsend, William, Norwich, N., lieut. 83rd Regiment of Foot	O.W. 316
1826	Townshend, Ann, Woodbastwick, N., widow	103 Davy
1844	Townshend, Edward, Hemsby, N., schoolmaster	667 Ebbage
1854	Townshend, Elizabeth, Acle, N., spinster	187 Day
1844	Townshend, George, Great Yarmouth, N., licensed victualler	671 Ebbage
1838	Townshend, Robert, Ranworth, N., husbandman	47 Skepper
1830	Tracey, Joseph, Brantham, S., yeoman	392 Pettingill
1837	Traice, Susanna, Downham, N., formerly of Hilgay, spinster	389 Warren
1841	Traxton, John, Stoke Holy Cross, N., cordwainer	1 Traxton
1831	Treadway, Legonier, Crostwick, N., clerk	O.W. 252
1835	Treadway, John Francis, Helmingham, S.	275 Harrowing
1820	Trett, Porter Elizabeth, Kings Lynn, N., spinster	39 Mack
1821	Tripp, Mary, Gillingham, N., widow	179 Dewell
1852	Tripp, Sarah, Lowestoft, S., widow	855 Latten
1839	Trollop, William, Wiggenhall St Germains, N., labourer	248 Calton
1853	Trollop, William, North Walsham, N., gent.	458 Veale
1837	Trott, Luke, Outwell, N., farmer	695 Warren
1827	Trott, Matthew, Upwell, Isle of Ely, C., labourer	100 Wood
1856	Trott, Matthew Martin, Kings Lynn, N., cabinet maker	38 Code
1842	Troughton, James, Norwich, N., surgeon	503 Canler
1850	Trower, Henry, Upwell, N., gent.	106 Cuthbert
1819	Trowse, Mary, Metfield, S., widow	Index only
1831	Trusson, Philip, Bruisyard, S., gent.	505 Hart
1838	Tubby, Elizabeth, Caister next Yarmouth, N., wife of Robert Tubby, farmer	256 Skepper
1843	Tubby, Elizabeth, Bawburgh, N., widow	272 Miles
1851	Tubby, Richard, Stratton St Mary, N., farmer	391 Friar
1834	Tubby, Robert, Caister, N., husbandman	413 Lane
1823	Tubby, William, Norwich, N., tinplate worker	69 Tann

1832	Tuck, Alexander Watts, St Peter Mancroft, N., butcher	13 Cooke
1857	Tuck, Fuller, Shipdham, N., butcher	427 Youngs
1845	Tuck, George, Syderstone, N., husbandman	369 Pedgrift
1852	Tuck, George, Great Walsingham, N., labourer	403 Latten
1820	Tuck, John, Outwell, C., farmer	508 Mack
1833	Tuck, John, Hoe next East Dereham, N., farmer	329 Cubitt
1848	Tuck, Joseph, Tunstead, N., labourer	659 Denny
1836	Tuck, Mary, Strumpshaw, N., widow	14 Smith
1829	Tuck, Robert, North Walsham, N., surgeon	146 Green
1830	Tuck, Robert	137 Pettingill
1835	Tuck, Sarah, Ipswich, S., widow	443 Harrowing
1837	Tuck, Thomas, Outwell, N., farmer	20 Warren
1822	Tuck, William the elder, Little Snoring, N., yeoman	90 Sadler
1829	Tuck, William, Hempstead, by Holt, N, publican and weaver	406 Farrow
1854	Tuck, William, Blakeney, N.	220 Day
1857	Tuck, William, Outwell, C., yeoman	36 Youngs
1842	Tucker, George Cooke, Cromer, N., innkeeper	569 Canler
1849	Tuddenham, Mary, Thetford, N., widow	196 Womack
1852	Tuddenham, William, Northwold, N., gent.	476 Latten
1831	Tudman, Stephen, Cawston, N.	169 Hart
1849	Tuffield, Elizabeth, Leiston, S., wife of Robert Tuffield, harness maker	58 Womack
1822	Tuffs, Mary, North Lopham, N., spinster	267 Sadler
1847	Tuffts, Mary, St Edmunds, Norwich, N., widow	279 Broom
1843	Tunbridge, Richard, South Walsham St Mary, N., tallow chandler and grocer	695 Miles
1821	Tungate, John the elder, Upton, N., carpenter	336 Dewell
1828	Tungate, John, Ormesby St Margaret, N., yeoman	212 Farrow
1852	Tungate, William, Docking, N., shoe maker	287 Latten
1854	Tungate, William, Norwich, N., clothes dealer	410 Day
1847	Tunmer, George, Ipswich, S., tailor and woollen draper	99 Broom
1837	Tunney, John, Great Dunham, N., gent.	672 Warren
1834	Turner, Charles, Paston, N., formerly of Edingthorpe, gent.	224 Lane
1835	Turner, Charles, Stowmarket, S., gent.	199 Harrowing
1852	Turner, Charles, Aldeby, N., yeoman	8 Latten
1853	Turner, Charles, Edingthorpe, N., farmer	538 Veale
1830	Turner, Edmund, Kelsale, S., gent.	199 Pettingill
1843	Turner, Edward, Ufford, S., farmer	141 Miles
1855	Turner, Elizabeth, Stoke Ferry, N.	633 Whitty
1840	Turner, Frank, Cowling, S., cordwainer	1 Turner
1830	Turner, George, St Cuthberts, Thetford, N.	396 Pettingill
1847	Turner, George, Norwich, N., tailor	556 Broom
1857	Turner, George, Norwich, N., carpenter, joiner and servant to Messrs. Grant and Co.	375 Youngs
1842	Turner, Girling, Melton, S., gent.	352 Canler
1827	Turner, Hannah, Woodbridge, S., spinster	204 Wood
1828	Turner, John, Felmingham, N., gent.	159 Farrow
1836	Turner, John, Pettaugh, S., farmer	288 Smith
1837	Turner, John, Forncett St Mary, N., farmer	230 Warren
1843	Turner, John Ellis, Scarning, N., farmer	53 Miles
1849	Turner, John, Gislingham, S., farmer	677 Womack
1857	Turner, John, Elsing, N., late farmer	741 Youngs
1832	Turner, Joseph, New Buckenham, N., general shopkeeper	263 Cooke
1835	Turner, Joseph, Snettisham, N., innkeeper	455 Harrowing
1825	Turner, Mary, St Etheldred, Norwich, N., widow	320 Hayward
1838	Turner, Mary, Felmingham, N., widow	698 Skepper
1850	Turner, Mary, Swefling, S., widow	50 Cuthbert
1852	Turner, Mary, St Martin at Oak, Norwich, N.	674 Latten
1856	Turner, Mary, Petistree, S., widow	512 Code
1827	Turner, Nicholas the elder, Norwich, N., bombasine manufacturer	149 Wood
1840	Turner, Nicholas, Norwich, N., gent.	223 Turner
1838	Turner, Philip, Aldeburgh, S., bricklayer	762 Skepper
1825	Turner, Robert, Freethorpe, N., husbandman	511 Hayward

1842	Turner, Robert, Halvergate, N., husbandman	22 Canler
1832	Turner, Rudd, East Ruston, N., miller	336 Cooke
1827	Turner, Samuel, Little Cornard, S., labourer	265 Wood
1849	Turner, Samuel, Woodbridge, S., woolcomber	683 Womack
1853	Turner, Samuel, Wood Ditton, C., harness maker	510 Veale
1835	Turner, Sarah, Carlton Colville, S., spinster	593 Harrowing
1842	Turner, Sarah, Paston, N., widow of Charles Turner	446 Canler
1855	Turner, Susanna, Kenninghall, N., widow	420 Whitty
1832	Turner, Thomas, Woodbridge, S.	405 Cooke
1819	Turner, William, Banham, N., cordwainer	173 Le Neve
1841	Turner, William the elder, Elmsett, S., farmer	370 Traxton
1848	Turner, William, Cley next the Sea, N., esquire	568 Denny
1855	Turrell, Abraham, Blyford, S., farmer	750 Whitty
1852	Turrell, Henry, Bungay, S., mariner	715 Latten
1853	Turrell, John the elder, Sustead, N., yeoman	344 Veale
1831	Turtle, John, St Augustines, Norwich, N., throwsterer	333 Hart
1849	Tuthill, Elizabeth, Great Yarmouth, N., spinster	270 Womack
1847	Tuthill, Hannah, Halesworth, S., spinster	619 Broom
1821	Tuthill, Henry, Southwood, N., farmer	26 Dewell
1841	Tuthill, John Scarlin, Great Yarmouth, N., esquire	439 Traxton
1856	Tuthill, Martha, Halesworth, S., spinster	631 Code
1849	Tuthill, Sarah, Acle, N.	359 Womack
1835	Tuthill, Thomas, Walberswick, S.	533 Harrowing
1853	Tuttell, William, Wheatacre All Saints, N., gent.	223 Veale
1831	Twidney, Noah, Burgh St Peter, N., yeoman	500 Hart
1827	Twigg, Benjamin, Great Bittering, N., yeoman	117 Wood
1836	Twitchett, Elizabeth, Nayland, S., widow	413 Smith
1830	Tyce, John, Norwich, N., livery stable keeper	294 Pettingill
1856	Tydeman, Edmund, Creeting All Saints, S., farmer	466 Code
1830	Tye, Charles, Dickleburgh, N., labourer	134 Pettingill
1836	Tye, Procter, Ashwellthorpe, N., victualler	369 Smith
1823	Tye, Robert, Kenninghall, N., farmer	93 Tann
1838	Tyler, James, East Tuddenham, N., farmer	397 Skepper
1819	Tyler, William, Riddlesworth, N., yeoman	295 Le Neve
1854	Tyler, William, Riddlesworth, N., stud groom	280 Day
1856	Tyrell, George, Diss, N., butcher	120 Code
1844	Ulber, Mary, St Georges Tombland, Norwich, N., widow	489 Ebbage
1822	Ulph, Sarah, North Walsham, N., widow	354 Sadler
1843	Ulph, Thomas, Titchwell, N., victualler	155 Miles
1846	Underwood, Edward, Sudbury, S., carpenter	112 Baret
1841	Underwood, James, Norwich, N., bricklayer	297 Traxton
1842	Ungless, William, Mellis, S., farmer	476 Canler
1827	Unwin, Elizabeth, Kings Lynn, N., widow	40 Wood
1819	Upcroft, John, St Gregory, Norwich, N., ale draper	25 Le Neve
1837	Uperaft, William, Hinderclay, S., yeoman	675 Warren
1829	Upson, William, Grundisburgh, S., farmer	317 Green
1838	Urquhart, Hannah, Great Yarmouth, N., widow	723 Skepper
1837	Utber, William, Colkirk, N., gent.	42 Warren
1852	Utbert, William Henry, Beccles, S.	780 Latten
1833	Utley, Elizabeth, Great Yarmouth, N.	378 Cubitt
1854	Utting, Charles, Brandeston, N., yeoman	476 Day
1848	Utting, Elizabeth, Beccles, S., formerly of Oulton Hall, S., widow	23 Denny
1844	Utting, James, Felthorpe, N., farmer	236 Ebbage
1854	Utting, John, Swaffham, N.	517 Day
1855	Utting, Mary Ann, Brandeston, N., wife of Charles Utting, yeoman	41 Whitty
1834	Utting, Rebecca, Catton, N.	3 Lane
1846	Utting, Samuel, Melton Constable, N., gent.	438 Baret
1828	Utton, James, Downham Market, N., gent.	432 Farrow
1854	Utton, James, Beccles, S., carpenter	130 Day
1828	Utton, Philip, Aldeby, N., farmer	508 Farrow
1825	Vale, Catherine, Great Yarmouth, N., widow	234 Hayward
1844	Vale, John, Southtown, S., gent.	518 Ebbage

1839	Varley, Amy, Reedham, N., widow	293 Calton
1829	Varley, Mary, Bungay, S., widow	308 Green
1835	Varley, Philip, Reedham, N., farmer	39 Harrowing
1854	Varvell, William, Loddon, N., farmer	495 Day
1839	Vassar, Charles, Mattishall, N., farmer	65 Calton
1853	Vassar, Lucy, Heigham next Norwich, N., spinster	430 Veale
1850	Vassar, Mary Ann, Heigham, Norwich, N., spinster	110 Cuthbert
1856	Vassar, Thomas, East Tuddenham, N., farmer	477 Code
1833	Vavazor, Thomas, Emneth, N., farmer	43 Cubitt
1853	Veale, Robert, Great Yarmouth, N., mast and block maker	1 Veale
1829	Veasy, John, Framsden, S., farmer	282 Green
1857	Vialas, Frances, Norwich, N., spinster	36 Youngs
1839	Vickers, John, Swannington, N., clerk	566 Calton
1854	Vince, Elizabeth, Downham Market, N., widow	403 Day
1854	Vince, John, Gunton, N., builder	155 Day
1855	Vince, Robert, Offton, S., yeoman	379 Whitty
1840	Vincent, Ann, Hillington, N., widow	303 Turner
1855	Vincent, Christopher, Happisburgh, N., gent.	462 Whitty
1820	Vincent, James, Fressingfield, S., yeoman	69 Mack
1839	Vincent, James, Whinburgh, N., farmer	499 Calton
1838	Vincent, John, Yaxham, N., farmer	686 Skepper
1852	Vincent, Robert, Denver, N., bachelor	300 Latten
1845	Vincent, Samuel, Westfield, N., farmer	287 Pedgrift
1852	Vincent, Samuel, East Bradenham, N., cordwainer	398 Latten
1854	Vincent, Samuel, North Elmham, N., formerly of Horningtoft, farmer	45 Day
1829	Vincent, William, Colton, N., kiddier	71 Green
1851	Vineyard, William, Frostenden, S., yeoman	532 Friar
1828	Vipan, Robert, Upwell, C., farmer	526 Farrow
1820	Vipond, John, Hardwick, N., carpenter	73 Mack
1841	Vyse, Edward, Diss, N., currier	449 Traxton
1844	Vyse, John, Thorpe Abbott, N., farmer	365 Ebbage
1848	Vyse, Keturah, Diss, N., widow	291 Denny
1822	Vyse, Rosamond, Dickleburgh, N., widow	382 Sadler
1834	Wabon, Jonas, Wells next the Sea, N., mariner	557 Lane
1827	Wade, Barnabas, Bedfield, S., butcher	277 Wood
1839	Wade, Benjamin, Stibbard, N., brazier and tinman	560 Calton
1826	Wade, Edmund, Halesworth, S., cooper	9 Davy
1849	Wade, Elizabeth, Great Yarmouth, N., widow	372 Womack
1852	Wade, Henry, Norwich, N.	O.W. 357
1829	Wade, Henry, Bressingham, N., butcher	184 Green
1836	Wade, James, Shipmeadow, S., formerly of Beccles, S., esquire	137 Smith
1839	Wade, John, Poslingford, S., farmer	187 Calton
1851	Wade, John, Norwich, N., cabinet maker	492 Friar
1852	Wade, Rose Maria, Hackford, N., widow	497 Latten
1841	Wade, Mary, Thorndon, S., widow	361 Traxton
1834	Wade, Thomas, Saham Toney, N., farmer	21 Lane
1837	Wade, Stephen, Saham Toney, N., yeoman	595 Warren
1822	Wade, William, Holt, N., common carrier	228 Sadler
1842	Wagg, William, Sutton, N., gent.	412 Canler
1837	Wainford, James, Saxlingham, N., farmer	318 Warren
1830	Waite, George, Norwich, N., tailor	306 Pettingill
1857	Wake, Elizabeth, West Winch, N., spinster	317 Youngs
1832	Wake, Henry, Grundisburgh, S., farmer	354 Cooke
1822	Wake, John, Ipswich, S., groom	196 Sadler
1842	Wake, Thomas, Dickleburgh, N., yeoman	559 Canler
1837	Wakefield, Francis, Norwich, N., publican	121 Warren
1819	Wakelin, John, Great Cornard, S., wheelwright and victualler	343 Le Neve
1849	Wakeling, Martha, South Elmham All Saints, S., widow	629 Womack
1852	Wales, Charles, Wangford, S., general shopkeeper	731 Latten
1830	Wales, Elizabeth, Kings Lynn, N., widow	104 Pettingill
1848	Wales, James, Freethorpe, N., harness maker	259 Denny
1833	Walford, Joseph, Woodbridge, S., gent.	O.W. 234

1834	Walford, Joseph Parmenter Naunton, Rushmere, near Ipswich, S., gent.	696 Lane
1822	Walford, Mary, Woodbridge, S., spinster	O.W. 174
1835	Walford, Mary, Stowmarket, S., widow	562 Harrowing
1842	Walford, William, Long Stratton, N., clerk	O.W. 290
1844	Walker, Allen, Hopton, S., army lieutenant	661 Ebbage
1834	Walker, Ann, Bungay, S., widow	672 Lane
1841	Walker, Ann, Norwich, N., wife of Isaac Walker, gunsmith	187 Traxton
1855	Walker, Ann, Great Witchingham, N., widow	O.W. 344
1856	Walker, Elizabeth Melvin, Kings Lynn, N., widow	333 Cuthbert
1829	Walker, Emery, Smallburgh, N., farmer	76 Green
1825	Walker, James, Terrington St Clements, N., farrier	469 Hayward
1848	Walker, Jeremiah, South Creake, N., labourer	765 Denny
1827	Walker, John, Hapton, N., carrier	206 Wood
1850	Walker, Louisa, Botesdale, S., spinster	397 Cuthbert
1834	Walker, Robert, Alderton, S., wheelwright	859 Lane
1845	Walker, Robert, Framlingham, S., gent.	140 Pedgrift
1854	Walker, Robert the elder, Ellingham, N., farmer	443 Day
1824	Walker, Samuel, Feltwell, N., yeoman	190 Borrett
1839	Walker, Samuel, Beccles, S., gunmaker	327 Calton
1824	Walker, Sarah, Blickling, N., wife of Matthew Walker, carpenter	136 Borrett
1856	Walker, Susanna, South Creake, N., widow	342 Code
1832	Walker, William, Stuston, S., rector	323 Cooke
1834	Walker, William Sheen, Burston, N., farmer	221 Lane
1836	Walker, William, Gaywood, N., miller	179 Smith
1852	Walker, William, Little Bittering, N., farmer	606 Latten
1838	Walkley, Thomas, Norwich, N., publican	818 Skepper
1829	Wall, Mark, Tasburgh, formerly Norwich, N., gent.	117 Green
1849	Wall, Samuel, Dennington, S., shoemaker	585 Womack
1849	Wall, Susan, Dennington, S., widow	584 Womack
1848	Waller, Charlotte, Great Yarmouth, N., widow	191 Denny
1835	Waller, Edward, Norwich, N., gent.	194 Harrowing
1853	Waller, Edward, Blakeney, N., bricklayer	434 Veale
1851	Waller, Elizabeth, Gatesend, N., widow	123 Friar
1835	Waller, George, Waldringfield, S., gent.	52 Harrowing
1839	Waller, Harry, Fakenham, N., gent.	136 Calton
1848	Waller, Henry, Gatesend, N., wheelwright	667 Denny
1848	Waller, Jabez, Saxmundham, S., brandy and porter merchant	834 Denny
1835	Waller, Jeptha, Hollesley, S., esquire	477 Harrowing
1823	Waller, John, Aylsham, N., farmer	260 Tann
1834	Waller, John, Cley next the Sea, N., auctioneer	477 Lane
1841	Waller, John, Benhall, S.	229 Traxton
1835	Waller, Mary, All Saints, Norwich, N.	631 Harrowing
1845	Waller, Robert, Cockthorpe, N., husbandman	569 Pedgrift
1852	Waller, Susannah, Roydon, S., widow	867 Latten
1834	Waller, William, All Saints, Norwich, N., gent.	633 Lane
1850	Wallman, John, Earsham, N., farmer	242 Cuthbert
1844	Walne, George, Weybread, S., husbandman	78 Ebbage
1836	Walne, James, Syleham, S., gent.	109 Smith
1843	Walne, James, Redenhall with Harleston, N., gent.	349 Miles
1823	Walne, William, Swainsthorpe, N., gent.	122 Tann
1857	Walpole, Charlotte, Great Yarmouth, N., widow	762 Youngs
1840	Walpole, John, Ormesby St Michael, N., husbandman	652 Turner
1829	Walpole, Robert the younger, Great Yarmouth, N., liquor merchant	193 Green
1854	Walpole, Robert Horatio, West Bilney, N., farmer	80 Day
1835	Walton, Nathan, Mickfield, S., farmer	344 Harrowing
1822	Walton, Thomas, Kings Lynn, N., yeoman	282 Sadler
1835	Wandby, Hugh, Upwell, C., land surveyor	163 Harrowing
1827	Ward, Ann, North Walsham, N., spinster	208 Wood
1851	Ward, Ann, London, formerly of Norwich, wife of James Ward	168 Friar
1846	Ward, Benjamin, Downham Market, N., yeoman	53 Baret
1849	Ward, Benjamin, Great Yarmouth, N., waterman	216 Womack

1820	Ward, Edward, Battisford, S., gent.	114 Mack
1831	Ward, Francis, Aylsham, N., bricklayer	57 Hart
1856	Ward, Henry, Southery, N., yeoman	524 Code
1822	Ward, James, Haughley, S., gent.	401 Sadler
1836	Ward, James, Brisley, N., gent.	105 Smith
1837	Ward, James, Lowestoft, S., fish merchant	501 Warren
1852	Ward, James, East Dereham, N., schoolmaster	610 Latten
1852	Ward, James, Thetford, N., schoolmaster	311 Latten
1829	Ward, John, Norwich, N., baker	394 Green
1830	Ward, John, Great Snoring, N., farmer	333 Pettingill
1845	Ward, John, Stoke Ash, S., clerk	784 Pedgrift
1856	Ward, John the elder, Necton, N., yeoman	680 Code
1850	Ward, Joseph, Alburgh, N., carpenter	2 Cuthbert
1850	Ward, Joseph, Beeston Regis, N., yeoman	45 Cuthbert
1842	Ward, Lucy, East Dereham, N., widow	311 Canler
1846	Ward, Lydia, Eye, S., widow and innkeeper	222 Baret
1833	Ward, Mary, Cawston, N., spinster	341 Cubitt
1840	Ward, Mary, Great Yarmouth, N., widow	295 Turner
1849	Ward, Robert, Norwich, N., gent.	619 Womack
1854	Ward, Robert, Potter Heigham, N.	108 Day
1855	Ward, Robert, Loddon, N., carpenter	202 Whitty
1857	Ward, Robert, Raveningham, N.farmer	721 Youngs
1853	Ward, Samuel, Stokesby, N., yeoman	115 Veale
1834	Ward, Simon, Redenhall with Harleston, N., husbandman	371 Lane
1833	Ward, Thomas, Hasketon, S., farmer	9 Cubitt
1838	Ward, Thomas, Feltwell, N., yeoman	137 Skepper
1850	Ward, Thomas, West Winch, N., farmer	473 Cuthbert
1842	Ward, William, Kirby Cane, N., farmer	450 Canler
1846	Ward, William, Stowmarket, S., minister of the Gospel	354 Baret
1831	Wardell, Martha, Wells next the Sea, N., widow	219 Hart
1831	Wardlaw, Henry, Sheringham, N., formerly of Cromer, N., farmer	455 Hart
1835	Wardlaw, Christian, St Peter Mancroft, Norwich, N., spinster	314 Harrowing
1848	Wardley, Samuel, Worlingworth, S., farmer	262 Denny
1829	Warmington, Mary Ann, Cawston, N., widow	316 Green
1841	Warmoll, John, Topcroft, N., farmer	451 Traxton
1856	Warn, William, Bedfield, S., farmer	575 Code
1853	Warne, Henry, Syleham Mill, S., manufacturer	101 Veale
1830	Warne, John, Norwich, N., gent.	Index only
1852	Warner, Eleanor, Gorleston, S., widow	219 Latten
1833	Warner, Hannah, Walcot, N., widow	199 Cubitt
1821	Warner, John, Newmarket, C., yeoman	19 Dewell
1849	Warner, John, Wrentham, S., miller, formerly of Thurlton, N.	407 Womack
1834	Warner, Mary, Framlingham, S., widow	198 Lane
1852	Warner, Robert, alias Drewell, Fakenham, N.	662 Latten
1828	Warner, Susanna, Fakenham, N., wife of Francis Warner, tailor	255Farrow
1820	Warner, William, Walcot, N., esquire	376 Pettingill
1839	Warnes, James, Sidestrand, N., farmer	465 Calton
1834	Warnes, Robert, St Paul, Norwich, N., twisterer	149 Lane
1854	Warnes, Robert, West Somerton, N., boatman	576 Day
1837	Warnes, Samuel, Ellough, S., farmer	41 Warren
1849	Warnes, Samuel, Southwood, N., farmer	84 Womack
1853	Warnett, Samuel, Hollesley, S.	23 Veale
1822	Warrant, William, Great Yarmouth, N., grocer	224 Sadler
1843	Warren, Ann Maria, Weybourne, N.	O.W. 266
1851	Warren, Anthony Paine, Woodbridge, S., yeoman	348 Friar
1820	Warren, George, Kersey, S., shopkeeper	204 Mack
1830	Warren, Hester, Holbrook, S., widow	106 Pettingill
1850	Warren, James, Great Yarmouth, N., gent.	223 Cuthbert
1834	Warren, John, Great Ellingham, N., gent.	727 Lane
1844	Warren, Mary, Kersey, S., widow	534 Ebbage
1853	Warren, Robins, Soham, C., farmer	643 Veale
1844	Warren, Thomas, Tibbenham, N., farmer	271 Ebbage
1820	Warren, William, Fressingfield, S., farmer	126 Mack

1837	Warren, William, Beachamwell, N., labourer	1 Warren
1840	Warren, William, Attleborough, N., farmer	143 Turner
1850	Warren, William, Starston, N., farmer	331 Cuthbert
1840	Warters, John, Methwold, N., yeoman	656 Turner
1842	Warth, Maria Langman, Heigham, Norwich, N.	539 Canler
1838	Warts, Augustine, Lessingham, N.	770 Skepper
1853	Warwick, Elizabeth, Lowestoft, S., spinster	621 Veale
1852	Wasey, Thomas, South Creake, N., cordwainer	813 Latten
1849	Wasey, William, South Creake, N., drover	57 Womack
1842	Watcham, Edward, Eye, S., formerly of Broomfield, Essex, yeoman	23 Canler
1834	Watcham, Stephen, Mendlesham, S., farmer	479 Lane
1850	Waters, Ann, Gorleston, S., widow	510 Cuthbert
1849	Waters, Azariah, Herringby, Stokesby, N., farmer	347 Womack
1851	Waters, Benjamin, Hemsby, N., farmer	516 Friar
1852	Waters, Constance, Great Yarmouth, N., widow	833 Latten
1856	Waters, George, Ipswich, S., gent.	292 Code
1836	Waters, Harriet, Great Yarmouth, N., widow	502 Smith
1845	Waters, James, Wroxham, N.	643 Pedgrift
1838	Waters, John, Castle Acre, N., blacksmith	455 Skepper
1841	Waters, John, Hardingham, N., farmer	272 Traxton
1854	Waters, John, Gorleston, S., yeoman	332 Day
1839	Waters, Robert, Oxnead, N., farmer	626 Calton
1852	Waters, Robert, Southtown, Little Yarmouth, S., merchant	856 Latten
1827	Waters, Samuel, Strumpshaw, N., fisherman	14 Wood
1834	Waters, Samuel, Stowmarket, S., gent.	534 Lane
1838	Waters, Samuel, Leiston, S.	722 Skepper
1838	Waters, William, Great Yarmouth, N., fish curer	725 Skepper
1853	Waters, William, Great Witchingham, N., yeoman	374 Veale
1853	Waters, William, Upton, N., gent.	115 Veale
1843	Waterson, James, Sharrington, N.	352 Miles
1825	Waterson, John, Skeyton, N., late of Norwich, gent.	246 Hayward
1828	Waterson, John, Norwich, N., cabinet maker and chair maker	434 Farrow
1848	Waterson, John, North Walsham, N., farmer	390 Denny
1820	Watkins, Ann, Henley, S., spinster	36 Mack
1827	Watlin, John, Ipswich, S., master mariner	611 Wood
1856	Watling, Henry, Weybread, S., farmer	350 Code
1837	Watling, John, Worlingworth, S., common carrier	297 Warren
1843	Watling, John, Mendham, N., lawyer	250 Miles
1852	Watling, Mary Ann, Great Yarmouth, N., widow	187 Latten
1841	Watling, Robert, Southolt, S., thatcher	365 Traxton
1840	Watling, Susanna, Beeston next Mileham, N., wife of Robert Watling, shopkeeper	128 Turner
1822	Watling, William, East Dereham, N., labourer	414 Sadler
1846	Watson, Charles, Wood Norton, N., yeoman	304 Baret
1854	Watson, Charles, Little Ryburgh, N., farmer	529 Day
1856	Watson, Edward, Norwich, N., gent.	660 Code
1845	Watson, Elizabeth, Diss, N., widow	309 Pedgrift
1855	Watson, Ellenah, Wells next the Sea, N., spinster	217 Whitty
1844	Watson, George, Rackheath, N.	3 Ebbage
1849	Watson, James, Thorpe, Norwich, N., stone and marble merchant	576 Womack
1851	Watson, Joseph, Norwich, N., yeoman	620 Friar
1855	Watson, Martha, Ilketshall St John, S., wife of Robert Watson, labourer	606 Whitty
1821	Watson, Tabitha, Gorleston, S., previously of North Ealing, Middlesex, spinster	304 Dewell
1841	Watson, Thomas, Great Yarmouth, N., carter	6 Traxton
1839	Watson, Robert, Moulton, N., farmer	291 Calton
1820	Watson, Royall, Thetford, N., yeoman	130 Mack
1845	Watson, William Ryley, Terrington St Clements, N., schoolmaster	450 Pedgrift
1856	Watts, Amy, Cransford, S., widow	609 Code
1844	Watts, Elizabeth, Burnham Sutton, N., widow	687 Ebbage
1839	Watts, George, Downham Market, N., pig salesman	137 Calton

1842	Watts, George, Moulton, N., farmer	178 Canler
1845	Watts, George, Southtown, Little Yarmouth, S., gent.	628 Pedgrift
1847	Watts, Isaac, Barton Turf, N., yeoman	284 Broom
1855	Watts, James Meadows, Little Fransham, N., draper	43 Whitty
1857	Watts, Johanna, Great Yarmouth, N., widow	13 Youngs
1823	Watts, John Junior, Hackford, N., thatcher	217 Tann
1840	Watts, John, Little Plumstead, N., yeoman	381 Turner
1846	Watts, John, Great Yarmouth, N., yeoman	536 Baret
1852	Watts, John, Marsham, N., yeoman	103 Latten
1853	Watts, Mary, Hindolveston, N., widow	340 Veale
1853	Watts, Mary, Wood Norton, N.	Index only
1837	Watts, Richard, Kings Lynn, N., coach maker and wheelwright	372 Warren
1845	Watts, Richard, Kings Lynn, N.	Index only
1829	Watts, Robert, West Bradenham, N., farmer	202 Green
1833	Watts, Robert, Horstead, N., gent.	497 Lane
1834	Watts, Thomas, Norwich, N., ironfounder	780 Lane
1837	Watts, Thomas, St Peter Permountergate, Norwich, N., engineer	555 Warren
1844	Watts, Thomas, Wood Dalling, N., farmer	638 Ebbage
1838	Watts, William, Boyton, S., gardener	207 Skepper
1846	Watts, William, Norwich, N., yeoman	411 Baret
1855	Wayne, John William, Cratfield, S., congregational minister	595 Whitty
1838	Wayth, Sarah, Eye, S., widow	755 Skepper
1846	Wayth, William Francis, Southwold, S., master mariner	404 Baret
1836	Wearing, Mary, Norwich, N., widow	251 Smith
1854	Wearn, Barnaby, Wingfield, S.	469 Day
1843	Weatherhead, William, Burnham Westgate, N., gent.	545 Miles
1848	Weavers, John, Coggeshall, Essex, miller	847 Denny
1835	Weavers, Robert, Beccles, S., farmer	391 Harrowing
1846	Weavers, Robert, Wetheringsett, S., blacksmith	364 Denny
1845	Weavers, Sarah, Morningthorpe, N., spinster	874 Pedgrift
1844	Webb, Elizabeth Robinson, Holt, N., widow	394 Ebbage
1832	Webb, Henry, Hindringham, N., farmer	150 Cooke
1838	Webb, Isabel, Pulham St Mary the Virgin, N., widow	513 Skepper
1837	Webb, John Pitt, Broome, N., single man	767 Warren
1847	Webb, Martin, Newmarket St Mary, S., tailor	491 Broom
1839	Webb, Richard, Pulham St Mary the Virgin, N.	340 Calton
1844	Webb, Richard, Stowmarket, S., bricklayer	79 Ebbage
1830	Webb, Robert, Cromer, N., carpenter	346 Pettingill
1856	Webb, Sarah Hardingham, Stowmarket, S., spinster	308 Code
1827	Webb, Stephen, Cheveley, C., yeoman	630 Wood
1819	Webb, Thomas, Burwell, C., farmer	77 Le Neve
1838	Webb, William, Newmarket, S., blacksmith	744 Skepper
1833	Webber, Benjamin Dornale, Upwell, N., carpenter	172 Cubitt
1838	Webber, Catherine, Wells next the Sea, N., widow	459 Skepper
1819	Webber, Joseph, Friston, S., gent.	330 Le Neve
1820	Webber, Mary, Melton, S., widow	187 Mack
1822	Webber, Samuel, Hopton, S., surgeon	233 Sadler
1839	Webster, Ann, Kings Lynn, N., widow	476 Calton
1833	Webster, Charlotte, Heigham, Norwich, N., widow	125 Cubitt
1824	Webster, Hammond, Great Yarmouth, N., shopkeeper	245 Borrett
1824	Webster, John, Kings Lynn, N., cordwainer	182 Borrett
1835	Webster, John, Great Yarmouth, N., mariner	611 Harrowing
1844	Webster, John, Great Yarmouth, N., tailor	358 Ebbage
1852	Webster, John, Lowestoft, S., gent.	714 Latten
1852	Webster, Paul Thomas, Norwich, N., ironmonger	777 Latten
1834	Webster, Samuel, Ipswich, S., merchant	644 Lane
1857	Webster, Samuel, Thornham Magna, S.	728 Youngs
1849	Webster, Susan Staff, Stanton, S., widow	55 Womack
1834	Webster, Thomas, Southburgh, N., farmer	529 Lane
1857	Webster, Thomas, Norwich, N., gent.	795 Youngs
1831	Webster, William, Ipswich, S., merchant	603 Hart
1834	Webster, William, Norwich, N., innkeeper	620 Lane
1825	Weeding, John the elder, Walton, S., gent.	487 Hayward

1843	Weeding, Phillis, Grundisburgh, S., widow	23 Miles
1834	Weeds, John, Thorpe next Norwich, N., carpenter	185 Lane
1857	Weeds, John, Norwich, N., accountant	430 Youngs
1857	Weeds, Sarah, Thorpe next Norwich, N., widow	228 Youngs
1835	Weeds, William, Bungay, S., cordwainer	95 Harrowing
1835	Wegg, Harriett, Great Yarmouth, N., wife of John Wegg, gent.	569 Harrowing
1832	Weights, Samuel, Hethersett, N., husbandman	110 Cooke
1854	Welburn, Elizabeth, Kings Lynn, N., widow	105 Day
1840	Welch, Thomas, Strumpshaw, N., miller	300 Turner
1852	Welch, William the elder, Beccles, S., whitesmith	171 Latten
1830	Welham, John, Otley, S., late of Ashbocking, S., gent.	210 Pettingill
1848	Welham, Samuel, Kersey, S., drillman	309 Denny
1844	Welham, William, Woodbridge, S., maltster	62 Ebbage
1838	Wellingham, Edward, Great Fransham, N., farmer	629 Skepper
1852	Wellingham, Edward, East Walton, N., farmer	793 Latten
1855	Wells, Ann, Norwich, N., widow	216 Whitty
1853	Wells, Edmund, Norwich, N., waterman	631 Veale
1838	Wells, George, Ludham, N., farmer	308 Skepper
1856	Wells, Hannah, Sutton, N., spinster	595 Code
1837	Wells, Henry, Norwich, N., coal merchant	142 Warren
1854	Wells, Henry, Freethorpe, N., wheelwright	190 Day
1834	Wells, James, Kings Lynn, N., yeoman	177 Lane
1828	Wells, John, Panxworth, N., gent.	7 Farrow
1834	Wells, Jonas, Strumpshaw, N., farmer	253 Lane
1844	Wells, Jonathan, Hockham, N., farmer	357 Ebbage
1848	Wells, Joshua, Strumpshaw, N., farmer	206 Denny
1847	Wells, Martin, Catfield, N., farmer	276 Broom
1829	Wells, Mary, Strumpshaw, N., widow	203 Green
1832	Wells, Mary, Strumpshaw, N., wife of Joshua Wells, farmer	1 Cooke
1841	Wells, Thomas, Sporle with Palgrave, N., farmer	402 Traxton
1852	Wells, Thomas, Dersingham, N.	446 Latten
1849	Wells, William the elder, Southwold, S., cordwainer	165 Womack
1856	Wells, William, East Dereham, N., gardener	528 Code
1855	Welsh, George, Kessingland, S., commander in Her Majestys' Royal Navy	628 Whitty
1827	Welton, Deborah, Wickham Market, S., single woman	327 Wood
1857	Welton, Howard, Badingham, S., farmer	338 Youngs
1836	Welton, Isaac, Brandeston, N., husbandman	368 Smith
1840	Welton, Robert, Yaxley, S., blacksmith	222 Turner
1847	Welton, Sarah, Hopton, S., widow	376 Broom
1851	Wenden, Daniel, Yoxford, S., yeoman	192 Friar
1843	Wenn, Wardell, - alias Stuart, Downham Market, N., merchant	342 Miles
1823	West, Abraham, Stoke Ferry, N., grocer and draper	202 Tann
1847	West, Christopher, Felthorpe, N., miller and farmer	115 Broom
1838	West, Edward the elder, Soham, C., farmer	336 Skepper
1832	West, Edmund the elder, Kenninghall, N, yeoman	203 Cooke
1853	West, Elizabeth, Felthorpe, N, widow	320 Veale
1840	West, George, Kings Lynn, N, publican	122 Turner
1835	West, John, Croxton, N, innkeeper	209 Harrowing
1855	West, John, Soham, C., gardener	642 Whitty
1819	West, Jonathan, Kenninghall, N, husbandman	57 Le Neve
1855	West, King, Feltwell, N, labourer	461 Whitty
1835	West, Robert, Dersingham, N, farmer and victualler	520 Harrowing
1842	West, Robert, Thornham, N, blacksmith	233 Canler
1823	West, Sarah, Beccles, S., single woman	53 Tann
1852	West, Sarah, Stalham, N, formerly of Norwich, widow	740 Latten
1850	West, Susan, Barsham, S., widow	525 Cuthbert
1837	West, Susannah, Gorleston, S., widow	125 Warren
1832	West, Thomas, Lowestoft, S., gent.	324 Cooke
1838	West, Thomas the elder, Raveningham, N, farmer	383 Skepper
1852	West, Thomas the elder, Raveningham, N, gent.	203 Latten
1856	West, Thomas, Feltwell, N	211 Code
1830	West, William, Beccles, S., linen weaver	94 Pettingill

1842	West, William, Upwell, N, wheelwright	190 Canler
1850	West, William, Bungay, S., yeoman	284 Cuthbert
1844	Westby, Hannah, Diss, N, wife of Simon Westby, clerk	372 Ebbage
1849	Westby, Samuel, Norwich, N, gent.	400 Womack
1835	Westby, Thomas, Norwich, N, saddler and harness maker	12 Warren
1857	Westgate, Robert, Banham, N, farmer	176 Youngs
1846	Westley, John, Newmarket All Saints, C., farmer	507 Baret
1828	Westley, Ralph, Kirtling, C., yeoman	210 Farrow
1830	Westley, Samuel, All Saints Newmarket, C., carpenter	193 Pettingill
1840	Weston, James, Earsham, N, wheelwright	412 Turner
1842	Weston, Martha, Gorleston, S., widow	166 Canler
1856	Weston, Mary, Earsham, N, widow	544 Code
1855	Weston, William, Downham Market, N, gent.	174 Whitty
1857	Wetherell, Thomas, Fincham, N, farmer	627 Youngs
1838	Whaite, Sarah, Harleston, N, spinster	556 Skepper
1851	Whaites, Charles, Witton, N, gent, o.w. missing	565 Friar
1829	Whaites, John, Diss, N, carpenter and innkeeper	486 Green
1841	Whaites, John, Rougham, N, gent.	309 Traxton
1857	Whaites, John, Langley, N, gent.	196 Youngs
1852	Whaites, Martha Browne, Witton, N, widow	785 Latten
1836	Whaites, Robert, Ingham, N, gent.	384 Smith
1824	Whales, Miller, Little Fransham, N, carpenter	60 Borrett
1850	Whaley, John, South Elmham All Saints, S., farmer	97 Cuthbert
1820	Whall, Henry, St Martins at Palace, Norwich, N, coachman	58 Mack
1830	Whall, John, Seething, N, cordwainer	385 Pettingill
1841	Whall, John, Kirby Bedon, N, gent.	211 Traxton
1842	Whall, John, Scottow, N, innkeeper	568 Canler
1856	Whall, John, Great Yarmouth, N, carpenter	598 Code
1837	Wharton, George, North Lopham, N, gent.	241 Warren
1840	Wharton, Mary, North Lopham, N, widow	252 Turner
1841	Wharton, William, Stradbroke, S., farmer	572 Traxton
1839	Whatley, William, Diss, N, gent.	88 Calton
1845	Whatling, Robert, Denham, S., farmer	233 Pedgrift
1843	Whatson, Charles, Metfield, S., farmer	162 Miles
1828	Whayman, Isaac, Sudbourn, S., farmer	224 Farrow
1837	Whayman, Isaac, Eye, S., farmer and farrier	391 Warren
1821	Whayman, William the elder, Sudbourn, S., farmer	4 Dewell
1856	Whayman, William, Sudbourn, S., yeoman	607 Code
1849	Wheatley, Francis, Yarmouth, N, esquire	523 Womack
1832	Whibread, Thomas, Marham, N, yeoman	16 Cooke
1825	Whidby, George, Stanfield, N, farmer	30 Hayward
1845	Whidby, George, Stanfield, N, farmer	798 Pedgrift
1827	Whight, William, Sproughton, S., carpenter	466 Wood
1847	Whin, John, Kings Lynn, N, livery stable keeper	762 Broom
1848	Whincop, George the elder, Blythburgh, S., blacksmith	40 Denny
1834	Whistle, Elizabeth, Nacton, S., spinster	868 Lane
1838	Whistle, John, Ipswich, S., tea dealer	137 Skepper
1839	Whistler, Elizabeth, Wiggenhall St Mary Magdalen, N, widow	457 Calton
1852	Whistler, James, Brancaster, N, innkeeper	729 Latten
1848	Whistler, James, Docking, N, yeoman	89 Denny
1854	Whistler, John, Brancaster Staithe, N, innkeeper and common beer brewer	215 Day
1849	Whitaker, Ann, Barton Hall, N.	205 Womack
1857	Whitaker, John, Newton Flotman, N., farmer, brickmaker and lime burner	829 Youngs
1836	Whitaker, Richard, Warham, N., wheelwright	257 Smith
1830	Whitby, Elizabeth, Swaffham, N., widow	270 Pettingill
1826	Whitby, alias Priest, Joseph, Newton, N., formerly of Leeds, Yorks, baker	359 Davy
1826	White, Ann, Whinburgh, N., wife of Philip White, farmer	293 Davy
1829	White, Anthony, Norwich, N., worstead weaver	226 Green
1834	White, Bartholomew, East Dereham, N., currier	816 Lane
1837	White, George, Shouldham, N., labourer	394 Warren
1820	White, James, Gressenhall, N., farmer	212 Mack

1838	White, James George, Palgrave, S., schoolmaster, formerly of Attleborough, N.	879 Skepper
1853	White, James, Gressenhall, N., farmer	519 Veale
1855	White, James, Mattishall Bergh, N., machinist	721 Whitty
1839	White, Jeremiah, Loddon, N., bricklayer	225 Calton
1839	White, John, Ufford, S., farmer	395 Calton
1829	White, John, Walpole, S., house carpenter	84 Green
1827	White, Mary, Metton, N.	635 Wood
1836	White, Mary Ann, Halesworth, S., spinster	286 Smith
1842	White, Robert, Ipswich, S., shipmaster and owner	703 Canler
1855	White, Saul, Martlesham, S., yeoman	662 Whitty
1846	White, Warin, Bungay, S., gent.	290 Baret
1839	White, William, Foxley, N., farmer	411 Calton
1843	White, William, Kessingland, S., gent.	58 Miles
1850	White, William, Heigham, Norwich, N., blacksmith	224 Cuthbert
1822	Whitehand, Ann, alias Peterson, Norwich, N., shopkeeper	309 Sadler
1856	Whitehead, George, Beccles, S., stonemason	568 Code
1835	Whitehead, John, Beccles, S., stonemason	64 Harrowing
1850	Whitehead, John Fryer, Beccles, S., stonemason	592 Cuthbert
1827	Whitehead, Samuel, Wortham, S., bricklayer	662 Wood
1832	Whitehurst, John, Newton by Sudbury, S., rector	469 Cooke
1839	Whiteman, Ambrose, Gayton, N., farmer	285 Calton
1845	Whiteman, Edmund, Feltwell, N., widower	158 Pedgrift
1834	Whiteman, George, Bungay, S., bookbinder	558 Lane
1854	Whiteman, John, East Raynham, N., farmer	100 Day
1831	Whiteman, Mary, West Raynham, N., widow	494 Hart
1837	Whiteman, Mary, Norton, S., single woman	539 Warren
1856	Whiteman, Roper, Watlington, N., yeoman	198 Code
1845	Whiteman, Thomas, Billingford, N., gent.	884 Pedgrift
1832	Whiter, Walter, Hardingham, N., clerk	459 Cooke
1819	Whitesides, John Osborne, Great Yarmouth, N., mariner	175 Le Neve
1834	Whitethread, Robert, Stokesby, N., yeoman	765 Lane
1833	Whitfield, Thomas, Barton Bendish, N.	359 Cubitt
1832	Whiting, Ann, Wortwell, N., widow	269 Cooke
1842	Whiting, Frederick, West Bilney, N., farmer	357 Canler
1822	Whiting, Isaac, Heacham, N., farmer	222 Sadler
1831	Whiting, John, Kings Lynn, N., gent.	29 Hart
1853	Whiting, John, Soham, C., gent.	599 Veale
1824	Whiting, Joshua, Bungay, S., bricklayer	311 Borrett
1839	Whiting, Joshua the elder, Bungay, S., yeoman	651 Calton
1821	Whiting, Samuel, Wortwell, N., fogger	39 Dewell
1843	Whiting, William, Great Yarmouth, N., mariner	482 Miles
1822	Whitley, Jonathan, Norwich, N., bricklayer	O.W. 175
1826	Whitlow, John, Old Buckenham, N., yeoman	248 Davy
1851	Whitmore, Elizabeth, Feltwell, N., widow	241 Friar
1828	Whitmore, Thomas, Mellis, S., farmer	146 Farrow
1827	Whitrick, Israel, Wereham, N., yeoman	52 Wood
1849	Whittingham, Francis, Wenhaston, S., farmer	159 Womack
1847	Whittome, William, Hilgay, N., beerseller	791 Broom
1842	Whitton, Robert, Denton, N., farmer	358 Canler
1855	Whitty, Samuel, Snettisham, N.	1 Whitty
1843	Whyett, William, Westfield, N., farmer	156 Miles
1840	Wickes, Rice, Aylsham, N., gent.	448 Turner
1835	Wickes, William, Aylsham, N., esquire	506 Harrowing
1857	Wickham, Edward, Swainsthorpe, N., farmer	597 Youngs
1846	Wickham, Ejester, Swainsthorpe, N., farmer	577 Baret
1839	Wickham, Elizabeth, Southtown, S., widow	665 Calton
1847	Wickham, James, Rockland St Mary, N., waterman	617 Broom
1834	Wicks, Robert, Tharston, N., farmer	435 Lane
1839	Wicks, William the elder, St Johns Maddermarket, Norwich, N., innkeeper	214 Calton
1844	Wiffin, Jeremiah, Wendling, N., farmer	284 Ebbage
1834	Wigg, Elizabeth, Barnby, S widow	274 Lane
1839	Wigg, John, Mutford, S.	672 Calton

1849	Wigg, John, North Walsham, N., assistant overseer	449 Womack
1856	Wigg, Maria, Great Yarmouth, N., widow	460 Code
1834	Wigg, Martha, Wangford, S., widow	405 Lane
1840	Wigg, Mary, Acle, N., spinster	O.W. 266
1844	Wigg, Mary Ann, Great Yarmouth, N., spinster	270 Ebbage
1827	Wigg, Robert, Norwich, N., yeoman	534 Wood
1844	Wigg, Robert, Great Yarmouth, N., publican	98 Ebbage
1856	Wigg, Wright, East Dereham, N., gent.	126 Code
1844	Wiggett, Edward, Cromer, N., carrier	267 Ebbage
1819	Wiggett, James, Buxton, N., thatcher	217 Le Neve
1845	Wiggett, John, Norwich, N., cordwainer	769 Pedgrift
1853	Wiggett, Sarah, Cawston, N., widow	613 Veale
1829	Wiggett, William, Saxthorpe, N., gent.	177 Green
1844	Wiggins, Thomas, Norwich, N., coachman	363 Ebbage
1839	Wightman, Clement, Saxtead, S., farmer	363 Calton
1830	Wightman, Mary, Saxtead, S., widow	436 Pettingill
1831	Wightman, Richard, Bedfield, S., farmer	139 Hart
1835	Wighton, William, Hevingham, N.	612 Harrowing
1834	Wignall, John, Stow Bardolph, N., farmer	429 Lane
1847	Wilch, James, Norwich, N., baker	649 Broom
1850	Wilch, James, Norwich, N., baker	512 Cuthbert
1856	Wilch, Maria, Norwich, N., widow	367 Code
1842	Wilcockson, Jane, Blakeney, N., spinster	622 Canler
1823	Wild, Sarah, Worstead, N., widow	254 Tann
1842	Wild, Thomas, Erpingham, N., farmer	394 Canler
1833	Wilde, James, Kesgrave, S., auctioneer	455 Cubitt
1843	Wildee, William, Holt, N., blacksmith	88 Miles
1848	Wilden, Charles, Haughley, S., cordwainer	241 Denny
1837	Wilding, Thomas, Combs, S., farmer	610 Warren
1846	Wiles, Stephen, Upwell, N., farmer	236 Baret
1828	Wiley, Thomas Randall, Norwich, N., yarn factor	60 Farrow
1838	Wiley, Thomas, Norwich, N., wool factor	245 Skepper
1844	Wilkerson, Henry, St Margarets, Norwich, N., lawyer	507 Ebbage
1845	Wilkin, Jane, Soham, C., spinster	435 Pedgrift
1840	Wilkin, John, Little Ryburgh, N., labourer	626 Turner
1821	Wilkin, Matthew, Denver, N., wheelwright	334 Dewell
1833	Wilkin, Sarah, Norwich, N., widow	485 Cubitt
1821	Wilkins, James, Norwich, N., plasterer	34 Dewell
1855	Wilkins, Robert, Norwich, N., music teacher	617 Whitty
1852	Wilkins, Sarah, Norwich, N., spinster	666 Latten
1827	Wilkinson, Amy, Kings Lynn, N., widow	360 Wood
1841	Wilkinson, Amy, Kings Lynn, N.	Index only
1855	Wilkinson, Eleanora Ann, Mundesley, N., widow	630 Whitty
1839	Wilkinson, George, East Dereham, N., nurseryman	456 Calton
1842	Wilkinson, George, Great Yarmouth, N., yeoman	458 Canler
1834	Wilkinson, Jeremiah, Wiggenhall St Germains, N., cooper	178 Lane
1823	Wilkinson, John, Great Yarmouth, N., carter	371 Tann
1849	Wilkinson, Jonathan, Costessey, N., cattle dealer	680 Womack
1843	Wilkinson, Joseph, Norwich, N., saddler	545 Miles
1831	Wilkinson, Mary, Great Yarmouth, N., widow	176 Hart
1846	Wilkinson, Pinkney, Gaywood, N., cowkeeper	216 Baret
1835	Wilkinson, Thomas, Mattishall Burgh, N., shoemaker	546 Harrowing
1822	Willer, John, North Walsham, N., plumber and glazier	77 Sadler
1840	Willer, John, North Walsham, N., plumber and glazier	325 Turner
1851	Willby, Sarah Ann, Thorpe, Norwich, N., spinster	198 Friar
1826	Willement, Sarah, Norwich, N., widow	104 Davy
1822	Willett, Thomas, Feltwell, N., grocer and draper	174 Sadler
1855	Willett, Thomas, Bawdsey, S., single man	756 Whitty
1833	Williams, Catherine, Hill House, Rendham, S., spinster	90 Cubitt
1848	Williams, Dinah, Newmarket, S., widow	300 Denny
1857	Williams, Frederick, Tharston, N., yeoman, formerly of Forncett St Peter, N.	160 Youngs
1852	Williams, Isaac, Beachamwell, N., gamekeeper	429 Latten

1824	Williams, John, Petistree, late of Bedingfield, S., farmer	269 Borrett
1826	Williams, Peter Elwin, Hackford next Reepham, N., surgeon	249 Davy
1821	Williams, Thomas, Norwich, N., wine and spirit merchant	92 Dewell
1829	Williams, Thomas, Thornham, N., gent.	470 Green
1830	Williams, Thomas, Kirby Cane, N., farmer	381 Pettingill
1856	Williams, Thomas, Thornage, N., farmer	3 Code
1822	Williams, William, Norwich, N., victualler	414 Sadler
1835	Williamson, Elizabeth, Burnham Ulph and Sutton, N., widow	5 Harrowing
1850	Williamson, John, North Walsham, N., basket maker	184 Cuthbert
1853	Williamson, Thomas, Briston, N., farmer	532 Veale
1840	Willimott, Ann, North Walsham, N., widow	27 Turner
1853	Willimott, Elizabeth, North Walsham, N., spinster	197 Veale
1855	Willimott, John, Downham Market, N., hairdresser	177 Whitty
1855	Willimott, Robert, North Walsham, N., farmer and coal retailer	690 Whitty
1824	Willimont, Elizabeth, Whitwell, N., widow	44 Borrett
1845	Willis, John Farrow, Burlingham St Andrews, N., wheelwright, o.w. missing	545 Pedgrift
1828	Willsea, Peter, Norwich, N., plumber and glazier	122 Farrow
1839	Willson, Sarah, Wrentham, S., widow	642 Calton
1841	Willson, Thomas, Woodbridge, S., mariner	81 Traxton
1846	Wilson, Anna Maria, Kings Lynn, N., widow	140 Baret
1852	Wilson, Daniel, Bawdeswell, N., gardener	760 Latten
1820	Wilson, George, Kings Lynn, N., machine maker	660 Mack
1837	Wilson, George, Kirby Cane Hall, N., clerk	779 Warren
1857	Wilson, George, Norwich, N., shoemaker	295 Youngs
1837	Wilson, Grace, Great Yarmouth, N., wife of Crispin Wilson, mariner	269 Warren
1820	Wilson, James, Redenhall with Harleston, N., corn and coal chandler	123 Mack
1837	Wilson, James, Beccles, S., carter	577 Warren
1857	Wilson, Jane, Wereham, N., spinster	502 Youngs
1832	Wilson, John, Beeston Regis, N., fisherman	320 Cubitt
1857	Wilson, John, Billingford, N.	817 Youngs
1853	Wilson, Samuel, Swanton Abbott, N., farmer	604 Veale
1857	Wilson, Samuel, Swanton Abbott, N.	Index only
1848	Wilson, Sarah, Great Ryburgh, N., widow	243 Denny
1832	Wilson, Thomas, Sutton, S., farmer	466 Cooke
1822	Wilson, William the elder, Great Glemham, S., farmer	9 Sadler
1844	Wilson, William, Kings Lynn, N., labourer	177 Ebbage
1855	Wilson, Thomas, Norwich, N., gent.	228 Whitty
1856	Wilson, William, St Stephens, Norwich, N., household broker	160 Code
1843	Wilton, Samuel, Middleton, N., yeoman, formerly of Heacham, N.	135 Miles
1838	Wilton, Susannah Mary, Stowmarket, S.	787 Skepper
1853	Winch, Robert, Kings Lynn, N., yeoman	417 Veale
1838	Windett, James, Northwold, N., farmer	854 Skepper
1840	Windram, Mary, Snettisham, N.	108 Turner
1854	Windwood, John, Haughley, S.	236 Day
1844	Winearls, William, Horningtoft, N., yeoman	341 Ebbage
1849	Winfield, James, Thorpe, N., farmer	378 Womack
1827	Wing, Simon, Mildenhall, S., farmer	348 Wood
1844	Wingfield, Joseph, Downham Market, N., gent	111 Ebbage
1824	Wingham, Thomas the elder, Oxborough, N., servant to Sir Richard Bedingfield	220 Borrett
1842	Wink, Lucy, Dennington, S., widow	581 Canler
1854	Winkfield, Thomas, Castle Acre, N., farmer	177 Day
1836	Winkup, James Lindoe, Thetford, N., bookmaker	245 Smith
1843	Winkup, Susanna Frances, Norwich, N., formerly of Drinkstone, S., widow	413 Miles
1849	Winn, Charles, Gunthorpe, N., farmer	12 Womack
1830	Winn, Joseph, Kelling, N., yeoman	158 Pettingill
1847	Winnett, Elizabeth, Great Yarmouth, N., widow	76 Broom

1831	Winter, Ambrose the elder, St Saviour, Norwich, gent	468 Hart
1827	Winter, Betty, Halesworth, S., widow	319 Wood
1819	Winter, Daniel, St Georges Colegate, Norwich, N., cordwainer	225 Le Neve
1845	Winter, Henry, Beccles, S., seed merchant	501 Pedgrift
1854	Winter, Henry, Great Yarmouth, N., butcher	438 Day
1857	Winter, James, St Martin at Oak, Norwich, N., shoemaker	257 Youngs
1850	Winter, John, Beccles, S., seed merchant and shop keeper	262 Cuthbert
1820	Winter, Mary Ann, Norwich, N., widow	582 Mack
1831	Winter, Thomas, Lingwood, N., husbandman	355 Hart
1847	Winter, Thomas, Langham, N., publican	733 Broom
1850	Wiseman, Anthony, Kings Lynn, N., coal porter	498 Cuthbert
1836	Wiseman, Jeffrey, Thorpe, Norwich, N., farmer	449 Smith
1852	Wiseman, Miles, Worstead, N., husbandman	225 Latten
1846	Wiseman, Robert, Norwich, N., bricklayer	415 Baret
1857	Wiseman, Thomas, Heigham, Norwich, N., farmer	258 Youngs
1856	Wiseman, Vincent, Docking, N., boot and shoe maker	586 Code
1834	Wiseman, William, Walcot, N., gent	647 Lane
1842	Wiseman, William, Norwich, N.	O.W. 288
1849	Wiseman, William, Pentney, N., victualler	168 Womack
1851	Wiseman, William, Burgate, S., farmer	367 Friar
1827	Wisker, Sarah Ann, Blakeney, N., wife of Thomas Cook Wisker, tailor	599 Wood
1830	Witham, Richard, Kenninghall, N., farmer	447 Pettingill
1832	Witham, Robert, Norwich, N., bricklayer	103 Cooke
1841	Witham, William, Great Yarmouth, N., mariner	434 Traxton
1837	Withers, John, Hellesdon, Norwich, N., gardener	677 Warren
1838	Withers, John the elder, Stibbard, N., farmer	763 Skepper
1845	Withers, Robert William, Scottow, N., blacksmith	553 Pedgrift
1853	Withers, Robert, Helhoughton, N., formerly of Tattersett, farmer	393 Veale
1827	Withers, William, Holt, N., gent	351 Wood
1836	Withers, William, Thornage, N., yeoman	279 Smith
1849	Witting, Daniel, Redgrave, S., farmer and tea dealer	476 Womack
1834	Witting, Sarah, Redgrave, S., widow	284 Lane
1820	Wittred, John, Marham, N., farmer	354 Mack
1830	Wivearls, William junior, Marham, N., farmer	339 Pettingill
1837	Wix, Edmund, Weasenham All Saints, N., blacksmith	94 Warren
1835	Wodehouse, Martha, Great Yarmouth, N., widow	478 Harrowing
1822	Wollard, John, Ipswich, S., cordwainer	357 Sadler
1830	Wolno, Nathaniel, Otley, S.	268 Pettingill
1840	Womack, Amy, Attleborough, N., formerly of North Lopham, N., widow	472 Turner
1849	Womack, Mary Ann, Diss, N., spinster	1 Womack
1845	Womack, William, East Somerton, N., farmer	373 Pedgrift
1857	Wood, Benjamin, Alderford, N., clerk	553 Youngs
1847	Wood, Christopher, Kings Lynn, N., bricklayer	55 Broom
1825	Wood, Hannah, Gaywood, N., widow	15 Hayward
1827	Wood, John, Gaywood, N., farmer	1 Wood
1841	Wood, Margaret, Ipswich, S., spinster	281 Traxton
1843	Wood, Sarah, Woodbridge, S., widow	518 Miles
1837	Wood, Susan, Stowmarket, S., widow	503 Warren
1831	Wood, William, Barham, S., yeoman	406 Hart
1851	Woodards, Ann, Norwich, N., spinster	591 Friar
1834	Woodards, Robert, Norwich, N., worstead weaver	162 Lane
1843	Woodbine, Clarke, Kings Lynn, N., whitesmith	519 Miles
1840	Woodbine, Philip, Burnham Westgate, N., blacksmith	100 Turner
1846	Woodcock, Charles, Norwich, N., coachbuilder	381 Baret
1857	Woodcock, Joseph, Newton St Faiths, N., yeoman	364 Youngs
1851	Woodcraft, William, Moulton, N., farmer	313 Friar
1854	Wooden, Francis Bullman, Great Yarmouth, N., innkeeper	127 Day
1852	Woodgate, Nathaniel, Stratford St Andrews, S., tailor	588 Latten
1834	Woodhouse, Ann, Worstead, N., widow	252 Lane
1831	Woodhouse, Brown, Worstead, N., farmer	265 Hart

1845	Woodhouse, John, Sculthorpe, N., husbandman	58 Pedgrift
1828	Woodhouse, Matthew, St Simon and St Jude, Norwich, N., fishmonger	466 Farrow
1836	Woodroffe, Thomas the elder, Beccles, S., yeoman	148 Smith
1834	Woodrow, Benjamin, Swanton Abbott, N., yeoman	621 Lane
1847	Woodrow, Charles, Lessingham, N., shopkeeper	672 Broom
1837	Woodrow, Cremer, Trunch, N., gent.	444 Warren
1850	Woodrow, Elizabeth, Neatishead, N., spinster	594 Cuthbert
1829	Woodrow, John, Hingham, N., schoolmaster	370 Tann
1832	Woodrow, John, Norwich, N., esquire	113 Cooke
1844	Woodrow, John, North Walsham, N., gent.	401 Ebbage
1848	Woodrow, John, Carlton Rode, N., farmer	582 Denny
1854	Woodrow, Richard, Felthorpe, N., farmer	397 Day
1832	Woodrow, Sarah, Neatishead, N., widow	116 Cooke
1830	Woodrow, William, Thornham, N., plumber and glazier	351 Pettingill
1845	Woodrow, William, Norwich, N., gent.	465 Pedgrift
1856	Woods, Ann Elizabeth, Stradbroke, S., widow	370 Code
1847	Woods, Daniel, East Dereham, N., gent.	776 Broom
1857	Woods, Edmund, Mendlesham, S., common carrier	15 Youngs
1838	Woods, Elizabeth, Rushbrooke, S., widow	242 Skepper
1851	Woods, Harriet, Pulham St Mary the Virgin, N., wife of Esau Woods, labourer	617 Friar
1838	Woods, Henry, Snettisham, N., gardener	415 Skepper
1820	Woods, James, Magdalen Street, Norwich, N., weaver	35 Mack
1845	Woods, James, Sutton, S.	3 Pedgrift
1854	Woods, James, Thurgarton, N., harness maker	407 Day
1853	Woods, John, Saxmundham, S., saddler and harness maker	276 Veale
1842	Woods, Mary, Salhouse, N., spinster	138 Canler
1820	Woods, Presgrave, Wiggenhall St Peters, N., farmer	79 Mack
1831	Woods, Richard, Gorleston, S., pilot	282 Hart
1822	Woods, Robert, Winfarthing, N., yeoman	12 Sadler
1853	Woods, Robert, Saxmundham, S., grocer, draper and general shopkeeper	251 Veale
1840	Woods, Samuel, Wiggenhall St Germains, N., tailor	91 Turner
1838	Woods, Sarah Marion, Beccles, S., spinster	619 Skepper
1840	Woods, Thomas, Wyverstone, S., farmer	127 Turner
1853	Woods, Thomas, Corton, S., farmer	363 Veale
1841	Woods, Timothy, Mickfield, S., farmer	62 Traxton
1831	Woods, William, Stradbroke, S., yeoman	121 Hart
1850	Woods, William the elder, Stoke Ash, S., farmer	58 Cuthbert
1854	Woods, William, Melton, S., wheelwright	242 Day
1857	Woods, William Currie, Kings Lynn, N., fishmonger	497 Youngs
1856	Woodthorpe, Charles, Toft Monks, N., farmer	621 Code
1834	Woodthorpe, Sarah, Carlton Colville, S., widow	316 Lane
1821	Woodthorpe, Thomas, Corton, S., gent.	71 Dewell
1832	Woodthorpe, Thomas, Carlton Colville, S., yeoman	52 Cooke
1855	Woodward, George, Heigham, Norwich, N., baker	671 Whitty
1836	Woodward, John, Gorleston, S., labourer	65 Smith
1839	Woodward, Maria, Norwich, N., widow	320 Calton
1841	Woodyard, Sarah, Wood Dalling, N., wife of William Woodyard, shopkeeper	523 Traxton
1855	Woodyard, William, Halesworth, S., bricklayer	256 Whitty
1831	Wooll, Hugh, Upwell, C., farmer and grazier	403 Hart
1826	Wooll, Richard, Upwell, N., gent.	329 Davy
1843	Woollard, Allenton, Kirtling, C., yeoman	316 Miles
1846	Woollard, Samuel, Snailwell, C., victualler	145 Baret
1844	Woollsey, Benjamin, Norwich, N., formerly of Panxworth, N., gent.	248 Ebbage
1827	Woolner, John, Beccles, S., common carrier	404 Wood
1822	Woolner, James, Shadingfield, S., yeoman	74 Sadler
1848	Woolner, James, Great Yarmouth, N., lamplighter	449 Denny
1831	Woolner, William, Belton, S., thatcher	280 Hart
1845	Woolnough, Benjamin, Linstead Magna, S., gent.	706 Pedgrift
1825	Woolnough, Hannah, Walton, S., widow	55 Hayward

1837	Woolnough, James, Bungay, S., formerly of St Lawrence, Ilketshall, farmer	209 Warren
1828	Woolnough, John, Carlton, S., farmer	132 Farrow
1841	Woolnough, John, Ufford, S., gent.	444 Traxton
1850	Woolnough, John, Bungay, S., tailor	217 Cuthbert
1842	Woolnough, Thomas, Halesworth, S., innkeeper	201 Canler
1831	Woolsey, William, Kirby Bedon, N., gent.	270 Hart
1831	Woolston, Benjamin the younger, Scratby, N., farmer	58 Hart
1849	Woolston, Benjamin, Scratby, N., farmer	607 Womack
1830	Woolterton, John, Norwich, N., gent.	322 Pettingill
1852	Woolterton, William, Denton, N., farmer	688 Latten
1843	Woolverton, Henry, Great Yarmouth, N., fishing merchant	494 Miles
1857	Woolverton, Sarah, Great Yarmouth, N., single woman	224 Youngs
1831	Worby, John, Carbrooke, N., farmer	251 Hart
1853	Wordingham, St John, West Barsham, N., farmer	431 Veale
1830	Wordingham, William, Warham, N., farmer	76 Pettingill
1830	Worledge, Robert, Cotton, S., farmer	103 Pettingill
1836	Worledge, Sarah, Eye, S., widow	399 Smith
1829	Worledge, Thomas, Great Yarmouth, N., bricklayer	59 Green
1838	Worledge, William, Battisford, S., labourer	759 Skepper
1841	Worman, Robert, Starston, N., gardener	421 Traxton
1850	Worman, William, Diss, N., carpenter	167 Cuthbert
1850	Wormer, John, Brisley, N., farmer	219 Cuthbert
1825	Worrell, John the elder, North Creake, N., yeoman	421 Hayward
1849	Worship, William Taylor, Gorleston, S., clerk	265 Womack
1855	Worters. William, Groton, S., farmer	244 Whitty
1835	Worth, John, Oakley, S., captain	Index only
1845	Wortley, John, Smallburgh, N., carpenter	797 Pedgrift
1856	Wortley, Robert, Norwich, N., solicitor	641 Code
1836	Worts, Augustine the younger, Lessingham, N., farmer	512 Smith
1844	Worts, Jemima, Great Yarmouth, N., widow	512 Ebbage
1842	Worts, Mary, Stalham, N., widow	84 Canler
1854	Worts, Mary Ann, North Walsham, N.	451 Day
1838	Wragg, Jonathan, Winfarthing, N., farmer	193 Skepper
1842	Wrench, William Butter, Morston, N., farmer	195 Canler
1843	Wright, Alexander, Framingham Pigot, N., yeoman	585 Miles
1846	Wright, Alfred, North Walsham, N., carpenter	102 Baret
1826	Wright, Ann, Wheatacre All Saints, N., spinster,	
1867	Wright, Ann, Yaxley, S., widow	457 Broom
1845	Wright, Anne, Haverhill, S., wife of Isaac Wright	217 Pedgrift
1844	Wright, Benjamin, Ringstead, N., farmer	450 Ebbage
1841	Wright, Charlotte Elizabeth, Norwich, N., widow	616 Traxton
1833	Wright, Cook, North Walsham, N., yeoman	139 Cubitt
1854	Wright, David, Barningham, S., farmer	134 Day
1852	Wright, Edward, Horning, N., labourer	608 Latten
1857	Wright, Edward, Thrandeston, S., carpenter	653 Youngs
1822	Wright, Elizabeth, Pulham St Mary the Virgin, N., widow	339 Sadler
1825	Wright, Elizabeth, Shipdham, N.	79 Hayward
1841	Wright, Elizabeth, Moulton, N., widow	75 Traxton
1856	Wright, Elizabeth, Norwich, N., widow	592 Code
1856	Wright, Emma, Stonham Aspal, S., widow	118 Code
1827	Wright, Frances, Wells, N., wife of Thomas Wright, esquire	483 Wood
1846	Wright, Frances, Fakenham, N., spinster	417 Baret
1832	Wright, George, St Peter Mancroft, Norwich, N., printer	545 Cooke
1836	Wright, George, Upton, N., marshman	348 Smith
1854	Wright, George, Trimingham, N., farmer	317 Day
1846	Wright, Hannah, Holt, N.	608 Baret
1824	Wright, Henry, Hilgay, N., farmer	25 Borrett
1838	Wright, Henry, Wymondham, N., farmer	569 Skepper
1847	Wright, James, Happisburgh, N., carpenter	273 Broom
1847	Wright, James, Sculthorpe, N., yeoman	229 Broom
1819	Wright, John, Redgrave, S., wheelwright	O.W. 174
1827	Wright, John, Fordham, N., farmer	648 Wood
1830	Wright, John, Tasburgh, N., nurseryman	252 Pettingill

1834	Wright, John, Runton, N., farmer	149 Lane
1837	Wright, John, West Bradenham, N., carpenter	631 Warren
1838	Wright, John, Hilgay, N., gent.	737 Skepper
1839	Wright, John, Bilderstone, S., blacksmith	190 Calton
1841	Wright, John, Metton, N., farmer	71 Traxton
1843	Wright, John, North Walsham, N., carpenter	562 Miles
1844	Wright, John, Walberswick, S., farmer	601 Ebbage
1845	Wright, John, Woodbridge, S., yeoman	210 Pedgrift
1846	Wright, John, Sibton, S., yeoman	58 Baret
1847	Wright, John, Thursford, N., gent.	386 Broom
1848	Wright, John, Mendham, N., harness maker	638 Denny
1850	Wright, John Carman, Attleborough, N.	187 Cuthbert
1852	Wright, John Lane, North Walsham, N., draper	345 Latten
1852	Wright, John, Rendlesham, S., shoe maker	790 Latten
1853	Wright, John, Norwich, N., carpenter	483 Veale
1854	Wright, John, Erpingham, N., farming bailiff	547 Day
1843	Wright, Jonas, Fakenham, N., cordwainer	59 Miles
1847	Wright, Joseph, Hainford, N., farmer	364 Broom
1820	Wright, Mary, Swaffham, N., widow	377 Mack
1837	Wright, Mary, Redgrave, S., widow	496 Warren
1830	Wright, Priscilla, Hasketon, S., widow	336 Pettingill
1842	Wright, Robert, Earsham, N., farmer	341 Canler
1845	Wright, Robert, Oulton, S., yeoman	690 Pedgrift
1846	Wright, Robert the younger, North Creake, N., farmer	458 Baret
1852	Wright, Robert, North Creake, N., farmer	4 Latten
1857	Wright, Robert, Attleburgh, N., farmer	589 Youngs
1857	Wright, Robert, Southwold, S., gent.	755 Youngs
1846	Wright, Robins Steed, Downham Market, N., brewer	70 Baret
1820	Wright, Samuel, New Buckenham, N., yeoman	311 Mack
1844	Wright, Samuel, Besthorpe, N., farmer	559 Ebbage
1857	Wright, Samuel, Stowmarket, S., saddler	123 Youngs
1850	Wright, Sarah, West Winch, N., spinster	204 Cuthbert
1831	Wright, Sergeant, Northwold, N., farmer	497 Hart
1820	Wright, Thomas, Brockdish, N., farmer	381 Mack
1825	Wright, Thomas, Mattishall, N., gent.	295 Hayward
1849	Wright, Thomas, Norwich, N., musician	68 Womack
1852	Wright, Thomas, Downham Market, N., gent.	192 Latten
1853	Wright, Thomas, Foxley, N., farmer	235 Veale
1857	Wright, Thomas, Little Walsingham, N., yeoman	646 Youngs
1824	Wright, alias Reeder, William, Swaffham, N., gent.	164 Borrett
1826	Wright, William, Horning, N., yeoman	16 Davy
1832	Wright, William, Suffield, N., gardener	179 Cooke
1835	Wright, William, Wretton, N., farmer	581 Harrowing
1836	Wright, William, Norwich, N., dyer	211 Smith
1836	Wright, William, Wighton, N., innkeeper	324 Smith
1844	Wright, William, Kelsale, S., yeoman	307 Ebbage
1846	Wright, William, Bacton, N., farmer	639 Baret
1848	Wright, William the elder, Carlton Colville, S., carpenter	277 Denny
1850	Wright, William, Newton St Faith, N., labourer	510 Cuthbert
1854	Wright, William, Poringland, N., carpenter	348 Day
1843	Wurr, Edward, St Stephens, Norwich, N., yeoman, late innkeeper	671 Miles
1847	Wurr, Sarah, Bunwell, N.	266 Broom
1852	Wurr, Susanna, Norwich, N., widow	229 Latten
1837	Wyand, Benjamin, Halvergate, N., innkeeper	799 Warren
1834	Wyatt, John, Burwell, C., farmer	544 Lane
1828	Wyburgh, Hannah, Nordelph, Upwell, N., widow	55 Farrow
1842	Wyer, Elizabeth, Thetford, N., single woman	Index only
1838	Wyer, John, Caston, N., miller and farmer	349 Skepper
1842	Wyer, John, Southery, N., farmer	380 Canler
1847	Wyett, Henry, Beeston, N., innkeeper	413 Broom
1844	Wymer, George, Reepham, N., gent.	662 Ebbage
1830	Wymer, John, Blofield, N., husbandman	36 Pettingill
1845	Wymer, John, St Michael at Thorn, Norwich, N., innkeeper	339 Pedgrift

1819	Wymer, Robert, Norwich, N., gent.	Index only
1848	Wymer, William, Norwich, N., innkeeper	88 Denny
1827	Wynter, Philip the elder, Aldeburgh, S., merchant	432 Wood
1857	Yallop, Elizabeth, Hillington, N., widow	690 Youngs
1830	Yarham, Edmund, Themelthorpe, N., farmer	338 Pettingill
1839	Yarington, Peter Master, Norwich, N., gent.	51 Calton
1825	Yarington, Samuel, Norwich, N.	204 Hayward
1834	Yates, William, St Peter Mancroft, Norwich N., china-man	388 Lane
1834	Yaxley, Ann, Binham, N., wife of William Yaxley, labourer	793 Lane
1835	Yaxley, James, Heacham, N., innkeeper	448 Harrowing
1830	Yaxley, John Pardon, Great Yarmouth, N., mariner	19 Pettingill
1843	Yaxley, John, Doughtys Hospital, Norwich, N.	42 Miles
1830	Yaxley, William, Whissonsett, N., yeoman	318 Pettingill
1848	Yea, Tabitha, Lowestoft, S., widow	505 Denny
1829	Yeames, Elizabeth	O.W. 240
1827	Yeldham, Thomas, Soham, C., yeoman	183 Wood
1846	Yell, Samuel, Wiveton, N., farmer	Index only
1837	Yeomans, Anne, Norwich, N.	O.W. 347
1838	Yeomans, James, Pockthorpe, Norwich, N., cordwainer	454 Skepper
1853	Yeomans, Roger, Great Ellingham, N.	12 Veale
1852	Yexley, Henry Hagon, Cromer, N., pensioner	35 Latten
1843	Yonge, Fanny, Swaffham, N., single woman	76 Miles
1850	Youell, John Fuller, Great Yarmouth, N., ironmonger	22 Cuthbert
1849	Youell, Sarah the elder, Norwich, N., widow	639 Womack
1850	Young, Andrew, Thetford, N.	328 Cuthbert
1827	Young, John, Northwold, N., farmer	139 Wood
1852	Young, John, Scarning, N., farmer	696 Latten
1839	Young, Margaret, Barwick, N., formerly of East Rudham, wife of John Young, gent.	145 Calton
1838	Young, William Thomas, Woodbridge, S., tailor	457 Skepper
1841	Young, William Wabe, Methwold, N., gent.	510 Traxton
1842	Younghusband, William Howard, Thetford, N., farrier	172 Canler
1841	Youngman, Dorothy, Beccles, S., widow	454 Traxton
1838	Youngman, Mary, Walsham le Willows, S., widow	889 Skepper
1834	Youngman, Thomas, Letheringsett, N., millwright	824 Lane
1820	Youngman, William, Walsham le Willows, S., gent.	Index only
1827	Youngman, William, Stoke Ferry, N., carpenter	168 Wood
1837	Youngman, William, Aylmerton, N., shopkeeper	800 Warren
1839	Youngs, Elizabeth, Norwich, N., widow	255 Calton
1845	Youngs, Elizabeth, Great Yarmouth, N., single woman	216 Pedgrift
1848	Youngs, Elizabeth, Heacham, N., widow	511 Denny
1848	Youngs, John, Great Yarmouth, N., yeoman	421 Denny
1857	Youngs, John, Alburgh, N., farmer	1 Youngs
1847	Youngs, Robert, Strumpshaw, N., yeoman	558 Broom
1849	Youngs, Sharman, Wortwell, N., farmer	45 Womack
1841	Youngs, Thomas, Moulton, N., husbandman	575 Traxton
1851	Youngs, Thomas, Stowmarket, S.	601 Friar
1850	Zipfel, Joseph, Norwich, N., watch and clock maker	19 Cuthbert
1824	Zipfell, George, Norwich, N., clockmaker	137 Borrett

INDEX LOCORUM

Note (2) indicates two or more references on one page

INDEX OF OCCUPATIONS

Note (2) indicates two or more references on one page